WOMEN'S VOICES

An Untold History of
the Latter-day Saints

1830-1900

Kenneth W. Godfrey
Audrey M. Godfrey
Jill Mulvay Derr

Deseret Book Company
Salt Lake City, Utah

©1982 Deseret Book Company
All rights reserved
Printed in the United States of America
First printing May 1982

Library of Congress Cataloging Production Data

Godfrey, Kenneth W.
  Women's Voices.

  Includes bibliographical references and index.
  1. Church of Jesus Christ of Latter-day Saints—
History—19th century. 2. Women in the Mormon
Church—United States—History—19th century. I.
Godfrey, Audrey M. II. Derr, Jill Mulvay. III. Title.
BX8611.G6   289.3'3 [B]   82-5006
ISBN 0-87747-909-7   AACR2

Contents

Acknowledgments

Shortly after he became Church Historian, Dr. Leonard Arrington wrote a letter and asked me to write a book containing selections from the letters, diaries, and journals of Mormon women. Prior to receiving Dr. Arrington's letter I had published at least one article regarding Mormon women and had, furthermore, given several talks on the same subject. Because of my great interest in the subject and because of the glaring lack of material regarding our pioneer sisters in the major histories of the Church, I readily accepted the assignment.

Just a few weeks thereafter, my wife and I decided to do the book together, because she, too, had developed a great interest in the feminine aspects of Mormon history. In January 1974 the Church Educational System granted me a sabbatical leave to do the research. Working in the Church Historical Department Archives, Audrey and I read more than 250 women's diaries, letters, and journals and selected those we thought were the most moving, important, and informative to be included in this book. After we received a call from the First Presidency to preside over the Pennsylvania-Pittsburgh Mission, Jill Mulvay Derr kindly consented to work on the manuscript and selection of materials. Soon it was concluded that the three of us would be authors of what we believed to be a very important book.

In order to facilitate the reading of this book, footnotes have been kept to a minimum. However, readers who desire full documentation of material referred to are invited to study fully footnoted manuscripts on deposit in the LDS Church Historical Library in Salt Lake City and the Brigham Young University Library, Provo, Utah. Furthermore, it became apparent as the manuscript was being prepared for publication that due to space limitations, some of the original material would have to be deleted; with some reluctance, though with great care, this was done. Thus, the published book is somewhat shorter than was originally intended; however, we do not believe that the quality of the book has been significantly diminished by reducing the quantity of material presented.

We wish to acknowledge the assistance of the staff of the Church Historical Department in helping us locate material and in granting permission to publish the same. Special thanks are due to Maureen Ursenbach Beecher for editorial assistance and to Carol Cornwall Madsen and Susan Staker Oman for assisting in the research. We also appreciate the help of the descendants of the women included in this book. Special thanks go to our families for love, encouragement, and support. Furthermore, this book would not have been possible without the assistance of Arlene Patterson and Louise Palmer, my secretaries, and Debbie Lilenquist, secretary in the Historical Department. The authors also express appreciation to former Church Commissioner of Education Neal A. Maxwell and Associate Commissioner Joe J. Christensen for granting the sabbatical leave that made the research possible. Profound gratitude also goes to Leonard Arrington, director of the Joseph Fielding Smith Institute for Church History at Brigham Young University, and to the Church Historical Department, with Earl E. Olson, assistant managing director, and Donald T. Schmidt, director of Library Archives, for granting permission to use much of the material found in this book.

Finally we wish to express not only our gratitude but our admiration to the women whose writings we have published. We have been made better because of their courage, their faith, their love, and their deep devotion to their families, their faith, and themselves. We believe they represent the very best of Mormonism and womanhood. We hope you find as much satisfaction in reading what they wrote as we did in spending the past six years in their presence. In many ways we feel that we know them better than we know many of the people with whom we associate from day to day.

Kenneth W. Godfrey
February 1982

Chapter One

Introduction

"A True Record . . . of Some Worth"

Mormon women are not unsung heroines. Throughout the last half of the nineteenth century they were celebrated within The Church of Jesus Christ of Latter-day Saints almost as readily as they were censured by its critics. Long after they lost the rapt attention of American journalists and antipolygamy crusaders, they survived in the Mormon consciousness as sturdy and faithful foremothers. More recently, in the wake of new scholarship in LDS Church history and a concurrent surge of interest in women's studies, Mormon women have received new consideration from Mormons and non-Mormons alike. These sister Saints are not unsung, but neither are they fully understood.

"There are few lives so uneventful that a true record of them would not be of some worth," Martha Cragun Cox wrote in the preface to her 300-page autobiography.[1] In fact, the "true records" or personal writings of Martha and dozens of other Latter-day Saint women are of critical importance to anyone who wants to understand Mormon women. Through their letters, diaries, journals, reminiscences, and autobiographies we can begin to reconstruct their experience as Mormons and as women. To those interested in that experience, the following selections from the writings of Latter-day Saint women will be of some worth.

While recent studies of Mormon women have focused primarily on women's achievements and contributions, their personal writings have not been overlooked. Excerpts from diaries, journals, and autobiographies have served to illustrate the spiritual dimension of sisters'

1

lives, for example, or their birthing and medical practices. Women's accounts have animated discussions of women's involvement in Mormon colonization, politics, and plural marriage.[2] Few of the studies of Mormon women published during the past decade are devoid of extracts from first-hand accounts. The sources are simply too plentiful to be ignored.

The Church's long-standing commitment to record-keeping has resulted in a rich cache of personal records produced and preserved by Latter-day Saints. The LDS Church Historical Department, Brigham Young University, the University of Utah, the Utah State Historical Society, and other local and regional archives have opened their Mormon holdings to scholars.[3] From 1939 to the present the Daughters of Utah Pioneers have reproduced in serial publications various women's writings. And some Mormon families have privately published journals or memoirs of their foremothers. *The Early Autobiography and Diary of Ellis Reynolds Shipp, M.D.*, edited and published in 1962 by her daughter Ellis Shipp Musser, is one of the most significant. More recently, scholarly editions of Mormon women's documents have been made widely available. The University of Utah Tanner Trust Fund's *A Mormon Mother: An Autobiography of Annie Clark Tanner* (1973) and *Dear Ellen: Two Mormon Women and Their Letters*, edited by S. George Ellsworth (1974), and the Utah State Historical Society's *Not by Bread Alone: The Journal of Martha Spence Heywood, 1850-56*, edited by Juanita Brooks (1978), are noteworthy examples.

As these recent documentary editions have shown, the personal writings of Mormon women are valuable studies in and of themselves. *Women's Voices: An Untold History of the Latter-day Saints, 1830-1900* is a collection of twenty-five women's documents, each with particular intrinsic value. Detailed letters, thoughtful journals, reminiscences carefully aggregating lives, events, and feelings—these begin to answer the question: What was the actual experience of Mormon women?[4]

Shared commitment to the restored gospel of Jesus Christ was the common root of that experience. It distinguished these women as Mormons, as fellow citizens with the Latter-day Saints and part of a modern household of faith. Most of the women in this collection chose that distinction; they were first-generation Mormons who left

2

behind the traditions of their mothers and fathers to join with others who shared the conviction that Joseph Smith, Jr., was a prophet of God raised up in the latter days to restore the gospel of Jesus Christ in its original purity. The heavenly visions Joseph Smith experienced as a youth in upstate New York resulted in the 1830 publication of the Book of Mormon, a religious history of ancient America that he had received from a heavenly messenger, Moroni, and translated by the power of God. Many, like Sarah Studevant Leavitt, confirmed Joseph's testimony through their own spiritual experiences. When she heard "the whole of Joseph's vision and what the Angel Moroni had said," she recalled, "it came to my mind in a moment that this was the message . . . for me and not for me only, but for the whole world, and I considered it of more importance than anything I had ever heard before."[5]

It was this personal witness of truth that anchored men and women to The Church of Jesus Christ of Latter-day Saints. While for Sarah Leavitt the witness or testimony came fast and forcefully, others labored long months or even years before deciding that Mormonism "laid a foundation that could be built upon that was permanent." Eliza R. Snow, poet and prominent leader of Mormon women, was five years in determining whether or not to be baptized a Latter-day Saint. But after extensively counting the cost, she "laid my earthly all / Upon the altar, and with purpose fix'd / Unalterably . . . am determind now *to be a Saint.*"[6] For Eliza, purpose once so fixed never altered in her fifty-two years as a Saint. Thousands of women likewise kept their faith intact through seemingly endless hardships that came as a result of their membership in the Church.

Few nineteenth century Mormons escaped the sting of persecution. Doctrines that challenged accepted values and peculiar economic and political practices kept Mormons in prolonged conflict with their neighbors in New York, in Ohio and Missouri, in Illinois, and later in Utah. For women this meant the frequent interruption of the home life they tried to establish and maintain. Mary Ann Weston as a young bride in Tirley, Gloucester, England, found her fondest hopes dashed when her husband died from wounds incurred during a mob attack on a gathering of Saints in their home. Even at the century's close some Mormons, such as Nancy Clement

Williams, were on the run, not from mobs but from marshals who sought to convict them for their involvement in the practice of plural marriage. The times, places, and circumstances changed, but the written response of early Mormon women usually echoed that of seventeen-year-old Nancy: "Feel very much my dependence on my Heavenly Father."

Those who actively confronted the Mormon community found that Saints could be evicted from a place, but not successfully scattered. Committed to the literal gathering of Israel, they moved as families and often as a community to "Zion," where God's elect would "be gathered in unto one place upon the face of this land."[7] Mormon missionaries declared the restored gospel first in the United States and later abroad, and those who received it were called to go to a promised land. The location of Zion changed, but those who chose to join with this "holy nation" and "peculiar people"—whether in Kirtland, Independence, Far West, Nauvoo, or the Great Basin— made a common sacrifice in leaving behind their former homes and ways of life. British convert Jean Rio Griffiths Baker observed, as she set out in 1851 "to gather with the Church of Christ, in the valley of the Great Salt Lake in North America," that she had taken "leave of every acquaintance I could gather together, in all human probability never to see them again on earth."

Gathering to Zion usually meant long and inconvenient, if not arduous, travel; most early Latter-day Saints experienced at least one trek. In 1843 Sally Randall traveled the Ohio and Mississippi rivers from Buffalo, New York, to Nauvoo, Illinois. Jean Baker's journey by water was considerably longer. She sailed the route from Liverpool to Salt Lake City via New Orleans; others went by way of New York. The Mormon Trail across the plains of Iowa and Nebraska was well worn and well documented by Mormon women, many of whom kept a diary or journal only when traveling. These records reflect a concern for the life and beauty surrounding the writers.

Writing about new sights and experiences allowed women to absorb and remember them. It also provided an outlet for frustration and grief. Mary Ann Weston Maughan graphically described how, after she was bitten by bedbugs in her riverboat cabin, her feet and legs swelled until she could not walk.

At best, nineteenth century emigration meant annoyance and discomfort. At worst it meant death. Patience Loader journeyed to Zion with the Martin Handcart Company, a group that left Iowa late enough in the season in 1856 to be caught by early winter snows. Patience later told the story of greatly reduced provisions, observing: "Our provisions would not have lasted as long as they did had all our breathren and sisters lived but nearly half the company died and caused our provisions to hold out longer."

Though the Saints anchored themselves firmly to the Great Basin in 1847, migration did not stop. Latter-day Saint efforts toward colonizing extended into the 1880s, when Saints moved into Mexico and Canada. Nancy Clement Williams's reaction to Colonia Diaz, Mexico, in 1890, with its "mud houses & mud fences; the street full of Mosqueat," was about as disappointed as that of Angelina Farley, who arrived in the Salt Lake Valley in 1850, complaining in her journal that "everything seems lifeless and tasteless. I can anticipate no rest or pleasure."[8] For these women, the process of settlement usually meant that home was a tent or wagon until a dugout or log or adobe shanty could be built, sometime later to be replaced by a multi-roomed home with walls of lath and plaster.

Fixing up homes, however permanent or temporary, occupied a fair amount of women's thoughts and energy and provided them some pleasure. Twenty-nine-year-old Caroline Barnes Crosby had been married a year and a half when she began keeping house for the first time in Kirtland, Ohio. "I felt like a child with a new set of toys," she recalled. Mary Jane Mount Tanner remembered when Saints in Payson, Utah, "were beginning to tear down their old unsightly cabins and make themselves pleasanter homes."[9] Even with the frontier absent as a prominent motif in their writings, women continued "settling in." Just prior to her daughter's wedding in Salt Lake City in 1874, Emmeline B. Wells recorded her pleasure with new carpets she had received: "I am pleased with them also the parlor furniture. I never expected to have been so well off in my life. . . . nothing extravagant but all in exact keeping and conformity." With years of privation as a base of comparison, women like Emmeline found themselves delighted with prosperity.

Settling new frontiers often involved women in activities beyond

Unidentified women and children sewing carpet rags, ca. 1900.
(George Edward Anderson Collection. LDS Church Archives.)

housekeeping. Some helped build their homes and carried on farm
work. One woman hauled manure on the land, sheared the sheep,
plowed, planted, and made irrigation ditches. For the most part,
however, when men were absent, women hired the heavy work
done, usually with money they earned on their own. Mary Fielding
Smith taught school; Patty Sessions was a midwife; Eliza Partridge
Lyman sold homespun candlewicking for a time; Martha Cragun Cox
wove cloth. The reality of life in nineteenth century America
demanded that most women supplement the family income in some
way. This was particularly true in the Mormon culture, where men
were frequently absent. In addition to serving missions and
performing other Church work, during each period of initial
settlement, men were called upon to participate in community
projects such as clearing the land, constructing public buildings, and, in
the Great Basin, digging ditches and canals.

Both men and women contributed to the community's economic
well-being and its self-sufficiency. Through the 1870s Brigham Young

stressed the importance of home industries and home manufactured goods, even attempting to establish a United Order, a society that "would never have to buy anything . . . and always have something to sell and bring money, to help increase their comfort and independence."[10] In 1874 sisters were told by Eliza R. Snow, president of the Church's women's organizations, that those who stepped forward and assisted efficiently in home industries (including silk culture, straw weaving, tailoring, and home canning) would be "doing just as much as an Elder who went forth to preach the Gospel."[11]

The Saints' efforts at economic cooperation would not only lessen their dependence on the "Gentile" or non-Mormon world, but would also increase community interdependence, bringing these modern Saints closer to New Testament Saints who "were of one heart and of one soul: neither said any of them that ought of the things which he possessed was his own; but they had all things common." (Acts 4:32.) Martha Cragun Cox, living in St. George, Utah, sensed that her own large household might have come close to this ideal of sharing, recalling, "We had in our home an almost perfect United Order." Large-scale efforts at economic sharing ultimately proved unwieldy and unprofitable, though they seem to have strengthened the Saints' commitment to consecrate time and money to the Church and to care cooperatively for poor and distressed members.[12]

The emphasis on economic cooperation pushed Mormon women into some unique ventures, such as forming women's cooperatives and buying, storing, and selling grain; but for the most part the sisters' economic activities were much like those of their American counterparts. However, in this as in all things the women's vision was influenced by their faith. Told in a scripture from the Doctrine and Covenants (29:34) that "all things unto [God] are spiritual," women often invested their midwifery, schoolteaching, weaving, storekeeping, farming, cooking, sewing, or nurturing with spiritual significance even though they acknowledged such activities as temporal necessities.

The Mormon community's image of itself as a "holy nation" where all things were spiritual excluded and offended many non-Mormons. Yet this covenant-people self-concept was central to Mormonism, and Saints gathered regularly to reaffirm it. "We never

missed a meeting for we loved the Saints and had confidence in them,"
wrote Drusilla Dorris Hendricks of life in Missouri. It is apparent from
Mormon writings that much social life revolved around gathering
with the Saints in such meetings—stake and general conferences, Sunday School, sacrament meeting, fast and testimony meeting (held on
Thursdays instead of Sundays until 1896), ward parties and picnics—
and for women, meetings of the Relief Society, Young Ladies' Mutual
Improvement Association, and Primary Association, as well as
officers' meetings and conferences for women who directed these
auxiliaries. The meetings became more numerous and specialized as
the century progressed and the Church and its organization grew.

In addition to these things, of course, were the theater, concerts,
bands, and balls typical of life in nineteenth century America. Each
community seems to have had societies or clubs for music, debate, and
drama. During long, cold winters, dances were popular and frequently
lasted late into the evening.[13]

Though such activities were a diversion, they were also a way of
strengthening community bonds. Young people were admonished to
seek amusement among Church members rather than among "outsiders," and often Latter-day Saint women penned the sorrow they felt
when a son or daughter courted or married outside the faith. "O how
glad I would be if he would only be one of our faith, and go down into
the waters of baptism. My heart would rejoice with joy unspeakable,"
wrote Emmeline B. Wells of one of her daughter's non-Mormon
suitors.[14] Mormons were a community of believers, a literal household
where members addressed one another as brother and sister. Those
who were outside the covenant were clearly outside the family, a
separation apparent to Mormons and non-Mormons alike.

Reverence for the community meant a reverence for its leaders,
especially its prophets or Church presidents. That the well-being of
these men was a dominant concern is shown in the frequency with
which women mentioned it. Sisters noted the sermons they heard
from these leaders, often showing their own thoughtful consideration
of the ideas presented. Rebecca Mace was unafraid to challenge
bishops and stake presidents when she believed they erred in what
they preached, and she became a recognized gospel authority in
Southern Utah. But even so, she supported these leaders in their posi-

tions. Most women were not blind to human failings, but they sustained priesthood leaders with the personal conviction that they had been "called of God by prophecy, and by the laying on of hands ... to preach the gospel and administer in the ordinances thereof."[15] Some members left the Church when they felt authorities had advocated ideas contrary to their own personal interests or convictions. Others wrestled with doctrines or situations they found difficult to understand. Caroline Barnes Crosby "felt very sorrowful, and gloomy" when friends apostatized in Kirtland, but she said she "never had the first idea of leaving the Church or forsaking the prophet."

The early nineteenth century Saints often mixed civil with ecclesiastical leadership. Joseph Smith was a candidate for the U.S. presidency when he was murdered. Even at the end of the nineteenth century, when as a part of attaining statehood for Utah the Church actively advocated the separation of church and state and the replacement of a church-sponsored party with partisan politics, the first loyalty of most remained with the Church. When Ruth May Fox undertook a position as secretary of the Republican Women's League in 1895, she commented: "I do hope they will not engender bad feelings in their division on party lines. For my part I care nothing for politics. It is mormonism or nothing for me."

Nineteenth century Mormonism as shared by both men and women included conversion, persecution, migration and settlement, and efforts at building a community-kingdom. However, these commonalities were not the total of the Mormon experience, and they certainly were not the total of Mormon women's experience. One expert in the field has suggested that "what we call women's history may actually be the study of a separate women's culture,"[16] and indeed the writings of Latter-day Saint women indicate that the women lived much of their lives in a subculture separate from men. It was a culture whose chief occupations were nurturing and housekeeping and whose primary rituals centered around women's relationships with other women, children, and men. Nurturing was often extended beyond the home into schoolteaching, nursing, and midwifery; and there was also a ready market outside the home for such homemaking skills as weaving, sewing and tailoring, cooking, and cleaning. The visiting that consistently strengthened bonds among women had its public counterpart in the gathering of women in Relief Societies, Mutual Improvement Associations, and, at the end of the century, women's clubs. These female occupations and rituals form the basis of a cultural history long untold—a history that women's writings tell best.

"Got breakfast then made some mince meat for pies," recorded Julina Lambson Smith in 1886. Kitchen work seems to have merited frequent mention in the diary she kept during her stay in the Hawaiian Mission. If women were not often the sole providers for their families' food, clothing, and shelter, they were frequently the most immediate providers. About to leave Missouri in 1838 because of mob action against the Saints, Drusilla Hendricks gathered her cabbage and made it into sauerkraut; and Eliza Lyman noted in her diary her concern when she "cooked the last of our flour to day and have no prospect of getting any more untill after harvest." Forced to be resourceful, women fed their families with whatever was available, and likewise cleaned and clothed them.

Providing personal and family necessities seemed a sometimes insurmountable task for women, many of whom found, like Mary Jane Mount Tanner, that "one day comes and goes, and the next follows; the same routine of work is gone through, and the same remains to be done." Totally ignored in some diaries, housekeeping tasks formed the bulk of other diaries and even of some reminiscences. When Bathsheba Smith wrote to her husband in 1851 to keep him abreast of what she had been doing during the winter, she indicated she had done "nearly all Fathers folks house work, nine in the family most of the time. . . . Maid father two fine shirts, mother twoo dresses. . . . Maid her some pillow cases. . . . Helped quilt two quilts. . . . I maid my carpet, made George A a pair of pants and coat and siss some clothing. . . . Maid me a nice hearth rug, maid some nice soap, maid a cushion for my rocking chair. . . . Maid me a dress and bonnet, Bathsheba an Apron and various other things, besides cooking, washing, mending, milking, churning, feeding my cow, pigs, chickings and visiting the sick as well as the well."[17]

Such careful accounting of domestic work reflected where women spent their time, but it may also have reflected their consciousness of the standard of "feminine domesticity" evident throughout nineteenth century America.[18] Popular journals idealized happy homemakers, but

Mormon women's personal writings show they responded variously to woman's work—some, like Bathsheba Smith, with obvious pleasure, others with ambivalence or nonchalance, and some with outright disdain.

Domestically inclined or not, women usually took delight in those for whom they provided, particularly their children. The birth of a child was an occasion of great joy. Wrote Martha Cragun Cox on January 11, 1871, in Southern Utah: "I recieved from Heaven the gift of a daughter, a mite of a creature weighing 7 lbs and 11 oz. As I looked at the waxen figure beside me on the bed I felt I had all I needed in this life to make up my sum of happiness." Babies' gaining of teeth and words and mobility merited mention in many accounts, giving a clear sense of how children and the accompanying pregnancy, birthing, nursing, and tending had impact on women's lives. In nineteenth century Mormondom the primary responsibility for nurturing children clearly rested with women. Many, like Martha Spence Heywood, expressed in quiet moments gratitude for "the rich blessing of children to give tone & exercise to the long treasured up woman's feelings."[19]

Because of their constant contact with children, mothers seem to have felt the loss of their children most keenly. In 1874, at age forty-six, Emmeline B. Wells found her teenaged daughters spending more time away from home, and hardly knew "how to endure being deprived of the society of my children but must bear it with what grace I am capable of sustaining." Missions, military service, and marriages meant sons and daughters would leave home to provide or be provided for elsewhere. Drusilla Hendricks so dreaded sending her son away with the Mormon Battalion that at first she refused to let him go. When the final call came for more men, Drusilla remembered, "William raised his eyes and looked me in the face. I knew then that he would go as well as I know now that he has been. I could not swallow one bite of breakfast but I waited on the rest thinking I might never have my family all together again. I had no photograph of him but I took one in my mind and said to myself, If I never see you again until the morning of the resurrection I shall know you are my child."[20]

Such goings away decidedly changed relationships, but the death Drusilla so feared suspended them. Infant mortality was high, and few

11

nineteenth century Mormon women escaped the loss of one or more children. For Martha Cox, the death of her firstborn was "my first real sorrow and the bitterest disappointment I had ever known." Sorrow was long remembered by some mothers who marked the passing days, months, and years since the birth or death of a deceased child. Emmeline Wells noted in her diary that September 1, 1874, was the anniversary of the birth of her first and only son, Eugene. "He would have been thirty today," she wrote. "If he were living how much happiness he might bring to me." Faith in a resurrection to life after death did not eliminate the pain the women felt, but it seemed to ease it somewhat. Upon the death of her youngest son, Sally Randall reflected: "I know he is better off than the rest of us, but it seems hard to part, but I think the separation will not be long if we are faithful."

Not all Mormon women were married, nor did all those who married have children, but nurturing and strengthening of family ties seem still to have played a prominent part in the lives even of nonmothers. If they pursued work, it was usually home-related work such as weaving, sewing, cleaning, or cooking, or nurturing work such as teaching or nursing or midwifery. Almost none of the single women were financially independent, nor did they live alone. They were a family's "maiden aunt" or were otherwise assimilated into existing households. Many single Mormon women, such as Hepzibah Richards, played out their dominant familial role as sisters, providing for parents or siblings or nieces and nephews, but not for children of their own.

Not until the last quarter of the nineteenth century was the single career woman nonsuspect in American society, and the Mormon culture was not substantially different in this regard. Latter-day Saints and Americans at large had prescribed separate spheres and roles for men and women: woman's sphere was the home, and her role was that of nurturer and housekeeper or homemaker or manager. As the nineteenth century woman's movement challenged these assumptions, Latter-day Saint women, too, considered whether or not the home was their only legitimate sphere of activity. Through the 1870s and 1880s, with the active support of their church leaders, Mormon women extended their sphere to include church and community activities as well as some nontraditional trades and professions. "My sphere of usefulness is being enlarged," wrote Susa Young, a music student at the Brigham Young Academy in 1879.

Acknowledging this expansion of women's activities, Eliza R. Snow, president of Mormon women's organizations, told her sisters through the 1870s and '80s that home was "a mother's first duty, but it is not *all* her duty."[21] Brigham Young also encouraged women to contribute to the larger community, but strongly emphasized the priority of women's duties at home, indicating that the woman who rose at the resurrection to find that her duty as wife and mother had been sacrificed in order to pursue any other duty would find her "whole life had been a failure."[22] The oft-expressed desire of women to train children "in the ways of truth and righteousness" or "in the fear of God and of wrong doing" conveys the pervasiveness of what they believed to be a divinely designated responsibility to establish and maintain individual households of faith.

If Brigham Young saw eternal rewards for this commitment to child-bearing and child-rearing, he saw temporal benefits as well. Declaring that women should not worry whether their marriages met expectations for intimacy, he asked them to find comfort and satisfaction in turning their attention to rearing their children. There are not extant statistical studies on the absenteeism of Mormon husbands and fathers, but one cannot read Mormon women's personal writings without surmising that their husbands were often away with church and community responsibilities.[23] "I well recollect the sensations with which my mind was actuated when I learned the fact that my husband had been called and ordained to the Melchisedek priesthood and would undoubtedly be required to travel and preach the gospel," wrote Caroline Crosby. For Bathsheba Smith, whose husband left Nauvoo for the fifth of a series of missions, the sensation was one of pain. She wrote her husband, George A. Smith, that she had watched his boat travel down the river "untill I could not see it any longer then I held my head for it aked [ached]."

Louisa Barnes Pratt, whose husband was sent from Nauvoo to Tahiti, found her own grief at saying goodbye compounded by that of four children: "The parting scene came. The two eldest daughters wept very sorely. We walked with him to the steamboat landing: he carried the youngest child in his arms. . . . He would be absent three years. . . .It was unfortunate at the last as he stept on to the steamboat the children saw him take his handkerchief from his eyes, they knew he was wiping away his tears, it was too much for them. They commenced weeping; the second daughter was inconsolable, the more we tried to soothe her, the more piteous were her complaints; she was sure her father would never return."[24] Louisa reported that she wept for three days before a calmness came over her and she could smile again.

Jenetta Richards with her husband, Willard, and son Heber John, Nauvoo, 1845. (LDS Church Archives.)

Women sent husbands away on missions with faith that this was part of the Lord's work, a "high and holy calling," in the words of Caroline Crosby. Mary Haskin Parker Richards, a young bride left with her husband's family at Winter Quarters, Nebraska, told her

14

uncle Willard Richards she would rather remain alone for even ten years than see her husband return home "before the Lord wanted him to."[25]

While church and community service and even employment could make for painful separations between companions, some Latter-day Saint women also expressed anxiety over the physical and emotional distances that resulted from involvement in plural marriage. When Latter-day Saints first publicly acknowledged in 1852 that plural marriage was widely taught and practiced among them, the response of most non-Mormons paralleled that of Eliza R. Snow in Nauvoo, who wrote, "The subject was very repugnant to my feelings —so directly was it in opposition to my educated pre-possessions."[26] Polygamy incurred heated public opposition until 1890, when the Church formally abandoned the practice.[27] Women who gave husbands their permission to take additional wives, and women who agreed to become plural wives in established families, usually struggled to attain a spiritual witness that the principle was divine.

In spite of such spiritual anchors, plural marriage forced women to cope with jealousy. Jane Charters Robinson Hindley of American Fork, Utah, herself a second wife, expressed in her diary the dread she felt when Mr. Hindley "returned and brought two I cannot call them wives yet it seems so strange. Oh what my feelings are thiss moment. . . . M[a]y God help me in my weakness and forgive me if I falter in my duty and affection to him I love."[28] Patty Sessions found that the bringing home of a second wife, Rosilla, resulted in a tense marital triangle. "I feel bad again," she wrote on September 8, 1847. "He has been and talked to Rosilla and she filed his ears full and when he came to my bed I was quite chled [chilled] he was gone so long and I was so cold I had been crying."[29]

Many women, however, found within the plural marriage system tolerable or even good marital relations. Bathsheba W. Smith and Lucy Meserve Smith were both plural wives of George A. Smith: each rejoiced in his affection, which neither seems to have measured, and both corresponded with and often lived with other wives in the family. Martha Cragun Cox said she and her two "sister wives" "loved each other more than sisters, children of one mother love." According to Martha, "We enjoyed many privileges that single wifery never

15

knew," including the sharing of child care and housekeeping responsibilities.

Marital relations were a major concern in the writings of nineteenth century Mormon women. Plural marriage dominates the excerpts included in this compilation, even though it was practiced by only about 15 to 20 percent of the Mormon population. Indeed, plural wives seem to be disproportionately represented among Mormon women whose writings have been preserved in archival collections. Perhaps this faithful fifth heeded the commandment to keep personal records as diligently as they heeded the commandment to enter into plural marriage. Or perhaps they or their posterity or archivists sensed the uniqueness of the experience and sought to preserve it. In any case, the variety of records well represents the variety of experience.

Individual plural wives even viewed their own experience variously. Emmeline B. Wells, who privately sorrowed that she felt "no protection or comfort in my husband," and longed for him to "love me even a little and not seem so perfectly indifferent to any sensation of that kind," publicly declared the other side of the coin: that plural marriage "gives women the highest opportunities for self-development, exercise of judgment, and arouses latent faculties, making them more truly cultivated in the actual realities of life, more independent in thought and mind, noble and unselfish."[30] This latter statement is taken from one of Emmeline's editorials for the *Woman's Exponent,* a semimonthly paper published by and for Mormon women. The *Exponent* was, among other things, part of the public campaign in defense of polygamy in which Mormon women were actively engaged from 1870 to 1890. Mass meetings were held, testimonials published, and memorials sent to the United States Congress in hopes of countering the national opposition to plural marriage. While Mormon women played a unique role in countering attacks upon the Church, their defense, however articulate, did not prevent passage of stringent federal anti-polygamy legislation in 1882 and 1887. However, women's rallying in defense of themselves, their families, and their religion provided them, as one author has suggested, "a chance to build their own identity. . . . their own meaningful and supportive self image."[31]

Active defense of plural marriage was only one aspect of women's increasing public involvement during the last third of the nineteenth century. The Relief Society, established for women in Nauvoo, had flourished there for two years and seen a brief revival in Utah in the 1850s. Brigham Young's reinstitution of the society in 1867 resulted in an organized sisterhood that exists to the present day. The Relief Society's early efforts were simply a formalization of work commonly performed by women in the family or community. Within or outside the auspices of the society, women provided for the poor, comforted the bereaved, and cared for the sick, all of which figure largely in their writings.

Lucy Meserve Smith found that in providing for the poor she "never took more satisfaction and I might say pleasure in any labour I ever performed in my life." And Rebecca Mace recorded her experience with Relief Society sisters who in 1897 visited the family of a son who had committed suicide. "Oh how welcome we were," she wrote. "The poor Mother clasped me to her in her helpless grief."[32]

After 1868 local Relief Societies, then established churchwide, rapidly added to these traditional womanly activities. They built and owned Relief Society halls, ran cooperatives, raised silk, bought, stored, and sold grain, and collectively supported the medical education of women as doctors and nurses, eventually establishing their own Deseret Hospital "with a lady M.D. as Principal." The *Woman's Exponent* provided jobs for women as editors, business agents, and compositors, and served as an outlet for dozens of women who wanted to write poetry and prose. It carried news of the Young Ladies' Mutual Improvement Association and the Primary Association, organizations for young women and children that the Relief Society staffed and mothered. And it featured the progress of the national suffrage movement in which Mormon women became involved. This flurry of activity meant increased opportunities for women to plan and conduct meetings, organize programs, balance budgets, and speak publicly.[33]

In addition to expanding women's community involvement, the building of a formal sisterhood strengthened the bonds between women. The informal gathering of women to share and visit was an integral part of American life all through the nineteenth century.[34] Some Mormon women's diaries describe days so filled with visits that one wonders how anything else was accomplished. Mary Haskin Parker Richards records that on December 6, 1846, she made separate calls on "some of my friends," including Brother Van Cott "to see his wife and mother"; Sister Noon, "to carry home a hood Which I had borrowed"; a friend, Ellen Wilding; her aunts Rhoda and Amelia; Sister Rushton "morning the loss of her child"; and in-laws Maria and Jane. Women washed, sewed, cooked, ate, and traveled together, making all such activities occasions for visiting.

Board of directors of the Deseret Hospital, founded by the Relief Society in 1882. Standing, left to right: Dr. Ellis R. Shipp, Bathsheba W. Smith, Elizabeth Howard, Dr. Romania Pratt Penrose. Seated, left to right: Phebe C. Woodruff, Mary I. Horne, Jane S. Richards, Eliza R. Snow, Emmeline B. Wells, Zina D. H. Young, Marinda N. J. Hyde. (LDS Church Archives.)

Letters between women lend a glimpse of some of the subjects they shared. "When you write to me write much news," Elizabeth Haven wrote from Missouri to her New England cousin. "[I] want to hear from old Holliston: marraiges, births and deaths." Other conversations were much more personal. Talk turned to husbands and work and children. "I want to be a good housekeeper and I just mean to be one, in due time," Martha Spence Heywood wrote her friend Emmeline Free Young in 1855. "I feel my awkwardness so keenly," she confided, confessing she "did not know how to wash my clothes till I was about thirty years old never cooked or kept house till after I came to Nephi."[35] "Where is Miss Crawford and Miss Cook?" asked Elizabeth Haven. "If you see them tell them not to be in a hurry about getting married, for I am not. O . . . don't you think that I am very silly?"

Lighthearted or soul searching, sharing among women was serious business. It was one means whereby they reaffirmed the reality and significance of their female culture. It was also often an opportunity for reaffirming a common commitment to the restored gospel. When faith entered into the sharing, the bonds of sisterhood seem to have been not only strengthened but sanctified. "Remember the Prophet and afflicted Zion at the throne of grace and receive this letter which is full of love and affection from a sister in the everlasting gospel," Elizabeth Haven wrote a female cousin. That women gathered together to feast upon spiritual things is evident from their writings. Patty Sessions noted frequent meetings of men and women during the Saints' extended stay at Winter Quarters, making particular mention when "none but females [were] there." These were occasions when spiritual gifts were exercised to the "joy and rejoicing" of all present. "They spoke in tongues. I interpreted. Some prophesied," Patty recorded of one such meeting.

In addressing the first Relief Society in Nauvoo, Joseph Smith discussed such gifts, indicating (in reference to Mark 16:17-18) that "no matter who believeth, these signs, such as healing the sick, casting out devils, &c., should follow all that believe, whether male or female."[36] Women exercised all these gifts, particularly the healing of the sick. Though such dramatic manifestations of the Spirit were certainly not part of every gathering of Mormon women, they seem to have had widespread impact on sisters through the end of the nineteenth century and during the early years of the twentieth century.[37] In 1895 Ruth May Fox recorded, between notes of more formal meetings for Relief Society, the Women's Press Club, and the Utah Woman's Suffrage Association, an informal gathering where women spoke in tongues and prophesied, describing in some detail the "glorious time."

"Diversities of gifts" within "the same Spirit" (1 Corinthians 12:4) is a phrase fittingly descriptive of the diversity of women within the latter-day household of faith. United by their conviction of the restored gospel of Jesus Christ, and sharing many common experiences, they nonetheless lived separate lives. Sarah DeArmon Pea Rich began married life as a wealthy, young bride; Emmeline B. Wells lost two husbands by the time she was twenty-four; Hepzibah Richards never married. Some of these women had their origins in the Southern States or New England; others in the British Isles or Canada. Scandinavians, who are not represented in this compilation, which consists of records originally written in English, were a significant part of the nineteenth century Mormon population. From their homelands, women came to Zion with families of various sizes, ages, and financial well-being and social status.

The Zion to which they came also varied. Mormonism was lived in different climes and at different times. The church meetings Nancy Clement Williams attended in the 1890s, even as she pioneered a new colony in Mexico, differed in number and variety from those Mary Fielding Smith attended at the Kirtland Temple in 1837, though there was continuity in content. Programs and policies were flexible. The cooperative movement so religiously stressed in the 1860s and '70s was not a major part of women's lives at the end of the century. Predictably, some of the practices of nineteenth century Mormons seem strange to modern Latter-day Saints. Emphasis on the Word of Wisdom, for example, was not as great during the nineteenth century as it is at present within the Church, and frequent mentions of wine, tea, and coffee in women's records should not bring sisters' faithfulness into question.[38]

Beyond these external differences are the differences within the women themselves. Emmeline B. Wells was intensely introspective and prone to extended analysis of each day's experience, while Patience Loader and Lucy Meserve Smith seem to have spent a good deal more time laughing and making others laugh. Ruth May Fox's middle years were a rush of public meetings, while Rebecca Mace filled her sunset years with quiet, private meetings with family and friends in need. In Kirtland Caroline Crosby felt a sense of personal achievement in studying Hebrew with the texts from her husband's class. Susa Young expressed a sense of pride in the poem she published in the *Woman's Exponent*, and Julina Lambson Smith was pleased that during her stay in Hawaii she could help manage the mission kitchen, sew new bathing suits for herself, her husband, and others, and learn a little native language on the side.

Of course, the picture of these women that comes from their personal writings also varies according to the nature of the writings themselves. Bathsheba Smith wrote letters to her husband, Susa Young to her mother, Mary Fielding Smith to her sister, Hepzibah Richards to her brother, and Elizabeth Haven to her cousin. The readership was clear, and some of the information shared was not intended to go beyond the family. Daily diaries, as well as journals, which were more sporadic and more reflective than diaries, were not so clearly audience-oriented. Some women seem to have used them to vent feelings they said could not be publicly expressed, at least at the time the record was made. The journal of Jean Rio Baker, however, was originally intended for the family back home in England, and reminiscences or autobiographies were definitely written with posterity in mind. "Just think of it, my dear reader," Sarah Rich prefaced her account of crossing in a canoe a river wild with running ice when she was far advanced in her first pregnancy.

Each of the following selections is preceded by a brief introduction to the writer as well as her personal writings. If the record exists in the woman's own handwriting, the authors have attempted to reproduce the original holograph as accurately and readably as possible. For this reason the original spelling has been maintained and minimal punctuation has been added. That is, sentences have been designated by capital letter beginnings and period endings, and commas inserted, when the lack of such punctuation in the original blurred the sense or readability of the text. Crossovers and repeated words have been deleted. Common abbreviations have been let stand as abbreviations, including the ampersand (&). Paragraphs have been designated for readability. For records existing only in typescript or whose original holograph is otherwise unavailable, the authors have standardized punctuation and spelling unless otherwise indicated. This is because the accuracy of the typescript could not be determined in the absence of the original holograph. The authors have marked with brackets in all selections the addition of any clarifying material, such as family and place names and unclear words and dates. Deleted sections have been noted with ellipses. Material needing further elucidation has been footnoted or explained in the introductory notes to each chapter.

William Mulder has suggested that in the "unpretentious subliterature of Mormon journals we come close to understanding history. In them," he writes, "we find something of the daily living and dying of men and women both weak and valiant. Their story is not epic except as life and many days together give it sweep—it is the sweep of daily existence, the great movement that is the result of countless little movements, each life a tiny capillary, a vein, an artery contributing to the strong heartbeat of their collective existence."[39] By chronologically presenting these selections from Mormon women's writings, the authors hope in some degree to chronicle the "great movement" of nineteenth century Mormonism. The history of its leaders has been written and rewritten, yet "the body is not one member, but many." Women are among the many who deserve greater recognition and understanding, and now "upon these we bestow more abundant honour." (1 Corinthians 12:14, 23.)

Chapter Two

Becoming a Mormon

"Fire in My Bones"

Even before The Church of Jesus Christ of Latter-day Saints was officially organized April 6, 1830, disciples of this new American religious movement had been seeking converts. Such proselyting activity was intensified after June 1830 when Samuel Smith set out as a missionary from Fayette, New York, with copies of the newly published Book of Mormon. The following October four elders were called to take the gospel to the "Lamanites" or native Americans, and during 1831 some fifty-eight Mormon missionaries proselyted for converts. By 1844 there were over five hundred missionaries in the United States, Canada, and Europe.[1] Even the Prophet Joseph Smith engaged in missionary work at various times in his life.

These Latter-day Saint elders bore witness of the restored church, citing the New Testament pattern for the gospel and the Church of Christ. They stressed the need for faith, repentance, baptism, and the gift of the Holy Ghost, and emphasized the organization of the primitive church and the spiritual gifts bestowed upon its faithful members. They declared that the apostasy foreseen by the ancient apostles had taken place, and that the anticipated restoration had been realized in God's establishment of his church in the latter days through Joseph Smith. For some who listened to their message, "the Bible seemed an unsealed book." One woman said she could suddenly see "fields of light and intelligence in it."

Missionaries encouraged those seeking the truth to read the Book of Mormon, which evidenced Joseph Smith's prophetic calling; and thousands who believed it were baptized into the new church. By

1835 some revelations given to Joseph Smith had been published as the Doctrine and Covenants of the Latter-day Saints, and in 1837 the Church's first missionary tract appeared, Parley P. Pratt's *A Voice of Warning*. Latter-day Saint monthly and semimonthly periodicals were published in Missouri, Ohio, Illinois, and, by 1840, England.

The word went forth, and not without effect. In the first decade of the Church from 1830 to 1840, membership swelled from 6 persons to 30,000. But the opposition swelled also. Attempts were frequently made to disrupt meetings and to harass and confuse Latter-day Saint missionaries. And persecution was often directed against new converts, many of whom left hostile families and neighbors to join the main body of the Saints and help establish Zion.

Hearing the restored gospel preached by Mormon missionaries, being converted to their message, and changing one's life to meet the demands of the Church were experiences shared by a whole generation of Mormons. They are still being repeated as a part of the Mormon experience, but to a lesser extent since many Mormons all over the world have "grown up in the Church." This chapter appropriately focuses on women in the process of becoming Mormons. That process is outwardly simple. It involves baptism by immersion and the receiving of the gift of the Holy Ghost by the laying on of hands. But the individual inward process is not so easily described. Some studies have identified patterns among early Latter-day Saint converts by comparing their social and religious backgrounds and geographical origins. These lend limited understanding as to which people responded to the message of the restored gospel. But conversion is an individual process, and fortunately, individual Mormons have been eager to relate their personal conversion experiences often in the meetings of the Saints and frequently in journals, letters, and reminiscences.

The two women whose accounts of their early Church experiences comprise this chapter provide a sampling of the women the Church attracted and the thoughts and feelings involved in their conversion. Sarah Studevant Leavitt and Mary Ann Weston Maughan were introduced to the Church early in their adult lives. Each woman had been a serious student of the scriptures and had been anxious to live a good Christian life long before she became acquainted with Mormonism.

Sarah believed from personal experience that the Lord could communicate with man through dreams and visions. Both were prepared for the message taught by the missionaries.

Religious courage is reflected in the autobiographical sketches that follow. Each woman believed in her own spiritual sensitivity and ability to recognize and act upon the truth. Each, in spite of painful opposition from family and friends, stood firm in her conviction of the truth. The reminiscences composed by these women living in late nineteenth century Utah stretch back to the early years of the century in Canada and England. The accounts are related by women mellowed and firm in the faith, but each account in its own way reflects the hope and enthusiasm characteristic of a new convert.

Sarah Studevant Leavitt (1798-1878)

Raised in New Hampshire by Presbyterian parents, young Sarah Studevant regularly studied the Bible and prayed on her own. Like many early Mormon converts, she was seeking a church similar to the early church described in the New Testament. Sarah married Jeremiah Leavitt (1797-1846) in 1817, and the young couple moved to Hatley, Quebec, Canada, where Leavitts had been established for some twenty or thirty years. There were Mormon elders in Canada in the 1830s, but none of them found their way to Hatley. A traveler who had attended a Mormon gathering elsewhere loaned the Leavitts a copy of the Book of Mormon and Parley P. Pratt's *A Voice of Warning.* "We believed them without preaching," Jeremiah Leavitt later wrote. In July 1837 the extended Leavitt family, including nine children of Jeremiah and Sarah, started as a group to gather with the Saints in Missouri. Delays kept them from joining with the Saints at Far West, but they later moved to Nauvoo, and finally to Utah, settling first in Tooele and later in Washington County.

The following extract is taken from an autobiographical sketch by Sarah Studevant Leavitt dated April 19, 1875. The sketch was edited and published by Juanita Leavitt Pulsipher (Brooks) in 1919, and an excerpt from the published version has been reprinted here with clarifying material added in brackets and spelling and punctuation standardized. The original is in private possession.

> I was born in the town of Lime, County of Grafton, New Hampshire, [date torn off] and am now seventy-six years, seven months, and fifteen days old. My father was Lemuel Studevant and my mother was Priscilla Tompson. My parents were very strict with their children, being descendants of the old Pilgrims. They taught them every principle of truth and honor as they understood it themselves. They taught them to pray and read the Bible for themselves. My father had many

books that treated on the principle of man's salvation and many stories that were very interesting and I took great pleasure in reading them. He was Dean of the Presbyterian Church. For years his house was open to all denominations, so his children had the privilege of hearing the interesting religious conversations, but as I had the privilege of reading the Bible for myself, I found that none of them understood the Bible as I did. I knew of no other way to understand it only as it read. The Apostle said, "Though we, or angels from heaven, preach any other gospel than that which we preach, let him be accursed,"[2] and it was very evident to my understanding that they all came short of preaching the doctrine that Paul preached, but I was confident we should have the faith.

From childhood I was seriously impressed and desired very much to be saved from that awful hell I heard so much about. I believed in the words of the Savior, that said, "Ask, and you shall receive." I prayed much and my prayers were sometimes answered immediately; this was before I made any pretentions to having any religion. When I was eighteen years old the Lord sent me a good husband. We were married at my father's house, March 6, 1817, in the town of Barton, County of Orleans, State of Vermont. The next June we moved to [Hatley] Canada, fifteen miles from the Vermont line, into a very wicked place. They would swear and drink and play cards on Sunday and steal and do any wicked act their master, the devil, would lead them to. This was very different from what I was brought up to [do]. My father would never suffer any profane language in his house. The next February I had a daughter [Ann] born. She lived only twelve days. There was some things very strange connected with the birth of this child, which I do not think best to write, but I shall never forget, which I never shall know the meaning of until the first resurrection, when I shall clasp it again in my arms.

The next January I had another daughter [Clarissa] born. When she was about six months old I had a vision of the damned

27

spirits in hell, so that I was filled with horror more than I was able to bear, but I cried to the Lord day and night until I got an answer of peace and a promise that I should be saved in the kingdom of God that satisfied me. That promise has been with me through all the changing scenes of life ever since.

When I was getting ready for bed one night I had put my babe into the bed with its father and it was crying. I dropped down to take off my shoes and stockings, I had one stocking in my hand. There was a light dropped down on the floor before me. I stepped back and there was another under my feet. The first was in the shape of a half moon and full of little black spots. The last was about an inch long and about a quarter of an inch wide. I brushed them with the stocking that was in my hand and put my hand over one of them to see if it would shine on my hand. This I did to satisfy others; as for myself, I knew that the lights were something that could not be accounted for and for some purpose. I did not know what until I heard the gospel preached in its purity. The first was an emblem of all the religions then on the earth. The half moon that was cut off was the spiritual gifts promised after baptism. The black spots were the defects you will find in every church throughout the whole world. The last light was the gospel preached by the angel flying through the midst of heaven, and it was the same year and the same season of the year, and I don't know but the same day that the Lord brought the glad news of salvation to Joseph Smith.[3] It must have been a stirring time among the heavenly hosts, the windows of heaven having so long been closed against all communication with the earth, being suddenly thrown open. Angels were wending their way to earth with such a glorious message—a message that concerns everyone, both in heaven and earth. I passed through all this and not a neighbor knew anything of it, although I prayed so loud that my husband was afraid they would all hear me.

After this there were two of his aunts came in and commenced talking about being slighted in not being invited to a quilting. I had no relish for any such talk and said nothing. They saw that I made no comment. Being astonished that I was so still, they asked me what I thought about it. I told them I didn't know or care anything about it, all I cared for was to know and do the will of God. This turned the conversation in the right direction. My telling my experience to these women and the effect it had on their minds was probably of much good, as they spread the news through the neighborhood. The result was, the whole neighborhood were convinced that the manner that they had spent their time was wrong, and instead of taking the name of God in vain they cried to Him for mercy. In short, the whole course of their former lives was abandoned. There were some exceptions, for the leopard cannot change his spots. How then can men do good that are accustomed to do evil, so says the prophet.

But there was a minister come from the states and formed a church, called the Baptist, which I joined because I wanted to be baptized by immersion. I had been sprinkled when an infant, but as I said before, I did not believe in any church on earth, but was looking forward to a time when the knowledge of God would cover the earth, and that glorious time is rolling, all glory to the Lord. I lived very watchful and prayerful, never neglecting my prayers, for I felt that I was entitled to no blessing unless I asked for them, and I think so yet.

We took a free-will Baptist paper that I thought always told the truth, but there was a number of columns in this paper concerning a new sect. It had a prophet that pretended he talked with God. They had built a thing they called a meetinghouse, a huge mass of rock and wood, on the shores of Lake Cryenth (I am not sure as to the spelling of this word) to make the blue waters of the lake blush for shame. In this Joe would go talk, he said, with the Lord and come out and tell them what the Lord said. But if I should go on and tell all the lies in that paper, how they healed the sick and managed their affairs, it would be too much for me. If you ever read the Arabian Night tales, you might guess of what importance they were, for I could compare them to nothing else. No person of common sense would believe a word of it, and yet they wrote it for truth, thinking that would hinder Mormonism from spreading. But in this the devil overshot himself, for they were too big lies for anyone to believe.

But I will go on with my experience. I had a place that I went every day for secret prayers. My mind would be carried away in prayer so that I knew nothing of what was going on around me. It seemed like a cloud was resting down over my head. If that cloud would break, there was an angel that had a message for me or some new light. If the cloud would break, there would be something new and strange revealed. I did not know that it concerned anyone but myself. Soon after this there was one of my husband's sisters came in, and after spending a short time in the house she asked me to take a walk with her. She had heard the gospel preached by a Mormon and believed it and been baptized. She commenced and related the whole of Joseph's vision and what the Angel Moroni had said the mission he had called him to.[4]

It came to my mind in a moment that this was the message that was behind that cloud, for me and not for me only, but for the whole world, and I considered it of more importance than anything I had ever heard before, for it brought back the ancient order of things and laid a foundation that could be built upon that was permanent; a foundation made by Him that laid the foundation of the earth, even the Almighty God; and he commanded his people to build up the kingdom of God upon the foundation he had laid, and notwithstanding the heathen raged and Satan mustered all his forces against the work, it has gone onward and upward for more than forty years, and will continue until the work is finished.

I read the Book of Mormon, the Doctrine and Covenants, and all the writings I could get from the Latter-day Saints. It was the book of Doctrine and Covenants that confirmed my faith in the work. I knew that no man, nor set of men, that could make such a book or would dare try from any wisdom that man possessed. I knew it was the word of God and a revelation from heaven and received it as such. I sought with my whole heart a knowledge of the truth and obtained a knowledge that never has nor never will leave me.

The next thing was to gather with the Saints. I was pondering over in my heart how it was possible for such a journey with what means we could muster. We had a good farm, but could not get much for it, but the voice of the Spirit said, "Come out of Babylon, O my people, that you be not partakers of her plagues." From the time the voice spoke so loud, clear and plain to my understanding, I knew the way would be open for us to gather with the Saints. For the Lord never gives a commandment to man but what he gives them a chance to obey. From this time we set out in earnest and was ready to start with the rest of the company July 20, 1835.[5] The company was made up of the Leavitt family, Mother Sarah Shannon Leavitt, and her children, consisting of twenty-three souls. Franklin Chamberlain, her oldest son-in-law, took the lead. He did not belong to the Church, but his wife [Rebecca Leavitt Chamberlain] did.

We had a prosperous journey of eight hundred miles to Kirtland, Ohio. I had no chance to be baptized and join the Church until I got there. My daughter, Louisa, and myself and some others were baptized at this place and were confirmed. Louisa had been sick for a year, under the doctor's care, and had taken very much medicine, but all to no purpose. She was very feeble, could sit up but little. She had been in the states with my friends for more than a year. Her father and myself went after her with a light carriage. As she was eighteen years old, I gave her her choice to go home with us or stay with my sister. My sister told her if she would stay with her she should never want for anything, but she said she would go with her father and mother. My sister said, "Louisa, if you ever get well, don't say that Mormonism cured you." So much for her judgment on Mormonism. She was rich, high spirited, and proud, and belonged to a church that was more popular than the Latter-day Saints.

Now I will go back to my story. We stayed at Kirtland about a week and had the privilege of hearing Joseph preach in that thing the Baptists said they called a meetinghouse, which proved to be a very good house. We went into the upper rooms, saw the Egyptian mummies, the writing that was said to be written in Abraham's day, Jacob's ladder being pictured on it, and lots more wonders that I cannot write here, and that were explained to us.

But our money was all spent, we could go no further. We had to look for a place where we could sustain ourselves for the present, while the rest of our company went on to Twelve Mile Grove in Illinois.[6] We promised them we would follow them the next year. This was the first of September. My husband found a place ten miles from Kirtland—Mayfield, a little village with mills and chair factories, and every chance for a living we could wish. Someone asked my husband why he went there. There was everything gathered out of that place that could be saved, but he was mistaken, although it was a very wicked place. There was a man by the name of Faulk, that owned almost the whole village. Of him we hired a house. It was about twenty feet from his tavern, so I could stand in my door and talk with those in the tavern. But they opposed Mormonism, so I said little about it. I thought I would first get their good will and then perhaps I could have some influence over them. Of course, so long as they thought me an enemy it would be of no use to preach over to them. I was persecuted and abused in many ways, but not by Faulk's family. But I paid no attention to vulgar expressions, for I cared nothing about them. I had something of more importance that was shut up like fire in my bones.

But it was a hard case when the children would come from school with their noses bleeding and crying, saying that they had been pounded most unmercifully. I went to the teacher very candid and told her that unless she could stop the scholars from abusing my children I should have to take them out of school, which I did not want to do. She said she would.

I wanted very much to get the good will of my neighbors, for I knew that I could have no success in preaching Mormonism unless I did, and I was so full of that spirit it was hard to hold my peace. Consequently, I mingled in the society of all, was cheerful and sociable as though I was a great friend, but kept on the side of truth and right. I would go into the tavern when they had balls and help set the table and wait on ladies and was very sociable and talkative. By and by, being free with all, I soon got the good will of some of them. If we had commenced telling them of their faults and that they were all wrong, which was the case, and they must repent or they would be damned, we could not have got along in that place but should have had to leave.

Mary Ann Weston Maughan (1817-1901)

Mary Ann Weston was born and reared a Methodist near Gloucester, England. She was the daughter of a prosperous realtor and often traveled with her father to purchase and sell houses and land. Seeking an apprenticeship as a dressmaker in 1839, Mary Ann took up residence with Mr. and Mrs. William Jenkins, through whom she heard of the Latter-day Saints. The excerpt that follows describes Mary Ann's experiences as an early Latter-day Saint in England.

Other portions of her autobiography tell something of Mary Ann's life after she left her father's family in England and married Peter Maughan in Kirtland. The Maughans eventually settled in Cache Valley in northern Utah, and Mary Ann noted with pride that Weston, Idaho, just north of Cache Valley, was named after her.[7]

Mary Ann's autobiography was written in the 1890s when she took notes and daybooks accumulated over the years and compiled them in journal form. This explains the frequent shifts in her narrative from past to present tense. Though the autobiography was published by the Daughters of Utah Pioneers in 1959, excerpts printed here are taken from the first volume of the original three-volume holograph in the Historical Department of the Church. Minimal punctuation has been added for clarification.

> In the spring of 1840, Mr Jenkins went to visit his friends in Herefordshire. Brother [Wilford] Woodruff was there preaching and Br Jenkins was Baptized into the Church of Latterday Saints. He came home and told us about [the Church]. This was the first we had heard of it. Soon Brother Woodruff came to our house. There was no one at home but me. He sat by the fire and soon comenced singing, Shall I for fear of feeble Man the Spirits course in me restrain. Br Jenkins had told us that he had left his home in America crossed the sea and come to Preach this Gospel to the people in England. While

Mary Ann Weston Maughan in later years when she wrote her autobiography.
(Daughters of Utah Pioneers.)

he was singing I looked at him. He looked so peaceful and happy I thought he must be a good Man and the Gospell he preached must be true.

There was a small Society of United Brethren in this place. I think they all joined the Church and emegrated to Navoo. Soon as the people were baptized the per[se]cution comenced. One sunday afternoon while some were being Bap[tized] a man threw a dog in the Pond saying he would Baptize the *Dog.* There was a man standing near me that had walked 8 or 10 miles that morning to be Baptized. He had a bundle of clothes in his hand. I saw a man from the other side of the pool come up to him and asked to borrow his clothes. They were willingly lent. The man went away, put them on, was Bap[tized] and returned them and Brother Rock carried them home wet. He afterwards joined the Church and we have laughed about his carrieng his clothes so many miles and not useind [using] them. Brother Woodruff Bap Mrs. Hill, Hannah Simonds now (M. Philips of Kaysville [Utah]) and myself at midnight in the pond in the centre of the village. We could [not] be Bap[tized] in the daytime on the acount of percuse-tion.

In the early spring my year [of apprenticeship] being up, Mrs Jenkins said I did not need to work a month on trial (as was the custom) as I was a good hand when I came to her, and another Aprentice haveing come to work on trial, I went home. I had plenty of work, but I was glad to take my old place in traveling when I could spare the time. Father would like to have me go with him. But I did not like to give up my Bissines [business].

In 1839 Uncle John Bishop died. I sat up with him the night before he died. He did not suffer much pain that night and the next day passed quietly away. This summer and winter [1840] I was at home working at my Bissiness and helping Father in his traviling. In the spring my sister Maria had a Powder Flask Burst in her hand. Her hand was very badly cut and bruised but no bones were Broken, and we were thankfull

it was no worse. She was laid up this summer with her hand
and I again took control of the House. I was very busy
haveing much sewing to do for our family as well as others.

My relatives did not obey the gospell (but they did not opose
me) and this made me sorrowfull and lonely. I attended all the
meettings I could often walking many miles alone to and from
them. One ship load of Saints has gone to Navoo from Glous-
cester and another will go soon as they can get ready. These
are the first from this country. On the 18th day of May 1840
I attended a Tea Meeting at Dynnock near Ledbury with
some friends. Bro Smith and Sister Smith now of Kaysville
and Bro John Davis of Tirley were Bap and Bros Smith and
Davis were ordained Priests on the Bank of the pond in which
they were Baptized.

This summer I became Engaged to Mr John Davis. He lived at
Tirley [and] was a Cooper and Carpenter by trade and a
young Man of much promis. On the Joseph Smith's Birthday
Dec 23d 1840 we were maried in Goucester by a Clergyman
of the Church of England. My husband had a home nicely
furnished in Tirley and we went there to live imeaditialy. We
both had good treads [trades] and plenty of work and were
very happy. The Elders soon called to see us. Brothers Willard
Richards and Leivi Richards, [Wilford] Woodruff, Rushton and
others that I do not remember their names. There was no
Saints in that place so Brother Richards counciled us to open
our house for meetings. We did so and the first held in our
house a lot of Roughs led by a Apostate Methodist came and
made a disturbance. They threatened the preacher with
violence, but we surrounded him and sliped him through a
door upstairs. When the Preacher was gone the Mob dispersd
and we were left alone. Notice was given for a Meeting in
two weeks and the Mob came again, but we succeeded in
hiding the Preacher and one of the Brethren took him away.
The Mob then turned on my husband, knocked him down
and kicked him. He was bruised Internaly and was never well
afterwards.

About this time he had a fall that hurt him some and he soon commenced to Bleed at the lungs. I sent for our family Physician. He gave Directions that he must remain in Bed and be kept very quiet, no noise or excitement alowed near him. We followed his advice and he soon begun to recover. Soon he had a dispute with his mother about Mormonism. This excited him and I was forced to ask her to leave the room. She did, but alase to late. He fainted. I was alone with him and could not move him, but a friend called and h[e]lped me to get him upstairs to bed. From this he took a relaps, and comenced to bleed at the lungs again. I sent for our Doctor but he gave no hopes of his recovery and quick Consumtion set in and he gradually failed from this time.

This was a very trying time for me as we were the only Saints in this place, and worse still we were surounded by per[se]cutiors who watched our house and if the Elders called would send word to his Mother. She was sure to come in, and thus we were deprived of the privilige of conversing with the Elders as we very much desired to do, or else I must ask his Mother to leave the room. There was no Saints within miles of us. We were alone most of the time, and this we prefered as it was better than having those who were not of our faith and would ridicule our Religion.

My husband did not suffer much pain but graduly grew weaker every day. He was confined to his Bed on the 14th of feb and I did not leave him by day or night or lie down to sleep during his Illness. The last few days some one or two kind friends staid with us, but he would not take anything from any hand but mine. I will pass by part of this trying time. He passed peacefully away on the 6th day of Apr 1841. That was the day on which the foundation stone of the Navoo Temple was laid. He was a good kind Husband and a faithful laterday Saint. I wished his funeral to take place on the Sunday but that being Easter Sunday his grandmother did not wish him buried on that day or on Good friday so he was laid to rest on Saturday the 10th of Apr 1841.

We lived near the Church so there was no need of a hearse. He belonged to a Club, but I do not remember the name of it. The Members all Attended his funeral. They were a fine lot of noble looking Men dressed in Black with long crape hat bands, and a Mourning Badge on their arm. Each one carried a long stafe trimed with crape. They marched two together with a very steatly step. I had not heard anything about them, and when I saw them coming I thought my heart would Break. His will was read by a lawyer by the side of his coffin. His friends disputed the will, and this made me feel worse than ever but the Lord sustained me in all my greifs and sorrows. When all had taken their last farewell of their loved one and the coffin closed, the Club then took charge of his remains and I was alone in the wide world.

He was Buried in a nice quiet corner of the grave yard of Tirley, Gloucestershire, and I have never lost sight of that place altho fifty years ago. It is the custom for the Mourners to attend the Church on the next Sunday when the funaral Sermon is preached by the Clergyman of the Church but my relative[s] were called to attend the funaral of a Cousen at Grandthackwells at Staunton so I went with the Ralatives of my late husband. I covered his grave with flowers and then attended the services in the church. My dear brother Thomas is attending the other funaral so I miss him from my side. I am worn out with greif and sorrow. Thomas has staid with me as much as he possible could through this sore Affliction, and stood nobly by me in all emergenecys. May God Bless him for his kindness to his sister who is now far away.

Our Physician a good kind man came to see me and advised me to leave that place imeaditily for my health or I would soon follow my husband. The next day I left my home a sad lonely Widow, where less than four Months before I had been taken a happy Bride. I did not go home for I felt that my Parents would try to stop me from gathering withe the Saints. I had many homes offered to me, by friends, but I went to Board with Mr & Mrs Hill of Turkey Hall. They were getting ready to go to Navoo. I prayed for strength to settle our Bissiness and then I would gather with his Saints. I had no debts to pay and the Lord Blessed me with success in collecting the Money due my husband and myself or the most of it. My health continued very poor, but I joined with a Company that was getting ready to go to Navoo.

The Co[mpany] sent a Agent to Bristol to Charter a Vessel. He found a good sailing Ship that was going to Quebeck for lumber and the Captain would have Berths put up in her for our Accommodation. This was the best he could do, and it proved a success in the end. My nice furniture was made by my husband before our marrage. I have a knife Box now that he made. It belonged to a long Dresser with three shelves. These were filled with beautifull setts of Dinner dishes of all kinds. Many of these I brought with me & some were sold, with my furniture. Carpenters and Coopers tools and other things were sold at Auction with Mr Hills goods, and I realized Money enough from my sale to pay my Passage and Board to Navoo. This was a very trying time for me. Every day I had to take leave of some dear friend that I never expected to see again in this world. The company was to start on Monday morning the fourth of May. Thus in three weeks I had settled up our Bissiness and was ready to start with them.

The last and hardest triel was to take leave of my Father, Mother, Brothers, and Sisters. My dear good Mother was most Broken hearted to see me go but Father was more calm. I wondered at this for I was his favorite child. He asked me the name of the ship and when she would sail. I told him all particulars, thinking he would come and bring Mother, to see me at the last before we set sail. I took some Books with me and in giveing them to my Sisters said here are som Books for you to read when I am far away and they never forgot those words. My two little sisters clung around my neck, sayying, we shall never see you again. I had not told them this for I knew the parting from them would be very hard. Little Jane wantd to come with me but this was impossible for she was only 8 years old. The next morning my youngest Brother, Charles, came to Turkey Hall to see me once more but we had gone and he was broken hearted.

An excerpt from Mary Ann Weston Maughan's autobiography. (Holograph. LDS Church Archives.)

Oh, the greif and sorrow of this time I can never forget, thus on the 4th of May 1841 I left all that was near and dear to me to travel some thousands [of] miles alone, and cast my lot with the people of God. We hired teames to take us to Gloucester and some of us started to walk a little way, when we came to the place where we would lose sight of Fathers House. I sat down and I might have staid there if some of the Company had not came bak for me. I was sick and quit [quite] over come with the greif and sorrow I had passed through in the last three months.

It is now forty six years since that time but to me it seems only yesterday. We were a sorry Company that traveled to Gloucester that morning. Myself and others wept all the way. I had been to Gloucester once since our Marrage, the occasion being the wedding of two of my husbands friends. John was Groomsman and I was Bridemaid. The Cermony was performed by the same Clergyman and at the same Church in which we were Married. On seeing the Church, I thought of the girl I was not six months ago. Now I had left all and was traviling alone to a land unknown to me, but I had cast my lot with the people of God and in him I put my trust.

Chapter Three

Kirtland

"We Set Our Faces Zionward"

Life in Kirtland, Ohio, was no harder and no easier for the three women represented here than it was for the rest of the Saints. The Ohio years of Mormonism's history were tumultuous and trying for all those who, like Caroline Crosby, Mary Fielding, and Hepzibah Richards, gathered to this first Zion of the restored gospel.

This gathering took place over a six- or seven-year period during which the infant Church expanded significantly. Missionaries continued to travel to the eastern states and Canada, and finally in 1837 to England—Mary Fielding writes of her brother Joseph's call to that mission. In fact, it was their brother James whose kindness in offering the missionaries his pulpit for a time started the elders on their way to mass success in the Liverpool area.

In Kirtland itself the Mormon experience became increasingly social as members met together in singing schools, prayer circles, and worship services. The Kirtland Temple, under construction from 1833 to 1836, was dedicated in the spring of 1836 with nearly one thousand Saints participating in the services.[1] In this "house of the Lord" members assembled regularly to pray, listen to sermons, sing, and exercise the spiritual gifts, such as speaking in tongues and prophesying, promised in the New Testament. Mary Fielding reports the times of love and refreshing "in the pentacostal outpouring of the Thursday meetings," and the "quiet, comfortable waiting upon God" of the Sunday services there.

Many Saints later recalled the Kirtland experience as a rich education in the "things of the Spirit." Joseph Smith received almost half of the revelations now included in the Doctrine and Covenants in or near Kirtland during this period. One such revelation designated Jackson County, Missouri, as the "Land of Zion," ultimately the land of inheritance to which Saints would gather, and some began to assemble there as early as 1831.[2] While the Church was centered in Kirtland until 1838, there were significant numbers of Saints in Missouri, first in Jackson County and later in Clay and Caldwell counties, and legal and organizational difficulties required that Church leaders travel frequently to Missouri.

But this geographical separation was less disjunctive for the Church than were the anti-Mormon persecution and internal dissension that eventually drove the Saints from Kirtland in 1838. Opposition had mounted against Mormons in Ohio from the arrival of the missionaries in 1830. Many of their early converts had been Campbellites, and the leaders of that sect, Thomas and Alexander Campbell, used pulpit and press to kindle a hot campaign repudiating Mormon claims and doctrine. The apostasy of some early Church members added fuel to growing anti-Mormon sentiment. Ezra Booth, a Methodist preacher turned Mormon, then anti-Mormon, composed nine letters for the Ravenna *Ohio Star* to satisfy those who had "solicited an exposure of Mormonism." And Philastus Hurlburt left the Church three months after his baptism to write an exposé of the origin of the Book of Mormon, later published as E. D. Howe's *Mormonism Unvailed.* Growing resentment against Mormons erupted in a mob attack on Joseph Smith and Sidney Rigdon at Hiram, Ohio, in 1832.[3] During the next six years mobs plotted and assembled; and though for the most part their attacks never materialized, their threats were a constant source of anxiety for the Saints.

The non-Mormon community at Kirtland feared that large numbers of poor Mormons would become town charges. Some non-Mormons refused to employ Mormons or sell them provisions. This situation was complicated by the steady arrival of Saints from eastern branches of the Church who had no means of support. By 1836, the year in which this section's writers arrived in Kirtland, economic conditions were improving among the Latter-day Saints, and work and housing were increasingly available. Even so, Caroline Crosby records her anxiety over having to vacate the house in which she and her husband had settled and return to a shared dwelling.

That November some Church leaders formulated articles of agreement for a new banking institution, the Kirtland Safety Society. But this budding prosperity was cut short by the failure of the bank a year later and the economic devastation wrought by the nationwide panic of 1837. Having involved themselves in land speculation and extensive credit buying, some Kirtland Mormons were particularly hard hit.

Tensions increased between faithful Latter-day Saints and dissenters in league with anti-Mormon forces, and many members lost faith and left the Church. Mormon hopes turned away from Kirtland and toward Missouri, where Latter-day Saint settlements were being established in Caldwell County. Joseph Smith and his family left Kirtland for Far West in January 1838, and small groups of Saints followed, the last , the five - hundred - member Kirtland Camp, leaving under the direction of the First Council of Seventy in July.

The reminiscence and letters that follow were composed by women who lived in Kirtland between 1836 and 1838. Hepzibah Richards went there to study and investigate the gospel, which she had heard preached in New England. "We had set our faces as flint Zionward and were ready to forsake all to gain that part," Caroline Crosby wrote, describing her and her husband's departure from Massachusetts for Kirtland. Both she and Mary Fielding were newly baptized converts who obeyed the commandment to gather to Kirtland as soon as they had sufficient means.

Each woman's writings reflect her ambivalence toward Kirtland, where "wheat and tares to such a height had grown" that Saints could hardly be distinguished from hypocrites. Each speaks with deep feeling of the spiritual manifestations to the faithful Saints and at the same time details her frustration with the scarcity of work, food, and housing, and the ever-present Mormon, anti-Mormon tensions. None of these women found her hopes in the promised Zion shattered by the Kirtland experience. All three feared for their own safety and that of their leaders, but the frettings in their accounts do not dim their courage, a combination of personal stability and faith that contrasts sharply with the fragmented Kirtland community they describe.

Caroline Barnes Crosby (1807-1884)

Caroline Barnes Crosby was baptized a Latter-day Saint in January 1835. She had been studying the Bible and the Book of Mormon for several months, and in November 1834 she had married Jonathan Crosby, who was already a Latter-day Saint. For almost a year the couple lived in Wendell, Franklin County, Massachusetts, with Jonathan's family, but in November 1835 they left the family to gather with the Saints at Kirtland, traveling first to Dunham, Quebec, Canada, to visit Caroline's parents. They stopped briefly near Fredonia, New York, where Caroline visited friends while Jonathan traveled on to Kirtland to arrange for employment and housing and then returned to complete the journey with Caroline. The excerpt that follows begins with the arrival of the Crosbys in Kirtland in January 1836.

The Crosbys and their son Alma traveled to Utah in 1848 with the main body of the Saints. Caroline began writing her memoirs early in the 1850s while she and her husband were working as Latter-day Saint missionaries in the Society Islands (Tahiti). Concurrently she began keeping a journal, a practice she continued almost to her death in Beaver, Utah, in 1884. The following excerpt from her memoirs, presented here with minimal punctuation added for clarity, is taken from a microfilm of a holograph in the Historical Department of the Church. The holograph original is in the Utah State Historical Society, a gift of S. George Ellsworth, professor of history, Utah State University, Logan, Utah.

> We reached Kirtland the 7th day of January. The first person that we saw was Evan M Green, one of the young men who first brought the gospel to Mass[achusetts] at the time my husband was baptized. He assisted us in getting our wagon up the hill near the temple, which we found very difficult in ascending consequence of the ground being clayey. We went

Caroline Barnes Crosby, center, with her husband, Jonathan; son, Alma; and a niece, Francis Pratt. Photo was taken in San Francisco ca. 1854, upon the Crosbys' return from a mission to the Society Islands (Tahiti). (Daguerrotype. Mae Crosby White family collection.)

directly to Parley P Pratts, whare they had engaged to board us awhile; and were soon introduced to a score of brethren and sisters, who made us welcome among them. I ever felt myself quite at home in their society.

Shortly after our arrival my husband was ordained to the office of an elder, and chosen into the second quorum of seventies. I well recollect the sensations with which my mind was actuated when I learned the fact that my husband had been called and ordained to the Melchisedek priesthood and would undoubtedly be required to travel and preach the gospel to the nations of the earth. I realized in some degree the immense responsibility of the office, and besought the Lord for grace and wisdom to be given him that he might be able to magnify his high and holy calling. The brethren had meetings of some kind almost every evening in the week. Besides singing schools in which all ages took a part, from the young adult to the old gray heads. Consequently we also took a part with them, and met two[?] evenings in a week. The quoir was large. Meuriel C. Davis was our leader for a year or more.

Father Joseph Smith sen, was the first and then the only patriarch in the church. Acordingly we went to him for a blessing, and received as good, and as great promises, as any mortal being could ask. I will therefore record them, for the perusal of my posterity, and friends. [Patriarchal blessings for Jonathan and Caroline Crosby follow.] These blessings cheered and rejoiced our hearts exceedingly. I truly felt humble before the Lord, and felt to exclaim like one of old, "Lord what am I, or what my fathers house, that Thou art thus mindful of us." They led me to search into my own heart, to see if there was any sin concealed there, and if so, to repent, and ask God to make me clean, and pure, in very deed. The Patriarch con-versed with us sometime, told us we had come togather right. And when we told him our ages, and places of birth, he ob-served that he thought we were both born under one planet. But merely by way of merriment. Mother Smith was in the room. She also added her blessing, or confirmed what we had already received.

Our meetings were held in the printing office, or rather in a room under it. The room was not large enough to contain the people who came. It was quite a curiousity to see them coming so early, almost as soon as light in order to get a seat. And finally they decided on taking their turns in staying away, as the weather was so cold, and it was unpleasant for those who stood outside. The females usually had seats. My husband worked for three months on the temple before it was dedicated, which was nearly the first he had ever done at the business.

I enjoyed myself well with sister Thankful Pratt. She was a very sociable interesting woman, but had very delicate health. The brethren attended meetings almost every evening, which left us togather considerably. When they all left us, she would look about her and say, "well it is you and I again, Sister Crosby." She was afflicted with severe spells of sick headache which came upon her monthly.

About the middle of March we went to Harpen Riggs to board. They were a young lately married couple, near our ages. They lived in a new house, which was situated on the cross street, which led from the Boston house, to bishop [Vinson] Knights. It was quite a pleasant situation. Sister R was a Mass[achusetts] woman, and seemed very near to me. We enjoyed ourselves togather finely. Chapman Duncan also came and boarded there several weeks, before, and after, the dedication of the temple, which transpired on the 27th of March AD 1836. I believe however, it was continued several days in which time the spirit of God was manifested in healing the sick, casting out devils, speaking in tongues, interpretation &c. We had some glorious preaching, that cheered and animated our hearts.

How often while listining to the voice of the prophet have I wished, Oh that my friends, parents, brothers, and sisters, could hear the things that I have heard, and their hearts be made to rejoice in them, as mine did. And I would frequently be led to exclaim with Dr Isaac Watts, Why was I made to hear thy voice, And enter while there's room, While thousands make a wretched choice, And rather starve than come. We had some joyful times that spring and summer. Many strangers came from various parts of the country, to see the prophet, and the temple. It certainly was a very pretty building, but my powers of description are inadequate to describe so complex a structure. Immediately after the dedication, many of the elders were sent on missions, some went to Missouri with families.

My husband purchased a lot west of the temple and began to make preparations for building. I followed braiding palmleaf hats for eight months after we came to K--tl--d. Braided near a hundred the first season, which brought me 70 doll[ar]s.

Kirtland Temple reflection, East Fork of the Chagrin River, Ohio, ca. 1908. (George Edward Anderson, "Church History in Photograph." LDS Church Archives.)

We had an invitation, and attended a family blessing meeting or feast that was held at the house of John P Greene. It was appointed for Father [John] Young to bless his family, and as sister [Rhoda Young] Greene was his eldest child (as I think she was) it was held at her house.[4] The house was crow[d]ed full. We had nice wheat bread and sweet wine all we wanted to drink, it was also called a feast, and so it was a feast of fat things. The brethren and sisters blest one another, but father Young I believe concluded to defer blessing his family untill he could have them by themselves. He seemed rather diffident in regard to speaking, or his mind so much affected by the subject, that he could not express his feelings. Brigham [Young] therefore arose and spoke in his behalf. The old gentleman wept freely, as well as many of his family, so that we had weeping, and rejoicing, nearly at the same time.

It was a general time of rejoicing for several months among the Saints. They frequently met from house, to house, to break bread, and drink wine and administer to the poor and afflicted. We also would attend a blessing at Dr Frederick G Williams. His eldest daughter had been lately married, and was about to leave for Missouri: he therefore blest her family previous to their leaving. He laid his hands upon each of their heads, and the scribe wrote them [the blessings]. The prophet Joseph was present, and had a vision of their journey, saw their wagon turn over, but no one was injured. It came to pass even as he said.

About the last of May, Elder Parley P P[ratt] went on a mission to Canada, and took his family. Mr Crosby rented his house and accordingly we went housekeeping. May the 27th, we moved our effects back again into br Pratts house and commenced providing for ourselves. We had then been married a year and a half, and had not kept house before. I felt like a child with a new set of toys. I cleaned the house from stem to stern, and arranged everything in the best of order.

51

Soon after we commenced housekeeping my brother Horace
Barnes came to see us from [New] York state, Chatauque Co.
He spent a week or more with us. We went with him to see
the prophet but I think he was absent. He saw Father [Joseph]
Smith [Sr.] and Emma [Smith], who showed him the records of
Abraham, that were found with the mummies, and explained
the characters to us as she had heard her husband explain
them. We said all we could to enlighten his mind. We also
invited a br[other] who had formerly been a member of the
presbyterian church to come and converse with him. He never
seemed disposed to contend against it. Br H brought me the
melancholy news of sister Catherine's sickness, with consumption, or liver complaint. We had a very good visit from him.
It was in the month of june. He left quite undecided in his
mind with regard to the truth of the work. I had some lonely
hours after his departure.

Several families came in at that time from [New] Y[or]k St[ate]
and as houses were very hard to be rented, every place being
filled, Mr C[rosby] rented the cellar kitchen to a man, and his
wife, with two small children. His name was Lewis, a black-
smith by occupation, and very poor people. But they found it
rather uncomfortable, and staid only a short time. About the
middle of July a co[mpany] came from Boston Mass. Among
them was John Boynton's parents, brothers in law and sisters.
Br Henry Herriman and Jonathan Hail [Hale]. And no house
could be found for their accomodation. John was building, but
could not get it ready in season. He therefore came to us and
offered to give us four times the amount of rent we paid, if
we would go in with sister Sabre Granger, a maiden lady near
by us, who was living alone, and let him have our house for
his friends. My husband left it with me to say, to which I
hesitated some time, but at length consented, rather reluc-
tantly. The remuneration I considered no object; [but] to leave
my pleasant little house, and go in with another, after living
by ourselves so short a time; but the idea of accomodating
friends, stimulated me to make the sacrifice.

Sister Granger's house was small, only one room, besides cellar, pantry, a small closet, and chamber. She had however a stove room, outside where she cooked her food. She had many peculiarities, which in some respects were not as agreeable to us, as we could wish. Notwithstanding being kind-hearted, and friendly, atoned in my estimation, for many imperfections.

My husband attended a Hebrew school that summer, and made some considerable improvement. I also learned to read, but not translate. He bought a nice set of books, consisting of bible, lexicon, and grammar. We had a small feast in co[mpany] with sis Granger while there. Father [Isaac] Morley presided. There were some great blessings pronounced upon some heads. One by father M upon Mr Crosby was that he should have a son a foot taller than himself, that he would be obliged to sit while his father blessed him. There was also a wedding there while we lived in her house. A br[other] by the name of Foster married a widow from Boston, her name I do not recollect. Shortly after we went in, Sister Mariann Sterns, came from the State of Maine. I think [she] came with Lyman Johnson, and put up at his house. She had one child, a little girl 9 years old. She soon became discontented there, and thought she was not welcome any longer. Sister Granger very kindly offered her a home, untill she could do better. Accordingly she came and stoped one month. Sis G was very kind in her own rough way. She brought home work, sewing and knitting for her, and fed her on vegetables, hard corn, and laugh [lake] string beans. We made her welcome to a share of what our table afforded, which was not very bountifully supplied at that time. I admired her very much, thought her an amiable, interesting woman. From there she went to house-keeping. Sister Granger had a sister come from Boston, who made her home there, a good share of the time.

The middle of Nov we got our house enclosed, and a loose floor, no windows, but my anxiety was so great, to get away by ourselves, that I determined to move in at all events. I truly felt rejoiced beyond measure to get into a house of our own after so long a time. My husband continued his labors incessantly untill he got the doors and windows in; and then we thought ourselves highly blessed. We had a nice cooking stove, a good cellar, and well, close to my door, which certainly were three great conveniences. But as yet we had no partition in the house. The weather continued very pleasant untill the middle of Dec, when a snow storm came on, which lasted sometime. The 19th of Dec 4 oclock PM Alma was born. That day, and night, the snow fell in profusion.

Dr W[arren] A Cowdry was my physician. Sisters Warren Smith, Sherwood, Vincent [Vinson] Knight, and sis Drury were with me. The latter staid one week, and then intended sending for her daughter, but as I did not get along as well as I could wish, we concluded to get a more experienced person. Sister John Goodson understood my situation, and very kindly offered her services, for one week. I found her to be an excellent nurse, as well as an interesting young woman. She had come from U[pper] Can[ada] a few weeks previous and had been married but a short time. We were much surprised at her offer. But I think she did it for a sort of a joke on her husband, more than anything else.

After she left, Ruth Drury came, and staid two weeks, and I then thought I could get along alone. I tried one month, took cold, which settled in my left breast, and caused me a severe sickness, with a broken breast, and all the disagreeable accompaniaments, of that distressing disease. We then hired a young woman by the name of Susannah Hidden, afterward the wife of Stephen Perry. After she left I had Lydia Chapman quite a young girl. I did not attend meeting until the next April. My babe was then 4 months old.

While I was sick I sent for Father Smith to lay hands on me. When he came he questioned us with regard to our faith and feelings towards the first Presidency. Said there were many murmurers about, and a spirit of dissensian in the church. I told him I had been confined at home, and had neither seen or heard scarcely anything of it, and I desired to continue in the truth, and keep the commandments of God. He then said he would shut the door and keep the devil out, after which he in co[mpany] with another elder laid their hands on me, and prayed. I felt that I had received a great blessing.

Times became very hard in Kirt[land]. It seemed that our enemies were determined to drive us away if they could possibly, by starving us. None of the business men would employ a mormon scarcely, on any conditions. And our prophet was continually harassed with vexatious lawsuits. Besides the great apostacy in the church, added a duble portion of distress and suffering to those who wished to abide in the faith, and keep the commandments.

We became very short of provisions, several times ate the last we had and knew not where the next meal was coming from. We then had an opportunity to try the charity of the brethren, who were many of them in the same predicament as ourselves. I recollect that Wm Cahoon called into see us one night, as he was going home with a few quarts of corn meal, and enquired if we had any breadstuff on hand, we told him we had not. He said he would divide what he had with us, and if my husband would go home with him, he would also divide his potatoes and meat which bore the same proportion to his meal. Joseph Young also divided with us several times in the same way, and we with him. We had numerous opportunities of dividing almost our last loaf with the brethren.

Mr C worked on br Joseph's house, as he was building tolerably large, but frequently got so straitened that he had nothing to give the workmen when saturday night came, and they were obliged to borrow or do without. They all left at one time, except Mr C, he worked on for several days alone. Sister Emma observing that he was laboring there alone, came in one day, and inquired of him whether or where he got his provision. He told her he was entirely without, and knew not where to look, as he had no money, and the boss who employed him had no means in his hands. She then went into

55

her chamber, and brought him a nice ham [weighing] 20 lbs.
Telling him that it was a present for his faithfulness, and that
he should bring a sack, and get as much flour as he could to
take home. Accordingly he came home rejoicing, considering
it a perfect Godsend. It was a beautiful white flour, and the
ham was very sweet. I thought nothing ever tasted half as
good.

About this time the Kirtland bank failed, which caused a great
deal of distress among the brethren. We had a little garden
which was a great help to us, we had no cow, and were
obliged to buy milk for the babe. My husband was sued once,
by the men who kept the meat market, Leonard Rich and
Roger Orton, and was obliged to sacrifice twice the amount of
the debt in property, to raise the money. Alas thought I, the
trials that I had heard the elders preach of were in reality
coming upon us. As to poverty we could endure that patiently,
but trials among false brethren, who can endure with patience?
Many of our most intimate associates were among the apostates.

Warren Parish was a sort of leader of a party of some 30 or
40 persons, among them was John Boynton and wife, Luke
and Lyman Johnson, Harpen Riggs, and others whose names I
do not recollect. These were some of our nighest neighbors
and friends. We had taken sweet counsel together, and walked
to the house of God as friends. They came out boldly against
the prophet, and signed an instrument which as I understand
by W Parish and others, renouncing all their allience with the
church. I met sister Riggs afterwards and asked her if it was
true that she had apostatized. She said she was dissatisfied
with some of the things in the church, but that she still
believed in the book of Mormon and thought she always
should. I felt very sorrowful, and gloomy, but never had the
first idea of leaving the church or forsaking the prophet. I was
feeble all through the summer but Alma grew, and was quite
fleshy, began to walk when he was 10 months old. As the fall
advanced I began to gain strength and felt much better.

We got our house a little more comfortable, the floor plained, and made very tight, a partition through, and floor over head. It began to seem more like living. About the first of Dec a number of elders were sent on missions. My husband was one that was appointed to go. He made what preparation he could, and the 7th of Jan 1838, in company with Warren Smith (who was afterward martyred at Hons [Haun's] Mill by the Missouri mob) he set off toward the east part of the state of Ohio, and went into Pennsylvania.

Mary Fielding Smith (1801-1852)

In 1836 Mary Fielding and her sister Mercy and brother Joseph were English emigrants, members of John Taylor's Methodist congregation in Toronto, Canada. With John Taylor they accepted the restored gospel taught them by Mormon apostle-missionary Parley P. Pratt and were baptized in May 1836. In the spring of 1837 all three Fieldings moved to Kirtland. By mid-June, however, Mary was left in Kirtland without family: Joseph Fielding had been called to serve as a missionary in England, and Mercy had married Robert B. Thompson and accompanied him on his mission to Churchville, Canada.

Mary's English education provided her with the necessary background to teach school, and when school closed she boarded with a family, caring for and tutoring several children. Through letters Mary maintained a close connection with her sister Mercy in Canada, reporting regularly on her personal living situation and feelings as well as on Church happenings. The following excerpts are taken from three of Mary's letters, which span the months between July and October 1837. In December of that year Mary married recently widowed Hyrum Smith and assumed care of his five small children. She lived with Hyrum in Far West and Nauvoo, and after his death journeyed to the Salt Lake Valley.

Original holographs of these and other letters written by Mary are located in the Historical Department of the Church. Ronald K. Esplin is preparing the complete correspondence for publication. Selections from three letters are included here. The first rather lengthy excerpt includes almost all of a letter from Mary to Mercy dated July 8, 1837. The last two pages of the holograph have not been included here because large torn sections on those pages make difficult an accurate rendering of Mary's prose.

The second letter was rather extensively edited by Susa Young Gates and published in the *Relief Society Magazine*, volume 2 (March 1916). Here the original holograph has been followed.

A nineteenth century portrait of Mary Fielding Smith. Artist unknown. (LDS Church Archives.)

The final excerpt is taken from a letter of October 7, 1837, addressed to Mercy and her husband, Robert B. Thompson. Much of the letter focuses on family matters and friends. This excerpt reveals something of Mary's feelings toward the presidency of the Church. In publishing parts of three letters here, the editors have preserved the original spelling and added punctuation and bracked material for clarification.

Kirtland July 8 [18]37

My dear Sister

As I have met with paper I feel inclined to commence the proposed corrispondence, as I hope you also do. I shall begin from the time my last letter was written. You would hear what a glorious meeting we had on the Thursday before Bro. Brunell left so I need give you no account of that.

On the Sunday following we had a quiet comfortable waiting upon God in his House. President [Sidney] Rigdon deliverd a very striking discourse from Daniel Chap[ter] 2nd Vrs 44. It would be useless for me to attempt giving you an idea of the manner in which he handled the subject. You must read the text and remember that he is a Masterpiece and then you may perhaps form some idea. He told us with great warmth indeed, that the Kingdom which was set up should never be destroyed, nor be left to other People. No, said he, nor yet change Governours. I realy thought from what he said that all opposers from that time rest satisfyed that their exertions would be fruitless, but I do not expect in the least that Satan will give up the contest. No hed [he'd] work in the Children of this World, and also in the Hearts of the Children of the Kingdom w[h]ere ever he can find access to them, untill he is bound. O may the Lord preserve us from his subtle power and keep us to that day.

It was truley gratifying to see the venerabl[e] Patriarch [Joseph Smith, Sr.] with his two aged Brothers in the upper stand and in the next, four of his Sons with president Rigdon in their midst, all I believe faithful servants of the living God.[5] Joseph & Hirum I know best and love much. While I lookd at them all my heart was drawn out in earnest prayer to our heavenly

Father in their behalf and also for the Prophetice their aged Mother [Lucy Mack Smith] whose eyes are frequently baithed in tears when she looks at, or speaks of them.

Our thursday meeting was again better than any former one. The hearts of the people were melted and the Spirit & power of God rested down upon us in a remarkable manner. Many spake in tongues & others prophesied & interpreted. It has been said by many who have lived in Kirtland a great while that such a time of love & refreshing has never been known. Some of the Sisters while engaged in conversing in tounges their countenences beaming with joy, clasped each others hands & kissd in the most affectinate manner. They were describing in this way the love and felicitys of the Celestial World. Altho the House of the Lord was more than half filld during this time their were few dry faces. The Bretheren as well as the Sisters were all melted down and we wept and praised God together.

Some of the prophecies delivered in toungs and interpretd were so great that I cannot begin to describe them but I do assure you Brother Hyrum Smiths prediction that from that hour the Lord would begin to bless his people has been verily fulfild, I believe as do many others that Angles were present with us. A brite light shone across the House and rested upon some of the congreation. What I felt that day seemd to out way [weigh] all the afliction and destress of mind I have sufferd since I came here. We have a promise of a still better meeting next Thursday if we humble ourselves as in the dust before the Lord. This will be our fast day. May the promise be verifyd indeed.

On Saturday July 8 We all received Letters from our Brethren [missionaries] in New York giving an account of their journey thither and their preparations for setting sail which did not take place til the 30 of June.[6] You will see that from various causes they were delayd 10 days in New York. They were all well and in good spirits tho much disapointed at not receiving the expected money, but they contrived to exchange some

Kirtland paper [bank notes] or to get provisions for it, so as to enable them to pay their expences amongst them. The fare was 20 dollars each in one of the largest Vessels that has ever saild 9 hundred tons burden. Joseph says I must send the money when the next Elders go which will probably be in the fall. But all uncertain they expect to land at Liverpool so that poor Brother James [Fielding] will soon have to recieve or reject them. Our prayer to God must be unceasing that he may become as a little Child that he may enter in to the Kingdom.[7] Sisters [Vilate] Kimball & [Marinda] Hyde are begining to wright to their Husbands at Preston [England]. They continue to be in good spirits.

While the Brethren were in new York they endeavourd to do all the good they could by conversing with the people and destributing the prophetic warning to all the Priests they could find. About 105 they were put into the Post Office.

Elders [Thomas B.] Marsh & [David W.] Patten have arrived from missouri. They met Elder [Parley P.?] Pratt 300 miles on his way thither and brought him back with them. Elder Marsh is a most excelent Man. He seems to be a Man of great faith. He says he believs the difficultys between the Presidency & the twelve will very shortly be settled.[8] And then we can expect better days than ever. *[The remainder of the letter is badly torn, and only parts of the sentences remain.]*

[ca. September 1, 1837]

My dear Sister

I have this day received a very short note from you and am glad to learn by Brother [Almon W.] Babbit that you are well and comfortably situated. He tells me he is expecting soon to return to Canada so that it is unnecessary for me to say much as he can inform you of the state of things here verbaly better than I can by writing. But still I can hardly refrain from sending a few lines.

I am now in a school which I took for one month. The time expires tomorrow when I expect again to be at liberty or without imployment, but I feel my mind pertty much at rest on that subject. I have called upon the Lord for direction and trust He will open my way. I hope you will not fail to remember me at the throan of grace. I have no doubt but you have many trials but I am inclined to think you have not quite so much to endure as I have. Be this as it may, the Lord knows what our sutiations [situations] are and he will support us and give us grace and strength for the day if we continue to put our trust in him and devote ourselves unreservedly to his service.

I do thank my heavenly Father for the comfort and peace of mind I now enjoy in the midst of all the confusion and perplexity, and rageing of the devil against the work of God in this place. For altho here is a great number of faithful precious souls, yea the Salt of the Earth is here, yet it may be truely called a place where Satan has his seat. He is frequently stering [stirring] up some of the People to strife & conttention and dissatisfaction with things they do not understand. I often have of late been led to look back on the circumstances of Korah and his company when they roase up against Moses and Aaron. If you turn to and read 16th Chap[ter] of Numbers you will there find the feelings and conduct of many of the People and even the Elders of Israel in these days exactly described. Wheather the Lord will comeout in a similar way or not I cannot tell. I sometimes think it may be so, but I pray God to have mercy upon us all and preserve us from the power of the great enemy who knows he has but a short time to work in.

We have had a terible stir with W[arre]n Parish the particulars of which I cannot here give you at length. We are not yet able to tell where it will end.[9] I have been made to tremble and quake before the Lord and to call upon him with all my heart almost day and night as many others have done of late. I believe the voice of prayer has sounded in the House of the

Lord some days from morning till night and it has been by these means that we have hitherto prevaild and it is by this means only that I for one expect to prevaile. I feel more & more convinced that it is through suffering that we are to be made perfect and I have already found it [to] have the effect of driveing me nearer to the Lord and so has become a great blessing to me. I have sometimes of late been so filled with the love of God and felt such a sense of his favour as has made me rejoice abundantly indeed, my Heavenly Father has been very gracious unto me both temperally and spiritu**a**ly.

Since I commenced this Letter a kind Sister has proposed my going to stay for a while with her to take charge of 2 or 3 children who have been in my School. They propose giving something besides my board & I think this will suit me better than a publick School if it is but little. I expect to go there in a day or too and hope to be quite comfortable as I know the family to be on the Lords side. The Mother is a Cousin of Brother Josephs and took care of him when a child. Their name is Dort.[10]

I felt much pleased to see Sisters Walton and Snider who arrived here on Saturday about noon,[11] haveing left Brother Joseph S[mith] and Rigdon about 20 miles from Fareport [Ohio] to evade the Mobbers. They were to come home in Dr [Sampson] Avards carrage and expected to arrive about 10 O clock at night but to their great disappointment they were prevented in a most greavous manner. They had got within 4 miles of home after a very fatueging [fatiguing] journey, much pleased with their visit to Canada & greatly antissipateing the pleasure of seeing their homes and familys, when they were surrounded with a Mob and taken back to Painsvill[e] and secured as was supposed in a Tavern where they intended to hold a mock trial. But to the disappointment of the wretches the Housekeeper was a Member of the Church who assisted our beloved Brethren in making their escape, but as Br J[oseph] S[mith] says not by a Basket let down through a Window, but by the Kitchin Door.[12]

No doubt the hand of the Lord was in it or it could not have been effected. The day had been extremely whet and the night was unusually dark and you may try if you can [to] conceive what their situation was. They hardly knew which way to stere [steer], as it had by that time got to be about 10 O clock. The first step they took was to find the Woods as quick as possible where they thought they should be safe. But in order [to reach] thereto they had to lay down in a swamp or by an old log just w[h]ere they happened to be so determinately were they pursued by their mad enemys in every direction. Sometimes so closely that Br J was obliged to entreat Bro Rigdon, after his exertion in running, while lying by a log to breath more softly if he meant to escape.

When they would run or walk they took each other by the hand and covenanted to live and die together. Owing to the darkness of the night their persuers had to carry lighted torches which was one means of the escape of our beloved suffers as they could see them in every direction while they were clim[b]ing over fences or travling through brush or corn fields untill about 12 O clock. When after traveling as they suppose in this manner 5 or 6 miles they found the road which led homeward and saw no more of their persuers. After traveling on foot along muddy sliperry roads till near 3 in the morning they arrived safe at home almost f[a]inting with fatuage [fatigue].

He Bro J told us that he decread in his heart when first taken that he would see home before Sun rise and thank God so it was. And notwithstanding all he had to endure he appeared in the House of the Lord throughout the Sabath in excelent spirits and spoak in a very powerful manner and blessed the Congregation in the name of the Lord and I do assure you the Saints felt the blessing and left the House rejoiceing abundently returning their blessing upon him. Brother Rigdon through his great weariness and a small hurt received from a fall did not attend the House but is now well. I suppose all these things will only add another gem to their Crown.

I did not think of takeing up so much room in relating these circumstances but I have been as brief as possible. I must now give you an account of [a very] affecting event which took place in Kirtland Sunday before last. You will of course remember a Mr. [Wycom?] Clarke, a Miller who has been a great opposer of our Church. As he and his Wife with some of their Children and other Friends were returning from the Prespeteran [Presbyterian] Meeting House in a very nice carrage, about one minuit after they passed the House of the Lord their Horses took fright and started off the side of the hill, overthrew the Carrage and hurt Mr C and one child considerably but Mrs. C so seriously as to prove fatal. She was burryd [buried] on the Wednessday following. She has left 6 weeping Children and a mourning Husband indeed. On the day preceeding the accedent she was heard to speak very unfavourabley of our Church but is now gone to prove whether it is the Church of Christ or not. I greatly desire that the visitation may be sanctified to the Family.

I believe it is not quite a year since Bro J S told Mr. C that the curse of God would be upon him for his conduct towards him and the Church. You may remember that our People wished to purchese his place, but he would not sell it on any reasonable terms and therefore kept it, and has been a trouble in the place but has prospered in buisness so much as to say he never prospered better and told a person some time ago that he was ready for another of Joseph Smiths Curses. I feel inclind to think he will never be heard to utter such words again. May the Lord forgive and save him and all others who raise their hand against the Lords anointed for I see more clearly than ever that this is no trifling sin in the sight of God. No it is as great as ever it was in any age of the world. I sincerely wish that all the members of the Church had a proper sense of their duty and privilege in this respect.

I expect to hear from you soon and also from England. I hope I shall not be disappo[int]ed. Tell [me] if you and Brother Thom[p]son have any idea of coming to Kirtland this fall, (if the Field of labour remains open there), and unless a change should take place in the state of affairs here for the better I should not advise it however much I might [like] to see you. Here are course [corps] of Men out of employ even in the summer and how it will be in the winter I cannot tell but I fear for Kirtland. O, that we as a people may be faithful this is our only hope and all we have to depend on. Give my kind love to Brother Thompson and all other Friends particularly Brother & Sis[ter] Law. I thank them for their kindness to you. I thank Brother Thompson for his last kind letter and should be pleased with [a]nother. I remain your very affectinate Sister

M. F.

[on margins]
Dadeus Sekins has marr[i]ed a widdower [with] 5 children
Sister Kimble desires her love to you Both

[October 7, 1837]

My dear Sister & Brother

. . . Brother Joseph [Smith] came to see us a few days since for the last time previous to his going on a journey to Messouri. I believe I felt as much at parting with him as an own Bro. He, Brother Rigdon, Bro. Hyrum S[mith], W[illiam] S[mith] & others are all gone on a very important business and are not expected back for some months. May the Lord have mercy upon us and guide us in their absence and preserve us here from the power of the devel & them also while absent. Indeed we all need to pray much. For as the great Wheels or Stone rolls forward as it is now doing with great success the grand adversary who knows he has but a very short time, will most assuredly rage with all his might.

Some important things were shown to Bro. Joseph in vision previous to his going off relitive to the enlargement of our Borders which has indeed become indesably [indispensably?] necessary for the Inhabitants of Zion both here and in the West are crying the Citys are too strait for us give place that we may dwell. The people are crouding in from all parts and as President Rigdon said in his last discourse *here,* they will gather and Earth and hell combined cannot hinder them for *gather they will.* Hence the necessaty of planting new stakes which they received a command to do before they left and it is expected that after they have set in order the Church in the West they will fix upon 11 new Stakes before they return but this is not spoaken of in publick for reasons you will be aware of. If this were generally known it would probably make their way much more difficult.

We had a very affecting time the last Sabbath. Our dear Brethren were present and took their leave of the Church. I suppose we had not much less than 1500 persons on the Congregation. Brother Rigdon receive[d] directions from the Lord in the morning as [to] the discourse he should deliver that day before he left us and truely it was marvelous, it was gareat it was glorious far beyond my power to discribe. The tears flowd plentifully from Bro. Josph Eyes during the service. When he looked over congregation and considered what had been done and then what was still to be done he seemed to be filled with feelings indiscribable. I am truely sorry that I am so unable to give you an idea of what passt. O what feelings ran through my soul while he was pouring his blessings upon all the sincere and faithful Saints. How I longed to have a share in them all. Brother R[igdon]s address was upon the enlargement and future glory and purity of Zion when she arises and puts on her beautiful garments which must be before long.

As it is quite useless for me [to] aim an entering into any particular subject, I must just tell you how he concluded his discourse. After showing us what we have to do & what our privileges are and what our future blessedness would [be] he spoak out with a loud voice from the fulness of his heart, And let all the people say Amen & Amen. When it seem[ed] as tho all the congregation in one simultainous voice responded with a loud Amen it was the opinion of most that they had never heard the like before. . . .

Hepzibah Richards (1795-1838)

Hepzibah Richards started for Kirtland with her brothers Levi and Willard in the fall of 1836. At their home in Richmond, Massachusetts, the three Richardses had learned of the restored gospel through their Latter-day Saint missionary cousin Brigham Young, and they were en route to Kirtland to meet Joseph Smith and learn more of the Mormons. Hepzibah remained in Waterville, New York, while Levi and Willard completed the journey to Ohio, but another brother, Phinehas, called for "Hepsy" a few months later, and with Phinehas and his two sons she made the anticipated trek to Kirtland.[13]

By the time she arrived, Levi and Willard had been baptized and Phinehas followed suit, but Hepzibah waited. By June 1837 Willard was already preparing to leave on his second mission, this one to England. The first of the letters that follow is from Hepzibah to Willard in England. The other Richardses, including Hepzibah's parents, two brothers, and two sisters, remained in Richmond, Massachusetts, skeptical about Mormonism, though by June 1838 the two sisters had been baptized Latter-day Saints and started for Missouri. The second letter from Hepzibah is addressed to her family in Richmond. Hepzibah was not baptized a Latter-day Saint until July 1838, after she had left Kirtland and traveled to Far West, Missouri. She died at Far West the following September.[14]

The first letter published here is taken from the original holograph in the Willard Richards Papers, Historical Department of the Church. Minimal punctuation has been added.

The second letter is taken from a typescript in a collection of Richards Correspondence, Historical Department of the Church. Spelling and punctuation have been standardized.

Kirtland Jan. 18, 1838

Dear brother Willard.—

I have rec'd. a letter from home dated Dec. 17. Mother was

suffering from rheumatism, sister N[ancy] with sore eyes. Other friends well. Uncles hand was gaining fast. Brother Wm. was to be married the 19th to Miss Sarah Lewis—sister to Mrs. Hinman. They had rec'd. yours of sept. & oct and were answering it. I have been watching the office for a letter from yourself. Last tuesday one arrived addressed, to cousin Brigham [Young]. He is not here to read or answer it. He left this place the 21 or 22 of Dec. in company with brother L[evi], Mr. [Daniel S.] Miles and his eldest son. They wrote us from New Portage 12 days after saying that they had concluded to go to Missouri.

Silhouette portrait of Hepzibah Richards, cut out with lace and curls sketched in ink. This and silhouettes of other Richards family members were made by Hepzibah, probably before the family left Massachusetts.

And now brother W. I must proceed to give you some account of the present state of things in this place. Would I had more cheering intelligence to communicate. For when you are so far separated from friends and home it grieves me to write any thing that is calculated to give you pain. You had an opportunity to learn something of the spirit which was beginning to prevail here last spring. That spirit has continued to increase; or if at any time it has appeared to be quelled it now appears that it was only preparing to operate with greater virulence, until it is generally believed that this place will soon be trodden down by the enemies of that gospel which you preach.

For some days past the aspect of things has been rapidly changing, and to the view of all appears to be gathering blackness. A large number have dissented from the body of the church and are very violent in their opposition to the President[cy] and all who uphold them. They have organized a church and appointed a meeting in the house [Kirtland Temple] next sabbath. Say they will have it, if it is by the shedding of blood. They have the keys already.

The printing-office has been attached on a judgment that [Grandison] Newel held against the Presidents of K[irtland] money.[15] Last monday it was sold at auction into the hands of Mr. Millican [Nathaniel Milliken], one of the dissenters. At one oclock the night following cousin Mary waked me, and said that Kirtland was all in flames. It proved to be the Printing-office—the fire was then in its height and in one hour it was consumed with all its contents. The Temple and other buildings badly scorched. Tuesday eve a meeting was held and a patrol consisting of 21 men 3 for each night in the week chosen to guard the city to prevent further destruction by fire. A part of these men are members of the church—a part dissenters. We feel that we are in jeopardy every hour; tho' we possess a good degree of confidence that we shall be preserved and guided to a place of safety.

I have written to Dublin, Indiana; where cousin Lorenzo [Young] resides. We think they will get it and some of them return to us immediately. Many are preparing to flee, believing that if they remain they shall be driven out by a lawless mob. Probably you will soon have no friends here to direct letters to, and where we shall be I cannot tell you. However, I am not pained at the thought of leaving K[irtland] for I have never felt at home here. Mr. [Albert P.] Rockwood, his wife and E.[?] have been baptised and some others in Holliston by Parley Pratt. Are much opposed. They and some few families from Holliston design to go to Missouri next spring. Cousin B[righam] will get his family there next spring. I know not what brother L[evi] will think best. I am pained at the idea of going so far away from eastern friends without the prospect of their following.

The presidents, Joseph [Smith] & Sidney [Rigdon] & Hiram [Smith] returned from Missouri a few weeks since. They are elected to the first presidency, or to preside over all the churches instead of this place only.[16] Are all going to Far-West. Joseph & Sidney are on the way with their families, or a part of them. Hiram has buried his wife [Jerusha] and is married to Miss [Mary] Fielding. Elder [John] Goodson's wife's mother, Mrs. Dorson was very much injured by a fall from a waggon about the time he concluded to return home [from England]. She was a very great sufferer and without proper medical attendance until he arrived. H[?] came for brother—took supper with us. L[evi] visited her a few times—as many as he could as he was then preparing to leave. Last saturday we heard she was improving. Was able to sit up an hour or more.

The Mummies and records have been attached. Mummies sold Records missing.[17] I will give you a sentence from a recent Revelation, published in the last paper printed in the office. After speaking of the different places which have been appointed for the gathering of the saints, the Presidents say, "Now we would recommend to the saints scattered abroad, that they make all possible exertions to gather themselves together unto those places; as *peace, verily thus saith the Lord,* peace shall soon be taken from the earth, and it has already began to be taken; for a lying spirit has gone out upon all the face of the earth and shall perplex the nations, and shall stir up to anger against one another, for behold saith the Lord, very fierce and very terrible war is near at hand, even at your doors, therefore make haste saith the Lord O ye my people, and gather yourselves together and be at peace among yourselves, or there shall be no safety for you."[18] It hardly requires a prophet's eye to see that perilous times are at hand.

With such prospects before us I can not think of your being left in England alone. Our family are scattered far and wide. Perhaps there is something for you to do for the good of your friends at home. Elders [Heber C.] K[imball] & [Isaac] R[ussell] will start for America the first of april. I have heard nothing for a long time respecting any ones' going out next summer. They are too much engrossed with their own perplexities and embarrassments to think or converse about it. I write not to advise but to express my feelings.

Brother P[hinehas] left here in Nov. designing to return with his family next spring. I think certainly they will not come. George [Phinehas's son] is here with us. Has been quite contented. My health was poor through the summer. Suffered much in consequence of my journey to Ohio. For 8 weeks past I have felt very well. Am with cousin Mary [Ann Angell Young]. Kept house 3 months before brother left. You say you have not seen a word of writing from A. Brother Wm. rec'd. yours last summer and answered it. I should be glad to exchange provision with you sometimes, and to mend your clothes which you say are getting ragged were it in [my] power.—Your sister, Hepzibah R.

Cousin Lucius has the care of 2 churches in the vicinity of Oberlin. His wife is with him. Had a visit from her and Mrs. Gates last fall. Cousins here send love to you. H.R.

Friday eve. 19 Jan.   I have given Mrs. [Vilate] Kimball an opportunity to write in my letter, but as [she] designs to write next week, to her husband, she declined. Cousin Fanny [Young] wished to write but was prevented by company. A letter to Mrs. Kimball and Mrs. [Marinda N.] Hyde arrived with yours; also one to Mrs. Russel. Elders [William] Marks, John Smith and Reynolds Cahoon have been elected and ordained to preside over Kirtland. Luke Johnson and John Boynton are no lo[nger] of the number of the 12. Elders John Taylor and John Page are chosen to fill their places. No good news respecting the [Kirtland] Bank. The Boston house is finished outside. Some few other buildings have been erected this summer; but in general K[irtland] wears the same aspect as when I first saw it. Mrs. [Nancy Young?] Kent is in this place about 6 miles from us with her family. Have seen her but little. Uncle [John] Young has been sick—is pretty smart now.

Joseph [Young] has another son. P[hinehas Young] and his family in Missouri. War in Canada between the republicans and those who prefer british laws.[19] Elder [Evan M.] Green is there—he writes that the father is against the son, and the son against the father.

I will tell you a little more about Richmond friends [family] as possibly their letter may fail. They feel that brother Wm. has made a wise and happy choice [in marrying]—friends on both sides acquiesce. I do not know that [there] is any prospect of their getting away from Richmond. Brother said he did not know as there was money enough in Berkshire County to purchase his property and brother [in-law William] Peirson's. Edwin [Peirson] is teaching in Barrington—Eliza Ann [Peirson] at home. Mrs. Edward Plummer died last fall in Mississippi. Mrs. Gray (old lady) recently of fever. There was much excitement in Holliston when elder Pratt preached there, and considerable disturbance—no one seriously injured. The church and the world joined hands in persecuting E[lizabeth Haven?] after was baptized. She has since been very sick, of putrid and Typhus fever, as uncle [John] Haven stated in a letter to father, but was recovering. Mr. Rockwood said in his letter that her life was despaired for 3 days by all except herself and those of them who held her by the prayer of faith. Cousin Walter R. owns a pleasant seat in Lenox. He and his wife were expected to accompany our people to Hinsdale the 20th of Dec. A letter from cousin F. Brigham a few weeks since informed me that friends in that region were well. Little Brigham [Young] and Mary [Young] are fine children. Mary has suffered much from whooping-cough, diseased lungs &c. Is getting smart now.

I think I desire to know and acknowledge the truth but do not yet see my way clear to be baptized not viewing these things as you do. I believe there are *good* people in K[irtland] but [it] is not a good place to make Mormons. You see I must stop. Must omit reading over my letter lest I should fail of sending it this morning. Sat. Hope to see you in the spring. Hepsy

[on margins]

The excitement respecting the burning of the printing-office appears to have subsided in a measure.

The lives of the Presidents have been seriously threatened. We do not dare to have Cousin B[righam] return to this place.

Miss Rhoda Richards, Richmond
Berkshire County, Massachusetts   Kirtland, 23rd, March, 1838

Dear Friends,

I received the letters which brought the sad news of our dear Mother's death early on Tuesday morning one week from the day it was mailed. I had worked very hard the day previous and in consequence of it had arisen with a sick headache. Was preparing to commence packing our goods for Missouri in the expectation of starting the next Monday morning for Wellsville, where I should have taken a steamboat bound for Missouri in the company with cousin [Evan M.] Greene's family who were already there. Thus situated I was obliged to proceed in business as far as my strength would allow; but I assure you it was one of the heaviest works I have ever experienced. Before Monday the traveling became so bad I was obliged to defer going. I had for months been impressed with the feeling that I should never see my parents again; and when I have been mourning this separation from all my former friends and have been told that our family were coming to me, have repeatedly said that I did not anticipate ever seeing them more.

I have never liked K[irtland] well enough to have one single desire in my heart that any of my friends should come here, but often I decided to go to Missouri and to use my influence to get our family there. I had strong hopes that I should see you all before many months. I expect to be ere long 1000 miles further from that spot which for many years I have

75

called home, and which is still dear to me because my dearest friends are there. The greatest trial I had in view of going further was to think how my dear Mother would feel when she knew it. But she was spared that pang; and notwithstanding I rejoice with heaviness, I will endeavor to rejoice that she has gone to her rest in the grave, and I trust to a better world. How should I prize the melancholy satisfaction of visiting that sacred spot and bathing it with my tears. But even this must be denied me. Those of you who are with Father will do all in your power to console him and make the remainder of his days comfortable. I can hardly be reconciled to the idea of never seeing him again; hope it will not be so.

I shall send our goods to the river as soon as the traveling is sufficiently improved. Do not expect to leave myself before May as I know of no company now that I should like to go with on the water. I care not how soon I am away from this place. I have been wading in a sea of tribulation ever since I came here. For the last three months we as a people have been tempest tossed, and at times the waves have well nigh overwhelmed us; but we believe there will yet be a way of escape. I have been backward in speaking to my friends at home, conscious that it would give them trouble, particularly my Mother, without doing me any real good. This people have experienced nothing yet worse than I have anticipated ever since I have been here.

A dreadful spirit reigns in the breasts of those who are opposed to this Church. They are above law and beneath whatever is laudable. Their leading object seems to be to get all the property of the Church for little or nothing, and drive them out of the place. The house of our nearest neighbor has been entered by a mob and ransacked from the top to the bottom under pretense of finding goods which it is thought they had stolen themselves. An attempt has since been made to set the same house on fire while the family were sleeping in bed. We suffer from fear, but we hope these days of suffering will not always last. For myself I have been less unhappy through all these disquieting scenes than I was last summer. Then I carried a steady burden which seemed almost too heavy to be borne. I cannot particularize on a sheet of paper; neither can I begin to say one half I wish.

I desire not my friends to make themselves unhappy on my account. I had learned before I came here to anticipate affliction and sorrow, knowing that it would surely come, and I am confident that nothing will be laid upon me which I shall not be enabled to endure. I would give up all the enjoyments I have had here for a long time for the happiness of seeing my friends at home for one short day, and the only hope I have that I shall ever see you rests on the probability that you will come to me. Still I wish none of you to come unless it is best on the whole.

Elder [Heber C.] Kimball's friends think he is on his way home [from England] hastened by the prospect of war. There is a cessation of arms in Canada; but in all probability it is only to prepare for a general combat. It has been reported here that American vessels were all detained in England; if so, our friends could get on board a French ship. I am not anxious that Brother [Willard] should hear of Mother's death until he gets among his friends who will be prepared to sympathize with him. My friends here are friends indeed as far as they can be; but they are so engrossed with their own cares and perplexities at present that they can do little for others. Brother L[evi] left Dublin [Indiana] the 14th of Feb. for Missouri, in company with our cousins and numbers who had gone from this place, all good company. He then designed to visit K[irtland] this spring, but it is my desire that he should not return, and I have written discouragingly to him about it. He could accomplish nothing desirable by coming. There is no business to be done here.

Brother William asks what he has done that L[evi] should neglect to write him? Nothing, I presume. He is not as much in the habit of writing as the rest of us. While in K[irtland] he had no leisure. I endeavored to persuade him that he must write to Father and Mother before he left but he did not.

I must give you some account of the plans and prospects of this Church relative to emigration. Many families have already left. Those that remain are going up in camp. They design to start the first of May, but may not before the 10th or later. Probably an hundred and 25 families or more remain. They will go in large wagons covered square on the top with canvas or something that will turn water. Will take their clothing, beds, and cooking utensils and tent by the way. Fifty yds. of common sheeting will make a tent that will accommodate eighteen persons. Women and children will sleep in the wagons. Some will take along light crick bedsteads, and other measures will be taken to prevent sleeping on the ground as much as possible. They will have runners to go before and lay up provisions, that the inhabitants may not take advantage of their necessities to increase their prices. They will travel five days in a week; stop on Saturdays to bake and wash. Sabbath hold meetings. Will be eight or ten weeks on the road. They design to take along the poor and the lame, deeming it wrong to leave those who have a desire to go but have no means. It will be required of them to refund it as fast as they are able. This will probably be accomplished, but it must be by mighty effort. Duck will be prefered for tent cloth—will turn rain better. The camp will move but slowly. The men will walk much of the way.

Cousin Joseph [Young] has given me the offer of going with them, and unless Brother L[evi] returns so that I can go with him by water, I shall probably improve it. They will have as good company and as few children in their tent as any. A Miss Millsam from the State of Maine—a fine girl—will probably be one of our number. How I should rejoice to have the company of some of our home friends if this is best. I fear to urge you lest you should be dissatisfied. I think if Father was here to go with the camp that he would be made comfortable. We shall have to suffer privations and inconveniences in so new a place. No fruit—small houses etc. But for our encouragement we shall have the prospect of better days, I hope. I have always desired that Rhoda [a sister] should stay there until Mother should come to accompany her. Now I want she should be company for Nancy [another sister], for I expect you will all come.

I think you will not see such days as you have seen if you remain in the Eastern States. They will ere long be involved in great calamities, we think. I think so much of Edwin [Peirson] in regard to the prospect of war. I cannot think of his being called into service young as he is, and subject to ill turns which would be likely to be brought on him by exposures. Wish he was here to go with me. Cousin Joseph [Young] thinks if he was here with twenty dollars it would be all sufficient to carry him through. I do not like to have him come here alone there is so much wickedness in these days. I mail a letter with this to Mr. [Albert P.] Rockwood that they may have an opportunity to come if they choose and go with us. They will drive cows enough to supply them with milk.

Did you save your keg of sprouts or scions? Save all the pie-plant seed this season and dry as much of the plant as you can. Dried fruit [would] be a treasure in Missouri. I am taxing you heavily with postage; but I have much to say and shall ere long be where you will not hear from me so often. If I think of any errands in future, I shall send a paper with dotted letters for you to spell out. . . .

What are Phinehas's family going to do? I feel interested for them. The probability is that cousin's property and the Doctor's [Levi's] together, which has been considered worth perhaps 2000 dollars, cannot be sold for enough to furnish a team for us. I have run till I have felt that I could run no more, to collect enough on all the Doctor's accounts to enable to send our goods to the river, without succeeding; but think I shall. Brother's coat that was left in our house will be sent to Missouri. Whatever is left here will be common plunder. . . .

Hepsy Richards

G[eorge] is well and thankful, is anxious to be in Missouri. I mailed a letter to Brother L[evi] the second of March. Am told the mail between this and Missouri is slow and uncertain. Shall write the first opportunity by private conveyance; but unless he returns, he will not hear of Mother's death for some weeks. . . .

Chapter Four

Missouri

"Zion Has Been Scourged"

Independence, Jackson County, Missouri, according to revelation, was to be the "center place for the city of Zion." In August 1831 Joseph Smith and other Church leaders had dedicated land west of there as the gathering place for the Saints. But by 1836-1837, when the three women whose writings comprise this chapter—Drusilla Hendricks, Sarah Rich, and Elizabeth Haven—gathered with their families to Missouri, it was not to Independence they came. The hundreds of Saints who had earlier built homes there had clashed with old Missourians, who resented them for socializing and trading exclusively among themselves. Mormon settlements in Jackson County had been attacked by old settlers, and by the close of 1833 all Saints had fled Zion's "center place."[1]

The Mormons sought temporary refuge in neighboring counties, mostly to the north in Clay County, anticipating that through legal operations they would soon recover their Jackson County lands. Drusilla Hendricks and her husband joined the Saints in Clay County, but they were not there long before they saw what Drusilla termed "the commencement of the compromise." When it became apparent that legal efforts to recover Jackson land were futile, the Saints "for the sake of friendship, and to be in a covenant of peace with the citizens of Clay County," agreed to leave that county. Church leaders had already been surveying possible areas for Mormon settlement further north in Ray County, and with legal assistance from non-Mormon Alexander Doniphan, they petitioned the Missouri state legislature for the formation of a new county from those lands. The creation of Caldwell County was the result.

During 1837 the population at Far West on Shoal Creek in Caldwell County mushroomed as Saints from Clay County and elsewhere gathered there by the hundreds. Far West quickly became Caldwell County's chief town, boasting almost five thousand inhabitants within two years of its settlement by Mormons. Drusilla and James Hendricks were among the first Saints arriving there from Clay County; Sarah Pea traveled there from southern Illinois to marry Charles C. Rich in 1837; later Elizabeth Haven, along with her brother and niece, moved there from Holliston, Massachusetts. In Far West industrious Saints built homes, cultivated the land, and set up schools.

Toward the end of 1837, as conditions in Kirtland deteriorated, Church leaders began to investigate "other stakes or places of gathering," deciding that the town of Far West should be enlarged and Kirtland Saints and those scattered elsewhere should gather there and to Missouri's other upper counties. Early in 1838 Joseph Smith moved his family to Far West, and over a period of several months the Kirtland Saints joined them.

The rapid migration to Caldwell County demanded new settlements, which the Prophet Joseph Smith authorized at Adam-ondi-Ahman in Daviess County and DeWitt in Carroll County.[2] This spread of Mormon settlements outside Caldwell County annoyed Missourians, who felt the Saints should confine themselves to the "Mormon County." "Our trouble began over the election," Drusilla Hendricks remembered, referring to the August eruption at Gallatin near Adam-ondi-Ahman when Daviess County non-Mormons attempted to prevent Saints from voting. In the skirmish none were killed, but several were seriously hurt. Exaggerated reports of the battle brought over a hundred Mormon volunteers from Far West, including Drusilla's husband, James.[3] The coming of more Mormons caused Daviess County residents to gather troops from neighboring counties. Tensions mounted, and both sides engaged in a series of conflicts referred to as the "Mormon War."

Battle broke out October 23, 1838, at Crooked River in southern Caldwell County when Mormon militia under command of David W. Patten encountered the encampment of anti-Mormon Samuel Bogart and his men. Three Mormons and one non-Mormon were killed in the contest—Drusilla Hendricks's husband was injured—but false information relating the "massacre" of fifty or sixty of Bogart's men created widespread alarm, and it was soon rumored that Mormons were on their way to burn Richmond, further south in Ray County. Missouri citizens, excited by such rumors, besieged Governor Lilburn W. Boggs to suppress the supposed Mormon insurrection, and on October 27 he hastily issued his infamous "extermination order": "The Mormons must be treated as enemies, and must be exterminated or driven from the state if necessary." Three days after the governor's order was issued, seventeen Mormons were massacred at an isolated settlement along Shoal Creek known as Haun's Mill.[4]

Angry anti-Mormon militias surrounded Far West, and several Church leaders there, including Joseph Smith, were taken prisoner. Sarah Rich found herself alone in the beleaguered city when her husband, Charles, was compelled to flee for his life for his participation in the Crooked River battle. The Mormons surrendered Far West on the first day of November, and through the winter Missourians picked at the spoils. "They robed me of my riding horse, stole my chickins and drove off my cows that gave me milk," Sarah recalled.

Arrested Church leaders were examined at Richmond, where testimony given by apostates and anti-Mormon Missourians confirmed the existence of the Danites, a secret, unofficial Mormon brotherhood committed to violence against non-Mormons.[5] For their alleged connection with the Danites, Joseph and Hyrum Smith, Sidney Rigdon, and others were held on several counts and were committed to Liberty Jail in Clay County.

In the months that followed, thousands of Saints left Missouri. "The stakes of Zion will soon be bereft of all her children," Elizabeth Haven wrote her cousin in February 1839. Most of the Saints moved to Illinois and Iowa, where they settled temporarily in small companies or branches. Hundreds were received with kindness in Quincy, Illinois. There Sarah Rich gave birth to her first child. Elizabeth Haven found work as a seamstress for "genteel people." And Drusilla Hendricks nursed her ailing husband. Mormon life went on, but with a note of sadness. "By the river of Babylon we can sit down," Elizabeth wrote. *"We weep when we remember Zion."*

Drusilla Dorris Hendricks (1810-1881)

In the spring of 1836 Drusilla Hendricks moved with her husband James and four children from their home in Tennessee to Clay County, Missouri. Here they settled for a time before moving further north to Caldwell County, where for two years they enjoyed relative peace and lived, Drusilla said, "as we supposed the Saints would live."

Drusilla Dorris Hendricks, standing right, with her mother and her husband, James. Undated. (Hendricks family collection.)

In the sketch that follows, Drusilla describes what happened to her family as tensions grew to crisis proportions near Far West in Caldwell County. Though the account is a reminiscence dictated sometime in the 1870s, there is enough detail to recreate the anxiety among Mormon settlers at the time of the Battle at Crooked River. James Hendricks was critically wounded in that battle and remained an invalid for the rest of his life, but the family would endure the Mormon experience in Missouri, then in Illinois, and cross the Plains to live long and useful lives in the Salt Lake Valley.

This excerpt is taken from *Henry Hendricks Genealogy*, compiled by Marguerite H. Allen (Salt Lake City: The Hendricks Family Organization, 1963). Spelling and punctuation have been standardized.

> We went on our way rejoicing until we reached Clay County, Missouri. We soon bought fifty acres of land there, and there were six families living on it. We went in the house with a man by the name of Jerome Benson. I put my beds upstairs.
>
> There were a number of Saints in this settlement that had been driven from Jackson County, and we had great times in talking of their trials in that county, not knowing that the same fate awaited us. It was not a week until my husband's father, brother and wife and sister came to see us. They lived near Independence but had never heard the gospel and said that they took no part in the driving of the Saints from that county. And now nothing would do but we must go home with them for a visit. The old gentleman said that James (my husband) must go; he knew that he would not be molested. But having told that his youngest son was a Mormon, it was not easy to stay the hand of the wicked and ungodly. So we went home with him, partly to satisfy the old gentleman and partly to satisfy our own curiosity to see Independence where the center stake of Zion should be. My husband also wanted to see the rest of his sisters that were there.
>
> After crossing the Missouri River, we had an excellent view of the country. When [we were] within about three miles of his father's house, the Baptist minister overtook us and the old

gentleman had to introduce his youngest son James, and lo and behold it was the *Rev. I[saac] McCoy*, that old Baptist preacher who was at the head of Jackson County's mob along with Col. Pitcher,⁶ and he was going to Independence, and he would tell the boys to be still and not molest him [James] for his father's sake, but he would not wonder if his wagon wheels were sunk in the mill pond, so he had better be kind of careful. That made his father and brother feel awful bad, but James seemed very cheerful and showed no signs of alarm.

They had said that we could not go home in less than a week. He must now go with them up town, but they did not stay very long. They found that McCoy was making up a mob to come that night so they thought that we had best go. His father said he could not stand to see James abused. They got our and their teams ready. They intended to go with us as far as the river and wept nearly all the way, but it gave us an opportunity to explain the gospel, and we did not fail to embrace it. They went on with us until within four miles of our house where they turned back with sorrowful hearts. We reached home all right.

Our wagons, some five or six in number, had stirred up the mob spirit for fear the Mormons would come and take away their place and nation. The mob was gathering within half a mile of where we stopped, and the brethren we bought of had bought quite a tract of land, and we had paid over money to them and they to the party they had purchased from who was also a Baptist preacher, and of course when his flock required him to do anything he had to do it. And they wanted him to rue bargains. He first sent his wife to tell the brethren they must give up the land, for his church was not willing that it should go to the Mormons. The brethren were not willing to give it up, for they had drawn up agreements and made the first payment and had given their notes for the balance, and everything was done according to law and now they were to have possession of the land. She made some threat [that] if they did not give up the land willingly then they would be forced to.

We found that the mob were still gathering at this place; I cannot remember their names. Our brethren began to gather and get ready to defend themselves. Lyman Wight stood the highest in the priesthood of any one there, and he was no coward. The next morning after the visit of the preacher's wife, there were twenty-five or thirty of the brethren there with their arms. I noticed they went upstairs and came down without their arms, and soon after I had to go upstairs for something and in stepping on my bed I was frightened and on removing some of the clothing found the bed full of guns, pistols, and swords.

The brethren stayed there, for the mob said if they could get Lyman Wight they could get along with the rest of them but would fight about four o'clock p.m. The land man rode up to the fence and four others stopped back four or five rods with broken horse whips in their hands. Eight or ten of the brethren were in the yard. He inquired for the man who had made the purchase of the land; they came out and asked what he wanted. He said he wanted the land he had sold back and was going to have it or he was going to do something terrible if they did not do as he said. He began to make some threats; I was looking out of the window not a rod from them. Lyman jumped over the fence and caught hold of his bridle, and in less than half a minute there were twenty-five or thirty brethren around him, and the man wilted, which was no surprise, for Lyman looked like he would tear him to pieces. He agreed to be rather decent, but those four men never came up to the crowd. If the brethren had of known what they had been doing, they would not have left a grease spot on them as they had caught one of the brethren alone and whipped him nearly to death, and that is what had broken their horse whips, and there was the commencement of the compromise in Clay County. We all gave up our land and agreed to go to Caldwell County.

We were to be let alone there, so we were glad to do so and not be mixed up with [the mobbers]. Our leading brethren worked day after day to accomplish this move. We were among the first to go, and Brother Emmet and family (the elder who baptized us) went with us. We soon selected a place, built a cabin, and cut hay, for we had but little time to prepare for winter. We got about twelve tons of hay stacked very nice. On looking out one evening we saw the prairie on fire and knew it was three miles away, but the wind was driving it direct to us. He [James] said he would go and fight against it. I went with him two or three hundred yards, but he had not time to light his fire until the fire was upon us. We were forced to run for life. The grass was tall and the flames were high, and when we reached the house the flames reached the stacks and burned them up. The house was filled with cinders but we saved it.

We now did not know what to do, but we found a man who had raised some corn a mile from us who wanted to sell it. My husband gave him sixty dollars for six acres in the field. We gathered and cribbed it, then we were provided for the winter again. I never lived happier in my life. I was always very sickly until now. I had quit taking snuff, tea, and coffee, and I became healthy and strong. Where before I could not walk half a mile, now I could walk three miles and not tire, for we kept the Word of Wisdom. I can bear my testimony to the world. I could run and not be weary, walk and not faint. I received health in my navel and marrow to my bones and hidden treasures of knowledge. I often made myself feel like the old Nephite women while they were traveling in the wilderness, for they became strong like unto the men.[7]

We never missed a meeting, for we loved the Saints and had confidence in them. We read considerable, mainly the Bible, Book of Mormon, and Doctrine and Covenants; had our children baptized when eight years old, and, in fact, could hardly keep them waiting until they were old enough.

We entered land at the land office, paid our money, and began to live as we supposed the Saints would live, to make their own clothing, etc. We bought some sheep and prepared to sustain ourselves, but when we were driven, we had to do the best we could to keep soul and body together. In the years of 1836-1837 we did pretty well, and on March 23, 1838, my fifth child was born and we called his name Joseph Smith Hendricks.

The summer passed until August without any trouble. We had had just three years of peace, but the first of August our trouble began over the election. My husband had to stand guard for three months, as the mob would gather on the outside settlements. The brethren had to be ready and on hand at the sounding of a brass drum. At three taps on the drum my husband would be on his horse in a moment, be it night or day, while I and my children were left to weep, for that is what we did at such times.

I was willing for him to go as I always was until he fell in defense of the kingdom of God. Our crops were nearly destroyed while he was on duty, but I gathered in all I could in his absence. This scene of things continued until October 24, 1838, when the mob gathered on the south of us and sent out word that they would burn everything they came to and that they already had two of our brethren as prisoners and the prairies were black with smoke. Joseph Smith and his brother Hyrum, with others of the brethren, came along, going upon the high places to try and discover, if possible, what was going on. They came back by the door of our house and stopped for a moment. They thought the mob was burning the grass and outer houses to scare the inhabitants to make them flee so they could rob and plunder them of what they had.

We had no chance of taking care of our vegetables, so my husband said that we had better make the cabbage into kraut, so we went to work and finished it at ten o'clock that night. He asked if I would go with him to get a stone to weight the

89

kraut. I walked behind him and watched his form, for he always stood erect. The thought came to me that I might never see him so straight and erect again. He got the stone and I still walked behind him, watching his form with those same thoughts and feelings on my heart and mind (that I might never see him like that again). I couldn't tell my feelings if I should try, but I said nothing.

We had prayer and went to bed and fell asleep. I dreamed that something had befallen him and I was gathering him in my arms when Bro. C[harles] C. Rich called at the door for him and told him what he wanted. They had word that the mob was on Crooked River ten miles south of us and was a strong band. He said they had two of our brethren as prisoners and were doing all the damage that lay in their power. I got up and lit a fire, for it was cold, while he brought his horse to the door. I thought he was slower than usual. He told me where they were to meet. I got his overcoat and put his pistols in the pockets, then got his sword and belted it on him. He bid me goodnight and got on his horse, and I took his gun from the rack and handed it to him and said, "Don't get shot in the back." I had got used to his going, so went to bed and went to sleep.

Just about the time he was shot I was aroused from my sleep suddenly, and I thought the yard was full of men and they were shooting. I was on my feet before I knew what I was doing. I went to the window at the back of the house but all was still. I was afraid to open the door. I could hear nothing, so I ventured to open the door. It was getting light enough, so I could see very little. I went out and around the house and found there was no one there. Then I was worse scared than ever, for I thought it was a token to me that they had had a battle. I got the children up and walked the floor and watched the road. I tried to work but could not. I tried to keep still but could not. Finally I saw Brother Emit [Emmet] coming through the timber. I watched and saw that he did not stop at home

but he hollered something about Bro. Hendricks. I could not
tell what it was, but he was on express to Far West.

The [Emmet] children soon came over and told me that their
father said that Brother Hendricks was shot. Then I went to
the field to give vent to my feelings, and while there I saw a
man pass through the field on horseback. It looked like he had
a great roll of blankets. I went back to the house and found
the children all crying. I went to the loom to try and weave to
let on to them that I did not believe the report about their
father. I could not weave at all, but had not sat there but a
few moments when I saw a Mr. T. Snider (he did not belong
to the Church, but a good man) get off his horse at the gate. (I
saw him wipe his eyes. I knew that he was crying.) He came
to the door and said, Mr. Hendricks wishes you to come to
him. I asked where. He said to the Widow Medcalf's and that
he had come for me. I asked where and how he was shot, and
he thought he was shot in the hip.

There was a woman in the house that I had taken care of for
weeks. I told her to do the best she could with the children,
and I mounted the horse behind Mr. Snider. We had four
miles to ride, and on reaching there we met nine of the
brethren that were wounded and they were pale as death.
They were just going to get into the wagon to be taken to
their homes. I went into the house. Sister [Ann] Patten had
just reached the bed where her husband [David Patten] lay,
and I heard him say, "Ann, don't weep. I have kept the faith
and my work is done."[8] My husband lay within three feet of
Brother Patten, and I spoke to him. He could speak but could
not move any more than if he were dead. I tried to get him to
move his feet but he could not. This was *Thursday*, October
25, 1838, and the next *Tuesday* was the battle of Haun's Mill,
where men and boys were slaughtered and thrown into a dry
well eighteen or forty-eight in number, out of which one (Ben-
jamin Lewis) received a decent burial.[9]

There were three beds in the room where my husband
lay—he in one, Brother David Patten in one, and Brother

91

Hodge was the one shot in the hip. Brother Obanyon [Patrick O'Banion] was on the floor begging for a bed, and some of the sisters ran and got him one. My husband was shot in the neck where it cut off all feeling to the body. It is of no use for me to try and tell how I felt, for that is impossible, but I could not have shed a tear if all had been dead before me. I went to work to try and get my husband warm but could not. I rubbed and steamed him but could get no circulation. He was dead from his neck down.

One of the brethren told me how he fell, for he was close to him. After he had fallen one of the brethren asked him which side he was on (for it was not yet light enough to see), and all the answer he made was the watchword "God and Liberty." On hearing this it melted me to tears and I felt better. Then I was told how many of the brethren were wounded and who they were and was shown the weapons used, and they bore blood from hilt to point. It makes me chill to think of it.

We stayed here until amost night when one of our neighbors, Brother [Stephen?] Winchester and wife came with a wagon and bed in it and took us to Far West. The brethren told me if I took him home the mob would kill him before my eyes. I left my children in care of the man and his wife that I had been taking care of for two months, who had been suffering with fever and ague. But when the army came in they ran and left everything, so the children had to go to the neighbors. But a Brother Stanley and his wife (who came from the east the day before the battle) gathered up my children and went and stayed with them and took care of things, for which kindness I shall always feel grateful.

We were compelled to stay at Far West until after the surrender, when we went home. The mob had robbed the house of bedding and, in fact, everything but my beds. My husband could not yet move hand or foot. Then we had to settle our business matters and fix to get out of the state. I went to work and sold what I could and gave our land for money to buy two yoke of cattle. Finally we had to leave everything, only what we could put into a little wagon.

About the middle of January [1839], Father Joseph Smith [Sr.] and Father [Isaac] Morley, with five or six others, came and anointed and administered to my husband. They stood him on his feet and he stood by them holding to each arm. He began to work his shoulders. I continued to rub him with strong vinegar and salt and liniments. The brethren were leaving the state as fast as they could. We did not know how we could go until Brother I[saac] Leaney [Laney], who was shot and wounded at Haun's Mill, came to see us and said we should not be left behind. He had been shot through and through from both sides, the balls passing through the lungs, but he was miraculously healed. He had twenty-seven bullet holes in his shirt. I counted them myself. He only had eleven wounds to be dressed.

The enemy was still on the alert. One night they were hunting the Danites about nine o'clock. It was very dark. The dog barked as if he was mad. I sat on the side of the bed where my husband lay. I was watching him and nursing my baby. My oldest son, William, said, "Mother, the mob is coming." They were swearing at the dog. We had the door fastened; they told us to open the door or they would break it down. I asked who they were. They damned me and said it was none of my business, and if I did not open the door they would break it down in one minute, so I told the children to open the door. I had a girl staying with us. She and the children were like a flock of chickens when they see the hawk flying around them. These men had false whiskers until they looked awful. One had a large bowie knife in one hand and a pistol in the other.

They came to the bed and told me to get up. I simply told them I was watching him [James] before they came. They took the candle from the table and turned down the bed clothes and asked what doctor I had. I told them I had none. They then asked me a great many questions. They told me they wanted to search the house, so one gave his pistol to another and took the candle. He told me to get up, as he wanted to look under my bed. I moved a very trifle higher upon the bed, for I thought of a dream which I had about three months before he was shot. I dreamed that he lay on the bed sick and was almost gone and two men came in to kill him. I told them they would have to kill me first. I thought they could not get me away from him; then they let him alone. But the men I saw in my dream and these of the mob looked as much alike as can be, so I was determined I would not leave him.

They looked under my bed and said they were looking for [Stephen?] Winchester. I told them to go to Illinois if they wanted to find him. They said his wife had been telling them that lie, but they did not believe it, so I told them when he started. After hunting under the beds at the back of the house, they must go upstairs. I told him where the children got up but said there was nothing there but meat. I had my meat up there to use on our journey. They finally concluded that Winchester was not there, so they came a second time to my husband's bed and turned the clothes down below his breast. I sat still on the side of the bed, for I was determined I would not leave him. They made him talk, but he was so weak and pale he looked more like he was dead than alive. They turned around and asked me for water. I told them that there was a pail and a cup by it, that I would not get up. They drank. I had wood in for the night. They sat down by the wood and put powder in their pistols. One said, "All is ready." Each man put his finger on the trigger of his pistol and said let us walk. I expected when they got back of the curtain they would fire at his head as he was bolstered up, but they stood about one minute and then went out. The mob had often sent me word that they were coming to help the Lord off with him. So I thought they had come for that purpose, but I acknowledged the hand of the Lord in it.

Then the doctor came and wanted to take his case in hand. He [James] said the doctor was on the side of the mob and he

knew he could do him [no] good. He wanted to lift the bone
in his neck that pressed the spinal marrow. He came a time or
two, but I could not engage him. Then he said he would give
me a receipt to make a liniment to rub him with to open the
pores of the skin. He also gave me some things to put in the
liniment. By this time my husband had got so he could stand
on his feet without helping him to get on them.

Brother Lainey [Laney] had secured one yoke of cattle as we
thought one yoke would haul all we could get in one wagon
that we had. We could then save the money we had to buy
our bread and clothing.

We started March 17, 1839, for Quincy, Illinois. On the first
of April as soon as the brethren found we were there, they
secured a bottle of oil, consecrated it, and came with Father
Joseph Smith [Sr.] at their head, (seven in number) while we
were camped out and got him [James] on a chair and anointed
and administered to him again, then assisted him to his feet
and he walked, between two of them, some thirty yards and
back.

We soon got into a room, partly underground and partly on
top of the ground. The room was very close, and he took sick
and I had to lift him at least fifty times a day, and in doing so
I had to strain every nerve.

We had the cattle which had hauled us here but could not sell
them, but could hire them out for a small sum to break
prairie, so we hired them. We had one small heifer that the
mob did not take that gave us a little milk for twice a day,
but in less than two weeks there came a drove of cattle from
Missouri and they drove her off with them, so we were like
Job of old and my husband as sore, for his blood cankered
and he broke [out] in sores all over his body so that you could
not put a pin point on him without putting it on a sore, from
the crown of his head to the soles of his feet.

In two weeks we neither had bread or meat so we sent our
oldest son, William, three miles out on the prairie to the man

95

who had hired our cattle. We had one spoonful of sugar and one saucer full of cornmeal so I made mush of the meal and put the sugar on it and gave it to my children. That was the last of the vegetables of any kind we had in the house or on the earth. We were in a strange land among strangers. The conflict began in my mind: "Your folks told you your husband would be killed, and are you not sorry you did not listen to them?" I said, No I am not. I did what was right. If I die I am glad I was baptized for the remission of my sins, for I have an answer of a good conscience. But after that a third person spoke. It was a still small voice this time saying, "Hold on, for the Lord will provide." I said I would, for I would trust in Him and not grumble.

Sarah De Armon Pea Rich (1814-1893)

Sarah De Armon Pea was born in St. Clair County, Illinois, in 1814. She married Charles Coulson Rich near Caldwell County, Missouri, in 1837, and the following sketch focuses on the young couple's life there. Charles C. Rich was a leader among the Saints during the Missouri persecutions. After Elder David W. Patten fell mortally wounded, Charles C. Rich assumed command of the Saints at the battle of Crooked River, and consequently incurred the wrath of the gentiles. He was forced to flee to Quincy, Illinois, leaving Sarah, pregnant with their first child, alone in Missouri "under mob law."

Sarah DeArmon Pea Rich standing right of the gate in front of her home at 273 North First West, Salt Lake City, with her daughter Elizabeth Rich Pratt and three of Elizabeth's sons, ca. 1880. (LDS Church Archives.)

Though Sarah's hopeful anticipation as a new wife was sobered by trials and terror, she was sustained by the support of close friends and family and by her commitment to her husband and the Church. The Church of Jesus Christ of Latter-day Saints was to determine the course of the Riches' lives as they moved with the Saints to Nauvoo and the Great Basin, and later, when Charles Rich was named an apostle, they founded Mormon colonies in San Bernardino, California, and Bear Lake Valley, Utah-Idaho.

This excerpt is taken from Sarah D. Rich's two-volume holograph autobiography written in 1885. The volumes are located in the Church Archives. Since the holograph contains no periods, minimal punctuation has been added here for clarity, but Sarah's phonetic spelling has been preserved. Capitalization of the letter s has been standardized since in the original holograph the upper and lower case s's are indistinguishable.

> As Far West was a place everybody lived in log houses so my husband had built a nice little hewed log hous and got it reddy to live in by the time we ware married. It was 4 miles from Farr west near my husbands fathers. So I left my fathers house in Farr West and we mooved to our coasey and happy home and we thought we ware the happyest couple in all the land. My husband had a beautifull prospect for a nice farm with plenty of timber and watter and our plans were laid for a comfortable and happy home in the near future o[u]r religion being first with us in all things.
>
> My father in fitting me out for to help us along gave me a nice riding horse, saddle, bridal and Martingills [martingales] as they ware fashenable in those days. And Mr Rich had a nice horse and rigg for riding so we attended meeting ever[y] Sunday at Farr West. So we rode horseback to meeting every Sunday and had the privalege of often list[en]ing to the prophet Joseph Smith preach and enstruct the people a priva- lege we both appreciated very much. Things went on so nicely during the summer we never once dreamed what was in store to brake up our happy anticipations and plans that were laid for our happyness with our home and friends.

Sometime in the fall rumers ware afloat that a Mob spirit was begining to trouble our Misourie kneighbors and there was prospect of trouble a head and those rumers soon turned into reality and we could foresee trouble for us instead of the quiat happiness we had layed out for us. My husband and myself talked over the matter and could see no way but to face the trouble[s] when they did come and as he was allwais well gifted in desearning what was coming [he] would let no time be lost in giving me good council and trying to have me pre-pare my mind to lean apon the Lord to give me faith that I might withstand the trials that was a head of us as a people.

He could foresee maney things that I had not yet learned to think of and he seamed to realise that the time was coming when we ware to be seperated from each other in the midst of our worst trouble and would often tell me if such a time did ever come that I must not let my faith fail me but pray for couriage to withstand trials when they did come. Little did I think the time was so near that he would be compelled to flee for his life and leave me as it ware in the midst of a howling mob with no one to look to for pertection but my Father in heaven.

But such was the case and thus it did accur as he had feared it would. For it was not long before the mob maney thousand strong gethered in apon us and surrounded our pleaseant homes and caused us to gether together into Far West in order that we could be better pertected in the absence of our men that ware out trying if it was posible to make peace with our enemyes and pertect the setlements that could not posibly leave there homes and gether in with the rest of us.

My Father and mother and sister had gone on a visit to Illinois to see my brother. They went just before those troubles com-menced and as it was not safe for them to travil and return to there home in Far West they wrote for me and my husband to moove into there house and look after the things they had left. Conciquently we did so and I took in those that had to leave there homes and flee into the city untill I took in seven

familys. By this time there was no room for aney more.
Among that number was John E Page and his sick wife. He
was then one of the twelve apostles of our church and about
one week after, his wife died. And as the mob was troubling
us so sevearley at this time it was impossible to have Sister
Page burried for three days and twice while she lay in the
house a corpse the mob entered the house and made a search
all through the house to see what they could find. They ware
at that time in a camp about a mile from our house and
would keep up screaming and yelling like a band of indian
war party.

And it was then that I stood in my door and watched my dear
husband as he was sent out to the guard of there camp bearing a flagg of truce. I see them shoot at him while bearing a
white flag with a message from our people to them in order
to try to make peace if possible. But thus he was received by
one of there guard a Methodist preacher by the name of
bogard [Bogart].¹⁰ He was the man that had a battle with our
people on crooked river when David Patton was killed one of
the twelve apostles of this church. My husband was allso with
David Patton when he was killed and Bogard knew him and
this is why he wished to kill him, and my husband and some
others ware compelled to flee for there lives as the mob swore
they would kill him.

I do not remember the names of all the brethren that left with
Mr Rich but Hose[a] Stout, Samuel Smith a brother of the
prophet and Seamor [Seymour] Brunson and Phineous Young
ware among that number that had to flee. And they had to
travil out into a willderness country where there ware no
settlement[s] in order to avoid meeting aney of the mob that
was prowling all through the country. Conciquently the[y]
expearenced maney hardships and [were] hungrey for food as
they only had one horse a peace. Conciquently [they] could
not take much provision with them and to help along they
ware five days lost and did not know where they ware nor
which course to travil. One of those days the company of six

100

only had one black bird among them to eat. They finely come upon a camp of indians who received them friendly and fed them and suplyed them with provision in there rude way and sent a pilot with them to the settlements. From thare they made there way to Quincy Illinois.

The company stoped there while Mr Rich went to the south part of the state where my brother lived and where my father and mother and sister was stopping and got my father to take a team and come to Fare West and bring me to him at Quincy. He was to meet me thare. This was in the month of January [1839] and the wether was veery coald for my father to travil 4 hundred miles but he made the trip in good time.

Now I must return to some of my expearence during the three months I was left alone in the midst of the mob after my husband had to leave. Him and I parted that night at one oclock. We had went to his sisters to stay that night befor he knew he had to leave. His sister lived at the store on the publick square of far West. Her husband kept the store. And when we parted not knowing whether we should meet again for a long time I felt confident it was the only thing he could do to avoid a madened mob from taking his life so I felt contented to have him go feeling that the Lord would spare us to meet again. So him and Hosey Stout made a covenent to stay together untill we should meet again and Hoseys wife and I made a coven[an]t that her and I would remain together as true friends untill we should meet our husbands again and apon this prommis we shook hands with our dear husbands and parted.

Her and I then went into my sistern laws house and went to bed praying the Lord to protect ourselves and our dear companions untill he saw fit to have us meet again. So in the morning after we had our brakfast we started to go home to my house abut 4 blocks away but found on the road the mob had placed more guards out to prevent any one from passing. We attemted to pass but was stoped by baynets pointed at us and told we could not pass. I told them I was going to my

101

home a short distance away. The[y] still refused and all that
we could do was to return to my brotherinlaws but when we
got thare and was telling in the store what had happened the
captain of the guards happend to be thare and here what I
said. He steped up to me and asked what was the matter. I
told him. He said was it your husband that capt boeguard
killed yesterday? I said yess sir for they thought he was killed.
He then said he would go with me to where the guard was
and see that I passed on to my home.

I told him on the way that I had sent my hired boy out with a
teame of oxen to git me a load of wood and that the boy was
taken prisner and the oxen kept in there camp. He told me to
give him the name of the boy and the discription of the cattle
and he would see they ware returned. So he told the guard to
let us two ladys pass which they did. We went to our home
and the captain hurried on to the camp and arived thare just
as the[y] had drove up my oxen to kill them for beef. He
called to them to hold on and asked for the boy that had
come for wood with that team. He then orderd some of his
men to hitch up the team and go and load on the wood and
guard that boy to his home with the wood. So I soon had the
boy, wood and team returned to me again.

So by his carr[y]ing the impreshian into camp that my
husband was killed it kept [them] from looking for him untill
he had time to git out of the way. But when they found out
he was not killed they felt awfull mad and would often come
to my house and tell me if I did not tell where he was hid
they would blow my brains out, at the same time pointing
pistols at me. For they thought he must be hid up somwher
never once thinking it posible for him to make his escape
when there was so maney troops of mobs in the country.

This was the kind of life I had to live under mob law for 3
months not knowing what time they might set fire to my
house for they thretned severl times that they would do so in
order to find my husband, and I at the same time in verry
delacate health. They robed me of my riding horse, stole my

chickins and drove off my cows that gave me milk. Thus
things went on untill my father arived. He found me verry
sick through excitement and hardships. But notwithstanding
my sickness with the help of Sister Samantha Stout we
gethered things together and packed up what little we had left
and on the 3rd of February in the cold storms we started in
wagons 2 in number. I mean 2 waggons to hawl all my father
had and all that myself and Sister Stout had allso Thomas
Richs effects for he drove one of the teames. We started for
Quincy Illinois. I was so feeble that I had to lay and [on] a bed
and travel over frosen ground for 4 hundred miles.

I must here mention the kindness of brother Thomas Rich to
me. He is a cousin to my husband and lived with us as one of
our family. He was so faithfull on this journey for I had to be
helped out and into the wagon ever[y] night and mourning
and he being young and strong to[ok] that care apon himself
and was so kind to me that I wish his name ever held in
remembrance by my children. Allso the name of Sister Samantha Stout the wife of Hose[a] Stout. She was like a dear sister
to me through all my trials and hardships in misouree she to[o]
passing through hardships and sorrow as well as myself. But
she bieing poor in health and verry young her hardships
shortend her days for she did not live a year after we landed
in Quincy where we met our husbands that had fled for there
lives some months before.

When we reached the mississippi river the ice had broke up
on the west side of the river and was running so the ferry
boat could not cross. So of cours I and Sister Stout felt quite
down hearted. We knew our husbands ware on the opasite
side in Quincy waiting for us and by this time quite a number
of the brethering ware allso there on the banks of the river
waiting to cross over. All the chance for crossing was to go
across in a skift or canoe through the ice untill they reached
the iland and from thare walk on the ice to reach Quincy on
the east side.

While I was setting on the bank of the river feeling so bad brother George D. Grant come along and knowing of my poor health and seeing me feel so bad he said to me, Sister Rich cheer up and I will go over and tell brother Rich you are hear. Some on hearing what brother Grant said remarked that it would be a verry daingerous undertaking as the ice was runing so swift. Said brother Grant, well I will try it live or die. So him and another man got into a canoe and started over. Sister Stout and I set on the bank and whched [watched] him untill he or they reached the iland and started across on the ice. They had not gone fare before we see the ice brake and one of the men fell into the river. We then see 2 men from the oppasit side run a cross to where the ice had broke. By this time it was gitting late near sunset and soon a man came back with the canoe and said George Grant had fell through the ice and they got him out just alive and that was all.

So when we heard this news we went back to our waggons clear discouriaged. I went into the waggon to cry while Sister Stout and my dear father and Thomas rich prepared the supper as I was not able to help them do aneything. But all this time my husband and brother Stout after seeing that brother Grant was well cared for ware planing to get over to us for they were the 2 men that we see go too brother Grant when he fell through the ice. They got him out of the river and conveyed him to a good place where he was attended to and then got a skift and carried on there shoulders to the lower iland beeing joined by brother Webb whose wife was allso in our company. They cross on the ice carr[y]ing the skift untill they reached where the ice was running. They then launched there skift and came down the river to where we ware camped and great was our joy to meet with our dear companyans who ware compelled to part with us 3 months before and flee for their lives from a howling mob.

And after there staying with us that night they concluded that it was best for us wimon [women] folks to cross the river at

once and not waite untill the ferry boat could cross which was
not likely to be the case for severl days. On my account it
was nessary we should cross over immeadiatly as I knew not
what moment I would be confined with my first child. So in
the morning us three wimon and our husband[s], that was
myself, Sister Stout and Sister Webb with our husband[s], got
into a canoe and they 3 men road [rowed] us over the river to
where we could cross the ballence of the way on the ice. Just
think of it my dear reader to see us undertake such a perilous
trip across the watter running with ice the cakes of which
ware so large that some times the men would have to jum[p]
out on the ice in order to puch it away and then jump back
into the canoe again and by hard work reached the ice on the
other side. And my poor oll [old] father had to be left with
the teams and waggons untill the ferry boat could cross. The
poor old man stood with tears in his eyes watching us, not
knowing whether we could rech shore or not. He said afterwards that sad was his feelings to see us start out to cross the
watters of the Miss[iss]ippi 6 of us in a canoe. But we reached
the shore in safty and was met on the banks of the river by a
brother George Crowch and his wife at whose house my husband had been stoping and they made us welcom and done all
for our comfort that they could untill Mr Rich could find a
place to rent which he found in a few days.

Elizabeth Haven Barlow (1811-1892)

Elizabeth Haven, a daughter of Elizabeth Howe and John Haven, was born and raised in Holliston, Massachusetts. Elizabeth was active in the town's Congregational church, but after reading the Book of Mormon given her by her cousins Brigham Young and Willard Richards, she decided to became a Latter-day Saint. She was baptized in September 1837, when Parley P. Pratt was proselyting in the Holliston area.

With her brother Jesse Haven and Ellen Rockwood, a niece, Elizabeth migrated to Far West, Missouri, in the spring of 1838. By February 1839 the family had taken refuge in Quincy, Illinois, with the main body of the Saints, and while there Elizabeth penned several letters to her cousin Elizabeth Howe Bullard in Holliston. The letters gravely portray the Saints' situation in Quincy as seen by a young woman committed to the restored gospel. But Elizabeth balances the weightiness of the Saints' trials with her own light-hearted humor and delight in everyday activities.

Elizabeth Haven married Israel Barlow at Quincy in 1840. The couple moved to Nauvoo and later settled in Davis County, Utah. The following letter, composed by Elizabeth over a two-week period, is taken from *The Israel Barlow Story and Mormon Mores* (Salt Lake City: Ora H. Barlow, 1968). The original letter is in private possession. Spelling and punctuation have been standardized.

Quincy Feb. 24th, 1839

Dear Elizabeth

With much pleasure I commune with my dear friends far away in the East, which my frequency in visiting will boldly testify. Weeks and months have rolled away in rapid succession since I left my friends far behind in N[ew] E[ngland] for the land of Zion. But O! how Zion mourns, her sons have

Elizabeth Haven Barlow with her husband, Israel, in the 1880s.
(*The Israel Barlow Story and Mormon Mores*. Salt Lake City,
Ora H. Barlow, 1968.)

fallen in the streets by the cruel hand of the enemy, and her
daughters weep in silence. It is impossible for my pen to tell
you of our situation; *only those who feel it, know.* Between five

107

and seven thousand men, women, and children driven from the places of gathering out of the state [Missouri] from houses and lands, in poverty, to seek for habitations where they can find them. The Saints are coming as fast as possible; they have only to the 8th of March to leave the state. The Prophet has sent word to have them make speed, haste out of the state. About twelve families cross the river into Quincy every day, and about thirty are constantly on the other side waiting to cross. It is slow and grimy; there is only one ferry boat to cross in. For three or four weeks past it has been beautiful weather and the roads great for traveling, which has made it very favorable for the brethren. But now it is rainy, the roads very muddy within three days. The stakes of Zion will soon be bereft of all her children. By the river of Babylon we can sit down, yes, dear E, *we weep when we remember Zion.*[11] *[There follows an eight-line verse by Parley P. Pratt.]*

We look upon our present with sorrow and much anxiety. We must now scatter in every direction just so we can find employment. Some of our dear brethren who have mingled with us in praise and prayer are now buried with the dead; some who a few months ago seemed to run well in the strait and narrow path have to our astonishment and grief forsook us and fled; our Prophet is still in jail, and many others whom we love. To look at our situation at this present time it would seem that Zion is all destroyed, but it is not so; the work of the Lord is on the march.

Never has there been a time since the Church was first organized that the work spread so fast as it has within the past six months. The Mormons have been the general topic of debate in this upper country, in the Western and Middle States and also in the Eastern States. I see by the papers that we have come up in remembrance there, though far from the truth sometimes. Many have now a curiosity to hear which previous to past difficulties would not so much as listen; but now anxious to hear both sides, the Elders can thereby preach the gospel to them. Much good will ultimately result in the past to bring about the purposes of Jehovah.

God moves in a mysterious way, his wonders to perform.
Many have been sifted out of the Church, while others have
been rooted and ground in love and are the salt of the earth.
I have understood that some of the Missourians begin to
tremble for driving us from the state and intend to leave also,
lest God should pour out his judgment upon the inhabitants. I
doubt not but that there are many honest hearts in Missouri.
You will learn from Charles's letter before you receive this,
that President Rigdon has been liberated from jail.[12] He gave
an account last Sabbath how he was set at liberty. He remarked that it was a miracle and indeed it is, but cannot stay
to recite the particulars. If I could sleep with you one night,
think we should not be very sleepy, at least I could converse
all night and have nothing but a comma between the sentences, now and then.

When we shall enjoy the society of the Prophet and know the
will of the Lord concerning the Church, we know not. We
sigh and long for his deliverance. The word of the Lord is
precious unto us, even as it was in the days of Samuel the
prophet, for since the ancient prophets and apostles have been
killed, the people have changed the ordinances and broken the
everlasting covenant, and there has been no open vision.

We want to know very much how the few Saints in H[ollis-
ton] have stood affected while Zion has been scourged. Have
any departed from the faith? I hope not. It is only those who
stand amidst all these trials unto the end that will at last be
found worthy of a crown of glory. These scenes try us exceedingly, and we are to be tried (everyone who inhabits the
celestial kingdom) like gold seven times purified. Therefore if
any think that they will not come among us because we are
tossed and driven about, rest assured that they will be tried in
some way until they are purified for the kingdom of Christ.

I often think of the church, the little branch which I left in
H[olliston], think that I shall soon see some of them in this
country. I presume that you often meet with those who
delight to boast over you concerning our situation here, and

109

you feel no doubt that it is as much as you are able to endure. God will lay no more upon us than what we are able to bear. I felt that trials were hard to endure alone there, but they were comparatively nothing to what I have passed through since. We want to know how many of the church are coming west: who? at what time they think of starting? and how they are coming, whether by water or by land? We wish to know all about it.

President Rigdon is now making out a history of the treatment of the Missourians toward the Mormons from the time that they were driven from Jackson County unto this present time, and he is going himself to Washington to plead at the feet of the President according to revelation. He has written to the Solicit[or] General of the United States court for a mandate or precept against the State of Missouri for redress of wrongs, also precepts against the Governor down to the private citizens who have [in] any way been concerned in injuring or driving us from Missouri. President Rigdon says he sees no way for the Prophet to be delivered only through the United States court.[13]

Those who were put into Liberty [jail] for treason and at Richmond [jail] for murder, have been false[ly] imprisoned, and they even now hold an action against the state [of] Missouri for this treatment. What these things will result in we know not. Things have transpired within one year which the Church looked not for, and what another year will accomplish is known only in futurity. When Heber Kimball (one of the Twelve) was in England he had a vision of future scenes. He remarked to me one day that the past scenes was not one tenth of the tribulations which I should soon see. Therefore, said he, "Sister, prepare thyself for greater things."

There has been a general commotion and stir among the Indians for months past. Several hundred Indian chiefs have had meetings this winter. What it is for, none can learn, but it is feared by the people in upper Missouri that [it] is a preparation for war. One tribe which has a prophet among them will

110

not allow the white missionary to be in their midst, because "they no preach the true God." I presume Sister Nurse has heard Brother Pratt speak of that tribe. The prophecies must all be fulfilled, and when the remnant of Jacob pass through there will be none to deliver. Micah 5:8. How soon they will pass through we know not. They are very wrathy toward the whites and we hear many things which they threaten, but God will not suffer them to rise until the Gentiles are ripe for destruction.

[February] 25. Dear E., After a day of sober reflection I resume my pen to converse with one [with] whom I have spent many happy hours in days past and gone, and hope to spend many, yes many more, but with far different objects in view. The understanding and knowledge we have of the scriptures makes *friends* and everything appear in a very different light to me. Mother wished me to write—in particular after I had seen the Prophet and had been to meeting—my testimony as to the truth of this work and let you all know. I have done so and several of you have my testimony. I wish that I had more of yours and the rest of the Church. Nancy will soon send her testimony to Mary.[14]

Past scenes have greatly strengthened my faith. If we were of the world, I believe that the people of Missouri would love us well enough to let us remain somewhere in the state. But they hate us, despise us, and persecute us, and when they kill us they verily think they do God's service. My faith is strengthened by seeing the prophecies beginning to be fulfilled. Verily thus saith the Lord, peace shall even be taken from the earth.[15] It is already taken from Missouri. They are troubled and perplexed, and since I have commenced this letter, [I] have heard that some who have fought against us are now fleeing their country, and also that the jailor at Liberty says if the government will not set the Prophet and the rest who are with him free, that he will, for such prayers as are offered up in that prison will never go unanswered. But the jailor would not dare to liberate them, for the mob surrounds them continually, determined to kill them if they are [liberated]. President Rigdon was let out of jail after dark, leaning on the sheriff's arm, and the next morning at sunrise he was forty miles from Liberty. When the mob learnt that he was gone they were much exasperated and are more bitter against those that are left.

Many fears are entertained in behalf of Brother [Parley P.] Pratt. The mob are determined that he shall be hung, but we hope not. He is a bold witness for Jesus, and his testimony has gone forth to the world in black and white. His wife has been with him in jail most of the time since their trial. We have written occasionally [of] the trials of the Saints of God within the past few months, but these are small to what we expect to pass through. Therefore let all who desire to live with the Saints count the cost before they set out on their pilgrimage to Zion, come prepared to suffer with the Church in all their afflictions, not to flee as many have, in the day of trial when labour was mostly needed. Yes this church

> Wants no more cowards in their bands,
> Who will her colors fly.
> The call's for valiant-hearted men
> Who are not afraid to die.[16]

President Rigdon was bailed out for $2,000, not that he was guilty, but to appease the wrath of the mob, and all the rest in Liberty jail have no cause of action found against them, but for their own safety they remain there, for the mob characters have threatened to [burn] Liberty if they are let out. We do not know how soon we will see them. Their families are in this place. The Prophet's wife says that she is not out of Missouri while her husband remains there. John Carroll [Corrill], formerly a brother in the Church but now a dissenter, a Representative for the State of Missouri, asked leave to introduce a bill into the legislature prohibiting anyone from prophecying or speaking in the name of the Lord in that state. Forty-one in favor, forty-four against it. Their cup of iniquity is fast filling up.

Brother Jesse [Haven] left us last Thursday on his way to
Springfield in this state to attend the conference of elders the
8th of next month. He intends to start from there to the East
in company with some elders preaching on their way to
N[ew] E[ngland]. He is in hopes to reach there by summer. I
suppose he intends to get his lost *rib* before he returns to
Zion.[17] Nancy wishes to say to Isaac [Bullard] to bring his rib
with him next time he comes to Zion, for she thinks it a poor
plan to travel 2,500 miles in these hard times to get a [wife].
Charles Nurse lives in this place and has gone to work in the
flour mill for eighteen dollars per month and boarded, likes
his employment, has a good boarding place, and lives very
high such as he has not been used to of late. He sends his love
to you and says you must come on, for there are many here
looking after [Y]ankee wives. He thinks he can speak a good
word for you. O Elizabeth, it is time for me to hush such nonsense.

[Albert] Perry [Rockwood] wishes Father to get his discharge
from military duties and send it to Quincy immediately. We
also want to have Father write us, as soon as you receive this,
to let us know about his coming to the West, how and when,
that we may know when to look for him. We all feel anxious
to know how he has felt while Zion has been scourged,
whether he is in prosperity or adversity. We want him to
write within one week after you get this, for we know not
how long we shall remain here, but if we are not driven and
can get into business very likely shall stay several months.
Our love to your dear mother, E[sther] Morton and finally to
all. Be sure and write me a *long*, yes *very* long letter soon.
Remember the Prophet and afflicted Zion at the throne of
grace and receive this letter which is full of love and affection
from a sister in the everlasting gospel, Elizabeth Haven.

*[There follow some fourteen separate postscripts written over a period of
time, which ask for news and give news of the Saints and Elizabeth's
work with "genteel people" in Quincy. The following notes are representative of these postscripts.]*

113

P.S. #1 When you write to me write much news. [I] want to hear from old Holliston: marriages, births, and deaths. Who is Deacon?[18] But be particular to let me know how the work of the gospel is. Are there any enquiries? Any been baptized? And who is coming to Zion or near its borders? Almost March, time draws nigh when I imagine you will leave N[ew] E[ngland]. Come as early as possible so that you can raise something in a garden to live on. That is about all that the Saints can do. We shall not stay long in a place at present.

P.S. #2 We want to know if Aunt Howe is coming? Elizabeth, fetch a bonnet block and bonnet thread. Think you could make it very profitable sewing bonnets here. Quincy is quite a handsome place. Some *beautiful buildings*. General handsome stores. Quite a city. Have seen many things here, which I have not seen before for ten months.

The people of Liberty have permitted the friends of those in prison to visit them but have just now heard that they refuse that privilege since P[resident] Rigdon was liberated, threatening to shoot the first Mormon that comes into the place. We are all in commotion in this country.

P.S. #3 One of the brethren died yesterday on the other side of the river and was brought over today, was carried into the courthouse, and President Rigdon preached a funeral sermon. Full house. Many of the citizens present. This forenoon President Rigdon, Brother [John] Taylor, one of the Twelve, Judge [Elias] Higbee and Elder [John P.] Greene of the high council met in Nancy's room to draw up a paper to present to the citizens of this place this evening, making known to them the situation of the afflicted among us.[19] Many in this place have great sympathy for us.

P.S. #4. The people of Quincy have contributed between four and five hundred dollars for the poor Mormons. God has opened their hearts to receive us. May heaven's blessing rest upon them. We are hungry and they feed us, naked and clothe us. The citizens have assisted beyond all calculation.

114

Great things await us, and this generation. Mr. P. has not heard from his father's family since we left M[assachusetts]. Wants to hear. Write about them whether sick or well.

March 3d. Have been to Mr. Wells two days sewing [for] genteel people, treat me with much attention and kindness. Have a sleeping chamber by myself. They live on the luxuries of the market. Do not let their maid come to the table. Quite a contrast to my situation from a log hut, to a palace. I am particular[ly] thinking father will be glad to know all about us. Often we change our situation.

P.S. #13. Where is Miss Crawford and Miss Cook? Are they married? My love to them. If you see them tell them not to be in a hurry about getting married, for I am not. O Elizabeth, don't you think that I am very silly? I do, but I don't feel sober just this minute. Do not read this to anyone. Wish you would write how many letters you have all received from me since August because the mail as been irregular.

P.S. #14. About two weeks after we left Far West three suns were seen to rise one morning which were seen by the people there. The sun, the great orb of the day was in the center, the other two were not quite so bright but produced shadows only dim. Light projected into the heavens from all three. They were seen several hours, but as the sun traveled towards the meridian of the day the others disappeared.

Elizabeth, fetch me two good apples. I have not tasted one this winter. Abby Ann Greene also wishes you to bring her one. Tell Maria and Eliza Ann to bring me a handful of chestnuts. Write me. E[sther] M[orton] must write a few lines too. Where is Adelia? Love to her in Holliston. Does she love the Truth?

Chapter Five

Nauvoo

Bonds of Affection and Affliction

Missouri Saints in exile in Quincy, Illinois, through the winter of 1838-39 began to leave that place in the spring and travel seventy miles up the Mississippi River to newly selected gathering sites in Hancock County, Illinois, and Lee County, Iowa. There Church leaders had secured for the Church thousands of acres, and many Saints were trading titles to their abandoned Missouri lands or Kirtland property for lots in the area. Commerce, Illinois, rapidly became the central gathering place, and during the summer of 1839 Saints renamed the settlement "Nauvoo," a word of Hebraic derivation signifying, according to Joseph Smith, a beautiful, restful location.[1]

In some respects Nauvoo did prove restful for Latter-day Saints as homes, farms, and businesses were established there over a seven-year period. Construction was a big business in the growing city, and log structures soon sketched a new skyline along the banks of the Mississippi. Newlywed Bathsheba Smith moved into her log home in 1842 and assumed responsibility for getting the rooms plastered, since her apostle-husband George A. Smith had left for a proselyting mission in the eastern states. Her letters to him detail the progress of their son, the new home, and a vegetable garden—one of the hundreds that flourished on Nauvoo city lots.

Elder Smith served a series of missions during the Nauvoo period, some indication of the rapid expansion of the Church's missionary program at the time. By 1846 nearly five thousand Saints had emigrated to America from Great Britain. Because new converts were encouraged to gather to Nauvoo, many made their way to the Midwest, including Sally Randall. She joined Mormon emigration in 1843, traveling from New York with two sons to meet her husband in Nauvoo. "I think it has been recommended full as highly as it deserves," she wrote her nonmember family upon arriving in the Saints' city.

"It is very sickly here at present with fevers and fever and ague and measles, and a great many children die with them," the letter continued. Swamps in the lowlands near the river made Nauvoo's climate unhealthy enough that scores died of malaria each year in August and September. Since children were particularly vulnerable, Bathsheba Smith was not unusual in feeling "uneaseey" when her year-old son, George, became ill. "I was afraid he was a going to have the feavor," she wrote her husband.

View of the Nauvoo House and the Mississippi River at the end of Main Street, Nauvoo, Illinois, ca. 1908. (George Edward Anderson, "Church History in Photograph." LDS Church Archives.)

In spite of the difficulties, population continued to increase until Nauvoo was one of the two largest cities in Illinois. Rejoicing in the blessings of being among Saints, Sally Randall remarked in an 1844 letter to her family, "I wish you could have the teachings that we have here at the conference." Though Nauvoo was without regular meetinghouses, the Saints assembled in homes Sunday mornings and then congregated out of doors, weather permitting, for afternoon preaching meetings. Here Joseph Smith, frequently the main speaker, expounded doctrines concerning the nature of the Godhead, man's free agency and godly potential, and ordinances for living and dead. A January 1841 revelation received by the Prophet commanded the Saints to build a temple that such sacred temple ordinances might be properly performed. In the spring of 1846 the Nauvoo Temple was completed and dedicated.

Women were not part of the public works crews who provided labor for the temple, but they contributed clothing and other provisions for workers as well as funds, through the Female Relief Society of Nauvoo. Bathsheba Smith was a charter member of the group organized in Nauvoo in 1842, with Emma Smith as president, to aid Nauvoo's poor and further the building of the temple. Joseph Smith frequently attended the society's weekly meetings and used the occasions to discuss doctrines concerning women's spiritual potential and responsibilities.

A new doctrine introduced by Joseph Smith at this time, but never publicly taught, was that of plural marriage. Many of the Saints eventually came to accept the new doctrine. Others never accepted it, and the concept became the focus of rumors and accusations against the Prophet and the Church.

Tensions continued to build between the Saints and their non-member neighbors in Nauvoo with the organization of the Council of Fifty, a group of priesthood leaders concerned with establishing a righteous government in preparation for the Millennium, and with Joseph Smith's candidacy in 1844 for president of the United States. Nauvoo, with its powerful city charter, had been seen by some as a threat to the political stability of Hancock and Adams counties, and the bloc-voting tendency of Mormons had had its impact on Illinois politics. Tensions erupted in June 1844 when a group of dissenting Church members undertook publication of the Nauvoo *Expositor* to publicize charges against Joseph Smith. The city council, fearing the libelous charges would arouse anti-Mormon mobs, declared the paper a nuisance and ordered press and paper destroyed.[2]

"Their has been some excitement in town, but I do not feel

119

alarmed," Bathsheba Smith wrote her husband regarding the incident. The situation proved to be more serious than she had assessed it, however. Joseph and Hyrum Smith were both illegally imprisoned at Carthage on charges of treason in connection with the *Expositor* affair, and both became martyrs when an armed mob rushed the jail.[3]

"They were Kililled at Carthag on the 27 of June and on 28 they weere braught home and such a day of mourning never was seen," Bathsheba later wrote.

"There are many that will rejoice and think Mormonism is down now but they will be mistaken," Sally Randall assured her family a few days after the martyrdom, "for the Lord has beguń his work and he will carry it on in spite of all mobs and devils." Brigham Young headed the Council of Twelve Apostles as they assumed leadership of the largest number of Saints. Through 1845, while construction and industrial development continued in Nauvoo, particularly work on the temple, the Twelve renewed interest in Joseph Smith's plans for colonizing missions in the west, beyond the current U.S. boundaries. In January of that year, as tensions flared, the Nauvoo city charter was repealed, and the following September the Twelve revealed plans for a mass exodus westward. Bathsheba Smith described Nauvoo as "one vast mechanic shop" that fall. Her own parlor became a paint shop for wagons. She and Sally Randall crossed the Mississippi before the fall of 1846, leaving whatever rest they had found in Nauvoo to seek, according to Bathsheba, "a home in the wilderness."

Bathsheba Wilson Bigler Smith (1822-1910)

When the gospel was preached in Shinnsten, Harrison County, West Virginia, in the summer of 1837, most of the members of Bathsheba Wilson Bigler's family were baptized, including her parents, Mark and Susannah Ogden Bigler, and three of her older sisters. Bathsheba's own baptism was witnessed by a cousin of the Prophet Joseph Smith whose second mission for the Church had taken him to West Virginia. What young George A. Smith called "an agreeable acquaintance" with Bathsheba deepened, and they were married in 1841 after Bathsheba's family had moved to Far West and then to Nauvoo and after George A. had served two more Church missions in the eastern states and England.

In the summer of 1842 the couple moved from rented housing in Nauvoo into their own new log house, where a few days later their first child was born—a son named after his father. That September George A. Smith set out on a mission through Illinois, and during the next two years he was frequently away on missions to New York and Boston with other members of the Council of Twelve, giving him and Bathsheba ample opportunity to exchange letters.

After the exodus of the Saints from Nauvoo to Utah, George and Bathsheba established themselves in a Salt Lake City home that came to be known as the Historian's Office. There George A. carried out his work as apostle, Church historian, and counselor to Brigham Young, and he continued to travel frequently on Church assignments. In the Historian's Office Bathsheba reared her two children and carried out her Relief Society responsibilities. Sustained as general president of the Relief Society in 1901, she served in that capacity until her death in 1910.

Several of Bathsheba's Nauvoo letters to George A. are included in this chapter. They represent a larger holograph collection of Bathsheba's letters to George A. now on file in the Church Archives. In the reproduction of the letters here, minimal punctuation has been added.

Bathsheba W. Smith in Utah, ca. 1875. (George Albert Smith Collection. Special Collections, Marriott Library, University of Utah.)

Mr. George A. Smith
Nauvoo Ill Oct 2th 1842

My Dear Companion I sit down this morning to write you a few lines—and feel thankfull to my heavenly Father that I have the privalege. We are well this morning and in midling good sperits. Some little disappointed. I had givven way to a faint hope that you would return with Br [Brigham] Yo[u]ng. Your father said he though[t] it was likely you would, but I was sadly dissappointed when I found not a single line from you. Br Yong hallowed to me and told me you was well and if I wished to send you a line to bring it to his house this evening. Truly that much was a s[a]ttisfaction to me.

George Albert was sick last saterday and sunday. He had quite a feavor. I was vary uneaseey about him. I was afraid he was going to have the feavor. I took him to the fount and had him

baptised and sinse then he has not had any feavor. He is about
well now. Looks a little pail. I anointed him with oil a good
many times and washed his little boddy with whisky and
water which was burning with feavor but it did not do the
good I wanted it should. I have written to you this will be
four times but William did not take one I wrote for him to
take. Br [George J.] Adams said he woul[d] take one for me,
but I did not much expect it would reach you there. But I
have thought since it has. Wheather you write or not I will be
vary apt to trouble you with a line evry time I have the
chance. I saw your Father friday. They ware all well.⁴ Had
received a letter from you. I do not know what to write that
well be the most sattisfactry to you. Br Yong will tell you all
that is going on.

I have got my corn and fodder secureed, broom corn, sunn[?]
flower seed and beeanes likewise. Mellissa⁵ and me did it.
Gilbert I expect will dig my potatoes. Uncle George is a going
to Keokuc [Iowa] to live. Br [Wilford] Woodruff to I expect
my most sosi[a]ble neighbor. Their baby has been vary sick.
Mary Ann has the ague [some?] since Jacob went away.
Nancy's children has been sick. Thadeas is now sick.⁶ Jeramiah
is ve[r]y low with the feavor. Br Alpheas and Jesse Harmon
have gone. Appleton [Harmon] intends to go tomorrow.
Mother Johnson sends her best love to you. Melissa likewise,
and so do I. Br Lightle says he has bespoke a man to plaster
my house and he will find lime and sand and hair. I think of
getting the two roomes plasterd. Br Canada was hear last
Satterday but one. Said he would bring some wheat heare and
get it growned [ground] and let me have some flower. Said he
would bring an half a bushel of salt and some shugar. I stay at
home. Am a fraid to go to meting. Ben a visiting once at
mothers. I have had somany melens and my dear was not
heare to help eat them. O I am so londsome all alone only
[except] baby.

[the writer guiding the baby's hand] I is a good boy. I write to you.

G. A. Smith, Jr.

(I do not no wheathe[r] you can read babys writing)

BWS

[on margin] Write evry chance. You do not know how I want to see you.

Mr. George A. Smith
Newyork City, Ny
Sabbath morning   Nauvoo July 16th 1843

My Dear husban, I sit down this morning to address you with a few lines and I pray my heavenly father that these lines may find you in good health and sperits, and likewise the rest of the breathren. My health is midling good at presant. I have had a vary severe coald but have got nearley over it. The baby is quite sick with a coald. He had a vary hot feavor last knight. Father will lay hands on him as he goes to meeting. Thare are a great many complaining with coalds. It is called the influaza. Caroline[7] has ben sick with a coald but is better now. Sister [Vilate] Kimball toald me Docttor [John M.] Burnhisel was a going to Newyork the middl of next week.[8] He said he would carry letters to Newyork for us. I have not much to write for I have not heard much since you left. It seemes a long time all though I think I have got a long quite as well as could be expected. Your Father visits us evry day. They ware all to dinner one day with me. We had a plenty of beanes, peas, beets, and sutch like things. O if you could have bin here we would have been quite happy.

I wish I could have been with you and staid untill you started for it seemed sutch a long time untill the boat came. I thought perhaps you would come home again a few minits, but I was disappointed. I wanted to see you vary much. I would have gone to you if I could. O my Dear it is nothing to cry when one feeles as I did when I saw the boat going down. I was pleased to think you would not have to wait any longer, but then how could I bare to have it carry you off so rappidly from me. I watched it untill I could not see it any longer then

I held my head for it aked. Soon your father and mother
came in. George A cryes pa. He feeles bad. He wants to see
you. He often goes to the door to see you. When we say
whare is Father, he will say a da pa. Br [Alvin] Hor has
brought me a load of wood. Evry thing has passed on smothly
sinse you left as yet. I want to heare from you vary mich.
Trust I may soon. I will close for the presant.

Sabbath morning July the 23—Dearest Albert as doctor Burnhisel has not gone as yet I again have the privalage of writing
to you this morning. My health and sperits are good. George
A has had the measels in addition to his coald and cutting
teath. He has been quite sick but is getting well fast. He
begins to play and croll about again. I expect he was exposed
to the measels on the fourth of July. I have not went to meeting sinse you left but stay at home. Sickness has kept me if
nothing else, but I think home is the best place for me, this
hot weather. Joseph [Smith] preached last sunday. I should
liked to have been thare very much. He preaches a gain to
day.

Br Far gave me a letter you sent me last friday. He said you
war all in good sperits. I shall not attempt to express the joy
that I felt when he gave it to me. When I read you had been
sick, I felt vary bad for I feared you had not got over it yet or
you might take coald agen. I expect it was the influanza the
same I had. I began to be sick the day you left, Satterday,
Sunday and monday I was quite sick, but thank the lord I am
well again a[s] usual, and think my baby will be soon.

I hope and pray you are well by this time. I should be pleased
to spend this afternoon with you. It seems to me I could not
wish to enjoy my self better than to sit under the sound of
your rich and lovely voice and hear you unfold the rich
treasure of your mind. Even the sound of your footstep would
be music in my eare. I all most forget I am a lone, whilest I
fancy to my self how happy I should be. The baby is a
waking. I must quit writing for the presant.

Wednesday July 26th

Dearest George A, I am well and in good sperits but want to see you vary much. I cannot help liking to see the time roll away. Little George Albert is nearly well. Has three more teeth. Sister Ridge and Barton are boath dead, died in Fortmaddison [Iowa]. Our folks have had a letter from Jacob [G. Bigler]. He writes he has gained the lawsuit. Their is know telling when he w[ill] get the mon[e]y, for the land will have to bee soald perhaps on six or twelve months credit.[9] Our gardon stands the drouth as well as any ones I have seen. We have had two or three small raines sinse you left. Our well hoalds out first rate. All the neighbour's come here fore water. I saw Sister [Phebe] Woodruff yesterday. She said she would write by mail for Dr Bernhisell kept putting off starting so much. I think he will go soon. She said she would write some for me so that would answer without me writing by mail.

August 1th 1843   tusday morning

Dearest, G. A. we are all well this morning with the exception of Malissa. She has the measels but is getting better. I received your vary kind letter yesterday. I was vary happy to heare you ware well and in good sperits. Amasa Lyman is sick.[10] Your Fathers about like you was last winter. John[11] is agoing to shcool. They are all well. They are all vary kind to me. I feel in good sperits. Think it will not be long untill I see you. I think I shall be able to get the house plastered soon. Dr. Burnhisell has given up going for a while yet so I will send it by mail. He has dissappointed us all vary much. We will try to be good children whilst you are gone. G A can go up stairs alone, but cannot walk qiute yet. Yesterday I received a skain of yorn sent to you by Rosell H. Smith Brown Co Ills. Your father says it is your cousin. Doctor [Levi] Richards was here yesterday. Says tell you we are all alive in Nauvoo only [except] those that are dead. He said tell you he had been heare, then he laughfed. I think he though[t] of what he said to you. Remain as ever yours sincearly B. W. Smith

Mr George A. Smith
Boston, Ms.
Nauvoo Sept 2th 1843

Dear Husban I sit down to write to you again to inform you
that we are all well at present and in first rate sperits. I
received a letter from you yesterday you wrote me in Phela-
delpha which gave me great sattisfaction, for a line from you
is the sweetest morsel I can posably get. I should like to have
been with you and have seen the things you wrote about
much, but I feel like I should be sattisfied if I could see you
with out seeing any more. The time rooles a way tolerable
swiftly. I hope it is half gone. My prayer is that you may get
home before coald weather sitts in.

We got the letter you sent to Presidend [Sidney] Rigdon last
Sunday which we was much pleased to get. When I get a
letter first all the rest come to heare it. The breatherns wives
have all been to see me this week. They are all well. I donot
think thar is much sickness. Thare is not in our neighbour-
hood. We have had several good raines or midling good
raines. I think our gardon will be tolerable good. Our potatoes
are poor. Vines are quite good. We begin to have plenty of
mellons which make many harts rejoice and ours are maid
glad. We have a plenty of tomatoes. George Abert feasts on
tomatoes and melons. He begines to walk and talk. I think I
shall wean him before you get home. He has had the bowell
and canke[r] complaint vary bad but is well now. I think it
hendered his walking. He has only six teeth as yet.

Our well is dry. We have to go to the Bishops for the last few
days. Our cow dose midling well. She dosenot go in the
drov[e] for she cannot get any more on the prary than she can
get at home. She comes home evry night vary well. With
your Fathers [and] others help I shall be enabled to get our
house plastered next week. Expect I have got it lathed up
stayers with the exceptions of the largest room overhead. I got
10 bushel of lyme of [William?] Nyswanger and uncle [Isaac]

Morley gote sand and maid the morter yesterday. I had money to get hair and nailes with the exceptions of one pickoon [picayune] which Melessa let me have. Josiah[12] let me have fifty feet of lumber and Amos did the carpenter work. Br Moss is sick. He cannot plaster the house. Br [Samuel] Flag says he will. Ickabad got me a gallen of whiskey for pickels. My cowcumbers do well. He said he would get some flower and honey and candells as he could as well as not, but has not as yet. I am a bout out of flower now. Father has brought nearley one bushel of meal[?] sinse you left. Have plenty as yet. Caleb[13] promest to bring me home the flower he borrowed this week. I think thare is not any danger but I shall get along.

Father and I thought perhaps you would get this before you left Boston and if not no harm done. I have had a fine ride in Josephs big carage. Went six or eigh[t] miles out. Amasa Lymon and family are at your Fathers. Have been thare two or three weeks. Amasa was vary sick but is so as to wride out now. His wife has the egue and feavor. The children have had it but are well now I believe. Perhaps your father will want to write some. Mr. Brown and Melessa talk so fast and so much it bothers me to write. You muss excuse this and look over all my imperfection. I am as ever yours in time and for eternity.

Bathsheba W. Smith

[There follows a short note to George A. Smith from his father, John Smith]

Mr. George A. Smith
Boston, Ms.
Nauvoo June 15th 1844

Dear Husband, I again take my pen to inform you we are well, and most earnestly desire this letter may find you so. We are just done mooping and cleaning the House. Melissa has maid or fixed three fine flower pots. We have got some new window curtens. We are a going to have a good dinner.

We have some appels a stewing for pies. Sister [Catherine] Clawson has just sent word for us to not get dinner, for she would send us some roasted veal.

O how I wish you could take dinner and chat an hour or two with us at least. We have been to the poast office again and a gain but cannot get one word from you. How I do wish I did know you ware well. I think I will get a letter to morrow. I expected one cirten last Wedensday. I sent but no letter. I thought you must be sick or you would have written, for I have been uneasy a bout you for you had to wride in the rain so much. At last I thought perhaps you had written to your Father and thought he would send it to me if you ware scarse of money, but the roads have been so bad, the bridges are most all washed away that it is all most inpossable to go to or come from Messedonia [Macedonia] here. Or perhaps the roads are bad othe[r] places so that the mail might be hendred. I flatter my self with these and other things that you are well and so I though[t] I would write to Boston and perhaps you would get it.

Uncel Asel Smith has been here and ate dinner with us. He says his famaly are weell. He said he was much pleased to see us so well, and getting along so well. I have not heard from Fathers for some time. They wer well the last I heard. Father sent me a quater of a dollar he got for your Books. George has gone to sleep and now I can finish my letter. He is quite well. Can walk nicely, begines to talk considerably begins to look helthy eats harty laugh's a gooddeal, is not half so much trouble stands on his stool to eat, has a plate to himself. Will not sleep with me more than half the time. Some time he will come in the bed an hour or two and be satisfied, but if I take him to bed with me it is against his will. So much for George. He ofen talks a bout you. I think he will not forget you.

We have had a gred deel of rain since you left. All most evry day for 7 weeks it has rained, a great many hard raines. Our sellar has water a considerable hier than the off set or the highest part. The well is vary full likewise. We have had the garden plowed. It looks vary well but wood [do] better if it did not rain so much. The wormes trouble all the neighbor's gardens, but have not mine but little. A great many people have had more or less out of our garden sutch as lettis onions Reddishes and greanes. Indeed I do not know what they would have done if it ware not for us. But to get any one to work in it is like pulling eye theeth. Our earley potatoes are getting quite large. The corn is in tossel. Cabbage looks well. Vines rather poore. Tomatoes in blow. Beets quite large. Will soon have peas. A good many of our flowers are in blossom. Our Cow has had the hollow horn. I believe she is well now. I have soald six pounds of butter since you left.

Their has been some excitement in town, but I do not feel a larmed. The lawites [William and Wilson Law and their associates][14] had got their printing press a going. Had printed one paper, and a scanlelous thing it was. The Citty Counsil exzamined its lease and found it a newicence so the atharites [authorities] went and burnt and disstroyed the press. This maid the Lawites mad. They tried to get a mob but failed. Joseph and those that were conserned in it have been tried but wer cleared. The Laws and a good many have gone and are going off.

I have not been to meeting since you left on the hill. I have been twice down to the meeting in Joseph['s] storehouse. I donot go any whar much. My health has been quite good ever since you left. I enjoy my self prety well. Would better if I could hear from you oftener. I received to [two] letters dated May 13th and a few lines May 21th. I have written three times. I do not know whether Sister Woodruff will write or not. I saw her this morning. She was well. I hope I will see you in two months from this day the lord willing. Be of good cheer and come home when you think best. You may besure I will be pleased let that be when it will. May the lord bless you and bring you home safe in health and prosperity. I remain yours affectionately.

B W S

[There follows a short note by Melissa Bigler]

Sister [Phebe] Woodruff has not received any word from
B[rother] W[oodruff] since th[e] 21 of May. She and I see ech
other and councel a bout writing and wonder why we cannot
get a letter. Give my love to Sister Loyd. Tell her I would be
pleased to see her. We have had rain evry day this week and I
believe it will continue longer by the looks of the time.

B W Smith

[There follows a note from Phebe to Wilford Woodruff]

Mr. George A. Smith
Newark, Kendall Co, Illinis
July 6th 1844

My Dear Husband I sit down this morning to let you know
we are all well, and in as good spirits as could be expected
considering all things. We have strange times since you left.
You will no doubt hear before this reaches you, of the death
of our beloved Breathren Joseph and Hirum Smith. They were
Kililled at Carthag on the 27 of June and on 28 they weere
braught home and such a day of mourning never was seen. It
paines me to write such a painfull tale, but the Lord has comforted our harts in a mesure. The Govener [Thomas Ford]
begines to open his eyes. He says we are a law abiding People
and he has pledged himself and the faith of the State that he
will protect us. The mob has tryed to get the govener to get
force to exterminate or drive the Mormons but he refuses. We
feel as though he would try to redeem his carecter. Br [John]
Talor was wounded but is getting bettr is quite weak but quite
cheerfull. Br [Willard] Richards was not hurt. They were boath
in Jail at the time of the masecree. I will not write any more
on that sub ject as I expect you will hear all the peticulars
before this reaches [you].

I received a letter on thursday from you dated June 14 and
this morning your Father sent me two letters from you one

dated June the 14 and one dated June 21. I canot express my joy on receivin thes letters. I was pleased to hear you was so well and goot a long so well and had terned torg [toward?] home. I was sorrow to hear you had not heard from home. I have written this makes five times since you left and I write thinking probably you will not get this. You, and the rest of the Twelve are sent for. I expect you will get heare about the same time the rest will. They were sent for to come home as soon as posable.

Br Adams has gone to Boston and J[edediah] M Grant to Washington.[15] Joseph toald Adams to go and tell the Twelve to come home when the Tragedy was over and a good many more things, whiche he should preache on sunday before he was killed, but the people did not enderstand it. Adams said he was a going to speak in parable. I have understood he said he did not understand all him self but it is explained now. I want you to take good care of yourself and not let the Mobbers get you. I shall pray for you much. I have not realy wished you here since our troubels but I cannot say I have not wished my self with you. A great many ould women expected our Citty to have been in ashes before this time but I have not been bad enought scared to make me trimble, though I have had some bad feelings.

George A is well as usuall has the Bowel complaint some but much better in health than he was when you left. He has been sick once or twice but generly tolerable well. I think he will know you when you get home. We get a long vary well. I have my health vary good. Our garden looks quite as well as anyones I have seen. We have had potatoes thre or four weeks. We have had several messes of boiled corn. Our peas are a bout write to eat. Wish you was here to help eat them. You must excuse this letter for we have had evry thing you could think of talked about since the flood and the worst pen I ever tried to write with by all odds. Sarah[16] and her children are here and other[s] have been here since I commencd to write. Your Father came out and fanely last Fryday. Staid untill Monday. They were all well. Thought all would come out write at last.

Jacob [Bigler] and Jesse came home in a week or to after you left. Brought some dried Appels but not any monney. I got one bushel of him. We have aplenty to eat. Do not be uneasey a bout us but come home as soon as you can and see how we get along. O my Dear I do want to see you come home. I pray the lord to bring you home safe. Jacob was maried in four weekes after he came home to Miss Ama [Amy Loretta] Chases of Nauvoo. I hav written evry thing up to the war in my letters to you. I received the five dolla[r] note you inclosed in your last. I will put this in the office and wish it may reach you. You are excuseable for not writin oftener. I did not think it was your falt, but I though[t] on account of the rain or the mob for the mail did not come in regular. Four m[ails]* come in this week. The cause of this I have [not]* lerned. I have sent twice a week to the office allmost ever since you left. Tell the good folk to send you home as soon as posable.

Sarah and Melissa sends their love to you. I will close by saying may the Lord bless you with food and ramont and with health and friends and preserve you from all evel and the hand of wicked men. I remain as ever yours for time and eternity.

Bathsheba W. Smith

---

*Page torn. Word supplied.

Sally Carlisle Randall (1805- ?)

Letters written by Sally Randall from Illinois and Iowa to her family in New England reveal something of the personality and values of a common woman for whom almost no other record is extant. Born in Westmoreland, New Hampshire, a daughter of George and Betsy Torrey Carlisle, Sally married James Randall, and the couple set up house in Warsaw, New York, about forty miles from Buffalo. Their older son, George, was fourteen and their younger son, Eli, ten years old when the family converted to Mormonism and laid plans to gather with the Saints in Nauvoo. In 1843 James traveled ahead to arrange housing for the family, and Sally and the boys met him in Nauvoo that fall, traveling, as did many Saints, on the Ohio and Mississippi rivers.

Anxious to send her nonmember family news of her new home among the Saints, Sally recounts everything from the cost of flour to the new doctrine of baptism for the dead, enlivening the details with her own feelings and opinions. Her last letter speaks of leaving Nauvoo, and the Randalls did travel west with the Saints, though they settled temporarily at a Mormon camp in Iowa before moving to Utah in the 1850s.

The Sally Randall letters included in this chapter have been taken from typescripts on file in the Church Historical Department. Spelling and punctuation have been standardized.

Nauvoo October 6, 1843

Dear Friends,

I take this opportunity to write a few lines to you, knowing that you are anxious to hear from us. We are all in as good health as usual. We had a very good journey and good luck. We did not leave Buffalo until Monday morning and got to Cleveland Tuesday before noon and left there the same day. The lake [Erie] was very rough Monday night. Almost all on

board were sick. I was not very sick nor the children, but we
had to keep pretty still to keep from it. Brother Williams was
very sick. We got to Beaver [Ohio] on Saturday and left there
Sunday morning. We landed in Nauvoo the 22 [September]
about 2 o'clock in the morning.

I found James in as good health and circumstances as I
expected. He has a lot with a log cabin on it and it paid for.
The house is very small but I think we can get along with it
for the present. He had a table and three chairs. We have no
bedsteads yet, but shall have soon. We have a cow is all the
livestock we have at present. Provisions are very cheap. We
can get good pork for four cents a pound, flour for one dollar
and fifty cents a hundred, sugar from 8 to 10 cents a pound.
Cows are from six to ten dollars.

As for Nauvoo I cannot tell you much about it at present for I
have not seen much of it yet, but what I have seen I think it
has been recommended full as highly as it deserves. It is very
sickly here at present with fevers and fever and ague and
measles, and a great many children die with them.

I expect it is a hard place for poor people that have no money
to get a living. There is so many poor that depend on their
work for a living that they can hardly get enough to be comfortable.[17] I am in hopes that we shall get some land to work
in the spring. I think if we have our health we shall get along.

I saw Elder [Charles] Thompson and his family last Sunday.[18]
He and Julia [daughter] are sick with the fever and ague. They
have another daughter. He says he hardly knows where its
birth place was. It was neither in Ohio or Kentucky but somewhere on the Ohio river. His wife said she wished they had
waited and come with me. His goods are now in the storehouse for freightage. For about sixty dollars he has moved
about twenty miles from here. Brother Williams sends his particular respects to father and wanted I should tell him how
much it cost me. It cost me twenty-two dollars beside what I
paid for provision and that was but a little. I could not had

better company than he was nor one that would have been more interest[ed]. I feel to respect him so very much for his kindness to me. Them people went from Alexander [New York] as we expected was all the company we had. The boats were all very much crowded that we were on. The last week we were on the water was the warmest weather. I think my butter was entirely melted and some run out, but did not hurt it. My cheese came full [aged] as well as I expected.

George is a little homesick I think, but he don't say much about it, but Eli is one of the contented sort. They have gathered some walnuts and hazelnuts. They miss grandfather's orchard very much. You may tell Mrs. Patterson that I have enough to eat yet and that is good enough, only I have no meat today, but may have tonight.

I don't want George to send any money in a letter at present.[19] Give my respects to all inquiring friends. I think you will not complain of me this time for not writing a full letter and I hope you will do the same and that soon too. I have wrote till I hardly know whether I am in Nauvoo or some other place. I should have written before, but I waited to see Elder Thompson. I shall write no more at present.

Sally Randall

I forgot to tell you we had a good well of water. I can work with it very well. We have two beef cattle to kill.

When George sends money I want it put in my hand.

Nauvoo November the 12
[1843]

Dear Friends,

I take my pen this morning to write a few lines to you, although with a trembling hand and a heart full of grief and sorrow, to inform you of our afflictions which are very great.

It seems more sometimes than we are able to bear, but it is the Lord that hath done it. Therefore, let us try to be reconciled.

George has gone to try the realities of eternity. He died the first day of this month about 3 o'clock in the morning. He was sick three weeks and three days with the ague and fever. He had it every other day about two weeks, and then every day till he died. We did not consider him dangerous only about three days before he died, and then medicine had no effect on him at all. He was taken in fits the day before he died and had them almost without cessation as long as he lived. When he breathed his last he went very easy, but oh the agonies he was in before it seemed I could not endure. He was not well after we got here, nor he was not contented and the Lord has taken him from the evils of this wicked generation. I know he is better off than the rest of us, but it seems hard to part, but I think the separation will not be long if we are faithful. His father took his death very hard and so did Eli. When we thought he must go, Eli said he wanted to tell George goodbye. It seemed as though my heart would break, but the Lord hath given and he hath taken his own to himself.

I have one request to make and that is that you will not cast any reflections and say if we had not come here he might have been alive, for we don't know. I believe it was the will of the Lord that we should come that his body might be laid with the Saints.

My health is good and has been ever since I got here and James has enjoyed good health. Eli is not well. He has a chill and fever every other day and I don't know but the Lord will take him to be with George. It seems as though my dependance was all gone, as though I had but little to live for. O mother, place not your affections too much on George for life is uncertain and death is certain.

I delayed writing sometime for it seemed to me that I never could write again. It is not as sickly here as it has been, but

137

there is a good many deaths now. People are coming in very fast. There was a boat load came in yesterday from England. I have not more to write at present. Give my respects to all inquiring friends. I want you should write soon.

Sally Randall

Nauvoo April the 21, 1844

Dear Friends,

I take my pen once more after a long time to write to you to let you know that we are all yet alive and in as good health as usual. James's health is not good. Mine is about the same it was last spring. Eli is much better than he was last fall. He goes to school this summer. He went three months in the winter. He is well contented.

George was not contented. He said after he was taken sick he was glad he hadn't got to always live here, but I don't think he thought he should die. After I found he must go he could not speak so that I did not talk with him about dying. I don't know that he spoke after Monday. He did not make Eli any answer when he bid him goodbye. Oh what a trying time that was to me and it seems yet that I cannot be reconciled to have it so, but I have no doubt but he is better off than he would be here and will come forth in the first resurrection, which will be in this generation according to our faith. His father has been baptized for him and what a glorious thing it is that we believe and receive the fulness of the gospel as it is preached now and can be baptized for all of our dead friends and save them as far back as we can get any knowledge of them.[20]

I want you should write me the given names of all of our connections that are dead as far back as grandfather's and grandmother's at any rate. I intend to do what I can to save my friends and I should be very glad if some of you would come and help me for it is a great work for one to do alone. It is father's privilege to save his friends if he will come into the

138

church. If not, some other one must do it. I expect you will think this is strange doctrine but you will find it to be true. I want to know whether Lettice was over eight years old when she died.[21] Oh, mother, if we are so happy as to have a part in the first resurrection, we shall have our children just as we laid them down in their graves.

I wish you could have the teachings that we have here at the conference. The 6th of April it was supposed there was from ten to fifteen thousand people.

Charles Thompson has buried his Julia and the people that came on with me from Alexander have buried their oldest child about three years old. It is quite healthy here at present. There are a great many coming in this spring. I understand John C. Bartholf is coming on this fall.

Eli wants you should send his cow bell and the rest of his little things that was left and if my shears and guage are there I want them sent. I have not seen them since I left. I have no news to write at present. I have not worked very hard since I have been here, but I have had enough to do. But I would have been glad to had some of mother's wool to spin last winter.

I expect you and the neighbors would like to know how we have lived. We have done very well. We have had a plenty of meat, milk, butter, flour, and corn. What fruit I bought has done very well. I have some left yet.

Now I want to know what father and the rest of the people thinks of Joseph Smith being president. If they want a righteous man at the head let them vote for him.

I shall write no more this time. Write to me and excuse me for not writing sooner. I received your letters about the first of March. Give my respects to all inquiring friends.

Sally Randall

Nauvoo July the 1st, 1844

Dear Friends,

I take this opportunity to write to you to let you know that
we are all as well as usual, and hope these lines will find you
enjoying the same blessing. We have had a very wet season
so far. It is hard times especially for poor people. I expect you
will have heard of something of our trouble before you get
this and will want to know the truth, and I will write it as
near as possible.

It has been about three weeks since the fuss begun. In the first
place there were six or eight apostates cut off from the
Church and from that time the devil has been raging with all
fury. They got up a printing press and went to printing all
manner of lies and abominations that could be thought of
against the prophet and the heads of the Church, and the City
Council held a council and agreed it was a nuisance and
ordered it destroyed and it was done. We have been expecting the mob upon us ever since.

The governor was sent for by Joseph [Smith]. He came to
Carthage, the county seat about fifteen miles from here, and
there he stopped. The mob were then gathered there and the
apostates with them. I would like to give you all the proceed-
ings of the governor but my pen would fail me. He sent for
Joseph and all that were concerned in destroying the press and
said if they would come then they should be protected and
have a trial according to law. They all gave themselves up and
went, but instead of having a trial they were put in prison.
The governor then sent and took away the state's arms and
sent in a company of troops he said to protect us.[22] The
prisoners were all set at liberty except Joseph and his brother
Hyrum and two of the Twelve, Elder [John] Taylor and Elder
[Willard] Richards. And Thursday the 27th of June the governor came to this town and said he had dispersed the mob
from Carthage and the same day about six in the afternoon
was one of the most horrible crimes committed that ever
history recorded!

Sampler embroidered by Mary Ann Broomhead, age 13, 1844. 13½" x 21". (Arts and Sites Division, LDS Church Historical Department.)

There were about one hundred and fifty of the mob made an attack upon the courthouse and the guards and went into the jail and the first one they shot was Hyrum. He was killed dead on the spot. Elder Taylor was badly wounded. Joseph then jumped out of the window. They shot him I know not how many times. The mob then fled as quick as possible. They were painted. There were some crossed the river the next morning and the paint was to be seen on them. There was only eight men left to guard the courthouse. The governor left this place the same day about sundown and took his troops with him. They got about four miles from here. They met a man coming to fetch the sad news and took him back, would not let him come. So we did not get the news till the morning.

If you can imagine to yourselves how the apostles and saints felt when the Savior was crucified you can give something of a guess how the Saints felt here when they heard that their prophet and patriarch were both dead and murdered, too, by a lawless mob. Never has there been such a horrible crime committed since the day Christ was crucified. It seems that all nature mourned. The earth is deprived of the two best men there was on it. They have sealed their testimony with their blood.

Joseph sent word to the Church after he went to prison to read the 6th chapter of Revelations and take particular notice from the 8th to the 12th verse. I have no doubt but that he knew he should be killed when he gave himself up. He told his wife when he left her he was going as a lamb to the slaughter and many other things give us reason to believe he knew what would befall him. He gave himself up to die for the Church that they might not be destroyed for it seemed all they [the mob] wanted was to kill him and they have done it. But I don't know as they will let us alone now, but I hope they will be easy a little while. They say there is nine more they are determined to have, and when it will end I don't know I expect.

There are many that will rejoice and think Mormonism is down now but they will be mistaken for the Lord has begun his work and he will carry it on in spite of all mobs and devils.

Now one and all of my friends as honest people, I entreat of you if you have any influence to use it now in our behalf among all people and in all places. I don't know how long we shall be permitted to stay here nor where I shall be next time I write if I ever have another opportunity. I am not sorry I am here at this time. I want you should write to me. I have not had but one letter from you since I came here. I have written you a long one this time. Give my respects to all inquiring friends. I have been braiding some this summer, but it is hard getting palmleaf. I intend to braid straw. I shall write no more at present.

Sally Randall

Nauvoo January the 15, 1845

Dear Parents and Brothers and Sisters

I take the opportunity to write a few lines to let you know that we are all yet in the land of the living and in good health, and hope these lines will find you all enjoying the same blessing. I have delayed writing a long time. I did not get the letter you sent by Mr. Bartholf. They left it to Elder [Almon] Babbitt's and they say there is no letter there and for that reason I have not heard anything particular from you since you wrote last winter. I have not seen Mrs. Bartholf but once since they came here. They live about 20 miles from here. She was well suited. I got the other things you sent by them and was very thankful for them.

Mrs. Bartholf told me Eliza had a son. I wish them much joy and hope it may live to be a blessing to them. I suppose Mother Nickols feels better if she has got to be a granny.

Eli talks and dreams a great deal about grandfather's folks and their apples, but when he wants an apple to eat he has to get a turnip. He is learning sword exercise this winter. As for myself I am not doing much of anything and yet have enough to do, but does not amount to anything. As to our living we have a plenty to eat and people can live as well here as any-where, all excepting fruit that is very high this year. But pro-vision is cheap: flour 2 dollars per hundred, wheat 50 cents, corn wt[?], pork from 2 to 3 dollars per hundred. Store goods are as cheap here as they were there although I have not bought anything but tea and a little sugar and hard work to get that, but people that have money can live as well as they please. But I think I have written about nonsense enough.

I expect you want to know something about the Church. It is peaceable times at present, but the mob characters and dissen-ters threaten of something in the spring, but we don't fear them much for we never shall be drove from here. We are too strong for them ourselves and besides that there is already ten hundred thousand of the Lamanites baptized into the Church and they are waiting very impatient to avenge the blood of Joseph and Hyrum. We have to keep men among them to keep them back or they would been here before this time.[23]

143

I expect you will think this is not right but the Lord will not suffer his people to be always afflicted as they have been and he does own this Church as a people and there is no other Church on the earth he does own and if you don't believe it now there is a day a coming when you will know it. I think if you could know the great things that are revealed from day to day you could not stay away. I want father and mother to be baptized themselves and when the temple is done come here and be baptized for all of their friends. They can save their progenitors clear back to the apostles' day and if they don't do it some other one will and take their crown.

I expect the temple will be done in a year from this time so that they will be attending to the ordinances.[24] It has gone on with great speed since the death of Joseph. If you knew what the Saints do I think you would not stay there long. If I could fly I would make you a visit once in a while and tell you some things, but I cannot write but a little and I must close for the present. Give respects to Brother Disbro's family. Tell them they are losing ground. My respects to all inquiring friends.

Sally Randall

I saw Charles Thompson the other day. He seems to enjoy himself very well.

Nauvoo June the 1, 1846

Dear Parents and Brothers and Sisters,

I now take the opportunity to write a few lines to you to let you know we are all well as usual. I received your letter written in March and was glad to hear from you once more. We expect to start in a few days for the West. Where we shall go I know not, but we are going into the wilderness. We go as Abraham went, not knowing whither we go, but the

Lord will go before us, and be our front and rearward. The Saints have been going steady since last February and are still going by hundreds. They cross the river in several places and cross day and night.

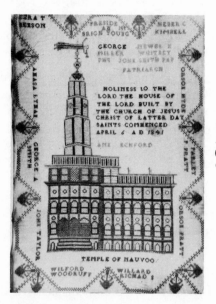

Sampler embroidered by Ann Eckford, ca. 1846. 13½" x 18½". (Arts and Sites Division, LDS Church Historical Department.)

The [word missing] room of the temple is finished and dedicated to the Lord. It is a most splendid building. We received our endowments last winter with the rest of the Saints in the temple, but those things are not for any only such as belong to the Church of Christ and I am very glad that I am worthy to have a name with the Saints of God and enjoy the privileges that I now do and I would rejoice if my friends would receive the gospel and go with me. If I could even have one friend, it would be great consolation, but if you will not receive the truth, the more I shall have to do for our dead friends. It is my privilege to be baptized for all of our friends that are dead and I intend to do it, unless some of my friends that are living will come and help me, and the more I do the greater will be the crown.

You think there is no need of going from here, but the mob are threatening continually to come upon us. We heard they were coming today but I have not seen anything in the least, for I believe there is faith enough in the city to keep them back until the Saints all get away. We have to make a great sacrifice in order to get away. The most of the Saints are selling out although at a very low price. I expect the temple will be sold. The Roman Catholics talk of buying it.[25]

Tell Mr. Disleno I expect he will make Mr. Holman's words true about going to Zion in his shirt. I think the time is not far distant when those that wish to be saved from destructions that are about to come upon this generation will have to flee for their lives. Tell Mrs. Disleno I have no notion of going to Wisconsin. I intend to follow the body of the Church and not be led about by every wind of doctrine nor by any false prophet that shall arise in these last days.[26] Mr. Bartholf and family are going to [word missing]. I have not heard anything of Elder [Almon] Babbitt's going to France. He is one of the trustees of the temple.

I expect you have heard about enough of this kind of talk but out of the abundance of the heart the mouth speaketh, and I will not trouble you much more. Lettice is married instead of coming to Nauvoo. I wish her much joy, but I do not think she has bettered her name. Eli goes to the prairie every day with the cattle to feed. We are going with a yoke of oxen and a mule. We have cows to drive. I don't know when I shall have another opportunity to write, but as soon as I have I will improve it, and I must close for the present so goodbye to all, earthly friends. Give my respects to all inquiring friends.

Sally Randall

Chapter Six

The Trek Westward

Refuge in the Wild

"My things are now packed ready for the west," Patty Bartlett Sessions began her diary in February 1846. She was to keep careful track of the hegira that took Latter-day Saints from Nauvoo, the City of Joseph, to the valley of the Great Salt Lake. The Saints' February departure from Nauvoo was some eight weeks premature. They had planned to leave in April when grass on the plains would sustain teams, but threats of interference from their antagonists made Church leaders decide to leave the city immediately, especially since nearly two thousand emigrants were already prepared to depart.

Eliza R. Snow was among those who crossed the Mississippi in February and gathered with the Camp of Israel on Iowa's Sugar Creek. There, under the direction of Brigham Young, some four hundred wagons were temporarily organized into companies, and on the first day of March the camp began its westward exodus. Across alternately frozen and muddy ground, Eliza traveled with Hannah Markham "seated in an ox wagon, on a chest with a brass kettle and a soap box for our foot stools, thankful that we are so well off." Wagons had been packed to utilize every possible inch of space. Pots, churns, and water barrels hung from the sides; pens of chickens were fastened to the backs. Some Saints had built extensions onto their wagons to make them roomier, but even then the one to three thousand pounds of provisions required, packed with what furniture, tools, and seeds could be squeezed in, made for close quarters.

"We divided a bag of flour at Richarson's point, another at Charidon and some more at the east fork of shoal creak, and have enough to

147

divide again if caled for," Patty Sessions recorded at the end of two months' travel. In spite of the time and admonitions the Saints had been given to prepare, many had left Nauvoo inadequately supplied; and as the journey advanced, families more amply provisioned were asked to share. At various points along the way the Saints refurbished their stores by exchanging labor for additional supplies.

By mid-May nearly twelve thousand persons had crossed the Mississippi River into Iowa. More than six hundred remained in Nauvoo under the leadership of Joseph Young, who was to direct the completion and dedication of the temple and supervise the final evacuation of Latter-day Saints from the city. Anti-Mormons, frustrated with the seemingly endless delay in the removal of the last few hundred Saints, grew restless through the summer of 1846, and in September they gathered on the outskirts of Nauvoo some eight hundred strong, armed with artillery and prepared to force the last of the Mormons out of Nauvoo. When Nauvoo citizens attempted to defend the city, a two-day exchange of gunfire ensued, and on the third day Nauvoo was invaded, several persons from both sides being killed in the skirmish. The Mormons surrendered the city, and destitute, they crossed the Mississippi River to join the rest of the Camp of Israel.

Organized into companies of about one hundred families each, the Saints journeyed across Iowa toward the Indian rangelands banking the Missouri River. The encampments there were plagued by sickness during the first summer when many persons contracted scurvy due to the lack of fresh vegetables in their diets, and others suffered with chills and fever.[1] Preparations for winter nevertheless went forward, and Winter Quarters on the west bank emerged at the end of September as a town of 820 surveyed lots with hundreds of log homes under construction. "The house into which we mov'd was partly chink'd & only mudded on one side & only covered on one side, the other having the tent thrown over it," Eliza Snow noted on October 28. A month later, winter winds blowing, she recorded with gratitude the completion of the chinking. Cabins of logs, willows, and dirt and some dugouts housed about 3,500 Saints at Winter Quarters through the winter of 1846-47. Thousands of Saints wintered at various other encampments near Winter Quarters or scattered across the trail on the Iowa side of the river.

To those who had been traveling for six months, the winter camps provided a much-welcome respite from the trail. Women, especially, found opportunity for activities long postponed. In her Winter Quarters diary, Mary Haskin Parker Richards reported her progress in making a black silk dress for herself. A young bride separated from her missionary husband, Mary was free not only to sew for herself, but also to attend singing school and dances and to act upon "many pressing invitations" to visit with friends.

By contrast, Patty Sessions did not have much time to herself. Her responsibilities as a midwife made for a rigorous schedule, even at the winter camp. But she had more spare moments for spinning, knitting, and making soap than she had found on the trail. And she had time to attend a variety of social and religious gatherings. At the Winter Quarters camp the Saints gathered on Sundays for meetings in their individual wards and for general assemblies where they received official instructions from Brigham Young and other members of the Council of the Twelve. High councils were appointed to similarly direct the affairs of other encampments. Patty noted her attendance at these general meetings and recorded with some care her participation in the frequent unofficial meetings of a small group of sisters where spiritual gifts were exercised and all enjoyed a "feast of the spirit of the Lord."

Patty Sessions and Eliza Snow left Winter Quarters in June 1847, following to the valley of the Great Salt Lake the band of pioneers who had left the winter camp in April. Mary Richards was among those who remained at the camp through the summer and a second winter. Each of these three women kept a daily record of her activities over a considerably longer period than that covered by the short excerpts included in this chapter, but these selections provide a revealing glimpse of the temporal and spiritual dimensions of the lives of three diverse women in the Camp of Israel. If cooking and washing were important, so were personal and collective considerations of the message and gifts of the restored gospel. If there was time to nurse the sick and mourn the bereaved, there was also time to dance or amuse oneself writing poetry. If the Mormon trek westward was a latter-day exodus, these were modern Miriams recounting the details of their deliverance with a pen for a timbrel.

Eliza Roxcy Snow (1804-1887)

By the time Eliza R. Snow left Nauvoo, she had earned a reputation as a woman of singular devotion, talent, and intelligence. A ream of published poems distinguished her as "Zion's Poetess," and she had served as secretary of the Female Relief Society of Nauvoo and officiated in women's ordinances in the Nauvoo Temple. Her agility with the pen and familiarity with Church leaders and organization have long made her two-volume trail journal of special interest to Mormon readers.[2]

Eliza left almost half of her life behind when she quit the Midwest. Her parents, Oliver and Rosetta Pettibone Snow, had moved from their western Massachusetts farm to the unsettled land near Lake Erie when Eliza was barely old enough to walk. The second of seven children, she grew up in Mantua, Portage County, Ohio, near the cluster of northeastern Ohio towns where Latter-day Saint missionaries baptized over one hundred settlers in late fall 1830. The following winter at Mantua, Eliza met Joseph Smith through Sidney Rigdon, a mutual friend, but she was not baptized a Latter-day Saint until April 1835.[3]

The Snows accompanied the body of the Saints from Ohio to Missouri to Illinois. When the Saints were forced to leave Nauvoo, Eliza became one of the plural wives of Brigham Young, and it was he who arranged for her to travel with the family of Colonel Stephen Markham in the journey from Nauvoo to Winter Quarters. Eliza joined a family of six for the trek, including the colonel and his wife, Hannah, their sons Warren, William, and David, and Warren's wife, Catherine Ann Jones Markham. Brother Markham was often ahead of the rest of his family, traveling in the van with the one hundred pioneers preparing the road on the journey through Iowa.

On the trail Eliza sewed, wrote poems and letters, and kept a regular journal. She spent considerable time visiting with other women. Among the friends mentioned in her journal are many women who were to work with her in Utah during her twenty-year term as general president of the Relief Society.

The original holograph diary, February 1846 to August 1949, is located in the Huntington Library at San Marino, California, with a microfilm copy (used here) in the Church archives. Minimal punctuation and some bracketed material have been added to clarify the text.

Eliza R. Snow, ca. 1850. (Daguerrotype Collection. LDS Church Archives.)

[February 1846]

Feb. 12th 1846. We left our homes and went as far as br. Hiram Kimball's where we spent the night and thro' the generosity of sister [Sarah M.] K[imball] & mother [Lydia] Granger, made some additional preparations for our journey.[4]

13th Cross'd the Mississippi and join'd the Camp. Found my br. L[orenzo][5] & br [David D.] Yearsley's families tented side by side; we lodg'd in br. Y.'s tent which before morning was covered with snow.

14th After breakfast I went into the buggy and did not leave till the next day. Sis. M[arkham] and I did some needlework tho' the melting snow dripp[ed] thro' our cover.

15th Sunday. Had a very pleasant visit with Sarah Lawrence.

17th Visited Sis. [Vilate] Kimball who had just arrived. Mov'd our tents to the upper end of the encampment. The day fine.

18th The weather fine. Received a visit from Loisa B[eaman] C[larissa] Decker & S[arah] Lawrence.[6] Last night very cold.

19th Snowstorm commenced in the night and continued thro' the day. It was so disagreeable out that I did not leave the buggy. Suffered considerably from a severe cold. Amused myself by writing the following.

The Camp of Israel.[7]
A Song for the Pioneers. No. 1.

Altho' in woods and tents we dwell
Shout, shout, O Camp of Israel
No christian mobs on earth can bind
Our thoughts, or steal our peace of mind.

Chorus.
Tho' we fly from vile aggression
We'll maintain our pure profession—
Seek a peaceable possession
Far from Gentiles and oppression.

We better live in tents and smoke
Than wear the cursed gentile yoke—
We better from our country fly
Than by mobocracy to die.
        Chorus.   Tho' we fly &c.

We've left The City of Nauvoo
And our beloved Temple too,
And to the wilderness we'll go
Amid the winter frosts and snow.
        Chorus.   Tho' we fly &c.

Our homes were dear—we lov'd them well
Beneath our roofs we hop'd to dwell,
And honor the great God's commands
By mutual rights of christian lands.
        Chorus.   Tho' we fly &c.

Our persecutors will not cease
Their murd'rous spoiling of our peace
And have decreed that we must go
To wilds where reeds & rushes grow.
        Chorus.   Tho' we fly &c.

The Camp—the Camp—its numbers swell
Shout, shout O Camp of Israel!
The King the Lord of hosts is near
His armies guard our front & rear.
        Chorus.   Tho' we fly &c.

Sat. 28th For several days past the weather has been extremely cold. People visiting us from the City think the
weather as severe as has been thro' the winter. This morning,
that portion of the Camp to which we were attach'd, was to
start out. Bishop [George] Miller's company left several days

153

before, but the intense cold prevented the body of the Camp from following soon as was anticipated.

We travelled but 4 miles and encamp'd in a low, truly romantic valley just large enough for our tents, wagons, &c. We arrived a little before sunset, and the prospect for the night seem'd dubious enough. The ground was covered with snow, shoe deep, but our industrious men with hoes soon prepared places and pitch'd the tents, built wood-piles in front of them, and but a few minutes with many hands transform'd the rude valley into a thriving town. On Indian Creek.

[March 1846]

Sund. Mar. 1st. The weather considerably moderated in the eve. The remainder of the Camp from Sugar Creek arrived with the Twelve, the Band &c. and tented on the bluff which surrounded us.[8] *[in margin]* Wrote to Sis. S[arah] M. K[imball].

Song for the Pioneers, No. 2.
The Camp of Israel.[9]

num'rous
Lo! a mighty host of people
    Tented on the western shore
Of The noble Mississippi
    They for weeks were crossing o'er.
At the last day's dawn of winter,
    Bound with frost & wrapt in snow,,
Hark! the sound is onward, onward!
    Camp of Israel! rise & go.

All at once is life in motion—
    Trunks and beds & baggage fly;
Oxen yok'd & horses harness'd—
    Tents roll'd up, are passing by.

154

Soon the carriage wheels are rolling
Onward to a woodland dell,
Where, at sunset all are quarter'd—
Camp of Israel! all is well.

Thickly round, the tents are cluster'd
Neighb'ring smokes together blend—
Supper serv'd—the hymns are chanted
And the evening pray'rs ascend.
Last of all the guards are station'd—
Heav'ns! must guards be serving here?
Who would harm the houseless exiles?
Camp of Israel! never fear.

Where is freedom? where is justice?
Both have from this nation fled;
And the blood of martyr'd prophets
Must be answer'd on its head!
Therefore to your tents, O Jacob!
Like our father Abra'm dwell—
God will execute his purpose—
Camp of Israel! all is well.

Mon. 2d According to the order of the preceding night, the whole Camp except some appointed to do a job of work move forward as early as practicable, and the weather having moderated considerably, after starting on frozen ground & ice, the travelling in the afternoon was in mud & water. Journey'd 12 m[iles] & encamp'd in a field where piles of small wood were scattered very conveniently for our fires as if prepare'd for the purpose, but they had been heap'd by the owner and left either thro' hurry or neglect. The last of the way being very bad, the last of the comp[any] only arrived in time for the next mor[ning] start. The country was timber land and quite broken, with high bluffs rising loftily over low valleys, and but little cultivated.

Tu. 3d. Camp mov'd in a body 8 miles which was on the bank of the Des Moine. The travelling much better than the previous day. The weather fine. Pass'd thro' the town of Farmington where the inhabitants manifested great curiosity and more levity than sympathy for our houseless situation. We join'd Bishop Miller's com. where he halted to perform a job of chopping & fencing on Reed's Creek.

Our encampment this night may truly be recorded by this generation as a miracle. A City rear'd in a few hours, and every thing in operation that *living* required & many additional things which if not *extravagances,* were in fact *conveniences.*

This eve. was very agreeably surpriz'd by sis. [Elizabeth Ann] Whitney's appearance in front of the buggy where I was seated eating my supper. I rejoiced much to learn that her family had arrived & were tented close by us, having before this time been separated from all old associates.[10]

Just before entering Farmington, finished the cakes which Sis. M. made at sis. [Sarah] K[imball]'s.

W. 4th This morning was usher'd in with the music of the Band which was delightfully sublime.

Stop'd this day to organize. Bishop M[iller]'s company went on. Others were appointed to finish the work he had commenc'd.

I spent some time with Sis. W[hitney] and Sarah A[nn Whitney Kimball].[11] Last night dream'd of being in elder [Heber C.] K[imball]'s mess. Thought myself quite awkwardly situated. Just at night Sis. Whitney came to our tent expressing much joy in her countenance & said we are all to go together in br. Kimball's com. the Camp being divided into different companys under The Twelve for the convenience of travelling.

Col. Markham exchang'd the buggy in which Sis. M[arkham] & myself rode, & which serv'd me as sitting room & dormitory, for a lumber wagon. Great numbers of the inhabitants of the country were to be seen walking in companys thro' this day, up and down the nameless streets of our magnificent & novel City.

Sis. M. and I took a walk this eve. Lost our way. Call'd at A[masa] Lyman's tent. After a little chat with E[liza Partridge Lyman] br. L. conducted us toward home until we came in sight of it, which we could hardly have found without a pilot.[12]

Th. 5th Our newly constructed City is razed and the inhabitants thereof take up their line of march. Return to the bank of the Desmoine which we had left at a half mile distance for our encampment. Sis. M. and I are nicely seated in an ox wagon, on a chest with a brass kettle and a soap box for our foot stools, thankful that we are so well off. The day fine. We travelled 2 miles on the bank of the river & cross'd at a little place called Bonaparte. I slung a tin cup on a string and drew some water which was a very refreshing draught. After crossing the river the road was thro' timber & intolerably muddy. The banks on this side rising almost perpendicularly the teams had hard work to draw the loads, as we ascended hill after hill. Our com. consisting of Pioneers, br. Markham's & br. Yearsley's families all of whom were attach'd to elder K[imball's] com. of fifty were only able to go 3 miles after crossing, when we came upon a prairie & encamp'd. The present division of our co. was rather awkward. The little boys had gone on with the cows, we knew not where, but afterwards learn'd they were 8 miles ahead with br. L. where most of the Camp had gone. Elder K. was ¾ of a mile beyond us and bishop [Newel K.] W[hitney] 1½ miles in the rear.

fr. 6th We cross'd the prairie & join'd the other encampment, on a small creek & uncomfortably muddy, but in good com. being directly in the neighborhood of the fifty to which we belong'd.

Sat. 7th Left the timber. Road very bad for a mile or more.
The weather warm & the ox-teams seem'd almost exhausted. I
got out of the wagon & walk'd for the first time on the journey. The face of the country quite broken for the first 5 or 6
miles; the timber principally oak, contrasting very much with
the beautiful sugar groves on the Desmoines. After a few
miles travel in small opnings interspers'd with strips of timber
land, we pass'd thro' several miles of rolling prairie, under
better cultivation than any we had seen since leaving Mon-
trose. Arrived at the place of our encampment after dark, tho'
not in the dark for the moon shone brilliantly upon our path.
10 or 12 miles this day.

Sun. 8th The day warm & fine. Heard this mor. of the birth
of Sarah Ann's son. Bishop W[hitney] did not come up last
night and the word was for the camp to remain thro' the day.
Call'd on Loisa [Beaman] Emily [Dow Partridge Young] &c.
Went to meeting, but when br. [Jedediah M.] Grant
commenc'd discourse I understood the citizens had requested
the meeting. Concluded it would be for their benefit & not so
interesting to us. L[oisa] and myself went to elder [John]
Taylor's tent & spent 2 or 3 hours very pleasantly with sis.
[Leonora] T[aylor] who was laboring under a rheumatic affection & felt quite disheartened. I told her she must not be dis-
courag'd. Could not feel that she would be long infirm. May
God heal her.

We went to Col. [Albert P.] Rockwood's tent. Father [Isaac]
Chase quite sick & Clarissa looking disconsolate.

Mon. 9th Our *town* of yesterday morning has grown to a *City*,
laid out in the form of a half hollow square, fronting east &
south, on a beautiful level, with an almost perpendicular, on
one side and on the other, a gradual descent to a deep ravine
on the west & north. At nine this mor. I notic'd but a few
rods from our tent, a black-smith's shop in operation, and
every thing indicated real life. Not a cooking utensil was idle.
Sis. M. baked a batch of eleven loaves but the washing busi-

ness was necessarily omitted for the want of water, an inconvenience the present location suffers more than any previous one. Had the pleasure of the first interview with Prest. [Brigham] Y[oung] since we left the City. Call'd on Sis. W. and Sarah with her fine boy.

Tus. 10th Rainy all day

Wed. 11th Rain'd all day. This mor. elder [Henry G.] Sherwood ascertain'd from observations, our geometrical distance from Nauvoo to be 55 and ¼ miles.

From the dampness of my lodging or some other cause, did not rest much & feel rather indispos'd. Took no breakfast, but for my dinner my good friend Sis. M. brought me a slice of beautiful, white, light bread and butter, that would have done honor to a more convenient bakery, than an out-of-door fire in the wilderness.

Th. 12th Rainy yet, intolerably muddy.

Fri. 13th Rain'd some in the night but colder before morning. Quite windy. Our tent blew down & with other accide[nts] upset a pail of potatoe soup which was intended for breakfast, but instead thereof we had coffee, fried jole [fish head] and *"jonny cake."* This mor. the subject of the fare of the pioneers of our *fifty* was call'd in question. H[eber] C. K[imball] said a distribution must be made and inasmuch as they did most of the labor they should have while anything remain'd. L[orenzo] Y[oung] said they must eat as he did which was a few slices of dried beef boil'd & a quart or two of milk added, in which he ate his bread. They said they would do so, but had neither the meat or the milk. Meat was furnished by some of the com. Our *mess* had divided with them at the large encampment on the other side the Des Moine among those who remain'd behind to finish B[ishop] Miller's job, who are said to remain there yet not having the means to come on. The rest that have been left at work having all come up including those who stopped about 6 miles back to do a job at rail splitting of

which I had not made mention. Sis M. and I made mother W
and Sarah A. a call in the eve. Heard the melancholy news of
the death of the amiable & much belov'd Mrs. Caroline C.
Spencer.

Also thro' the medium of letters receiv'd from Nauvoo, that
Wm. Smith & G[eorge] J. Adams were gathering on one side,
& John E. Page in conjunction with [James J.] Strang, on the
other, while Orson Hyde advocates the cause of truth in favor
of the Church. Has baptized Luke Johnson, who has gone east
for his family intending to join The *Camp of Israel*.[13]

Sat. 14th Cold & windy. Sis M Harriet, Elizabeth & myself
go to the Creek about a half mile distant, to wash, while Sis.
Y. & Catharine [Markham] stay to attend to the cooking department the result of which we receiv'd some tokens before
night, to wit, Catharine sent us some nice sweet biscuit for
dinner, & when B. came with the buggy for us at night, Sis.
Y. sent us a supper of rich pot-pie made of wild game, rabbits,
pheasants, quails, &c. which is the *fourth* dish of the kind on
which we have feasted since we left the City, being 4 weeks
yesterday. Our hunters have been very fortunate. I think few
have fared as well in this respect as our family which now
numbers 22, elder Sherwood being with us.

Before we left the *washing vale* it commenc'd raining. Turn'd
windy before morning & I was heartily glad to see the moon
shining on the wagon cover, a few inches above my head.

This eve. 2 of the ten pioneers left at the incampment on the
other side the Desmoine came up with their knapsacks on
their backs. The brethren get corn for 12 & 15 cents pr.
bushel which is the highest they have given except in one
instance when they gave 20.

Sun. 15th So intolerably windy, the men fail in their efforts
to keep the tent upright. I did not leave the wagon till night.
Sis. [Patty] Sessions made us a visit in the afternoon. Sis. M.
making the wagon comfortable with coals. The subject of
brotherly oppression was forcibly presented to my view, & I was

led to inquire "How long O Lord?" Is there no reward for patient submission? Will the insolent oppressor always go un-punished? How long shall some feast while others famish?

Mon. 17th [16th] The day fine. Took coffee with Sarah A. Went to br. A. Lyman's tent. Found a little child of Sydney Tanner at the point of death.

Tu. 18th [17th] Rainy & windy.

Wed. 19th [18th] Warm & pleasant. Had expected to leave the encampment but are detain'd by the death of br [Edwin] Little, a nephew of Prest. B. Young. A very busy day with us in overhauling and arranging wagons, baking &c. Prest. Y. shook hands with us.

Th. 19th Left the encampment. The day very cold & windy. The country mostly prairie, broken with strips of timber, mostly oak, sufficiently rolling for farming, not much culti-vated, but decorated with many new beginnings which promise beautiful homes with a few years improvement. Saw a few fine young peach-orchards. Our mess with the pioneers were belated & after travelling 9 or 10 m[iles] put up for the night, the body of the Camp being a mile & a half in advance. The road was good most of the way, a few mud-holes to ford by star-light.

[in margin] Wrote to Sis. L. & Mrs. K.

fr. 20th The cold more intense insomuch that we were obliged to close the front of the wagon. Traveled 8 or 9 m. & stopped on the bank of a creek with a pole bridge, called *Fox river.* Our com. still ahead. Much difficulty in getting feed for the teams. Saw Harriet & Sarah.

Sat. 21st The going very bad for 3 or 4 ms. after crossing the river, half of the distance timber'd land. We met Prest. Y[oung] who had return'd from his encampment to see to the repairing of one of his wagons. The day fine & the remainder of the road beautiful, over a prairie 15 miles. Encamp'd in the

161

edge of the timber that skirts the Chariton, 4 ms. from the stream. Having overtaken the Camp in the morning.

Sun 22 After passing the timber land which was very rugged, came to a bottom of 3 miles on which I counted upward of 80 wagons before me at one view. Cross'd the Chariton which at this place is a muddy looking stream perhaps 2 rods in wi[d]th with steep banks. The pioneers assisted the teams with ropes. Pass'd on about ¼ m. and encamp'd on a beautiful ridge, where the tents were arranged on each side the road. Saw sis. Rich for the first time. Encamp'd on the river. One of the girls sick with the measles.

Br. L[orenzo] came up just before night. Had not seen him before since crossing the Des Moine.

> *Song for the Pioneers of the Camp of Israel No. 3.*
> *Dedicated to Prest. B. Young & Elder H. C. Kimball*[14]
> *Let us go.*
>
> *Let us go—let us go to the ends of the earth—*
> *Let us go far away from the land of our birth;*
> *For the banner of "freedom" no longer will wave*
> *O'er the patriot's tomb—o'er the dust of the brave.*
>
> *Let us go—let us go from a country of strife—*
> *From a land where the wicked are seeking our life*
> *From a country where justice no longer remains—*
> *From which virtue is fled & iniquity reigns.*
>
> *Let us go—let us go from a government where*
> *Our just right of protection we never can share—*
> *Where the soil we have purchas'd we cannot enjoy*
> *Till the time when "the master goes forth to destroy."*
>
> *Let us go—let us go to the wilds for a home*
> *Where the wolf and the roe and the buffalo roam*
> *Where the life inspir'd "eagle" in "liberty" flies—*
> *Where the mountains of Israel in majesty rise.*

Let us go—let us go to a country whose soil
Can be made to produce wine, milk, honey & oil—
Where beneath our own vines we may sit & enjoy
The rich fruit of our labors with none to annoy.

Let us go—let us go where our rights are secure—
Where the waters are clear & the atmosphere pure—
Where the hand of oppression has never been felt—
Where the blood of the prophets has never been spilt.

Let us go—let us go where the kingdom of God
Will be seen in its order extending abroad—
Where the Priesthood again will exhibit its worth
In the regeneration of man and of earth.

Let us go—let us go to the far western shore
Where the blood-thirsty "christians" will hunt us no more;
Where the waves of the ocean will echo the sound
And the shout of salvation be heard the world round!

Mon 23 Commenc'd raining last evening. Rain'd thro' the night and this day.

Wed. 25th Commenc'd snowing Mon. night & snow'd with little intermission till this afternoon. The oak ridge on which we are encamped being of a clay soil, the mud of our street & about our fires, in our tents &c. is indescribable. Thro' the un-remitting kindness of Mrs. Markham, I do not leave the wagon & this evening we supped together thro' the kindness of Catharine, on jonny-cake & milk, the product of *"old whity"* the family cow. Having had a calf a few days ago, she affords us a fine treat.

We are now in Davies Co. having cross'd the line of Van Buren about 4 miles this side the 11 days encampment, which is 8 ms. from Keosauque [Keosauqua], the county town.

It is impossible to obtain grain here for the teams which live mostly on browse. 25 men of our "fifty" took a job of making

163

rails, for which they got 10 bush. of corn, which was distribu-
ted tues. night. They also got 100 [pounds] of bacon for the
pioneers, 100 more paid for. Thus the Lord opens the way for
his poor saints, thro' patience & industry to obtain the neces-
saries of life, as they journey towards the western wilderness.

Mary Haskin Parker Richards (1823-1860)

Mary Haskin Parker was among the 1,135 Saints who emigrated to Nauvoo from Great Britain in 1841. Her parents, John and Ellen Haskin Parker, and several of their children had been baptized in 1838 near Preston, one of the early centers of Mormon missionary activity in England. For a time local Saints held meetings in the Parker home, where elders Heber C. Kimball, Willard Richards, and Joseph Fielding were frequent visitors. Mary developed with these men friendships that remained important to her throughout her life. John and Ellen Parker emigrated to Nauvoo in 1840, leaving their youngest child, eighteen-year-old Mary, to follow on her own a year later.[15]

Mary Haskin Parker Richards.
(Daughters of Utah Pioneers.
Salt Lake City, Utah.)

Mary lived with her parents in Nauvoo until January 1846, the eve of the Saints' departure, when she married Samuel Whitney Richards, a nephew of her friend Willard. A few months after the newlyweds started out on the westward trek, Samuel was called to serve a mission in Great Britain. He departed in July, leaving Mary in the care of his parents. That she comfortably adopted the whole Richards family is evident from her diary, where she refers to Samuel's parents as "mother" and "father" and frequently notes evenings spent with Samuel's Aunt Rhoda, Uncle Levi, and Uncle Willard and his wife Amelia. Mary's own parents moved to St. Louis when they left Nauvoo, joining a strong community of Saints there for several years before traveling to Utah.

Mary Richards kept a diary during the two years she stayed at Winter Quarters awaiting Samuel's return from Scotland. The early portion of that diary is included in this chapter. Much of Mary's time was spent with Jane Snyder Richards, "Sister Jane," the wife of Samuel's brother Franklin, who was also serving a mission in Great Britain. Their husbands away, the young wives sought the help and company of the Richards family and of Jane's family, the Snyders. Mary and Jane, both without children at the time, were able to sew and wash and visit together and commiserate over the absence of their husbands. However, Mary's life was too busy and her spirits too light for her to spend much time languishing. Her diary is marked by an airiness that keeps the reader smiling.

The original holograph of the diary of Mary Haskin Parker Richards is in private possession, but a microfilm of the holograph is located in the Historical Department of the Church, and that has been used in preparing this selection. Minimal punctuation has been added for clarification.

A Journal & Memorandom of Mary H Richards, commencing Saturday November 28th 1846. In the PM went to Bro [James] Smithes expecting to get a letter from my father [John Parker], but was disappointed. Called at Uncle Willards, and talked with him about 20 minutes. Got a letter for mother and a paper for Sister Jane. Called to see Aunt Rhoda & spent a few minutes with her & Uncle Levis folks. Next called to see Bro [Ezra T.] Bensons folks, he having just retorned from his

mission to the East the Evening before. From him I got considerable information concerning my Husband. He also
brought me some presents which he sent me. A workbox in
which was 2 letters, a Sattin Ribon, & flowers, for a bonet, a
smelling bottle, 2 white An[?] & a Silk one for Henry, and a
purse containing 10 dollars.[16] Sister B took of[f] bonnet &
shawl and made me stay and make a visit. Took supper &
spent the eve with them. Enjoyed myself much. It was indeed
a day of rejoicing to me to hear of the prosperity an[d] well-
being of my dear companion. May Heavens ritchest blessing
attend him w[h]ere e'er he romes & retorn him in safty to my
bosem.

Sunday 29th In the AM went to meeting. Was addrest by Bro
[Heber C.] Kimball who gave us some good instructions how
we Aught to walk &c. Was followed by Bro Benson who
gave us an interressting account of his mission to the East, the
state of the different branches, the downfall of aposstacy &c
&c. In the PM Aunt Amelia E R[ichards] visited with us, &
read 5 letters which she had just received from Richmond
mass[achusetts]. Maria [Richards Wilcox] & Jane also visited
with us.[17] We had a joyfull time.

Monday 30th. The weather some what comfortable. After
doing up my work in the morn, I sat down and mended
fathers over Coat, and a dress for my self. After supper went
with Mother to Bro Van Cotts, & spent the eve. Had a pleasant visit.

[December 1846]

Tuesday December first. Windy day. After breakfast Mrs
Rebecca M Jones and babe from Mo. [Missouri] called to see
me. Was in great hast[e]. I accompanyed her to the River from
whence she retorns to Mo. On my retorn called at Bro [Edwin
D.] Woolleys, and spent the day. Had a good visit. Ellen
[Wilding Woolley] & Mrs. Smith acompanyed [me] home.[18]

Wednesday 2th. A cold day. Was makeing me a hood. Spent the eve at Bro Wm. Youngs. Enjoyed myself much.

Thursday 3th. The weather cold. Helped do the work and finished making my hood.

Friday 4th. A cold day. Was sewing in the AM and in the PM baked 3 loves of bread. [unclear] Br. Wm. Youngs. Eve was knitting.

Saturday 5th. The weather comfortable. Fixed Mothers hood for her & mended a dress for my self. In the eve read about an hour in the Bible.

Sunday 6th. The weather cold. In the morning got breakfast &c. Was no meeting. Went out to see some of my friends. Called at Bro Van Cotts, to see his wife & mother, they having been sick. Found them comfortable. Spent about & hour with them. Eat some bread and butter, Honey & chese &c. Next went to sister [Sarah] Noons, to carry home a hood Which I had borrowed. Spent a few minutes with them. Next called to see Ellen Wilding [Woolley]. At Br Woolleys had the pleasure of spending about & houre with her alone in the waggon. Next called at Uncle Levis. Found them well. Aunt Rhoda having kept [in] her Waggon for near 4 weeks on account of sickness. I went into her humble abode to see her. Found Amelia with her. Spent a short H[our] time with them. Next called at Uncle Willards house to see Bros [Thomas] Bullock & [John] Rushtons familys who had just arrived. Found Sister R morning the loss of her Child she having died the day before. Stayed a short time with them. Then called to see Maria, & spent a few minutes with them, &c. From there I went about ½ mile South to see Sister Jane. Found her suffering with face Ac[h]e & canker. Spent the eve & Nigh[t] with her. Had a good supper &c.

Monday 7th. A very cold day. Stayed until eve with Jane. She read her letter for me &c. Spent the evening writting in my Journal, knitting &c.

Tuesday 8th. A cold day. Was sewing, knitting, reading & cooking &c.

Wednesday 9th. The weather a little more comfortable. In the AM Sister Maria came to see us. Got her to fit the lining to my black Silck dress. I cut the waist and sewed on it the rest of the day. Eve was knitting.

Thursday 10th. A pleasant day. Was sewing on my dress all day, and in the [eve] was knitting.

Friday 11th. A lovely day. Was sewing on my dress. Eve was knitting.

Saturday 12th. A beautyfull day. Sister Jane & myself went out to do some buisness. In the first place went to the Store, which was very much crouded. Stayed a while. Bought some Cotton &c. Then called to see Bro Smithes folks & made a short stay with them. Next called at Uncle Willards house, w[h]ere we had the pleasure of being present at a Councel held between the Twelve & the Natives. There was present 10 Indians two Chiefs & two Interpiters, one a french Man or half breed. We was quite interessted to hear them talk & see them act.[19] After Councel was dismissed had some talk with W. I asked him which way he thought Samuel & F[ranklin] would retorn. Said he did not know, but he supposed they would come back by this place. Said we might make our selfs contented. All things should go right. After leaving there, we called to see Bro Bensons family, & spent a few minutes with them. On our way home called to see Bro Feelding [Joseph Fielding] & family, who seemed quite glad to see us. Stayed & conversed with him about 2 hours. Then came to Janes house & took Supper with her wich I enjoyed, & soon after had the pleasure of seeing Bro [Stephen H.] Godard direct from Nauvoo. In the eve he accompanyed us to Bro H[enry] Grows w[h]ere we spent about 2 hours, and then retorned home. Had quite a pleasant conversation with Bro G who brought to rememberance by gone days.[20]

169

Sunday 13th. The weather comfortable. After getting breakfast, washing dishes, &c. went to meetting. Heard a raugh discourse, delivered by Bro [Cornelius P.] Lot[t], and a few remarks by Bro Brigham [Young]. Spent the rest of the day at
home, reading, &c.

Monday 14th. Had a little snow this morning the first I have
seen this year, but it melted as soon as the Sun was out, and
was very pleasent to day. I commenced writing a letter to my
Husband, and in the eve was knitting reading &c.

Tuesday 15th. Had a little more Snow. The weather rather
cold. Went to Janes & baked a loaf of bread. PM was writing
in my letter. Eve Sewing &c.

Wednesday 16th. A cold day. In the morn cut a garment for
Henry. Was cooking writing in my letter &c.

Thursday 17th. A cold day. Was writing in my letter. Eve
Jane came to stay with me I being a lone. She was writing a
letter to Frankolin, and I was writing in my Journal. She read
me her letter, and I read her most of mine.

Friday 18th. A very cold day. Was sewing and wr[i]ting in
my letter. Eve borrowed a penn at sister Pratts and finished it.
Mother & father went out to spend the eve at Bro Hart's.
Henry & I was all alone.

Saturday 19th. The weather please[n]t. Had the head Ache all
day. Felt Sober in the morn. Sister Obanks [?] came to learn to
make baskets. Could not get room to sit down near Stove, So
I went to Sisters Janes and sewed on my dress, & baked a loaf
of bread. They were washing. Eve wrung & hung out some of
her cloth[e]s, then came home. Spent the rest of the night
knitting.

Sunday 20th. In the morn got breakfast, washed the dishes,
swept the Tent, washed me, changed my dress and sat down
& commenced to write a [s]crap to put in my letter. In about
ten minutes after the Temple Bell rung for meeting, got ready
& went. Bro Brigham preached a sermon that I think will be

long rememberd by all who heard it. He began by speaking of several Evils exsisting in the Camp, such as, swearing, stealing, eveil speaking, &c. Said if they did not repent & leave of[f] their Eveil doings, The door of kn[o]wledge should be shut up against them, and they should be wasted by sickness, by Pestilance, and the Sword, and those who were found righteous among them, should be taken out of their midst, and they should perish with their dead. Said many [things] that were interessting.[21] Had & excellant meeting. Evening, father & Mother went to spend the eve at Bro Rights, and sister Jane came to spend it with me. We were each writing a [s]crap to put in our letters. 'Twas a beautyfull day.

Monday 21st. A cold day. In the AM was sewing. In the PM went to visit Bro [Henry] Grows family, who appeard Glad to see me. We talked of by gone days, and of things that had trancepired during our absence from Each other. Had a very pleasant visit & stayed all night.[22]

Tuesday 22th. The weather cold. In the morn Bro Grow started for Mo. Spent the day with his family. In the AM was sewing on my black silck dress PM made an Apron for sister Grow &c. While there had the pleasure of seeing Sister Fairbanks and received & Introduction to Sister Veach. At Sun down retorned to Sister Janes house & spent the eve, & Night with her.

Wednesday 23th. The weather more comfortable. Was at home all day sewing helping my Mother &c. At dusk went with her to Bro Willys and spent the Eve. Had a very pleasent Visit.

Thursday 24th. A pleasent day. In the morn, Jane came & said if I wished to wash to day, I might have the privelige to do so in her house. If not she wanted father Mother, & my self, to go & make her a visit. Father & mother consented to do the latter, and I aggried to do both. So after breakfast, I went down to her house & washed me out 4 dresses, & as many Aprons & some other things. Put them out to dry. Then

washed of[f] the floor wich is the first time I have washed a
floor since the first of Aprial. Father & mother came. We had
an excellant Supper. Sister Jenne was with us also. We staid
the Eve. Talked of several things that had passed since our
leaving Nauvoo. Father spoke some things that hurt Jane's feelings, but she spoke Noble in her own defence, and made
father draw in his horns, and they parted still freinds. I remained with Jane all Night.

Friday 25th. A beautyfull day. In the morn went home an[d]
getherd together a large washing of clothes and retorned to
Jane's to spend Christmass over the washtubs. Was washing
with all my might til dark. Then put my cloth[e]s in water til
morning. Eve went with Jane to Bro Phinehas Youngs to see
about getting some flower. On our retorn, called on Maria, &
spent about 2 hours with them. Ate supper with her &c. Had
a pleasent little visit and retorned home. Spent the Night with
Jane.

Saturday 26th. Another fine day. In the morn went home &
getherd up all the clothes I could find, that needed washing,
and retorned again to Janes, to finish my washing. Rung out
my clothes that I had put to soak the night before and hung
them out to dry, then washed the remainder of my clothes.
Had a considerable large wash. Finished about dark. Washed
of[f] the floor & took supper. In the evening foulded my
cloth[e]s and put them out of the folks way. Felt very tired.
Staid all night with Jane.

Sunday 27th. The weather pleasent. Took breakfast with Jane
then came home changed my dress and at 12 oclock went to
meeting. Was addrest by Orson Pratt, on the Policy of the
removal of the Church in the spring. Said they intended to
send out a company as early as posable in the Spring, to put
in a crop at the foot of the mountains on the banks of the
Yellow Stone.[23] They also intended to send a company across
the mountains to put in a crop of Weat in the fall. He was
followed by Bro Benson on the same subject. He told the
brethren that none of them should leave this place to go any

farther without receiving councel to do so. Desired them to fix
their waggons & hold themselfs in readyness, so that if they
were called upon to go the[y] might be ready, to do so &c.
Exorted the Saints to be faithfull & reform from all their Eavil
doings &c&c. Had a good meeting. Came home and read a
while in the book of mormon, & helped mother get supper,
after wich Elcy Snyder called to go to singing Scool with me.
On our way there called on Abigal [Smith] Abbott, & took
her with us. Bro Godard led the C[h]oir for the first [time]
since the Dedication of the [Nauvoo] Temple. We had a good
sing. Enjoyed ourselfs much. Went & slept that night with
Sister Jane.

Monday 28th. The weather still good. Took breakfast with
Jane then Ironed my cloth[e]s. Finished about dark. After
supper took my knitting and went with Jane to spend the eve
at Bro Samuel Snyders.

Tuesday 29th. The weather cold. Spent the day with Jane
sewing. In the eve was reading until 8 oclock. Then Jane, Ellcy
& myself spent about two hours trying to see which could
Compose the best Poetry. Then retired to bed.

Wednesday 30th. A cold day. In the AM was at Jane's sewing
for my self. In the PM went with her to Bro Bakers. Had a
good visit, and an excellant Supper. Spend the eve and
retorned home with Jane & stayed all night with her.

Thursday 31st. A very cold day. In the morn, went with Jane
to Uncle Willards to help them do some sewing. Made an
Apron for Amelia & 2 handkerchiefs for Uncle W and helped
sew on his garment. After we dismissed our work, Uncle W
sat down to eat some supper. Asked me if I was grown proud.
I said if I was it was unknown to me. Then said he, Come &
Eat some supper with me. I did so, & Eat of[f] from his plate
while conversing with him. Aunt Rhoda came & kneeled
down by him & said she had bowed down on her benders to
recieve a blessing. He then took the word Benders for a text &
preached a sermon from it, about an half houre long, on false

modesty. After this, I went to Uncle Levis & slept with Aunt R[hoda]. Had a good nights rest.

[January 1847]

Friday Janawary first 1847. A Cold day. After wishing & being wished a happy New Year by Uncle L. & family I retorned to Uncle Ws to spend the day sewing for them. Helped make a garment for Uncle W. & a Apron for Ellen, &c&c.

Saturday 2th. A very cold day. Took breakfast at Uncle Ws. then retorned to Janes house to get some things. From there I went to Bro Everits to make a visit. Spent the day very pleasently conversing, reading &c. Stayed all night.

Sunday 3th. The weather cold. Went with Sister E to meeting at Bro Scots. Was addrest by H C Kimball, on the dutys of familys. Exorted Husbands to watch over their wives & Children, & to instru[c]t them in the knowledge, & fear of the Leord, not with severity but with meekness, & forbearance. Wives to be subject to their husbands, & to watch over their Children & set before them an example worthy of imitation. He desired the Saints to reform from all their Wickedness, & put away all their contracted feelings, &c&c. After meeting retorned to Bro Everits & took dinner. While there Ellen Wilding came & staid a short time, then accompanyed sister E & my self to Bro Willcoxs w[h]ere we staid about & houre & ½. Had a pleasent conversation with W[alter] & Maria on diferant points of doctring. From there sister E & I went to singing Scool and had a good sing. Bro Godard was present. Then went & staid all night with Jane.

Monday 4th. A cold day. Took breakfast with Jane, then retorned home and did some sewing, & wrote a little in my Journal, &c&c.

Tuesday 5th. A cold day. After getting breakfast, I went with Mother to the Store, w[h]ere she was going to trade out a bill.

Got me cloth for a pair of garments. On our way home called
to see Maria. After I got home, I cut out a garment for
mother then went to Bro Lambsons to make a visit. Met with
a very warm reception. Sister Robins who had lately arived
from Nauvoo finding I was there came & spent the PM with
us, then perswaided Mrs. La. to let me go and Eat supper
with her, which I did, as she lived in the next house. After
this we retorned to Bro L & spent the Eve very pleasently.
Then Br L accompanid me home. The Snow had been falling
all the PM & eve and was now quite deep.

Wednesday 6th. A very cold day. Got breakfast, then cut out
a garment for Mother & 2 for my self. Eve was sewing.

Thursday 7th. An exceeding cold day. Had only wood
enough to make one fire. Got breakfast, which took us til
noon then being froze out with the cold, I went to sister Janes.
When I got there my hands & feet ached severely. Felt quite
unwell all day from the effects of the cold. Was reading.
Spent the night with Jane.

Friday 8th. A bitter cold day. Staid with Jane. In the AM
Mother came & brought some bread to bake. In the eve Jane
& myself got supper. When it was ready father & Henry
came, and we all took supper together after which we washed
the dishes and spent the eve reading.

Saturday 9th. A very cold day. In the morn baked a corn
cake & sent it to fathers for their breakfast. Then spent the
day makeing a garment. Eve finished it.

Sunday 10th. The weather still very cold. Took breakfast with
Jane, then went to meeting at Bro Russels. Was addrest by
Bishop [Thomas] Lang, Br Russel, & father. Had a good meeting, after wich I called to see Br Harts folks & spent about an
hour with them. Then returned to Janes & took supper, after
which she accompanied me to the singing Scool w[h]ere we
spent the eve very pleasently. Then retorned home.

Monday 11th. A very cold day. Still with Jane. In the morn got breakfast for father & Henry. In the PM helped Jane to fix a dress. Then got supper for F[ather] & H. Eve went with Jane to Bro Fi[e]ldings w[h]ere we spent the eve very pleasently, after which Bro Fielding accompanied us home.

Tuesday 12th. The weather a little more comfortable. In the morn got breakfast for Father & Henry. Washed the dishes & then sat down & wrote a few lines in my Journal. PM baked a shoulder of Lamb. Got supper &c. Father & H Eat with us, Mother having been for 3 days with Maria. Eve I went with Jane & H to a meeting at Bro Allens house w[h]ere we was addressed by Elder W[ilford] Woodruff, who gave us some good instructions in relation to the resurrection of the dead, &c&c. Said if there was any under the sound of his voise who felt as if the journey was to great for them, or the trials to hard for them to endure, his advice too such would be to go into their Waggons & shut themselfs up, as the[y] had no closets, & pray to the Lord to take away their lives, & grant them a burial with the Saints of God, as their death would prove a blessing to their posterity who would ever beleve that their fathers died in full belief of the Gospel of Christ. And when the servants of God should retorn to the places w[h]ere they had buryed their dead, in the morn of the Resurrection, & sound the Trumpit, that should shake the Earth and call them from their slumbering tombs, then they also would receve a resurrection & come forth. W[h]ereas if they should go into Missouri & be buryed there, he did not know who would be to the truble to go there and hunt them up for the[y] would never once think that a Saint of God would be buryed there.

Wednesday 13th. A fair day. In the morn got breakfast, washed the dishes, made the bed &c. Sewed a little on my garment. PM baked a loaf of breads & cleaned a hogs bone and put it to boil & made a pot pye for supper. Then washed the dishes, & spent the Eve sewing.

Thursday 14th. A pleasant day. In the morn got breakfast, washed the dishes, scoured the table, &c. Then carried in some clay to make a new hearth, and pounded it about an hour. PM Bro Hunter called to see us, & staid about an hour. Had a pleasent talk with him after wich I took supper at Br Jennes, it being the next door, & Mother Jacob there on a visit we had a good supper. I then helped do up the work, then assisted Jane a little about her washing. Eve went with her to Bro Scrodshams, one of our neighbors w[h]ere we spent it sewing, and had a social conversation with them.

Friday 15th. A cold stormy snowey day. Morn got breakfast &c then went to Bro Chesters Snyders, & bought 10 pounds of flower for which I paid 31 cents, then returned home & hung out some Cloth[e]s on the line for Jane, wich froze before I could get them on the line. Tried to sew on my garment, but was unable to accomplish much for the cold. Eve helped bring in the cloth[e]s and wood.

Saturday 16th. The weather cold. After cooking breakfast, washing dishes &c&c Jane & myself went to Bro Smithes to make a visit. We spent the day very pleasently. Had an excellent Supper, and at 9 oclock was accompanied home by Bro S.

Sunday 17th. A very cold day. After doing up my work in the morning, I went with Sister Jane to Uncle Willards w[h]ere we spent the PM & took Supper. Then retorned home. On our way called at Bro Grants Scool room, expecting to have a sing, but was disapointed. While at Uncle Ws today Emelia [Amelia] loaned me a Josey to wear through the Winter which had belonged to Elize Ann.

Monday 18th. An exceeding cold day. Got breakfast as usual, then sewed on a garment for Mother. Eve got Supper &c, then sat down and read.

Tuesday 19th. The weather still cold. After getting breakfast, washing dishes, making the bed &c I accompanied Jane to Maria's w[h]ere we spent the day very pleasently. Mother was still with them. I was marking a garment for her. We had a good Supper. In the eve Maria played several tunes on her Accordian. About 9 oclock we retorned home.

Wednesday 20th. The weather more comfortable. Did my Work as Usual, then sat down and wrote a short time in my journal. PM baked a loaf of bread and got Supper. Eve went to Meeting at Bro Van Cotts accompanied by Elsie Snyder. Had a very good meeting.

Thursday 21st. The weather moderate. After doing up my work Sat down and wrote awhile in my Journal. PM was sewing. Also in the eve.

Friday 22st. The weather cold. Was cooking, cleaning house, sewing, &c. Eve Abagil Abbott came to inform me that Bro Van Cott had brought a letter for me from Mo. so I retorned with A to Br V Cs. Got my letter, and found it was from my Bro Johns wife informing me that they were well & prospering. I spent the eve & enjoyed my self much. Before I left Sister V C made me drink Tea & eat Gingebread, wich was quite a treat.

Saturday 23th. The weather cold. Was sewing, &c&c. The house smooked so bad that it was amost impossible to keep any fire.

Sunday 24th. The weather still cold. Went to meeting in Bro Curtis['s] Ward. Had a very good meeting. PM, I was writing. Eve was reading.

Monday 25th. A cold day. Was sewing most of the day. Eve was knitting.

Tuesday 26th. The weather comfortable. Early in the morn Sister Chester Snyder sent for Jane and my self to come to her house for a quilting. We went. Stayed a little while. Then Henry came and informed me that Bro Godard had come to invite me to a party at the Councel house. Sister Snyder excused me and I went up to our tent. Found Bro G waiting for me, so I got ready as quick as posable and accompanid him.

Called at Bro Hendrixs and got his wife, and about 4 oclock
enterd the Councel house. Bro G took me on to the floor for
the first dance. Here for the first time I joined with those who
praised God in the dance. When this figure was formed it
being the first, and Bro Rockwood being at the head, according to order, we all kneeled down and he offerd up a prayer.
We then arose & danced the figure, and so praised God in the
dance. I danced with Bros [Edward] Duwsette, W[illiam]
Cahoon & G[eorge] Grant, and others, and once with Bro
Brigham the mon[e]y musk. Had a very pleasent party and
some good refreshments. About 11 oclock every man took his
partner or partners & marched 3 times round the room. We
were then dismised with the blessings of God. Bro G accompanied me to sister Janes w[h]ere I spent the nigh[t].

Wednesday 27th. Moderate weather.

And Thursday 28th. Was sewing kniting &c&c.

Friday 29. We had a little snow. After getting breakfast &
doing up my work I went up to our Tent. Found a good fire
in the stove. Was there all alone for several hours, writing a
letter to my far absent husband. Felt very lonely although it
seemed good to be alone awhile communicating my thoughts
to that absent freind who is dearer to me yes far dearer than
all others. About 5 PM I returned to Janes. Got supper &c,
then went with Elsy Snyder to the Singing Scool. On our way
called at Maria's. Found her about ready so we all went together. There were more of C[h]oir tonight at the Councel
house than had ever been seen together since we left Nauvoo.
We sung for about an hour & ½ then danced til ½ past 11. I
danced with Godard bros Duzette, Chatman and others, and
once with little Brigham Young, and 3 Couple of little
Children. It was the Anniversary of the night I was marrid and
I told some of the Sisters that I was celebrating it &c. We had
a very pleasent time, but my thoughts were wandering on by
gone day[s] and I could not help recalling to mind the many
changes that have taken place since that night [a] year ago.
Then was I happy in the Sociaty of the only one I ever loved

179

but now more than 5000 miles separates us from each other, and the ever restless oacian [ocean] rolls between us but hope still whispers we shall meet again. About 12 oclock I came to Sister Janes w[h]ere I spent the night.

Saturday 30th. The weather somewhat comfortable. After doing my mornings work I again went up to the Tent and spent the day writing. Evening returned to Janes and got supper &c after which I was knitting.

Sunday 31st Weather cold. Went with Jane to meeting in her ward. Brother Curtis preached to us, & said we were now enjoying a day of Jub[i]lee, but days of truble were yet before us, in which we should be tried in every thing. But if we endured our trials patiantly, our reward would be great. His sermone was very interessting. In the PM we went to the Council House w[h]ere we were addrest by Bro [William W.] Majer & Bro from London. Bro Brigham bore testemony to what Bro M had said. The de[s]course was very interessting. After meeting I called at Watters, w[h]ere I stayed & took supper. I then called to see Sistern Benson and staid afew minutes with her. Had a pleasant little chat. Afterwards Maria & myself went to Singing Scool which was held at Bro G Grants scool room. We had a very good sing, after which I went with E Snyder to Janes w[h]ere I spent the night.

[February 1847]

Monday Febuary first. A cold day. Janes chimaney smooked very bad, so that it kept the tears runing down my cheeks about all the time. Was very uncomfortable. Did a little sewing, and in the eve was knitting.

Tuesday 2nd and Wednesday 3rd. The weather still cold. Did some writing sewing &c. The smook trubbled us considerable.

Thursday 4th. A Cold day. I was writing in my journal. Eve[n]ing, went to meeting at Bro Van Cotts. Had a very good meeting.

Friday 5th and Saturday 6. The weather cold. Was writing some in my letters sewing, knitting, cooking &c&c.

Sunday 7th. The weather comfortable. Went with Jane to meeting in her ward. From there we went to the Councel House to meeting, where we were addrest by Bro Zebedee Colt[r]en, followed by several of the Brethren on the subject of the Saints being united, showing the nessessity of their being so. I then went to Bro James Smithises w[h]ere I spent the night.

Monday 8th. The weather comfortable. I cut & fitted a dress for Sister S[mithies] and spent the day sewing on it. Eve I visited with Sister [Vilate] Kimball and had a sweet talk with her. Saw her little Son Solomon who was then but a few days old. Night slept with Sister Egan.

Tuesday 9th. The weather cold. Was at Bro Smithes sewing on Sister Ann's dress. Eve I went with them to the Council House w[h]ere there was a party assembled. This eve I danced with Bros Grant Duzette & Pitt & once [a] kethlian [cotillion] with Bro Brigham and when he took me to my seat he said Sister Mary you have learned me I am very much obliged to you, &c. We spent the evning very pleasently and about 12 oclock returned home. I spent the rest of the night with Sister Egan.

Wednesday 10th. The weather cold. Spent the day at Brother Smithes sewing on her dress. Eve I visited at Bro Orson [K.] Whitney's. Had a very pleasent visit with Ellen [Helen Mar Kimball Whitney]. She repeated or said over some verses to me that her Mother Sister [Vilate] Kimball had composed the next morn after her little Son Solomon was born. The first *verse is all I remember. It is as follows.* The Lord has blessed us with another Son Which is the seventh I have Born May he be the father of many lives. *But not the Husband of many Wives.* Before I left, Bro O orderd a bowl of hot Punch to be made, and Made us all drink of it freely. I then went to Sister Egans where I spent the night.

Patty Bartlett Sessions (1795-1892)

Perhaps because she was a midwife who daily ushered new spirits into life, Patty Sessions had a gift for tying together heaven and earth. Having lost six of her nine children, Patty could bid a dying friend take word to them and then join with other Saints in community dancing. She was as comfortable prophesying in tongues as she was planting horseradish, and her diary is a remarkable blend of things temporal and spiritual.

Born in Bethel, Maine, the daughter of Enoch and Anna Ball Bartlett, Patty was only seventeen when she married David Sessions. She was baptized a Latter-day Saint in 1834, and David followed her a year later. They joined the Saints in Missouri, taking with them their teenaged children Sylvia and David and their oldest son, Perrigrine, and his wife. A farmer and stockraiser, the elder David tried to establish a new home at Far West, but within a year he and his son Perrigrine lost what property they had collectively owned. During that same year Sylvia married Windsor Palmer Lyon and Patty lost her sixth child.[24]

The Sessions family followed the Saints to Nauvoo, and there Patty became known as "Mother Sessions," an experienced midwife whose assistance was to be in demand among the Saints for several decades. In connection with her midwifery, Patty was skilled in the medicinal use of herbs, and she served, in that sense, as one of the few "doctors" accompanying the Saints westward. Her skills were constantly put to use, as is shown by the daily accounting of her activities at Winter Quarters that follows. Patty continued her midwifery practice in Salt Lake City until 1872, when she moved to Bountiful, the settlement her son Perrigrine had founded north of the city. There she raised fruit and built a school to serve her grandchildren and the poor.

Several holograph volumes of her diary, 1846-1880, are located in the Historical Department of the Church. Minimal punctuation has been added to the excerpt presented here.

Photograph of Patty Bartlett Sessions, probably taken at the time of her death in 1892. (Portrait Collection. LDS Church Archives.)

[January 1847]

Friday Jan. 1 [1847] I had a new years party. Eliza Snow, Loiza Beaman [Young] Zina Jacobs &c were here. Enjoyed myself well. Opened and read the sixtyeth chapter of Is[a]iah. P G [Perrigrine Sessions] came home from Mo [Missouri].

Brought 30 bushels corn meal 8:00 lb pork—16 [pounds] shugar 4 gallons molases.

Saturday 2 Tried my lard. Went to a party to Br Winchesters.

Sunday 3 Wrote a letter to David.

Monday 4 Put Erastus Snows wife to bed. Helped take care of the meat.

Tuesday 5 I have been out all night had no sleep. Put sister Alexander to bed. Came home. Wrote a letter to Mother. Sent both to St Lo[u]is by Br Scott. P G has started off to go to the rush bottoms hunting. Broke down the waggon. Elsworth came back got another.

Wednesday 6 I have baked some mince pies. Cal[l]ed to sister Cynth[i]a sealed [to] G[eorge] P Dikes [Dykes].

Thursday 7 Put her to bed with her 20th child. I have visited the sick.

Friday 8 Put Loiza, Adaline & Melissa all to bed in 6 hours and a half.

Saturday 9 P G came home. Visited the sick.

Sunday 10 Visited the sick.

Monday 11 Cal[l]ed to sister Empy. Staid all night. She got better.

Tuesday 12 Brigham [Young], Heber [C. Kimball] & wives were here on a visit.

Wednesday 13. Put sister Hall to bed. Visited many sick.

Thursday 14 Put sister Knight to bed. Miscariage yesterday. Visited the sick today. Spun some yarn for a comforter.

Friday 15 Put Harriet F--- Wicksome to bed. Sister Empy sent for me. Child born before I got there.

Saturday 16 Put sister Egleston to bed.

Sunday 17 Had a good [unclear] meeting at the Marker[?]. Put sister Patsy to bed.

Monday 18 Put sister Avery to bed.

Tuesday 19 Visited the sick. We were chose in to Br Heber's Co[mpany].

Wednesday 20 Visited the sick. Eliza Snow was here. Made me a cap.

Thursday 21 Went to Br Leonards to a party. I visited the sick.

Friday 22 Eliza Snow was here again.

Saturday 23 Visited the sick.

Sunday 24 Went to meeting. Heard a revelation read then visited the sick.

Monday 25 [K]niting Mr Sessions a comforter.

Tuesday 26 Caled to Hannah Jones. Talked to her for her bad conduct then I went to the Bishop to have a bedstead fixed up for her and to make her comfortable although I thought she was a bad woman. Yet she lay on the ground and about to be confined and I pit[i]ed her.

Wednesday 27 Visited her again. Set her son to fix her bedsted.

Thursday 28 Put William Wicks[?] wife to bed. Caled on for counsel by Sabre Grible. Caled on again to visit Hannah.

Friday 29 Sabre came again for me. I went to see Sister [Elizabeth Ann] Whiteney and others that were sick.

Saturday 30 Visited the sick.

Sunday 31 Went to meeting.

Monday Febr 1st. Wet the down the seach[?] and visited the sick.

Tuesday 2 Out all night. Put Alvin Clements wife to bed.

Wednesday 3 Visited sick and baked mince pies.

Thursday 4 My birthday. Fifty two years old Febr 4 1847 in the camp of Isrial Winter Quarters. We had brandy and drank a toast to each other desireing and wishing the blesings of God to be with us all and that we might live and do all that we came here into this world to do.[25] Eliz Snow came here after me to go to a litle party in the evening. I was glad to see her. Told her it was my birthday and she must bless me. She said if I would go to the party they all would bless me. I then went and put James Bullock wife to bed then went to the party. Had a good time singing praying speaking in toungues[26] Before we brake up I was caled away to sister Morse then to sister Whitney then back to sister Morse. Put her to bed [at] 2 o clock.

Friday 5 This morning I have been to see sister Whitney. She is better. I then went to Joanna Rounda [Roundy]. She said it was the last time I should see her in this world. She was going to see my children. I sent word by her to them. I then went to the Silver Grey party.[27] Eliza Snow went with us. I danced with Br Knolton[?] Mr Sessions not being well. Joanna died this evening.

Saturday 6 Made soap. Visited some that were sick then went put sister Whitney to bed. She had a son born eleven o clock P M.

Sunday 7 Warm and pleasant. I went to meeting then visited the sick. Br Hathaway came here.

Monday 8 Finished making soap.

Tuesday 9 Visited the sick. P G gone hunting.

Wednesday 10 Visited the sick. Did me up some caps and caled to see sister Lamb.

Thursday 11 Put sister Lambs to bed. Came home eat breakfast then went to get some one to take care of sister Knight.

Traveled around untill afternoon. Eliz Mitchel said she would take care of her. I came home very tired. Br Kimbal said he would say for himself and in behalf of Joseph that I had done my part for her.

Friday 12 oclock [unclear] to Sister Dun. Child born before I got there. I then visited the sick. Br. John Young and wife visited us. Had a good time.

Saturday 13 Visited sisters Buel and Rockwell. Had the wild hairs puled out of my eyelids. My eyes very sore.

Sunday 15 [14] Went to meeting then in the evening collected Zina Jacobs, Eliza Snow, sister Marcum [Markham] at sister Buels to pray for Sylvia and child that they might be delivered from bondage and Windsor and David come here with them. We prayed sung in toungues spoke in tongues and had a good time. Then went to put Sister Oakley to bed. Child born 4 oclock A M.

Monday 15 I have been out all night had no sleep. Visited the sick all day.

Tuesday 16 We wash. Visited the sick. Sister Young died 15th at sister Holmons.

Wednesday 17 Visited the sick then carded some wool.

Thursday 18 Visited the sick.

Friday 19 Visited with sister Hyde at Loizas. She is making me a dress.

Saturday 20 Visited the sick. It snows. P G came home from hunting.

Sunday 21 There is more snow than I have seen at once since I left Maine. Dont go to meeting. Caled to sister Devenport.

Monday 22 Stayed all night. Visited the sick.

Tuesday 23 Visited the sick yesterday I cooked for the widow orphan and poor that they might feast and have thier hearts made glad today in the counsel house.

Wednesday 24 Spun 2 skeins then visited the sick.

Thursday 25 To sister Mary Ann Nobles. She was sick all day.

Friday 26 Wrote to Sylvia. Send two letters to her by Perrigrine. Put Mary Kimbal to bed. Out all night.

Saturday 27 Put Mary Ann Nobles to bed. P G starts this morning for Sylvia. I visited the sick.

Sunday 28 Br and sister Leonard and sister Buel was here last night. We spoke in tongues and had a good time.

Monday March 1st Spun. Went to Br Tomases. Put his wife to bed.

Tuesday 2 Carded and spun some wool. Strained some honey. I went to bed sick.

Wednesday 3 Not well to day.

Thursday 4 Visited the sick.

Friday 5 Not well.

Saturday 6 Not well. Picked some wool.

Sunday 7 Did not go to meeting. I visited the sick. Precinda [Huntington Buel] and Zina [Diantha Huntington Jacobs] was here.

Monday 8 Put Sister Mary Dykes to bed. Fornatus Duston Josiah Call and wives came here.

Tuesday 9 Fixed the [wool] cards. Set over some of the teeth.

Wednesday 10 Put Wm Davies wife to bed then visited the sick.

Thursday 11 Visited the sick all day. Got a [spinning] wheel. At night put Almira Devenport to bed.

Friday 12 Carded spun and visited the sick.

Saturday 13 Carded spun visited sister Gean [Gheen] with E[liza] R Snow sister Chase.

Sunday 14 To meeting to Br J Wolace. Br Kimball preached.

Monday 15 Put sister Stilman to bed. Visited the sick. Sister E R Snow came here last night. She has done me up a cap and wrote me some poetry which she composed which I shall write here.[28] *[There follows the poem, "Composed for Mrs Patty Sessions By Miss E R Snow March 15 1847," the first stanza of which reads:]*

> *Truth and holiness and love,*
> *Wisdom honor, joy and peace—*
> *That which cometh from above,*
> *In your pathway shall increase.*

Tuesday 16 Eliza Snow left here. I visited the sick and also Mary Pearce. She died to day.

Wednesday 17 She was buried. I went to the funeral. Brigham [Young] preached. I then visited the sick. Mr Sessions and I went and laid hands on the widow Holmans step daughter. She was healed. I was sent for to go to a private meeting with Brighams family. Did not go. Mr Sessions wished me to go another way. I went.

Thursday 18 I visited the sick.

Friday 19 Eliza Snow came here to dinner. We then went and visited sister Whitney.

Saturday 20 Scoured yarn.

Sunday 21 Went to meeting. Br Brigham told his dream of seeing Joseph the charge he had to this people from him [Joseph] to keep the spirit of the Lord. I then visited the sick.[29]

Monday 22 I commenced [k]niting a comforter. Harvy Call came down from Punchaw [Ponca, Nebraska].

Tuesday 23 Visited sister Martindale. She is very sick. Then visited sisters Buel Jacobs and Leonard. Mr Sessions came in the evening.

Wednesday 24. Visited the sick.

[A list of home remedies is included on the page between these two dates, including "for bowel complaint take tea one spoonful of rubarb one forth corbnet soda one table spoonful brandy one tea spoonful peperment essence half tea cup ful warm water take a table spoonful once an hour untill it opperates."]

Thursday 25 Finished comforter. Visited the sick.

Friday 26 Br Belnap sent me a quarter of dear meat. I divided it with sisters Kimbal and Buel then went to a special meeting. Brigham preached.

Saturday 27 Visited the sick.

Sunday 28 Went to meeting. All the twelve preached that was here. My leg is lame and I rode with Br Snows family.

Monday 29 I bought 5 cents worth of horse redish. Set some of it out, sowed some garden seeds in trays of dirt and put some more into the ground.

Tuesday 30 [K]nit on another comforter. I was sent for to go to sister Leonards. I went, in the evening they sent for Mr Sessions. We prayed spoke in tongues interpreted prophesied and had a good visit.

Wednesday 31 I [k]nit and visited the sick.

[April 1847]

Thursday April 1st Put Sarah wife P P Pratt to bed. Visited with sister Knight at Sister Buels. Mr Sessions and I then visited the sick and anointed and laid hands and [said] a blessing.

Friday 2 Took up our beaf. Sold 75 lb to Br Litle. I have finished the comforters one for Mr Sessions the other for Peri- grin. We have let the Pioneers have 24 pounds of pork, 2 bushels of corn meal. Let them have it March 31.

Saturday 3 Visited the sick. Sisters Buel & Knight were here visiting. I was caled to Br Waggoners wife in the evening.

Sunday 4 Went to meeting then visited the sick.

Monday 5 Commenced to [k]nit Marys mits. Visited the sick.

Tuesday 6 Went to conferrence. 12 o'cl[ock] ajorned sinedi [sine die]. I then visited the sick. Received a letter from Windsor & Sylvia dated 7 of Feb.

Wednesday 7 The Pioneers mostly started. Sister Holmon was here on a visit.

Thursday 8 Parley P Pratt has returned from England.

Friday 9 The most of the twelve have started as pioneers expecting to come back next monday. I visited the sick.

Saturday 10 Opened a chest aired the things mended some. Finished Marys mits.

Sunday 11 Went to meeting. Parley preach[ed]. Gave us a history of his journey to England. I then visited the sick.

Monday 12 I visited the sick. Sister Horn gave me 75 cents for Doctoring her when sick.

Tuesday 13 Visited sister E R Snow with sister Leonard. Had a good time. Spoke in toungues and prophesied. The spirit of the Lord was with us. I visited others that was sick also.

Wednesday 14 The twelve came back on monday as they expected and have started again this morning for the moun- tains. Br Taylor came home from England last night. He and Parley has not gone to the mountains.

Thursday 15 Lewis Robinson and family arived last night. Brought me a letter from W P Lyon. Sisters Leonard Lamb &

Miller visited me today. Mr Sessions and I were caled to anoint and lay hands on sister Holman. We then went to sister Leonards. Had a feast of the spirit of the Lord. [K]nit Lucina a pair of mits.

Friday 16 I have been to a number of places to collect pay that was due me but got but one half bushel meal. Mary Elen is here cut[t]ing Carlos some clothes. This evening visited sister Pitts child. It was dying.

Saturday 17 It is dead. I [k]nit me a pair of mits. Brewed some beer.

Sunday 18 It is quite cool this morning. Porter [Rockwell] and others starts to go on with the pioneers. I visited E R Snow & sister Leonard. They are not well.

Monday 19 Looked over my chests.

Tuesday 20 Sisters Leonard & Buel were here on a visit.

Wednesday 21 1 oclock P G and Sylvia and child come. I was almost overcome with joy and gratitude to God for our pres-ervation to see each other again. David could not get the team over the river and it raind and I could not go and see him. His father went and caried him some vi[c]tuals and see him.

Thursday 22 1 oclock David came. I was almost overcome again. My children all that were living were soon seated around the table with their Father and Mother. We rejoiced together and thanked the lord. I then was caled to see the sick.

Friday 23 We visited the sisters and brethren all day. In the evening David went to a party. They prayed and danced and prayed again. Sylvia her Father and I with a few more sisters met at Br Leonards. He was gone but Mr Sessions presided and we had a good time. We prayed prop[h]esied and spoke in toungues and interpreted and were refreshed.

Saturday 24 We visited and were visited all day.

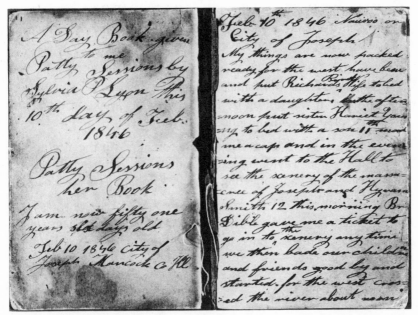

Inside front cover and first page of 1846-1849 diary of Patty Bartlett Sessions. (Holograph, LDS Church Archives.)

Sunday 25 Went to meeting. Br Taylor preached. We then visited sisters Nobels & Ashba.

Monday 26 Went to several places. Br Mager [William W. Major] is taking our portraits. Visited at sister Pearces with sisters Young Kimbal Whitney & E R Snow and others. In the evening we all went to the girls house. Had a meeting. It was good.

Tuesday 27 Visited Sister Kimbal and others and rode out to the bur[y]ing ground.

Wednesday 28 Visited Lucy & Francis & Laura Pitkins and many others. Put sister Van Waggoner to bed.

Thursday 29 Visited Sary Ann and sister Whitney. Sylvia had a chill at sister Buels as we visited her in the forenoon. We prayed and laid hands on her. She was better.

Friday 30 We visited the girls at Brighams. E R Snow and myself made arrangement to have the mothers in Isriel meet at sister Leonards and have a prayer meeting.

Saturday May 1st Sylvia and I went to a meeting to Sister Leonards. None but females there. We had a good meetting. I presided. It was got up by E R Snow. They spoke in toungues. I interpreted. Some prophesied. It was a feast.

Sunday 2 Went to meeting in the forenoon. In the afternoon visited sisters Taylor took dinner then took supper with sister Noon. Then had a meeting to sister Kimbals. There we had a feast of the good spirit.

Monday 3 Have been writing a letter to mother. Then went to sister Youngs. Visited in the afternoon. Had a meeting in the evening.

Tuesday 4 Sylvia packed up her things to go hom[e]. Br Calls came from Punckaw [Ponca].

Wednesday 5 They are here yet. David drove to the river. The wind blew so they could not cross. Came back. Sylvia and I visited Loiza. E R Snow has composed some poetry for Sylvia. I will write it here in my book.[30] [There follows the poem addressed "To Mrs Sylvia P Lyon by Miss E R Snow." The first stanza reads:]

> Go thou loved one God is with thee—
> He will be thy stay and shield,
> And fulfill each precious promise
> Which his spirit will direct.

May Thursday 6 Put Helen Kimbal to bed. The child still born. David could not get over the river.

Friday 7 Could not get over the river. We washed.

Saturday 8 Got the waggon over but concluded to wait for W W Phelps.

Sunday 9 It is Davids birthday 23 years old and the same time of day that he was born. He and Sylvia left me on the bank of Missouri river. Started for home. Mr Sessions went over and saw them leave the river. O may the Lord speed them in all safety home. May they keep the spirit of gathering and with all their connection[s] gather up their substance and come to us again as soon as the Lord will is my prayer. Mr Sessions an[d] I returned to the house. Went to meeting. Counsel was given for the saf[e]ty of our catle and also for raising a crop. In the evening I was sent for to go and lay hands on Zinas child. We had a prayer meeting.

Monday 10 We have over ha[u]led our chests.

Tuesday 11 Sister Lenard & Buel were here on a visit. Sister Buel had the toothache bad. We laid hands on her.

Wednesday 12 I have mended some. Visited the sick.

Thursday 13 E R Snow is here making me some caps.

Friday 14 Visited with E R Snow Loiza Beaman & sister Pearce at sister Taylors. Had a good visit.

Saturday 15 E R Snow here again. Finished my caps. Made me three.

Sunday 16 She staid all night. It rained. I went up to the girls with her. We had a meeting.

Monday 17 I was caled to George Grants child last night. I was sick. Visited the sick today. Saw Amos Davis. Heard from Sylvia & David. He met them fifty miles this side of Mt. Pisgah.

Tuesday 18 Visited the sick in several places. Anointed and laid hands on sister Murrys son.

Wednesday 19 Visited the sick then put Jedidiah Grants wife to bed. Then went to sister Levets to meeting. 18 sisters met. We spoke in toungue[s], interpreted and had a good time.

Thursday 20 Put sister Isaac Brown to bed and visited the sick in the rain.

Friday 21 Fair weather. Visited the sick and tacked a comforter. Got 4 lb coffee of sister Benson.

Saturday 22 Fixed the waggon cover. Visited the sick.

Sunday 23 Jed. Grant got home. I went to meeting.

Monday 24 Visited sick. A steam boat name[d] Archer came up today. A man fell off of the boat and was drowned this afternoon.

Tuesday 25 Went onto the steamboat Archer. Found the wife of the man that fell of[f] the boat. Took her to meeting at sister Buels. There we comforted her. I visited the sick before and after meeting.

Wednesday 26 Visited the sick. Isaac Browns child died while I was there.

Thursday 27 Made soap. Visited sister Cutler with E R Snow and others. Had a good [time]. Prayed and sung and spoke as the Lord directed.

Friday 28 Made more soap. Have got over 50 pound hard soap. Let a kind of a Br Lewis have 25 pounds of good grease. I have not got only soap to do a part of one washing and that was poor stuff for all the grease.

Sattyrday 29. Packed 186 pounds of pork for the mountains. I then went to collect some debts. Got nothing. Then went to a meeting to Eliza Beamans with many of the sisters. Sisters Young and Whitney laid their hands upon my head and predicted many things that I should be blesed with that I should live to stand in a temple yet to be built and Joseph [Smith] would be there. I should see him and there I should officiate for my labours should then be done in order and they should be great and I should be blessed and by many and there I should bless many and many should be brought unto me saying your hands were the first that handled me bless me

196

and after I had blesed them their mothers would rise up and bless me for they would be brought to me by Joseph himself for he loved litle children and he would bring my litle ones to me and my heart was fil[le]d with joy and rejoicing.

Sunday 30 Sister E R Snow and others had a good time at sister Buels with a few then all went to Sister Tomson. Many more came. Had feast of the good things of the kingdom there. In the evening we went to sister Kimbans [Kimball's?]. Had a glories feast of feeling and hearing.

Monday 31 Pack and loaded our waggon and slept in it.

Tuesday June 1 Sister E R Snow is here. The girls wash some for her. She lines Carlos hat. We had a feast in the afternoon at sister Millers. There we blessed and got blessed. I blesed sister Christeen by laying my hands upon her head and the Lord spoke through me to her great and marvelous things. At the close I thought I must ask a blessing at sister Kimbals hand but it came to me that I must first bless her and show Herbers girls the Order that duty caled them to perform to get many blessings from her upon them. I obeyed. Layed my hands upon her head although it was a great cross and the power of God came upon me. I spoke great and marvelous things to her. She was fil[l]ed to the overflowing. She arose and blesed the Lord and caled down a blessing on us and all that pertained to her. Sister Hess fell on her knees and claimed a blessing at my hands. I then blessed her. Sister Chase claimed a blessing of Sister Kimbal. She blessed her with me. She spoke great things to her. The power of God was poured out upon us. E R Snow was there and with many others. Thank the Lord.

Wednesday 2. It rains.

Thursday 3 Fair weather. We expect [to] start to morrow for the mountains. I caled to Sarah Anns this evening with E R Snow. Sisters Whitney and Kimbal came in. We had a good time. Things were given to us that we were not to tell of but to ponder them in our hearts and proffit thereby. Before we went down there E Beaman, E[liza or Emily] Partrige, Zina Jacobs came here laid their hands on my head blesed me and so did E R Snow. Thank the Lord.

Friday 4 We do not go today. Mr Sessions and I went to Br Leonards to a party. We had a feast of good things both temporal and spirutal [spiritual]. When going there I caled to Sister Kimbals and with E R Snow blesed Helen and Genette. Then in the gift of toungues E R Snow sung a blesing to all the rest of the girls. Then we went to Br Leonards.

Saturday 5 We start for the mountains or a resting place and leave Winter Quarters. Ten years today since we left our home and friends in Maine. We now leave many good friends here and I hope they will soon follow on to us. I drive one four ox team go 4 miles camp.

Chapter Seven

Immigration

"Some Little Description of My Travels"

"I am now, with my children, about to leave forever my native land in order to gather with the Church of Christ, in the valley of the Great Salt Lake." So wrote Jean Rio Griffiths Baker, a convert of two years, as she prepared to leave London in January 1851. Forty-nine years of age and recently widowed, Jean Rio was one of 15,000 British converts who left England for Utah between 1849 and 1857. Patience Loader was another; in 1856 she, with her parents and brothers and sisters, boarded a Mormon immigrant ship at Liverpool to begin the journey to the Zion newly established in the tops of the Rocky Mountains.

The gathering that had commenced when the Saints first assembled in Ohio, and had continued in Missouri and Illinois, took on new meaning and strength as the main body of Saints settled in Utah. They saw in the building of their Great Basin kingdom the literal fulfillment of Isaiah's prophecy "that the mountain of the Lord's house shall be established in the top of the mountains, and shall be exalted above the hills; and all nations shall flow unto it." During the 1850s missionaries were sent to Europe, Latin America, the Pacific Islands, India, Asia, and South Africa, carrying out the commission to teach all nations and gather together the dispersed children of Israel from the four corners of the earth.[1]

Elders instructed those whom they baptized—new members of the spiritual community of Saints—to join with the temporal community of Saints in Utah in order to "rear a Temple unto the Lord . . . to more fully keep the commandments of God than they can here in Babylon

River view of the city of New Orleans, after an illustration published
in *Harper's Weekly*, 1867. (Leonard V. Huber Collection. Historic New Orleans
Collection. New Orleans, Louisiana.)

. . . [and to] be near where the Prophets and Apostles of God reside."[2]
Missionary success outside of Europe was minimal during this early
period, but in Europe, particularly in the British and Scandinavian
missions, it was phenomenal. When Patience Loader sailed from Liverpool in 1856, she and her family accompanied nearly five hundred
Danish Saints to New York. At that time the Scandinavian Mission
was baptizing some one thousand converts each year, about one-
fourth of whom gathered to Utah.

This mass migration of new converts to Zion required organization
and means, both of which the Church provided through the Perpetual
Emigrating Company. Incorporated in 1850, the company supervised
migration and administered the Perpetual Emigration Fund, a fund
based on donations of cash and property from Saints in the Great
Basin. There were converts, such as Jean Rio Baker, whose personal
means adequately covered their journey to Utah, but thousands of
emigrants—butchers, shoemakers, weavers, clerks, farmers—depended on the rotating fund to assist in or totally finance their westward
travel. Ideally, as they repaid their indebtedness the PEF could finance
further migration. Despite the fact that many debts were never repaid,
the PEF financed emigration until its dissolution in 1887. By that time
the Church was firmly established, and Church leaders placed less
emphasis on building a stronghold of Saints in Utah.

Liverpool agents for the PEF chartered ships for emigrants or, if it
was not possible to charter a full ship, an agent arranged to have part
of the ship sectioned off for Mormons. On board, Saints were organized into wards or branches with returning missionaries presiding

over each group. Larger ships had as many as twelve wards, sometimes formed according to language groups. In her diary Jean Rio recounted aspects of daily life during her eight weeks on board the *George W. Bourne,* including such details as the role of the presiding elders and shipboard provisions for bathing. Conditions varied from ship to ship, though Mormons were generally well known for their organization and orderliness. Morning and evening prayers, ship-cleaning, and religious classes were typically part of the daily routine.

In 1851 the *George W. Bourne* carried Jean Rio and other Saints from Liverpool to New Orleans, where PEF agents booked their steamboat passage up the Mississippi River to St. Louis. By the mid-1850s, the New Orleans route was abandoned in favor of Atlantic crossings to New York, Philadelphia, or Boston with passage to St. Louis by rail. This was the route followed by Patience Loader and her family in 1856. From St. Louis the Saints continued to outfitting posts in Iowa.

PEF agents outfitted Saints with teams and wagons to prepare them for the overland journey. "A life of toil, fatigue, and privations, to which we are unaccustomed," Jean Rio anticipated. Five months of travel across the Plains was wearying but bearable for most. Many immigrant families encountered sickness and death in the course of the rugged crossing, but the only large-scale tragedies occurred in 1856 when two companies of European Saints, including the Loaders, left Iowa City late in the season. Church leaders had hoped that large numbers of poor Saints could walk across the Plains carrying their possessions in handcarts, and the safe arrival in Salt Lake City of the first three handcart companies in fall 1856 seemed to fulfill their hopes.[3]

In the meantime, however, the Willie and Martin companies had been stalled in Iowa City awaiting completion of their handcarts. Due to their late start, they were caught in early snows in Wyoming. Rescue teams arriving from the Salt Lake Valley in mid-October were shocked to learn that more than two hundred members of these companies had frozen to death. "We know that if God had not been with us that our strength would have failed us and bodys would have been left on the plains as hundreds of our poor brothers and sisters was," Patience testified after she arrived in Salt Lake City. By 1860, the last year for handcarts, over three thousand Saints had walked to Zion. Beginning in 1869 immigrating Saints came to Utah by rail.

The gathering to Zion was an experience of unparalleled newness for Saints who had never before been away from their native lands. Like many other immigrants, Jean Rio Baker and Patience Loader sought to capture the richness of their new experiences by writing them down for others. Patience loved to recreate her traveling companions by relating their very words and conversations. Jean Rio carefully drew word pictures to share new landscapes and cities with her family in England. "As you are aware," she wrote them, "I am not one to go through the world with my eyes shut." Her eyes since have opened more eyes than she might have imagined.

Jean Rio Griffiths Baker (Pearce) (1810-1883)

Unlike most of the immigrants who journeyed to the Great Basin, Jean Rio Griffiths Baker left England with a fine education and considerable means. Her daily accounting of the journey from Liverpool to Utah is the work of a woman of remarkable perception and literary skill. The record is not reminiscent, however, and only sketchy facts exist concerning Jean Rio's life previous to her immigration. The daughter of John Walter and Susanna Burgess Griffiths, Jean Rio married Henry Baker, a civil engineer, in 1832. The couple were baptized Latter-day Saints in London in the summer of 1849, following the example of their oldest son. Henry died that fall, leaving Jean Rio and seven children well provided for.[4]

When the Bakers boarded the *George W. Bourne* at Liverpool in January 1851, they were an even dozen among the 281 passengers en route to New Orleans. Jean Rio traveled with her six sons: Henry, William, Edward, John, Charles, and Josiah; her daughter, Elizabeth Ann; and four in-laws. Nearly all the passengers on the *George W. Bourne* were Latter-day Saints, and Jean Rio provides some telling glimpses of their interactions as a shipboard congregation.

The excerpt selected for this chapter includes the first four months of the diary Jean Rio kept for about fifteen months, until March 1852, when she settled in Ogden supposing she had "finished my ramblings for my whole life." A few additional entries indicate that she married Edward Pearce in 1864, but was widowed within six months. In 1869 she moved to California, and she returned to Utah only briefly to visit her children. The following excerpt is taken from a photocopy of a typescript in the Historical Department of the Church. The location of the original is unknown. Spelling and punctuation have been standardized.

> January 4, 1851. I this day took leave of every acquaintance I could gather together, in all human probability never to see

Jean Rio Griffiths Baker.
(Portrait Collection.
LDS Church Archives.)

them again on earth. I am now, with my children, about to leave forever my native land, in order to gather with the Church of Christ, in the valley of the Great Salt Lake in North America.

Jan. 5. Left London for Liverpool. On arriving at Euston found that the train had gone two hours [before]. Took lodging for the night.

Jan. 6. Arrived in Liverpool at 8 P.M.

Jan. 7. Passed our medical examination and went on board the ship *George W. Bourne,* on which our passage is taken. Myself, six sons, one daughter, one daughter-in-law and my late husband's brother and Uncle [Jeremiah Bateman] and Aunt [Mary Ann Bateman]. Also Mr. [Zachariah] and Mrs. [Mary Shepherd] Derrick and four children.

Jan. 8. Myself and eldest son paid a visit to Mrs. Naish at Oxton in Cheshire. I have now, I suppose, seen the last of all my friends in this country.

Jan. 11. The ship towed out onto the river to be ready for a fair wind.

Jan. 12. Sunday. Meeting on deck in the afternoon, spent the evening in singing.

Jan 13. Provisions served out for a week. Laughed heartily at our supply of oatmeal, 70 pounds![5]

Jan. 15. The ship has just got foul of the mooring chains of a government hulk, and lost her largest anchor and cable. The wind has been very high the last four days but against us. The ship rolls as badly as if she were off the North Finland in a gale and that is no joke, as I well know.

Jan. 17. The anchor has just been fished up.

Jan. 19 Sunday. Wind still contrary. Meeting held between decks.

Jan. 23. Shift of wind in our favor. At 10 A.M. the tug hauled us out of the [Mersey] river into the Irish Sea. At 6 P.M. the wind turned dead against us. More than half of the passengers sick, and we who have escaped are obliged to hold onto anything that comes in our way in order to keep on our feet.

Jan 24. The wind blowing tremendously—only 10 out of our company of 181, but are seasick. Myself, I am happy to say, with Eliza, are in the minority.[6]

Jan. 25. We have had a dreadful night; the ship has seemed as if she really must turn over several times. Some of the passengers terribly frightened, but as for myself, the sea has never had any terror for me at any time. One of the sisters delivered of a fine healthy boy this A.M.

Jan. 26. Sunday. Meeting between decks. Sacrament administered, after which a couple were married by our President Elder [William] Gibson.

Jan. 30. I went on deck today—the first time in a week, and a bad week it has been. All my children, except Eliza, have been sick. Contrary winds all the time. The wind has not advanced us twenty miles for the past six days.

Jan. 31. A clear view of the Irish Coast. It appears very moun-
tainous at this distance, quite as much so as the Welsh Coast.
Saw many fishing boats in Dublin Bay—also five ships. This
wind has changed in our favor, and if it continues, we hope
soon to be out of the horrible Irish Sea. My dear little Josiah
continues very weak, but is not, I think, any worse than when
we left home. Oh how I pray that the sea may return his
health.

Feb. 1. We are going at the rate of eleven miles an hour. Mr.
and Mrs. Derrick are very poorly, also Aunt and John. The
dear child has suffered more from sickness than any of us.
Josiah has escaped it and I hope is recovering.

Feb. 2. Sunday. We are now on the broad Atlantic, the wind
still favorable. Meeting as usual. Cooked our last piece of
fresh meat this day.

Feb. 3. Plenty of wind—going at twelve miles an hour. Seven
or eight porpoises playing around the vessel . Passed a Dutch
ship, which saluted us.

Feb. 4. Spoke to an English schooner. Wind not as good.

Feb. 6. Almost a dead calm the last two days. The folks at
home are, I suppose, sitting by good fire while we are on the
deck enjoying the view of a smooth sea in warm sunshine.

Feb. 9. Sunday. Meeting on deck. A fresh breeze has just
sprung up.

Feb. 14. Still favorable wind. We have averaged eight miles
an hour since Sunday. Preaching on deck this evening by
Elder Thomas Margetts. I can hardly describe the beauty of
this night—the moon nearly full, with the deep blue sky
studded with stars, the reflection of which makes the sea
appear like an immense sea of diamonds. And here we are
walking the deck at nine o'clock in the evening without
shawls or bonnets. What a contrast from this day three weeks
ago when we were shivering between decks and not able to
keep on our feet without holding fast to something or

another. If we managed to get on the upper deck the first salute we got was a great lump of water in the face. Well, I have seen the mighty deep in its anger with our ship nearly on its beam end, and I have seen it as now, under a cloudless sky and scarcely a ripple on its surface. I know not which to admire most. I cannot describe it as it should be described, but I feel most powerfully the force of those words "the Mighty God" which Handel has so beautifully expressed in his Chronicles.[7]

Feb. 15. Still a fine wind. Three sails in sight. My dear little fellow not so well tonight. Signs of squally weather.

Feb. 16. Sunday. We have had a heavy gale all night. Scarcely one in ten can keep our footing on the deck. The sea looks like a number of hills rolling over one another. We are obliged to sit on the deck to [eat] our meals and hold our plates pretty firmly to prevent their running away from us. My little Charles fell down the after hatch-way this afternoon. It seems almost a miracle that he is alive, having fallen on his head. Josiah very poorly.

Feb. 17. The wind has moderated a little but still squally.

Feb. 18. The weather very rough all night. Saw schools of flying fish this morning. Josiah rather worse than better. I am afraid.

Feb. 19. A good breeze in our favor.

Feb. 22. At half past 5 P.M. my little Josiah breathed his last. He had sank rapidly since last Tuesday, when he practically lost his speech. I did not think his death was so near, though when witnessing his sufferings, I prayed that the Lord would shorten them. He has done so, and my much beloved child is in the land of the spirits awaiting the morning of Resurrection, to again take possession of a tabernacle, purified and fitted to enter the presence of the Great Eternal, in the Celestial Kingdom. The Captain has given me permission to retain his little body until tomorrow, when it will be committed to the deep, nearly one thousand miles from land, there to remain until the word goes forth for the sea to give up its dead. Then shall I have my child again, and with those others who have gone before him, to present before the Lord, never again to be separated.[8] I do feel this trial to be a severe one. I had hoped to be able to take all my family safely through to the city atop the mountains. My poor little Charles, too, is suffering with inflammation in his eyes. Has been blind for two days. Spoke to a French war brig today.

Feb. 23. Sunday. The body of my dear little boy is removed to a snug little cabin under the forecastle, where the male adults of my family have watched it all night. The second mate with the assistance of Uncle Bateman have sewn up the body of the dear little fellow ready for burial. At eleven o'clock the tolling of the ship's bell told us that the time had come that the mortal part of my dear child was to be committed to the deep. Elder [William] Booth conducted the services, in Longitude, 44/4 West, Latitude, 25/3 North. This is my first severe trial after leaving my native land. But the Lord has answered my prayer in one thing—that if it was not His will to spare my boy to reach his destined land with us, that He would take him while at sea, for I would much rather leave him at sea than alone in a strange land. Charles's eyes are better today. He can open them a little. The rest of us are in good health.

Feb. 24. A most tremendous squall this morning with such a storm of rain as I have never seen before. It had the appearance of a dense fog. The deck was covered with water to a depth of three or four inches in less than five minutes, rushing through the scuppers in a torrent. The passengers were all ordered below so that I was unable to watch the effect of the storm, but our ship was in a greater bustle for a short time than I have ever seen it. Every sail was taken in, and in a minute or two the vessel began to roll and pitch as if she would turn us all into footballs. Keeping your footing was impossible, so that the only alternative was to sit on the deck and hold on as best we could. This lasted about an hour when we could go up on deck again. We found that the storm had passed away, but we had the effect of it in a heavy swelling sea during the remainder of the day. Charles's eyes are much better.

Feb. 25. Fine weather. Numerous schools of porpoises just ahead of us. One of the brethren struck one and hauled it on board. It measured five feet in length. It was soon skinned and cut up into pieces. A part of it was presented to me. I did not much admire it—it was like very coarse beef and in color, very black.

Feb. 26. Squally weather and the heat almost unbearable. Charles's eyes nearly well and the rest of us in good health. The sea is covered with foam and gulf weed, with a flying fish here and there springing out of the water and a few porpoises tumbling over and over as if enjoying the warm sun. Our ship is in the center of an immense circle bounded only by the clouds. All is grand and beautiful and fully repays me for the inconveniences of a sea voyage. By the by, I have said nothing as yet about our everyday life. A bugle sounds every morning to let us know it is six o'clock, when all who think proper, arise. At 7:30 it sounds again for morning prayer, after which, breakfast. We then make beds, etc.

We employ ourselves during the day according to our inclinations. Sometimes a few musical ones get together and have a few tunes. Sometimes [a few] get together and gossip and so the day passes. When we have rough weather we have enough to do to keep on our feet and laugh at those who are not so clever as ourselves! But we are most of us getting our sea legs as the sailors say. For my part, I can now walk the ship when she is rolling and pitching with tolerable care. I have only had two tumbles from the first. Sometimes a lurch will come of a sudden when we are at our meals, and capsize our teapot, and send us one over the other, but we are getting accustomed to it so we are on our guard. Our general custom is to sit on the deck and take our meals in our laps. Each family have their own department in front of their berths and can have their meals without being intruded upon by others. We can cook our food in any way we please and amuse ourselves in any way we please (within the bounds of decorum), go to bed and get up when we choose. Indeed we are under no restraint whatever. Our president is, I believe, a really sincere servant of God. His name is William Gibson, a native of Bonny Scotland, and his office is to watch over us as a pastor, to counsel, exhort, reprove if necessary. In short, to see that all our doings are in accordance with our profession as Saints of the Most High God. I much regret that we cannot have his company to the Valley. He will leave us at St. Louis.

March 2. Sunday. Meeting as usual. The last three days have been a succession of exceedingly heavy squalls, to the terror of many of our company who have been again attacked with sea sickness. I have much reason for gratitude that neither myself nor my family have suffered. I have gone on deck as often as I could, but the motion of the boat was so violent that I could not do so without difficulty. It was awful, yet grand to look at the sea. I could only compare it to an immense cauldron, covered with white foam, while the roaring of the wind and waves was like the bellowing of thousands of wild bulls. Conversation on deck was out of the question. I could only look on, and wonder and admire, for through our literal ups and downs I have felt no fear; and were it not that my bones ache with the incessant motion, I should feel no inconvenience. I was on deck this morning about six o'clock to see the sun rise but was disappointed, the weather being very cloudy, but not so boisterous as it was yesterday. We have now a fair wind and are progressing at the rate of nine miles an hour. I hope it may continue, for the last few days have driven us back some hundreds of miles.

March 9. Sunday. Fair wind and plenty of it for the whole of last week. We have passed the Bahama Islands and are happy in the expectation of seeing the land of America soon. We had a sad meeting this afternoon. Elder Booth was suspended from fellowship for inconsistent conduct.

March 10. I came on deck at five o'clock this morning to enjoy the cool breeze and see the sun rise. The heat is intense during the day, and it is dangerous to be on deck with the head uncovered. Nearly half our company are affected, more or less, with prickly heat. The Captain has supplied us with a large tub for the purpose of bathing the children, and the little ones are, many of them, dipped in it every morning. The men amuse themselves after another fashion: they don a thin pair of drawers and pour water over each other, proving the benefits they receive by the increased healthiness of their appearance. This evening we came in sight of the island of Abercoa.[9] It has a stationary light.

March 11. Passed the islands of Great and Little Isaacs, Green Turtle Island. The last we were within three miles of and could see the houses on it, with a number of small schooners lying at anchor. About the middle, on a rising ground stands a revolving light which made a brilliant appearance. The island is about forty miles across.

March 12. Passed Bush Island, also Double Headed Shot. This last is not exactly an island, but a long chain of rocks. At the distance we were, it had the appearance of long detached rocks or buildings. On one stands a tall light house bearing a stationary light. We are now in the Gulf of Florida. Held a meeting this afternoon in which three of the sisters were cut off the Church for levity of behavior with some of the officers of the ship, and continued disregard to counsel of the president. Also Elder Booth and Sister Thom. The conduct of these two has been most shameful ever since we came on board ship, and since they were placed under suspension it has been worse than it was before. Brother Thom is deeply grieved at the conduct of his wife. He is an excellent man and a pattern for every man in the Church. We all hope he will soon be able to forget her entirely. Such a woman deserves no place in the remembrance of a man of God.

March 14. Fine weather, intensely hot. Passed seventeen sails of various sizes. Upon measuring the water it is found that we have enough for twenty-three days supply. Our allowance has always been ample. I was on deck this morning to see the sun rise; there was not an atom of cloud to be seen in any direction. I have often read of the beauty of Italian skies, but I am sure they can not exceed in splendor that which at this moment arches over the Gulf of Florida, or Mexico, as it is mostly termed.

March 16. Sunday. Meeting as usual. Saw a water spout at half past eleven A.M. At seven in the evening a violent squall came on, driving most of the passengers below, myself, with a few others, remaining on deck, bidding defiance to the rain, for the sake of enjoying the lightning. It was very beautiful, seeming to illuminate one half of the horizon at once. We heard no thunder.

March 17. We have had a very rough night, and have rolled about nearly as badly as when skirting the Bay of Biscay. Aunt and Mrs. Derrick as sick as they were in the Channel. Foul winds all day. When I came on deck this morning, it was as much as I could stand, and to my astonishment, the sun was rising on our starboard bow instead of astern of us. It is now 8 P.M. and the wind has veered a little in our favor.

March 18. A fine boy has been born in the night. At 10 A.M. a boat brought a pilot, a horrid-looking fellow, the very fac-simile of a pirate. We can now see land plainly. At twelve o'clock a steamer came and took hold of us and at two o'clock we were at anchor at Belize, a pretty looking little village.[10] A boat has come alongside loaded with oysters, which has found a ready market.

March 19. Coming on deck this morning I was struck with the appearance of the water. It is a perfect mirror. The reflec-tion of the houses on shore is seen as clearly on the water as they are above it. There is a small schooner lying at anchor right by the landing place, and every rope and block in the rigging is seen reversed, exactly as if standing in an immense looking glass. The water is quite still as much so as in one of our cisterns at home. At 9 A.M. a steamer took us in tow, and we are now going up the river—the Mississippi.

March 20. Our ship is at anchor at New Orleans, 170 miles from the mouth of the river. We arrived here at 5 P.M. today. To describe the scenery on each side of this mighty river needs a better pen than mine. No description that I have ever read has done it anything like justice. Sugar and cotton plantations abound. The houses of the planters are built in the Cottage style, but large with verandas on every side and beautiful gardens. At a little distance are the Negro huts, from thirty to fifty on each plantation. They are built of wood, with a veranda along the front, painted white and mostly have either jasamine or honeysuckle growing over them. Each cottage has a large piece of garden or ground attached to it. In general appearance, they are very superior to the cottages inhabited by the poor in England. Groves of orange trees are very numerous, the perfume from which is delightful, as the breeze wafts it toward us. Thousands of peach and plum trees are here, growing wild, and are now in full blossom. We saw plenty of wild geese, also foxes and a racoon or two; storks fly by here in numbers, over our heads, and settle down on the river side, and stretching out their long necks look at us as if in astonishment. There is an endless variety of landscape. The only thing which detracts from its beauty is the sight of the hundreds of Negroes working in the sun. Oh Slavery, how I hate thee! *[There follows a description of the city and the slave market.]*

March 23. The steamer Concordia came alongside and received us and our luggage. So we start for St. Louis.

March 29. Arrived at St. Louis. Our portage up the river has been delightful. You must know that an American steamboat is nothing like our English one. If I describe the Concordia it may serve for a general description, though some are larger and some smaller. Its length is 300 feet, its width 60 feet. It is flat-bottomed and when heavily laden draws seven feet of water. She is built of fir and is consequently very light. The engines and boilers are on the deck; the stoke-hole is quite open on each side and the firemen have an uninterrupted view of the country. The head of the vessel is pointed, the stern circular. There is a clear passage of eight feet in width all around the boat, except where it is stopped by the paddle boxes, and these have good steps both up and down. From this, which is called the lower deck, you ascend by a handsome flight of steps to what is called the hurricane deck, which is an open gallery five feet wide entirely round the vessel, with a low railing next the water and roofed overhead. There are chairs here for the accommodation of the passengers. On the inner side of this gallery is a row of cabins with two doors each, one opening on to the gallery and the other into the saloon, which is 150 feet in length and thirty feet in width. Here the cabin passengers dine, etc. The ladies cabin is placed astern; its size is fifty feet by thirty, and [it] is splendidly furnished with sofas, rocking chairs, work tables and a piano. The floor (as well as that of the saloon) is covered with Brussels carpeting. There is also a smoking room for the gentlemen, opening out of the saloon forward, in which are card tables, etc. In front of this there is a large open space, the whole width of the ship, roofed over like the gallery and furnished with seats.

From this is another staircase leading to the upper deck, on which are built several neat cabins for the officers. The one forward encloses the steering wheel. Here stands the pilot completely secured from wind and weather. To the wheel two ropes are attached which are conveyed downward to the lower deck. Each rope is fixed to a lever which works the rudder. The whole arrangement is very simple and the elevated position of the pilot (forty feet above the lower deck) enables him to see and avoid any collision with snags, which are pretty plentiful still. Government has done much toward cleaning them away by sending out what they call snag boats, with men in them to either drag away the snags by force and let them float off, or by sending down divers to cut them off close to the mud. . . .

St. Louis is 1,250 miles from New Orleans in the State of Missouri. It is a large and fine city extending five miles along the river side and about half as far inland. The plan of New Orleans will apply to this city, so that no other description is necessary. I took a house for a month into which we had our luggage brought and once more found ourselves in a home, though but a temporary one. It contains two parlors, two bedrooms, and an outhouse answering all the purposes of kitchen and wash house, a large yard with back entrance, and a cellar, in which I found coal enough to last me three months, left by the last tenant. I suppose the reason for this apparent waste is to be attributed to the cheapness of the article. The mines are but seven miles from the city.

The next discovery that I made was that I wanted a cooking stove, which I purchased for $14 with all the utensils belonging. Early in the evening a gentleman by the name of Howard came to the door and introduced himself as a member of our Church, appointed by his branch to visit all newcomers, enquire of them if they are in want of anything, and see that their needs are supplied. Here I would say that I feel under much obligation to Brother Howard for his untiring kindness and advice to us all during our stay in St. Louis. His wife also greatly attached herself to me. She introduced me to the best stores of all kinds and was the means of saving me many a dollar. Their house is exactly opposite to mine, and they have a family. Their children and mine soon became acquainted and enjoyed themselves finely in their rambles about the town and the country beyond. The markets are extremely good. They open at four o'clock every morning except Sunday. All kinds of meat, poultry, and fish is very cheap. The flesh meat is good but not so large and fat as in English markets. Vegetables and fruit are abundant and of great variety. Groceries, wines, and spirits are very cheap. I have omitted to say that we have found the weather gradually cooler as we came up the river.

April 4. We had a heavy fall of snow and were glad to sit by a good fire. On the next day, to our astonishment we were glad to throw open the windows. And this I am told is the general character of the American springtime, but the summers are intensely hot. We had one day of heavy rain, with thunder. On the following morning I looked in vain for the road, but saw a perfect river in the place of it, and Mrs. Howard at her parlor window laughing at my very evident amazement. The sidewalks are all right, being raised so much above the road, and the lumps of stone I have before mentioned in describing New Orleans enable the pedestrians to get on pretty well. As to the horses, or oxen, which are more commonly used, except in private carriages, they dash through it without ceremony, sending the water in all directions—which, to those like ourselves who do not believe in sprinkling, is not very agreeable. The town, however, being built on a rising ground from the river, is soon dry again.

The churches are magnificent buildings. By the by, any place of worship, but let it belong to any denomination it may, has a steeple, and is called a church. The Catholics have three churches surmounted with a large gilded cross, the Presbyterians have three (two of them splits from the first), the Baptists have four, the Episcopalians and Independents several each. Too, there are the Methodists, Lutherans and Swedish churches, so that the religions are as plentiful as can be wished. The poor despised sons of Africa have a little church to pray and praise the Lord in, too. It is only lately that their white masters have allowed them this privilege. The Mormons have six meeting rooms. They also have the use of the Concert Hall on Market Street on Sundays, which holds 3,000 persons. I could but feel amazed to see that spacious room filled to overflowing and the staircase and a lobby crowded with those who could not get inside. They have an orchestral band and a good choir, ten of whom are trebles.

I went on Palm Sunday to one of the Catholic churches. I had as good a squeeze as I ever had on trying to gain admission to one of Julian's concerts. When I did get inside, the lay brother in attendance put me in a seat where I could both see and hear to advantage. The mass was splendid. They have a powerful organ and a fine set of singers. The solos and duets were beautifully performed; the organ gave the choruses a much finer effect. After the service was ended I was allowed to look around the interior of the building. At the upper end are three altars, the High Altar, of course, in the center. The altar cloth is of white satin, richly embroidered, edged with rich lace, half a yard in depth. The coverings for the cushions are in purple velvet. The altar rails are of black walnut, hand-somely carved and polished. On each side are seats for the scholars and nuns of the adjoining convent. Strange-looking beings these last! They wear black woolen shawls reaching down to the hem of their coarse black camlet gowns, a close bonnet made of black glazed cambric, and black crepe veils reaching to the knees. Well may they be called the Black Nuns. The attendant priests wear long black gowns with a hempen cord around the waist, to which hangs a rosary and a crucifix.

On each side of the building are confessionals with dark green curtains. The walls are ornamented with a number of finely-executed oil paintings, but horrible to look at, all of them rep-resentations of the martyrdom of the different saints. In the upper part of the church (over the gallery) are several little chapels dedicated to various saints. And gloomy places they are, but the altar in each of them is much ornamented. Ad-joining the church is a college, similar, I am told, to that at Marynorth. So much for public places!

I have purchased four wagons and eight yoke of oxen, each wagon to hold a fourth part of our luggage and provisions for our journey.[11] Our four wagons are to leave here in company with sixteen others on April 19 for Alexandria, by steamboat, and then travel overland to Council Bluffs to join the com-pany who intend to go on to the Valley this year.

April 19. At 5 P.M. went on board the Financier steamboat.
On each side of the vessel was lashed a barge, one of which
received our wagons, the other our cattle. Seeing this we
thought it better to waive our rights to berths in the steamer
and betook ourselves to our wagons, where we made our
beds and slept in comfort without the constant jerking which
is always caused by the action of machinery. In the morning
when I drew aside the curtains in the end of my wagon, I was
almost startled at finding myself close to what I took to be a
stone wall, but looking upwards, found it to be a pile of rocks
some hundreds of feet in height, the top of which was
covered with verdure. I cannot describe the grandeur of the
scenery—it was almost appalling. In some places it seemed
almost as if the pressure of a finger would have sent it
toppling down. These rocky shores are so perpendicular that
our boat could run, in safety close enough for us to pluck the
blossoms off the trees which grow at their base and in the
crevices within our reach here and there. Masses of the rock
had fallen, and trees and shrubs had grown in their places.

Every few miles we came to a town built near the river side,
the hills behind rising above the tops of the houses. Leaving
the towns, we every now and then saw the cottage of the
solitary settler, with its enclosure of perhaps forty or sixty
acres of land, the cattle and sheep grazing and pigs and
poultry running at liberty. The man and his elder children
would, in most cases, look at us as we passed, sometimes
waving by way of a salute, while the wife would stand watching at the door, usually with a child in her arms. We passed
hundreds of these farms and tens of thousands of acres without an inhabitant.

While [I was] gazing on the scenes, a gentleman passed me on
the edge of the barge, and looking up I saw that he was
intoxicated. I had scarcely turned my eyes from him when I
heard the shouts of the passengers that someone had fallen
into the river. Going around to the other side, I saw the same
gent who had just passed me, struggling for his life. The boat

was stopped instantly and every effort made to save him but to no purpose. As he sank he threw out his pocketbook, which was picked up by one of the men and given into the hands of the clerk in order to be restored to the relatives of the deceased. It contained his address and $275. It appeared that he was a citizen of the town of Hannibal in the state of Illinois. He was the owner of what is here called a flat, which is a sort of barge, very wide and long and made square in both ends. These are filled with produce of various kinds, roped in and the sides closed. At one end a cabin is built for sleeping in. These flats are taken down to New Orleans. The freight is taken out and sold. The vessel is then taken to pieces and the lumber sold, the owner taking his passage on a returning steamboat to his home, and when arrived there, set to and built another one, load it, and away again. These flats are built entirely of fir planks and are very light. They seem to just lie on the surface of the water and when laden will carry from fifty to eighty tons. Our unfortunate fellow passenger had been down to New Orleans and was returning with the profits of his journey when he met his death in the way I have described, not more than fifty miles from his home. Our vessel remained some time stationary, but we saw him no more. The probabilities are that he had been sucked in some hole, with which the bottom of this river abounds, or his clothing caught by a sawyer, from which he was unable to extricate himself. This occurrence cast a gloom over us for the remainder of the passage.

I was glad when we landed on the eighteenth in the evening. And a bad landing it was for our poor cattle, for the brutality of the men belonging to the boat was most shameful, and many of the poor beasts suffered much on consequence. However, we all got ashore at last and without losing any of our luggage, which was more than I expected. We drew up our wagons on an open space of ground, by the side of the river, close to the town of Alexandria in the state of Illinois, and here we made our first encampment. We then made a fire, there being plenty of wood lying about in all directions, and soon had our kettles boiling. We sat down to a comfortable cup of tea. Afterwards the men took our cattle to water and then placed them in a large yard near at hand, having procured some hay for their food for the night. During this time we got our beds made in our wagons, and on the return of the brethren we unitedly offered up our thanks to the God of Heaven for bringing us here in safety through unseen and unknown dangers, and then retired to rest, feeling sure of His protection during the night.

I should like here to say a little about this mighty river which I have seen in all probability for the last time. Mississippi is the name given it by the Indians, signifying "Father of Waters." It has been explored, I am told, for 4,800 miles without coming to its source, and is supposed by some to at last loose itself in the Pacific Ocean. It has more tributary streams than any river in the known world. It is of various widths, and on its surface shows many small islands inhabited only by birds and otters. The water is very muddy but perfectly sweet and as soft as rain water. The instant you leave the Gulf of Mexico the water is entirely free from salt, the current running only one way—that is, toward the sea. The distance from St. Louis to this place is 230 miles, so that I have traveled 1,630 miles, and I will say that such scenery, both wild and beautiful, I had never expected to look upon. It has seemed to repay us for all our inconveniences, and here we are all in good health.

I do not expect so much pleasure in our overland journey, as we must expect a life of toil, fatigue, and privations, to which we are unaccustomed. When I recall to mind the various scenes through which we have passed, and the thousands of miles we have traveled during the past three months, and the manifold instances of preserving mercy we have received at the hands of our Heavenly Father, I doubt not I shall still (if I remain faithful) enjoy the same protection upon land which I have done upon the water. I have told you as well as I could the major part of what I have come in contact with, and the future will most likely be an account of trials, difficulties, and privations such as at present I have no idea of, so as to be able to provide against them. But as you are aware I am not one to go through the world with my eyes shut. I expect to be able to send you some little description of my travels to amuse you in a winter's evening. In the meantime, may the God of Heaven bless you eternally. . . .

Patience Loader (Rozsa Archer) (1827-1921)

When James and Amy Britnell Loader were baptized near Oxford, England, in the winter of 1850-51, their twenty-three-year-old daughter Patience declined to join them because she liked fun, and to her religion seemed "long-faced." The fourth of the Loaders' thirteen children, Patience had been working in London for several years at the time her parents were baptized. When she moved closer to home and witnessed the daily lives of Latter-day Saints, she found their way of life attractive. She investigated the Church and was baptized in June 1853.[12]

Along with her parents, three sisters, and two brothers and in-laws, Patience emigrated to America in February 1856. The Loaders rented rooms in New York and planned to stay there for a year to earn enough money to outfit themselves for the westward trek. In May, however, they received word that they should leave immediately for Iowa City and prepare to travel west by handcart. Because the Loaders and other members of the Martin Company waited in Iowa City most of July while their handcarts were constructed, they reached Council Bluffs about three weeks behind schedule. Realizing that in starting so late they risked an encounter with early winter storms, the group still voted to go forward. More than one hundred members of the company lost their lives during the three-month journey. James Loader died on the trail at the end of September, leaving Patience, her mother, four sisters, and a brother to complete the trek by themselves. The following excerpt from Patience's reminiscence begins just after the death of her father and ends with the entry of the Martin Company into Salt Lake City on November 30.

In this reminiscence which she wrote in her later years in Pleasant Grove, Utah, Patience also detailed her early life and her marriage to John Rozsa.[13] The reminiscence exists in typescript at BYU, and the original is in private possession. The original spelling was preserved in the BYU typescript and has been maintained here. The typescript

Patience Loader Rozsa Archer in later years, when she frequently recounted her handcart experience. (Drusilla Loader Smith family collection. Pleasant Grove, Utah.)

contains no punctuation, but minimal punctuation has been added here for clarification. Capitalization in the typescript is very irregular, particularly with letters *g, m, k, s,* and *w,* which in some handwriting are neither distinctively upper or lower case. Since in most other

223

instances Patience's capitalization is regular, use of these letters has been regularized.

> The night and morning began to get very cold. About the begining of October we had the first snow storm. We was then at the black hills. We halted for ashort time and took shelter under our hand carts. After the storm had past we traveled on untill we came to the last crossing of the Platt river. Here we meet with the wagon company. Thay was campt for the night. We the hand cart [company] had orders from captain Edward Martin to cross the river that afternoon and evening here. Poor brother stane [Jonathan Stone] was missing. He was sick and laid down to rest by the road side. He fell asleep it was suposed. Some of the breathren had to go back in sea[r]ch of him and when thay found him he was dead and nearly all eaten by the wolves. This was a terrable death poor man. Br Stone was aloan [lone] man from London England.
>
> As I said we had to cross the river. Mother went to see Mrs. Ballen thay in the wagon company. Sister Ballen gave Mother three good sliceses of bread and molaces [molasses] for us girls. Br Nathen Porter from Centervell [Utah] had been to England on a mission. After landing in New York he was taken very sick. Bro Bestan took him to his home to take care of him. Here we became acquainted with Bro Parter. My sister Maria and myself took turns in siting up at night. He recou[p]ed in health suficant to go home to Utah. That season he bought a muel and road crossing the plains in the wagon company when we meet with him at the Platt river. He remembered our kindness to him through his sickness. His heart went out in sympathy for Mother and us girls when we told him that dear father was dead. He fealt so sorry to see us having to wade the river and pull the cart through. He took Mother on his muel behind him telling her to hold fast to him and he would take her safely through the water. Then he told Mother that he would return and bring our cart through the river.

This we did not know that he intended doing so we started to cross the river and pull our own cart. The water was deep and very cold and we was drifted out of the regular crossing and we came near beign drounded. The water came up to our arm pits. Poor Mother was standing on the bank screaming. As we got near the bank I heard Mother say for God sake some of you men help my poor girls. Mother said she had been watching us and could see we was drifting down the stream. Several of the breathren came down the bank of the river and pulled our cart up for us and we got up the best we could. Mother was there to meet us. Her clothing was dry but ours was wett and cold and verey soon frozen. Mother took of[f] one of her under skirts and put on one of us and her apron for another to keep the wett cloth from us for we had to travle several miles before we could camp. Here Mother took out from her Apron the bread and molaces Sister Ballen gave her for us. She broke in peices and gave each some. This was a great treat to us and we was all hungary. It seemed to give us new strength to travle on.

When we was in the middle of the river I saw a poor brother carreying his child on his back. He fell down in the water. I never knew if he was drowned or not. I fealt sorrey that we could not help him but we had all we could do to save our ownselvs from drownding. That night we had no dry cloth to put on after we got out of the water. We had to travle in our wett cloths untill we got to camp and our clothing was frozen on us and when we got to camp we had but very little dry clothing to put on. We had to make the best of our poor cercumstances and put our trust in God our father that we may take no harm from our wett cloths. It was to late to go for wood and water. The wood was to far away that night. The ground was frozen to hard. We was unable to drive any tent pins in. As the tent was wett when we took it down in the morning it was somewhat frozen so we stretched it open the best we could and got in under it untill morning. Then the bugle sounded early in the morning for us to travle seven miles as we could not get any wood to make a fire. There was snow on the ground.

We had a good many sick people more than could ride in the sick wagon so the captain apointed Brother Ward to take charge of the inveleads as he had traveld the plains so many times having been on several misseans. Captain Marten thought he would be the right man to put in charge of the sick and bring them sefe to camp but this araingment failed. The poor man misstook the road and thay got lost. The captain started Bro Ward out of camp along time in the morning before the main companys started so that thay should be able to get to camp before we arived there. It was aterrable day. It snowed and drifted and the wind blowed all day. We traveled seven miles and when we campt there was no signs of Brother Ward and his sick breathren. Then captain Marten called for some of the breathren to go back and find the company of Inveleads and when it was geting dark thay returned bringing in nineteen all f[r]ozen. I never knew if that was all that started out in the morning or not.

Now I must say after we got to camp we found we had to go along way to go for wood so my sister Maria and myself went with the breathren to get wood. We had to travle in the snow knee deep for nearly a mile to the ceders. We found nothing but green ceder as all the dry wood on the grown[d] was coverd over with snow. I ask one of the breathren to cut me down a shoulder stick so he kindly gave us quite alarge heavy log. My sister took one end on her shoulder and I raised the other end on to my shoulder and started back to camp. We had not gone very far when we boath fell down with our load. The snow beign so deep made it very hard work for us to get back to camp with our load but after much hard work we got there. My Mother and sisters was anxiously awaiting our return for thay was boath hungrey and cold in the tent.

As soon as I could get some wood chopt I tryed to make afire to make a little broath as I had an old beef head. I was

allways on the look out for anything that I could get to eat
not only for myself but for the rest of the family. We got of[f]
the skin from the beef head chopt it in peices the best I could
put it into the pot with some snow and boiled for along time.
About four o clock in the after noon we was able to have
some of this fine made broath. I cannot say it tasted very
good but it was flavord boath with sage brush and from the
smokey fire from the green ceder fire. So after it was cooked
we all enjoyed it and fealt very thankfull to have that much.
It would have tasted better if we could have alittle pepper and
salt but that was aluxury we had been deprived of for along
time. After I done with my cooking the beef head for that
day I took the pot into the tent for thay was all [waiting]
anxiously for there dinner and supper together. For after we
had eat what we could the remainen was left for the next day.
I put the fire into the bake oven and took it in the tent and
we all sat around it to keep us warm as we could. We young
folks had drank our broath. My Mother was still drinking
hers. The captain of the company came with two other
breathren and fetched poor brother John Laurey to our tent.
Since my poor father died this brother had staid in our tent as
he had no friends with him. He was alone. He was one of the
poor Inveleads that was lost. Brother Toone said to Mother
give him somthing warm. Mother said I have alittle hott soup
Patience made for us. I will share with him. Thay left this
brother with us to take care of. We tryed to give him alittle
with atea spoon but we could not get the spoon between his
teeth. Poor dear man. He looked at us but could not speak
aword. He was nearly dead frozen.

It got dark. We rapt him up the best we could to try to get
warm but he was two far gone. We all laid down to try to get
warm in our quilts the best we could my Mother and myself
and sister Jane in one bed my sister[s] Tamar Maria Sarah and
my little brother Robert in the other bed and poor brother
Laurey in his own bed. Poor man. He had only one old
blanket to rap him in. We had a buflow roab. This he had
over him. After we was in bed it was a dark loansome night

227

he commenced to talk to himself. He called for his wife and children. He had previously told me that he had a wife and nine children in London and that thay would come out as soon as he could make money enough to send for them.

He said he was counceld to come to this countrey first and leave his family in England for atime. He was told that he could earn more money in this countrey than in England. He was a taylor by trade and had never been acostomed to working out doors. Poor man. I doubt if he had lived to come to Utah that he would have made but very little money working at [h]is trade for in those days there was but very little call for Taylors as there was but verey few people could aford to employ a Taylor to mak there clothing. And another thing there was but very little cloth in Utah. Some folks was able to get own made geans and the sisters generly made all there husbands and boys clothing as they had nothing to pay for tayloring to be done.

In the night we could not hear him talking any more. I said to Mother I think poor brother [Laurey] is dead. I have not heard him for the last hour. Mother ask me to get up and go to him. I got up but everything in the tent seemed so silent and then was such a sadd feeling came over me. It was so dark and drear that I said to Mother I cannot go to him. She sais well get back in bed and try to get warm and wait untill daylight. Of course we did not sleep. Early as it was alittle light I got up and went to the poor man. Found him dead frozen to the tent. As I turned him over to look in his face never can I forget that sight. Poor man. I told Mother that he was dead. She said go and tell Brother Toone. I went to his tent. Told him Br Laurey was dead. He said well he will have to be buried. He told me we would have to rap him in a quilt. I said he has no quilts. He has only one small thin blanket and we cannot spare any of our quilts as we had allready used one to rap my dear father in when he died. So we rapt him in his own little blanked and the breathren came and took him away to burey him with eighteen more that had died dureing the night.

What a deplorable condition we was in at that time. Seven hundred miles from Salt Lake and only nine days full rations. That morning the bugal sounded to call us together. The captain ask us if we was willing to come on four ounces of flour aday. All answered yes. We had allready been reduced to half pound pr day.[14] Well we return to our tents. I had left the remainer of the beef head cooking on the fire. The next tent to ours was Br Saml Jones and sister Mary Ann Greening was traveling with Sister Jones and family. Sister Mary Ann was at her fire cooking something. I dont [know] what she had to cook. I am sure she had but little. We look around towards the mountains and she called out oh Patience here is some Californians coming. And as thay got nearer to us I told her no thay are not Californians. It is Br Joseph A. Young from the valley.[15]

He was acompanyed by brother Hanks or James Furgeson I cannot say which it was of those two breathren with there pack animal. Thay came to our fire. Seeing us out there Br Young ask how many is dead or how many is alive. I told him I could not tell. With tears streaming down his face he ask whare is your captains tent. He call for the bugler to call everybody out of ther tents. He then told the captain Edward Martin if he had flour enough to give us all one pound of flour each and said if there was any cattle to kill and give us one pound of beef each saying there was plenty provisions and clothing coming for us on the road. But to morrow morn-ing we must make a moove from there. He said we would have to travel 25 miles. Then we would have plenty of provisions and that there would be lots of good breathren to help us that thay had come with good teems and good coverd wagons so the sick could ride. Then he said that he would have to leave us. He would have liked to traveled with us the next morning but we must cheer up and God would bless us and give us strength. He said we have made a trail for you to follow. He bid us good bye.

Thees breathren had to go still further seven miles to the Platt river as the wagon company was still campt there and thay was in great disstres as there teems had given out. So many of them and there provisions was givingout and geting very short. After the Breathren had left us we fealth quite encuraged. We got our flour and beef before night came on and we was all busy cooking and we fealt to thank God and our kind brothers that had come to help us in our great disstress and miserey for we was suffering greatly with cold and hunger. When night came we went to bed. We slept pretty comfortable more so than we had done for some time. We fealt assured hope. We was all glad to make a moove from this place.

It seemed that if God our Father had not sent help to us that we must all have persihed and died in a short time for at that time we had only very little proveseans left and at the request of Br Martin we had come on four ounces of flour a day for each one to make the flour last us as long he could. I dont know how long we could have lived and pulled our handcart on this small quantity of food. Our provisions would not have lasted as long as thay did had all our breathren and sisters lived but nearly half the company died and caused our provisions to hold out longer.

Accordingly we struck tents in the morning and packed our carts and started on our journey again. It was a nice bright morning but very cold and clear. The snow was very deep in places. It was hard pulling the cart. I remember well poor Brother Blair. He was a fine taul man. Had been one of Queen Victoreas life guards in London. He had a wife and four small children. He made a cover for his cart and he put his four children on the cart. He pulled his cart alone. His wife helped by pushing behind the cart. Poor man. He was so weak and waurn down that he fell down several times that

day but still he kept his dear little children on the cart all day.
This poor man had so much love for his wife and children
that instead of eating his mosael of food himself he would
give it to his children. Poor man. He pulled the cart as long as
he could then he died and his poor wife and children had to
do the best thay could without him to help them. The poor
children got frozen. Some parts of there bodys was all sores
but thay all got in to Salt L City alive but suffering. Wether
the children lived or not I never heard as they went north of
the city and our family went South.

I will say we traveld on all day in the snow but the weather
was fine and in the midle of the day the sun was quite warm.
Some time in the afternoon a strange man appeard to me as
we was resting as we got up the hill. He came and looked in
my face. He sais is you Patience. I said yes. He said again I
thought it was you. Travel on. There is help for you. You will
come to a good place. There is plenty. With this he was gone.
He dissapeared. I looked but never saw whare he went. This
seemed very strange to me. I took this as some one sent to
encurage us and give us strength.

We traveld on and when we got into camp there was five or
six of the breathren with there wagons camped there. They
had been and got quantitys of wood and thay had allready
made about adozen big fires for us and there was plenty of
lovely spring water. That was agreat treat to us for the last
water we had seen was when we crossed the Platt river. We
had nothing but snow water and that did not taste very good
as we had to melt it over the campfire and it tasted of sage
brush sometimes ceder wood smoke. We fealt very thankfull
to our breathren for making us thees good fires and suplying
us with wood so abundantly. I realy must say that I was very
thankfull for since our dear father died it had fallen on me
and my sister Maria to get the most of our wood and I
thought it was so good that we did not have wood to get that
night after such hard pulling all day through the snow and it
was nearly dark when we got in camp.

It seemed good to get apound of flour again. That night the
breathren fetched out some provisions and clothing but thay
said thay had not got much to give us as thay did not know
how long thay would be there that thay would have to wait
untill the wagon company was heard from. Thees breathren
was very kind and good to us did everything thay could for
us. This place was Willow Springs. Here it was that poor
William Whittacar died. He was in the tent with several
others. In one part of the tent he and his Br John occupied and
the other part of the tent another family was sleeping. There
was ayoung woman sleeping and she was awoke by poor Br
Whiticar eating her fingers. He was dieng with hunger and
cold. He also eat the flesh of his own fingers that night. He
died in the morning and was burid at Willow Springs.

Before we left camp that day we traveld a good many miles.
We meet several wagons load with provisions and clothing.
From this time we began to get more to eat and some shoes
and warm under clothing which we all needed verry much
some worse than others. I was thankfull to get a nice warm
quilted hood which was very warm and comfortable. I also
got apar of slippers as I was nearly bear foot. We still had to
pull our handcart for atime as there was not wagons suficiant
for all to ride. Only those that was sick could ride but every
day or two we would meet teems & wagons and those that
was the most give out was taken into the wagons.

When we campt one evening abrother from the valley came
to our camp fire. He enquired of me if I knew if there was
afamily by the name of I cannot remember the name. But I
well remember the circumstance. I told this brother that there
was the two children living. The father got disscuraged and
staid at Laremy and the mother had died. At this the poor
man broak down. He said she was my poor dear sister. As
soon as I heard of the trouble and disstress of this handcart
company I made ready to come in search of my poor sister
and family. He said whare are the two children. I directed him
to the wagon they was in as he wanted to take them to his

own wagon. He said he had fetched a feather bed and good warm blankets and quilts for his sister to keep them warm and provisions for them.

I told this brother that thees two poor boys had suffered severly with cold and hungar since there poor mother died. One morning as we was geting ready to leave camp I saw those two dear boys. The Eldest was eleven years old I beleive and youngst not more than four or five years. The Eldest was crawling along on his hands and knees. His poor feet was so frozen the blood runing from them in the snow as the poor thing was making his way to the sick wagon. The other dear child crying by his brother side his poor little arms and hands all scabs with chilblains and scarcely anything on to cover his body.

This good brother, there Uncle, ask me if I knew any good sister that will come and wash and take of[f] there old clothing. He said I have plenty to keep them warm and good bed and blankets. Sister Reed was standing near by. She said, I will wash them and make them comfortable and she washed thees two poor boy. There Uncle made them anice warm bed in his wagon and this was the Last I saw of them untill we arived in Salt Lake City. Then I was told that thay was boath living and that there Uncle had taken them to his home north of the city. Many years after I heard that thay was still living and doing well. Then thay was grown young men. I was also told that there father came in search of his two boy. He was then getting old and wanted to come and live with them but the boys did not feel very good towards there father for leaving them in such a helpless condition.

Another family by the name of Holiton boath father and mother died leaving four or five children. The Eldest daughter a fine young womaman eighteen years old was so frozen [she] had big wound in her back. Her sufferings was so great that she died after we got to Salt Lake City. Another poor girl eleven years old father and mother boath di[e]d of hunger and

233

cold but there little daghter lived to get to Salt Lake but her poor feet was so frozen that boath had to be amputated above the ankle. This poor [girl] was crippled for life. I saw her several years after and she was agreat sufferer and had to go under another operation and have the bone taken of[f] still further up the leg as the flesh and bone was still roting. I dont know if she lived through the second operation or not poor afflicted girl.

The breathren that came to meet us was very kind and good to [us] and as wagons and teems arived our handcarts was left and we could ride in the wagons and sometimes we could sleep in them. One day I well remember we had avery hard days travel and we came to Devels Gate that night to camp. The snow was deep and terrable cold freezing. When we got to camp we found several big fiars. There was several log huts standing there and several breathren from the valley was camping there. Brother Joel Parish was cooking supper for the rest of the breathrens. We was all so hungory and cold many ran to get to the fiar to [get] warm but the breatheren ask for all to be as patint as possable and that we should have some wood to make us afiar so we could get warm.

Brother George Grant was there.[16] He told us all to stand back for he was going to knock down one of those log hutts to make fiars for us. For he sais you are not going to freeze to nigh[t]. Now he called out again stand back and said this night I have the strength of a giant[?]. I never fealt so strong before in my life. And at once he raised his axe and with one blow he knocked in the whole front of the building took each log and split in four peices and gave each family one peice. Oh such crawding for wood. Some would have taken more than one piece but Bro Grant told them to hold on and not to be greedy. There was some that had not got any yet. He said there is one sister standing back waiting very patintly and she must have some. I called out Yes brother Grant my name is Patince and I have waited with patience. He laugh and said give that sister some wood and let her go and make afiar. I was very thankfull to get wood. I had waited so long that my clothing [was] stiff and my old stockings and shoes seemed frozen on my feet and legs.

My poor dear Mother was siting down waiting untill we got back with wood to make afiar. As soon as we could get this log cut in peices we soon got our fire going and took of[f] our wett stockings and dryed them ready for morning and we had to wait some time before we got our flour for supper. During the time we was waiting a good brother came to our camp fiar. He ask if we was all one family. We was six in nomber. Mother answerd Yes we are all one family. She told him we was her daughters and the boy was her youngst son. He ask Mother if she had no husband. She told [him] her husband had died two month ago and he was bured on the plains. He had been standing with his hands behind him. Then he handed us a nice peice of beef to cook for our supper. He left us and came back with a beef bone. He said here is a bone to make you some supe and said dont quarel over it. We fealt suprised that he should think that we would ever quarel over our food. Mother said Oh brother we never quarel over having short rations but we feel very thankfull to you for giving us this meat for we had not got any meat neither did we expect to have any.

We camped here for two days or rather two nights and it was reported around camp that we would not have to pull our handcarts any further that we would leave them at Devels Gate and that we would all be able to ride in the wagons. This was dileghtfull news to us to think we would not have to pull the cart any more. I fealt that I could still walk if I did not have the cart to pull. But oh what dissapointment the next morning. We faunt it was only those could ride that was to sick and weak to pull their carts and so we girls all pretty well in health we had to start out with our cart again. As we started out from camp there was quite a nomber of the breathren from the valley standing in readyness to help us across the streem of water with our cart. I was feeling somewhat bad

235

that morning and when I saw this stream of water we had to go through I fealt weak and I could not keep my tears back. I fealt ashamed to let those breathren see me sheding tears. I pulled my old bonnet over my face as thay should not see my tears. One brother took the cart and another helped us girls over the water and said we should not wade the cold water any more and tryed to encourage us by saying soon we would all be able to ride in wagons.

We traveld on for some few miles. Then we came to the Sweet Water. There we had to cross. We thought we would have to wade the water as the cattle had been crossing with the wagons with the tents and what little flour we had and had broaken the Ice so we could not go over on the ice. But there was three brave men there in the water packing the women and children over on there backs. Names William Kimble, Ephrem Hanks, and I think the other was James Furgeson. Those poor breathren was in the water nearly all day. We wanted to thank them but thay would not listen to [us]. My dear Mother fealt in her heart to bless them for there kindnes. She said God bless you for taking me over this water and in such an awfull rough way. [They said] oh d--- that I dont want any of that. You are welcome. We have come to help you. Mother turned to me saying what do think of that man. He is arough fellow. I told her that is Brother William Kimble. I am told thay are all good men but I daresay that thay are all rather rought in there manners. But we found that thay all had kind good hearts. This poor Br Kimble staid so long in the water that he had to be taken out and packed to camp and he was along time before he recovered as he was chil[le]d through and in after life he was allways afflicted with rhumetism.

After we was over the Sweet Water we had to travel some distance to agood place to camp. In between the mountains we had avery nice camping place. Here we remained for nine days as we had to wait untill more provisions came to us. What suplys had allready been sent to us had to be left for the breathren that had to stay all winter at Devels Gate as the cattle had nearly all gave out boath in the wagon company and our company and a great deal of freight had to be left there at Devels Gate untill spring. And we was on four oz. of flour aday nearly all the time we was in camp on the Sweet Water but the morning we had orders to leave there we was told to leave our handcarts. We was all very glad to leave the cart but we had to walk for several days before we could all ride in the wagons. It seemed good to walk and not have aload to pull through the snow. We got dear Mother in the wagon to ride and we girls was young and we was willing to walk untill such times as it was conveniant for us to ride.

During our nine days camping on the Sweet Water many of the stout young men went out and got raw hide and anything thay could get to eat. On one occasion I got a bone gave me with scarcely any meat on it. I was cooking it to make alittle supe for breakfast and the breathren from the valley came and ask [us] to go to there camp and sing for them. So we left Mother to see to the cooking of the bone. The breathren had cut down logs and formed seats for us all around there camp fire but thay said thay had nothing to give us to eat as thay themselvs was short of food. Well we sang and enjoyed our-selvs for two or three hours and then went to our own tent.

When arived there our fiar was out and Mother was gone to bed and my ten year old brother was also in bed. Mother said I fetched the pot with the soup. We said allright Mother we staid longer than we ought too but the breathren did not want us to leave but we told them we would go and sing for them another night. We was so hungory. We had nothing to eat so we went to bed but Mother sais it is to bad you have nothing to eat and it makes you more hungory to sing. You had better not go to sing for the breathren again. But I must tell you that I got so hungary that I took the bone out of your soup and picked the little meat of[f] it and put the bone back into the pot. It seemed that I could not go to sleep without telling you for I knew you would not find anything on the bone in the

237

morning. We told her that was allright. We fealt glad that our
dear Mother found alittle bit to eat and we all went to sleep
and slept comfortable and warm untill morning not withstand-
ing it was a terrable cold freezing night.

Then we got up and prepared our bone soup for breakfast.
We did not get but very little meat as the bone had been
picked the night before and we did not have only the half of
asmall biscute as we only was having four oz. of flour aday.
This we devided into portians so we could have asmall peice
three times aday. This we eat with thankfull hearts and we
allways as[k] God to bless to our use and that it would
strengthen our bodys day by day so that we could performe
our dutys. And I can testefie that our heavenly Father heard
and answerd our prayers and we was blessed with health and
strength day by day to endure the severe trials we had to pass
through on that terrable journey before we got to Salt Lake
City. We know that if God had not been with us that our
strength would have failed us and our bodys would have been
left on the plains as hundreds of our poor brothers and sisters
was. I can truthfully say that we never fealt to murmer at the
hardships we was passing through. I can say we put our trust
in God and he heard and answerd our prayers and brought us
through to the valleys.

I remember on one occasion when we was camping on the
Sweet Water thees same breathren came to our tent and ask
us girls to go to there camp and sing for them again. My dear
Mother told them she thought we had better not go to sing
that night. It made us still more hungary to sing and we had
nothing to eat after we came back to the tent. They fealt
sorry for us but thay could not give us anything for thay was
short of provisions themselvs untill thay got suplys from
home. That night was a terrable cold night. The wind was
blowing and the snow drifted into the tent onto our quilts.
That morning we had nothing to eat if we got up not untill
we could get our small quantity of flour. Poor Mother called
to me come Patience get up and make us afiar. I told her that

I did not feel like geting up it was so cold and I was not feeling very well. So she ask my sister Tamar to get up and she said she was not well and she could not get up. Then she sais come Maria you get up and she was feeling bad and said that she could not get up. With this Mother sais come girls this will not do. I believe I will have to dance to you and try to make you feel better. Poor dear Mother. She started to sing and dance to us and she slipt down as the snow was frozen and in a moment we was all up to help our dear Mother up for we was afraid she was hurt. She laugh and said I thought I could soon make you all jump up if I danced to you. Then we found that she fell down purposely for she knew we would all get up to see if she was hurt. She said that she was afraid her girls was going to give out and get disscuraged and she said that would never do to give up. We none of us had ever fealt so weak as we did that morning. My dear Mother had kept up wounderfull all through the journey. Before she left England she had been in delicate health. For many years she had not been able to walk amile and after we started on our journey to Utah she was able to walk all across the plains only some times we put her on the hand cart to rest her alittle.[17]

After we left the Sweet Water whare we campt for nine days she was able to ride in the wagon. We was so glad to get Mother in the wagon. If we girls could not ride it did us good to know that Mother could get arest and not have to walk in the snow any more. And when we got into campe that night the good brother that owned[?] the wagon told us that we could sleep in his wagon and he would make a hole in the snow and make his bed there. He thought we would be warmer in the wagon. We made our bed there but we only had one old quilt to lie on and in the night I woke up and called to Mother I am freezing the side I had laid on was so benomed with cold. Mother got up and helped me out of the wagon. There was some big fiars burning in several places in the camp and lots of the sisters siting and sleeping near the fiar to keep warm. So I went to the fiar and staid there the remainer of the night.

In the morning we traveld on again as usul. One great blessing
we had more food to eat. We got our pound of flour a day
and sometimes alittle meat and very soon we was all able to
ride instead of walking and we could stay in the wagon at
night. After we baked our bread we put the hott coles in our
bake kittle and took in the wagon and that made it quite comfortable and warm for us to sleep in.

I can well remember how kind the breathren was to us poor
disstresd looking creatures. I think we must have looked a
very deplorable set of human beigns to them when thay first
meet us camped in the snow. When Joseph A Young first
arived in our camp the tents was half coverd in snow. Oh
how thankfull and delighted we was to see those two
breathren. What brave men thay must have been to start out
from Salt L City in the midle of winter in search of us poor
folks that was away back campt near the last crossing of the
plat river. When thay left the city thay did not know how far
thay would have to travle in the snow before they would find
us.

When the word came to Presedent Brigham Young on Sunday
he was in the Tabernacle in meeting. Those days the people
use to go from the settlements by teem to attend meetings.
And when the word came that there was hand cart company
back on the plat river with scarcely any provisions and that
many was dieing with hunger and cold Brigham Young told
the people this message had come to him. And he also called
on all the men to take there teems and wagons and gather up
all the food and clothing thay could get and start out at once
and not to come back untill thay found the people. He said
that if thay did not go that he would go himself and he
started out himself with the breathren. He got as far as the big
mountain. He took cold and the breathren prevailed on him
to return back home. Then he gave orders for everybody to
go to work and bake bread and gather up all the clothing and
quilts all thay could get together and every teem and wagon
that could be got was loaded and sent out. Every day the road

was kept open by teems coming to us every day with provisions and clothing of some kind. After the breathren came out
to us there was not so many deaths.[18] My Sister Mrs Jaques
dear little two years [old] girl died near Fort Bridger.[19] She rapt
her in a blanket on quilt and fetched her into Salt L City and
she was burid in Franklin D Richards lot. I well remember that
when we campt in Echo Canyon that Sister Squires was
confined in the morning. She had alovely baby girl and thay
named her Echo. The morning she was born the father was
running around camp enquiring of everybody if thay had apin
to give him to pin somethig around the baby but I dont think
that he was able to get one. The breathren fixed the wagon
very warm and comfortable for Sister Squires and boath her
and baby arived safe into the City.

I will now conclud my hard journey across the plains by
handcart and say that we that lived through this terrable
journey arived in Salt L City Sunday noon the thirtieth day of
November 1856. We was met and warmly greeted by our
kind breathren and sister and taken to there homes and made
comfortable and welcomed to share there home and food with
them. Brother William Thorn Bishop of the Seventh Ward
took home with him my Mother and my brother Robert myself and sisters Maria, Jane, and Sarah. My sister Tamar went
with Br. Thomas Ricks to Farmington. This is the kind brother
that gave us the beef at Devels gate and told us not to quarel
over it. The next spring he marr[i]ed my sister Tamar. . . .

When first we arived in the city to us everything looked
dreary and cold. The streets was all coverd with snow but the
people was kind and good and tryed to encourage us and make
us feel as good as thay could. The next day my Mother and
three sisters and my brother left the city with my brother in
law John Dalling for Pleasant Grove Utah County.[20] I myself
staid in the city for some weeks. At that time the city was not
built up very much. The houses was scatering. To me it
seemed a very loanly place in the Seventh Ward. I had been
living eleven years in the city of London before I left England

and to me it seemed avery loansome place. I said to my old friend Annie Thorn if this is Salt L City what must it be like to live in the country. I dont think I will go to Pleasant Grove. So I concluded to stay in the city for atime as I had several friends living in the city that I was acquainted in the old country and I thought it would be better for me to stay in the city and let my Mother and sisters go to Pleasant Grove which I did. I visit two or three familys and enjoyed myself very much for several weeks untill I began to feel quite rested.

Chapter Eight

Colonization
of the Great Basin

"The Foundation of a Life to Come"

Lucy Meserve Smith arrived in the valley of the Great Salt Lake in October 1849, so delighted "to sit at the table with long absent relatives and friends" that she called it "a foretaste of the resurrection of the just." It was another beginning—a new gathering of Saints "in the top of the mountains." Fifteen years of Mormon exodus caused Eliza Partridge Lyman to describe her 1848 arrival in the Great Basin less enthusiastically. It was merely "our journey's end for the present." But this place was to serve both Lucy and Eliza as a permanent home, and for generations to come the Great Basin would be the heartland of latter-day Zion.

After Brigham Young and the Pioneer Company (143 men, 3 women, and 2 children) arrived in July 1847, Mormon wagons continued to stream into the Salt Lake Valley. Following the vanguard by a few days was a community of Saints who had wintered four hundred miles southeast of the valley at Pueblo. This group of families, some of whom had traveled with the Mormon Battalion and others who had emigrated from Mississippi to join the gathering Saints, tripled the population. By the end of 1847 two thousand settlers had arrived, and over the next decade emigration swelled the number of residents in the Salt Lake Valley and surrounding Mormon settlements—to 11,380 by 1850 and to some 40,000 by 1857.

In preparation for the thousands of converts who would continue to gather to Zion, and as an important part of building a self-sufficient Mormon economy, Church leaders planned for widespread colonization of the Great Basin—a vast region including most of present-day Utah and Nevada as well as portions of present-day Idaho, Wyoming, and California. Over a period of more than forty years the Saints were called or assigned to settle various parts of this region for agricultural or industrial purposes. "Mr. Smith was sent by the Presidency with a Co[mpany] to Iron Co[unty]," wrote Lucy Meserve Smith of her husband George A.'s call to the "iron mission." Martha Cragun Cox remembered leaving the Salt Lake Valley when she was ten years old and her father "received [a] call to the Dixie country as a pioneer." Unlike men called on proselyting missions, those assigned economic missions were usually expected to take family members with them. Whole households moved from barely built homes back into wagons to trek to the site of a new community.

The same cooperative procedure used in building up the Salt Lake Valley was followed in outlying Mormon settlements. Land, water, and timber were publicly owned, and their use and distribution were regulated by local Church leaders. Families were housed in dugouts or lean-tos (Eliza Lyman chose to stay in her wagon box) while city plots were laid out, surrounding farmland assigned, and log or adobe homes built. Order, unity, and community being highly valued among the Saints, men continued to contribute at least a portion of their efforts to public or semipublic works such as meetinghouses, mills, and ditches.

As they attempted to create a self-sufficient commonwealth, the Saints encountered considerable political hostility. With the 1850 organization of Utah as a U.S. territory, Church leaders entered into long-term conflict with the federal government over control of Utah's territorial affairs. Though numerous federal appointees were sent to Utah starting in 1851, Brigham Young served as territorial governor, the legislature was comprised primarily of local Church leaders, and local probate judges held both civil and criminal jurisdiction. While Saints were accustomed to church and civil government working closely together (the provisional State of Deseret had run smoothly for two years), federal officials deemed the practice un-American, and some went so far as to accuse the Saints of disloyalty to the U.S. government. Their malicious reports prompted U.S. President James

Buchanan to replace Brigham Young as governor of Utah Territory in 1857. Having been misinformed that this action would throw Mormons into a state of rebellion against the government, President Buchanan sent along a military force to assure acceptance of the new appointee. Brigham Young had received no official announcement of the coming of the governor or troops, and he declared martial law as they approached. The ensuing Utah War was bloodless, but it was evident that for the Church, building an isolated kingdom was impossible. In fact, the freedom of the Saints to choose their own political, economic, and social norms was to remain a source of conflict until after Utah achieved statehood in 1896.

By the 1870s Mormon women would be actively involved in that conflict, but through the 1850s and '60s their concerns of necessity seem to have been more insular. All three of the women whose writings comprise this chapter played a critical role in providing food, clothing, and shelter for their families. Self-sufficient households were rare; most acquired some of the essentials through purchase or bartering. "We are spinning some candle wick which we shall try to sell for bread stuff," wrote Eliza Partridge Lyman. Lucy Meserve Smith and Martha Cragun Cox wove cloth and taught school in exchange for commodities and services. Since church and community obligations kept their husbands away for extended periods, these women bore the major responsibility for managing family resources.

If their peculiar circumstances often demanded unsought independence, women found what Lucy Smith termed "solid comfort . . . in our association together." Plural marriage sometimes strengthened bonds between women. Both Lucy and Eliza mention sister-wives with deep affection, and Martha gives a particularly warm and detailed account of female relationships in a plural household. In Eliza's journal, visiting female family members and friends appears as much a part of the daily routine as eating, and with characteristic gusto Lucy seems to have regularly relished gathering with neighbors to spin. As was the case with their American sisters to the east, Mormon women formed among themselves strong networks for support and companionship.[1]

There was much in community social life to bring men and women together, however. One sister's memoir reconstructs a "Leap

245

Year Pic Nic Party" at Provo's gristmill, and another rather soberly considers the personal impact of all the "theaters, music, and balls, concerts" in St. George. Through the 1850s in Salt Lake City and other settlements, small cultural societies—musical, dramatic, scientific, literary, "polysophical"—typically involved both men and women. Brothers and sisters assembled in church meetings and cooperated on special projects such as Sunday School. The official church organization for women, the Relief Society, was briefly reestablished during this period, giving sisters' "willing hands," as Lucy Smith recounts, and various opportunities to assist the brethren.

Taking on the commission to make the desert "blossom as the rose," the Saints who first settled the Great Basin began transforming a wilderness into their promised land. But establishing Zion was more than a matter of laying out streets and building meetinghouses; it required a people pure in heart. The following writings show that women self-consciously struggled to cultivate the soul as well as the sod. As they reminisced, Lucy Smith and Martha Cox seem to have been more aware of whom they had become than of the development of the land they had helped to settle. If, as Martha said, they "laid the foundation of a life to come," they conquered both outer and inner frontiers to do it.

Eliza Marie Partridge Lyman (1820-1886)

In the fall of 1848 Eliza Lyman arrived in the Salt Lake Valley with her two-month-old son Platte (named for the river the Saints had followed during their journey from Winter Quarters) and her sister, Caroline Ely Partridge Lyman. These sister-wives of Amasa Mason Lyman had made the journey across the Plains together, taking care of their own housing and food just as they had at Winter Quarters when Amasa had gone first to the Salt Lake Valley with the pioneer company and then on a mission to the southern states. He was captain of the "hundred" in which his wives, seven of them, traveled from Winter Quarters to the Salt Lake Valley, and the demands of his position required that the women be self-sustaining.

The journal of Eliza Marie Partridge Lyman shows that she maintained considerable independence after the family arrived in the Great Basin. Amasa Lyman, a member of the Church's Quorum of Twelve Apostles, was often away, and when he was in the valley, he had to share his time among several families.[2] The process of settlement unfolds in Eliza's journal as she describes the daily activities involved in establishing a household in the wilderness.

The daughter of Edward and Lydia Clisbee Partridge, Eliza was born and raised on the frontier in northeastern Ohio, learning in her youth the schoolteaching and tailoring that she later employed to sustain herself. Eliza had lived in the homes of two prominent Church leaders before she married Amasa Lyman. Her father served as presiding bishop of the Church from 1831 to 1840, and she later lived in the home of the Prophet Joseph Smith in Nauvoo.

A reminiscence at the beginning of Eliza's journal describes her early life. She began making daily diary entries in February 1846 when she left Nauvoo, and continued writing long after her move to Millard County, Utah, in 1863, though her entries were frequently sporadic. The holograph journal is located in the Historical Department of the Church. Minimal punctuation has been added here, mostly periods after the dates of each entry, which in the original are set off in the margin.

Oct 17th [1848]. Reached the place of our destination in the valley of the Great Salt Lake. I have been quite as comfortable on the journey from Laramie as could be expected under the circumstances. Some of the time the weather has been very cold with rain and snow, so that I could not be comfortable anywhere as I had no stove in the wagon, but I and my child have been preserved through it all and I feel to give thanks to my Father in Heaven for his kind care over us. We are now at our journey's end for the present. The weather is beautiful. The country barren and desolate. I do not think our enemies need envy us this locality or ever come here to disturb us.

[April 1849]

18th. Moved into a log room. There are [eight] of us to live in this room this winter. My Mother and Sisters Caroline and Lydia and Br Edward, Mr. Lyman a part of the time, one of Maria's children to go to school and myself and Babe.³ We are glad to get this much of a shelter but it is no shelter when it rains for the dirt roof lets the water through and the dirt floor gets muddy which makes it any thing but pleasant.

April 8 1849. During the past winter we have had some sickness. My Baby was very sick with whooping cough. Many children around us died with it.⁴ My brother Edward also had it, they are both quite well of it now. We are intending to have our houses moved out of the fort onto our lots in town. Cooked the last of our flour to day and have no prospect of getting any more untill after harvest.

13th. Br Lyman started for California in company with O. P. Rockwell and others.⁵ May the Lord bless and prosper them, and return them in safety to their families and friends. Br. L has left us that is Paulina, Caroline and I without any thing to make bread, it not being in his power to get any. The family at Cotton wood have some.[6]

Watercolor of Eliza Marie Patridge Lyman as a young woman. (Daughters of Utah Pioneers. Salt Lake City, Utah.)

Sunday 15th. Mr. Hakes and family here. Took Sarah and Dionitia home with them.[7] We gave Sarah some cotton yarn for stockings, some tallow and soap grease. Samuel White a man in Br Lymans employ says they cannot move our houses till after harvest so I think I shall move onto the lot without a house and live in a wagon box and tent.

Monday 16th. David Frederic[8] and brother Edward gone to Cotton wood.

Tuesday 17th. Br Frederic and Edward returned from Cotton wood. Brought a quarter of beef also drove our cow Frosty to us so that we can have some milk. Drove a yoke of Mother's cattle to work.

18th. Made preparations for moving onto the lot where we can make garden. Called on Sister Holmes in the evening. We are spinning some candle wick which we shall try to sell for bread stuff. There is an old Lady who goes round and peddles whatever any one has to sell and as there are no stores in the town or Territory she has very good success.

Thursday 19th. Moved onto our lot to live in wagons again. We are 4 in family, Sister Caroline, Br Frederic and myself and Babe. Sold a ball of candle wick for 3½ quarts of corn. Sold another ball for 3½ quarts of meal which has to be divided between Paulina Lyman, Mother, and my family.

Friday 20th. Visited at Mother's with Sister Lucinda Bingham.

21st. Sister Emily brought us 15 lbs flour. Said Presnt Young heard that we were out of bread and told her to bring that much although they have a scanty allowance for themselves. I sincerely hope I may be able to return it before they need it.

Sunday 22nd. Staid at the wagons. Sister Emily spent the day with us. Br Hakes brought some shoes to Carolina and Paulina.

24th. Went to Mother's and staid all night.

25th. Carded and spun 3 balls candle wick. Br Frederic setting out fruit trees on the lot. Jane James a colored woman let me have about 2 lbs of flour it being about half she had.

26th. Caroline gone to tend sister Emily's babe while she washes.

28th. A military organization, more men together than I have seen before in the valley. Samuel White gave Paulina 1 dollar to buy corn with. Sister Caroline gave 2¼ dollars for a calico dress pattern. Gave Charles Burk 25 cts for his trouble in getting it for her.

Sunday 29th. Staid at the wagons with the babe while the rest went to meeting. Wind blows hard and cold. Went to Mother's who is still in the Fort and staid all night.

Monday 30th. Carded and spun some cotton yarn. Came home in the afternoon and cut out 2 shirts for D. Frederic.

[May 1849]

May 1st. Made a pair of pillow cases, the baby an apron and sewed on a shirt for D.F.

2nd. Went to the Fort and visited at Sister Holmes' with sisters Fuller and E.R. Snow. Had quite a rain with high cold wind. Went to Mother's and staid all night.

Thursday 3rd. Fast day.[9] Went home found Caroline going to washing. Assisted her. Paulina bought a ½ bushel of corn of Mr Shoemaker.

4th. Sewed and went to the Fort.

Saturday 5th. Did sundry kinds of work. Priscilla and Cornelia Lyman and Charles Burk came from Cotton wood. Brought Dionitia home and took me back with them. Slept at Mother Hakes with her.

Sunday 6th. Went to meeting, heard an excellent discourse from Wm Crosby. Took dinner with Sister Crosby who is a most excellent woman. Went from there to Sidney Tanner's where I staid all night.

7th. Spent the day with Mother Shepherd. She gave me some tea for Mother. I bought some soap and cotton cloth for which I am to sew. In the evening went to Cornelia Lyman's.[10] Heard from home. Learned that Sister Caroline had taken a school about 10 miles north of us because she has nothing to eat at home, and is under the necessity of doing something as there is nothing to be bought although we have the money to pay for flour if there was any.[11]

Tuesday 8th. Maria Louisa born. She is the daughter of Maria Lyman.

10th. Attended a sewing party at Mrs Hakes'. Br Erastus Snow happened along and took dinner with us.

12th. Visited at Sister Crosby's. She gave me some nice stuff to make my Boy a cap.

13th. Went home in br Hake's carriage. Found Sister Caroline there but going back again in the evening to her school. Have got sister Lydia to stay with me till I can do better, or some other way.

14th. Washed &c. Lent D. B. Huntington the spy glass by B. Young's order.

Wednesday 16th. Visited at Wm Walker's with sisters Emily and Louisa Young and Sarah Ann and Lucy Kimball also Presnts [Brigham] Young and [Heber C.] Kimball.[12]

18th. Cut and made a pair of pants for J. Holmes. Staid at Mother's all night. Came home the next day but the wind blew so hard and cold that I went back to Mother's again.

19th. Our tent burned down, burnt the rocking chair while I was away.

Sunday 20th. Staid at the wagon. Caroline came home but went back the same day. I went to the Fort again in consequence of a cold rain.

21st. Paulina and Dionitia moved into John Hess' room in the Fort. Sister Emily visited us.

Tuesday 22nd. Tremendous rain and snow storm with high winds.

23d. Snow blowing furiously. We were so very uncomfortable although we had a stove in the wagon that we thought best to go to the Fort to Mother's. We did so and found her worse off than we were, for the rain was running through the roof and every thing in the house was wet, and the ground perfectly muddy under her feet. We thought it would never do to live that way so took her and her effects up to the wagons deeming it more prudent to live out of doors than in such a house as this. In the afternoon br Frederic went to look for the cows that had strayed away during the storm but did not find them. Spent several days hunting them. Found them at last. Bought 11 lbs flour and 11 lbs shorts of T[itus] Billings at 10 cts pr lb.

25th. Edward went to Cotton wood to get br Frederic's cow, but S. Driggs forbade his taking her so he had to come back without her. Charles Burk brought us some beef. Some of old Mike which was tougher than a boiled owl. Sarah Clark came up on a visit.

26. Sister Emily Young and Lucy W. Kimball here on a visit. Caroline came home.

Sunday 27th. Took my babe to meeting. Went to sister Emily's to dinner with Caroline and sister Brown.

28th. Washed &c. Had company in the afternoon sisters Sarah Clark and Helen Callister.[13] Bought 9½ lbs corn meal of Sister Holmes. Paid 50 cts in work for it.

29th. Cut and made a pair of pants for br Holmes.

30th. Saw a head of wheat which looks encouraging in this time of scarcity. Visited at Paulina's with Sarah Clark. Bro Frederic shearing sheep for Charles Rich.

31st. Spent the afternoon at Br T[homas] Callisters.

[June 1849]

June 1st. Sister Emily spent the day with us.

Saturday 2d. Caroline came home. We washed &c. Went to the Fort and staid all night.

3d. Came home and staid at the wagon all day. Br Tinney and S[amuel] White here to dinner. Caroline went to her school in the evening.

4th. Spent the afternoon at Sister [Augusta Adams] Cobb [Young]'s with Sister Emily Young.

6th. Edward went to Cotton wood and got the white cow and calf. Paid Washburne's boy 1 dollar for herding.

7th. Edward moved the hen house from the Fort to the lot.

8th. Br Frederic ditching, Edward building hen house. Mother spinning cotton, Lydia helping Emily wash. Caroline teaching school and myself making pants for D. Frederic, taking care of Baby &c.

9th. Washed some. Finished pants &c. Let D. Frederic have 2 dollars to buy summer coat.

Sunday 10th. Sister Caroline came home. We all but Lydia went to meeting.

11th. Br Frederic and Edward pulling down houses in the Fort and hauling the logs to mill to get the split. Mother carried the cotton yarn that she has carded and spun to the weavers. Maria Lyman sent us some cloth for pillow cases and a few dried apples.

June 12th. Let Paulina have 1 dollar to buy flour. This morning the mountains are covered with snow which makes the air quite cold.

Wednesday 13th. Sister Emily spent the day with us. Lydia

and I washed &c. Washed wool for D. Frederic. Bought some coarse flour.

14th. The Indian Chief Walker here to day.[14]

15th. Bought a ½ bushel wheat of sister Richardson. Paid 20 cts for grinding wheat.

16th. D. Frederic at the mill sawing the logs for our house. Edward hunting oxen in the forenoon, and went to the mill in the afternoon to haul logs. Very high wind in the evening.

Sunday. Staid at the waggon. Sister Caroline does not visit us to day. Some rain and wind. Bought 4 pints of coffee for Mother for which I pay 50 cts.[15]

Monday 18th. Picked wool &c.

19th. Went to the warm springs and took a bath.[16] Went to Cotton wood with C. Burk and staid till the 1st of July. Spent the most of the time at Br Wm Crosby's. He and his wife went home with me. Sister Crosby gave me a pair of cotton stockings some bleached cloth for my boy Platte some shirts a box of pins a box of wafers and a cheese weighing about 16 lbs. a can of whey for vinegar &c. Sister Elizabeth Brown gave Platte some calico for a dress.

[July 1849]

July 4th. Had green peas out of our own garden.

5th. Br Summy worked ½ day on our house.

6th. Same as yesterday.

7th. Br Summy worked on the house all day. Sister Caroline came home. Went back next day. Paid 1½ dollars for 12 lbs flour.

Sunday 8th. Attended sister Abbott's funeral. Paid br Summy 4¾ dollars in gold dust and some cheese.

9. Br Summy worked on the roof and br Hughes on the chimney and next day finished it.

10th. Visited at br James Ferguson's.

16th. Sister Caroline home to stay, having finished her school.

17th. Paulina moved out of the Fort onto the lot by us and will occupy one room of our house if it is ever finished.

18th. Went to the warm spring to bathe.

21st. Have some flour that was made from wheat grown this year. We are in hopes that we shall not be troubled any more for bread as the harvest has commenced.

22nd. Sunday. Staid home all day. Have been very busy all the week preparing for the feast that is to be enjoyed in the Bowery on the 24th.

23d. Made a shirt for br A[braham] O. Smoot.

Tuesday 24th. Great celebration which we all attended. Took dinner with the Cotton wood ward. Had a pleasant time. Plenty of victuals, music and mirth, and some good preaching.

Wednesday and Thursday. Washed &c.

[August 1849]

Aug 18th. Maria Lyman sent some red calico for Platte a dress, a birthday present. Also a dress pattern for Caroline or me.

20th. Platte DeAlton Lyman one year old to day. Made a dinner in honor of the event. Sisters Billings, Warner, Burk, Walker, Paulina and Priscilla Lyman, Emily Young and Sarah Clark took dinner with us. Not a man there but one who will be a man if he lives a few years.

25th. Sisters Clarisa Robison, Eliza Duzett and Catharine Foutz visited us.

28th. Caroline and I visited as [at] Sister Keziah Burk's.

[September 1849]

Sept. 2nd. Attended meeting. Heard P[arley] P. Pratt preach in the forenoon and Erastus Snow in the afternoon. Br Frederic gone to Cotton wood for wheat. Br Crosby and Tinney here to dinner. We have very cold nights and our house if house it can be called is very uncomfortable. The logs laid up part of the roof on and a very little chinking in.

4th. Mother visited at br Riser's.

Wednesday 5th. Took my year old babe and went to the field to glean wheat. I spread a quilt under the wagon in the shade for the baby while I gleaned, but the sun was so warm that I could not work long.

6th. Made a Babies dress for sister Rich, for which I get 1 lb of wool. Br Kimball called on us. Wrote to br Lyman.

7th. Visited at Lewis Robison's with sisters Caroline, Lydia and Paulina. Took two quilts to piece for Sister Billings also a shirt to finish.

8th. Received 6 lbs 3 ounces wool from Cotton wood to be divided among several of us. Br Frederic put up an adobie wall between the rooms.

Sunday 9th. Sidney Tanner and S[amuel] White here to dinner. Staid at home.

10th. Tremendous shower of rain and hail.

11th. Washed &c. S. Driggs sent us two lbs 10 ounces tallow, it being our portion out of a very fat cow.

12th. S. Tanner and wife here to dinner. Lucy Ferguson here visiting. Mr Frederic mudding the house.

13th. Visited at Dr D[arwin] Richardson's with Mother, Caroline and Sister Van Cott's.

Sunday 16th. Attended meeting. Heard a discourse from the Reverend Mr Marble an emigrant.

17th. Gleaned wheat.

18th. Went to Sister Billing's to sew. Cut and partly made a pr of pants for John Warner, took them home and finished them.

19th. Samuel White gave us an invitation to attend his wedding the next week at Mrs Foutz's.

21st. Sewed all day.

22d. Made a cap for Oscar Lyman[17] and helped Paulina on her dress. Father Gould called on us, just from the States.

Sunday 23d. Staid at home all day. Brs Tinney and White here to dinner.

24th. Making preparations for the wedding.

26th. The wedding came off in good style and every one seemed pleased with themselves and every body else. Staid till one oclock at night and danced. Went home and rested till morning then went to Cotton wood and had another party and dinner at the residence of the bridegroom. Had a very pleasant time.

28th. Came home again and found all well. Sarah Clark came with us to spend a week. Bought a ½ doz cups and saucers for 1½ dollars, an ounce of indigo for 20 cts.

29th. Saw br T[homas] Grover just from California. Read 2 letters from br Lyman, one to Caroline and one to D. Frederic.

Sunday 30th. Attended meeting and heard Levi Hancock and Lorenzo Snow preach in the forenoon and Father Isaac Morley in the afternoon.

[October 1849]

Oct 1st. Received some goods that Br Lyman has sent from California to his family.

3rd. Several of the friends from Cotton wood here to dinner. D. Frederic divided the goods that br Lyman sent. 11½ lbs coffee to each woman or family counting S[amuel] White and wife and Sarah Clark in the family. 13 lbs sugar, less than a lb of tea, 18 yds cotton cloth to the most of us. 1 bolt calico each, Lydia one bolt, Mother ½ a bolt, br Tinney 1 bolt, John

Gleason 1 bolt. He also sent 1 bolt pants cloth, 1 Doz hickory shirts, 1 bolt white flannel and one red, 2 bolts blue drilling which has been divided into dress patterns of which we each took one that is 7 of us. I let mine go to Sarah Clark to pay for one that I had been under the necessity of borrowing before the goods came.

4th. Our company from Cotton wood all gone home except Sarah Clark who is spending the week with us.

5th. Finished a pr of pants for D. Frederic.

6th. General Conference.

10th. Br White and Hakes here to dinner. Mother went home with them. Caroline and I visited at Sister Summy.

Sunday 21st. Mother came home from Cotton wood.

23rd. Visited at Father Lott's with Mother, Emily, Sister Pierce and her daughter Margaret. Making shirts to pay for soap. Spent a week at cotton wood with Cornelia.

Nov. 15th. Commenced weaning Platte DeAlton.

16th. Sister Emily moved home after staying with us for a time. Sister Lydia went with her to stay awhile.

18th. S. Tanner and wife and Br Brown here to dinner. Br Glover called on us in the afternoon.

Eveline Rollins moved into one room of our house.

Dec 3rd. Had company, namely, sisters Caroline and Harriet Huntington, Priscinda Kimball, Emily and Zina Young, Lydia and Mother, Dionitia and Paulina. Presnt Young and Kimball joined us at supper. Snowed all day. Edward commenced going to school.

4th. Mother has gone to live with Emily this winter.

12th. Caroline and I went to Emily's visiting. Platte and I staid all night. Edward drew Platte home on his sled.

15th. D. Frederic gone to board with Paulina.

16th. Paulina made a dinner for some of her friends in honor of Oscar's birth day.

17th. Br Haskins making sash for our windows.

Lucy Meserve Smith (1817-1892)

As a young woman, Lucy Meserve Smith worked in a cotton factory in Lowell, Massachusetts, in order to earn enough money to gather with the Latter-day Saints in Illinois. The skill she acquired with a hand loom assured her a livelihood in Nauvoo and later in Utah. Lucy took great pride in the hundreds of yards of cloth she wove. As any reader of her reminiscence is bound to discover, she had a pronounced sense of accomplishment about everything she did, from weaving to battling grasshoppers to teaching Sunday School.

The daughter of Josiah and Lucy M. Bean Meserve, Lucy was born in Newry, Maine. She lived there until a few years after her baptism in 1837, when she left for Lowell. After she arrived in Nauvoo, she hired out as a spinner and weaver, spending some time in the employment of Emma Smith, wife of the Prophet Joseph. At age twenty-seven Lucy became the second wife of George A. Smith, a member of the Church's Council of Twelve Apostles. (Letters of Bathsheba W. Smith, George A.'s first wife, appeared in Chapter Five.)

The Smiths were an exceptionally happy family. George A. Smith had six wives, who lived in various settlements in the Utah Territory.[18] The wives were in many regards as close as sisters, and Lucy referred to them as such. Sister Bathsheba and Sister Susan lived in Salt Lake City, Sister Zilpha in Parowan, and Sister Hannah in Provo with Lucy, where the two of them raised the son of Sister Sarah following her untimely death. George A. Smith was heavily involved in Church responsibilities, serving with the Council of the Twelve and as Church Historian. He became a counselor to Brigham Young in the First Presidency in 1868. Though he was more often away from Lucy than with her, she found happiness in their relationship and in her own achievements in maintaining a household.

The "Historical Narrative" of Lucy M. Smith recounts her ancestry and early life as well as her activities in Utah. The following excerpt begins with the arrival of the Smiths in the Salt Lake Valley in 1849.

The original holograph is in Special Collections, Marriott Library, University of Utah, Salt Lake City, Utah. Minimal punctuation has been added here. Some portions of the manuscript appear twice, and the version revised and rewritten in Lucy's own hand is used here.

Lucy Meserve Smith.
(George Albert Smith Collection.
Special Collections,
Marriott Library, University of Utah.)

Oct. 27th [1849], we arive in Salt Lake City quite late in the evening tired and hungry, but I must cook supper for myself and teamsters, and then I could go back to my wagon and go to bed, and thank my Heavenly Father for my safe arrival. We found my husband's Father and Mother well and pleased to greet us.[19] They made a feast next day, had us all to partake. It was a great treat to sit at the table with long absent relatives and friends. I feel that it must be a foretaste of the resurrection of the just.

I slept in my wagon til into January, cooked and washed for ten persons over a fire in a little fireplace in a little log cabin floor only over part of the room belonging to the widow Smith Mother of Silas S. and Jesse N. Smith. Aunt Mary Smith died at Parowan Iron County.[20] Sister Zilpha moved into Father [John] Smith's house as they moved into their new

house. There her Joseph was born and I went and took care of her. The following Aug. 6th [1850] I gave birth to a still born son, then I nursed Sister Caroline's babe at my breasts six months, which is now br. F[rancis] M. Lyman's wife. [21]
[added later] Clara

Mr. Smith was sent by the Presidency with a Co[mpany] to settle & found Iron Co[unty].[22] He took sister Zilpha with him. Sister Bathsheba must take her two children and go and do the work for Father Smith's family, and I must go to br. Calisters and nurs baby as we had no wood, although we had bread stuff & meat groceries &c. Sister Sarah and hannah with their babes went into a little adobie house belonging to br Henry Bigler (as he was away with the Mormon Battalion.) The next June 12.th, 1851. Sister Sarah died leaving her son John Henry who was three years the 18.th, of Sep. following. I was teaching school at that time in the 17.th, ward. I taught 4½ months, I had 56 pupils. Miss Sarah J. Rich was my assistant.

I weaned Clara at the age of 11. months. I then went to stay with sister Hannah, as Father Smith wished me to go and help raise the boys.[23] We colored, hired wove a web of gingham to make ourselves and boys some clothes. When Mr Smith returned from Iron Co he was appointed to go to Utah Co. to preside. He took me and sister Hannah with the two boys, and settled us in the City of Provo, where I lived, til the boys were Married, being seventeen years. *[added later]* I think.

The first winter we lived in Provo Br. Kelting's and Br. Roberts ladies got up a Leap Year Pic Nic Party and I was presented with a Ticket also Sister Hannah, and all we had to do was to present our Ticket to a gentleman. That I could do very well but when the time came for me to invite my partner to dance first, "I that was the rub."[24] Some one must lead me to him. My courage failed me. Then we had a nice dance, nice supper, and the Ladies ate on their partner's plate rather than wash them as both could not have room at the table at the same time the room was so small being the upper story of the Grist Mill.

The next Leap Year Party was conducted by Lucy M. Smith, Ann K. Dunyon, Hannah M. Smith, and Martha Bullock. We had our house trimmed with evergreens globes baskets and flowers, many of them manufactured by sister Abbey Brown and her daughter sister Dunyon. The trimmings were nice and very tastefully arranged, which gave the rooms a delightful appearance. When the company assembled the four managers steped out on the floor and it fell to my lot to open the ball by prayer, then we invited our partners to dance until supper time, then we made the table look inviting as posible by loading it with all the variety of luxuries obtainable at that time, and then we had a green Fir tree in a keeler of dirt covered with a whitecloth and the tree was trimmed neatley besides having six lighted candles which contributed to give the table a delightful appearance.

We had a very dry warm spring and summer, and we were very destitute of sweet, so the Good Provider sent Honey Dew on to the Cottonwood and Willow leaves, and so br. Geo. Adair and wife, Sister Hannah and myself took the necessary utencils, went among the bushes, cut bows, washed off the sugar flakes into tubs strained the sap cleansed with milk and eggs then skimmed as it boiled. I understood the prossess nessessary, as I had seen my Mother manufacture sugar from the Maple sap. We four worked two days, made 50. lbs. of nice sugar, besides feasting on Pancakes and Molasses, and making a quantity of candy for the children. Br. Adair carried our Tithing to the Bishop. He said ours was the best of any brought in. He wished to know the reason. Br A told him that he had an old sugar hand along that understood the business.

Before we could raise any fruit, the fields abounded with ground Cherries growing spontaneously, which we appreciated as a great favour from the Giver of all good. I used to take Jonny and Charly long before the Sun peeped over the mountain and go to the field a mile and pick a five galon can full of the precious fruit and go back in time to eat our breakfast, as sister H. would have it ready, and then I would go to my school. Sister H. would fetch her babe sit her on the floor go and pick another can of Cherries. What we did not eat we could sell for a good price as fruit was scarce every where in the Territory.

When things got a little more plenty myself Sister Eliza Terril, Sister Rua Angeline Holden and Sister Hannah Maria Smith took our spinning Wheels and went to a large room in the Seminary and tride our best to see who could reel of the greatest No. of knots from sunrise to sunset.[25] Sister Terril 100,11. knots. Sister Holden not quite so many but better twist on hers. Sister H.M. Smith and I made the best yarn. It was equal for twist but I had a few knots the most but she spun and reeled 80. knots. On the whole we concluded we all beat. We had refreshments four times during the day, indeed, we took solid comfort in our days labour, and our association together.

We used to have Ward Parties in cold weather beside numerous others. Sometimes they would be kept up til nearly daylight. We had not much work to do in cold weather those days, so we had our dancing parties for exercise, then we had our meetings our Concerts and Theaters to while away time til work came on in the Spring, then we did not need any more dancing for exercise, but we could play on the Whimmikie Whammikie two Standard Lillikie Strikiety Huffity Whirlimagig. (Flax Wheel)

While Johnny and Charley were little boys down came myriads of grasshoppers, eating everything before them. I was teaching school. Mr. Smith had gone to Washington to intercede for a State Government.[26] He calculated that we had sufficient provisions to last til he returned, but we had more or less company so we got out and were oblige to resort to bean bread. It was rather light food to teach school on. Sister Hannah's Sarah M. was a little baby, and Sister Redfield had a feeble babe at the time, and wished Sister H to nurse it what her own babe could spare. She did so and Sister R. gave her a few lbs. of flower, so we could have one pancake a piece in the morning. The little boys seemed satisfied, being told they could have only one. I would come home at noon and go back to my school without a bit of dinner til some one threshed, then I could get wheat on schoolbill.

One day an Indian brought some Sarvis berries, which I bought. [I] picked some green Currents, found a few weeds for greens, and made a Pie of the berries, and we had a way up dinner. We must have felt as thankful as the Pilgrims did over their dinner of clams they ate off the chest lid that good Elder Brewster gave thanks over. When we got our Wheat flowered, then we could eat and give thanks for more than one Pancake.

I had planted a little patch of sweet Corn. One Sunday the Hoppers came. I suppose they thought I would not meddle with them because they succeeded[?] in others of my neighbours garden on Sunday, but I said it was right to do good on the Sabath so I fought and saved my corn, and my *good* neighbours was glad of it.

While I was in School at Provo two of the Brown boys and John H. Smith, were out of School one day, and the Provo River being very high and running very swiftly, they thought they could have a nice boat ride. They accordingly procured a Skiff and started out. They paddled to the oposite side. When their boat capsized the two Browns managed to get back into the boat, but John Henry sank and came up and was sinking the second time, when to the surprize of the people on the shore there came a great swell in the water without a breeze stirring and went right down under John H. lifting him up out of the water and throwing him up the high straight bank, and as he struck on his stomach the water poured out of his mouth very profusely.

His Father (George A. Smith) was at Salt Lake City at the time, and at that moment as near as we could learn, a feeling came over him, that all was not right with his boys at Provo.

He hastened to his prayer-room, and prayed to our Heavenly Father that his boys might not be swallowed up in the Provo River. When I got out of school, J.H. looked very pale. I asked the cause and he related to me the whole circumstances also of his mirraculous deliverence, saying I took one good drink while I was in the River. Said I, Jonny the Lord has a great work for you to do. He has already been on two missions to Europe, once 15. years ago, and once since he was a member of the Quorum of the Twelve Apostles, in 1884-5.[27]

[There follows a "school composition" prepared by Lucy in 1862 in commemoration of the Fourth of July.]

Sister Hannah and I took in spinning and weaving, and I learned to cut clothes so I could cut the boys suits myself. I taught school a No. of quarters. I attended Proff Charles C. Wandell's school one quarter at Provo in the old Seminary. I met with the Provo Choir of Singers twice a week two years and a half in succession which I injoyed very much. In the mean time sister Hannah and I wove hundreds of yards of cloth such as bed coverleds, diaper, geans, kearsey flannel linsey carpets &c. The draft work was very hard and dificult to get every figure right, and that I would have if I had to undo a half yard.

In 1856. the saints were called upon to confess our sins, renew our covenants, and all must be rebaptized for a remission of our sins, and strive to live more perfectly than ever before.[28] Then we had greater manifestations of the power of the evil one. I fasted two days to obtain a testimony from the Holy Spirit that I was accepted of my Heavenly Father. At the same time I kept at work in my loom both days without breaking my fast. One evening after the rest of the family had retired I knelt down to pray and I was grasped by the wrist very tightly and it seemed as though there was something held over my face so it was very difficult for me to breath or utter a word. Said I old felloa you can figure away, but you've got the wrong pig by the ear this time. I kept praying every breath I could draw which came very hard and loud, but I did not hurry, nor I could not be frightened. I went to bed when I got ready, but they followed me still trying to smother me, and after I got into bed I was struck on the shoulder quite hard.

The Holy Spirit said to me they can do no harm where the name of Jesus is used with authority. I immediately rebuked them in the name of the Lord Jesus Christ, and by virtue of the Holy Priesthood conferred upon me in common with my companion in the Temple of our God. All that evil sensation left me immediately. I soon fell asleep and was troubled no more at that time, but those wicked spirits seem to go from house to house annoying the saints after that, as they commenced their operations on me first I knew not why.

I was then chosen set apart and blessed to preside over the Relief Society with Sister Rua Angeline Holden for my first, and Sister Nancy Bigler Flemming for my second councelors, Sister Sarah Jane Goff Blackburn Sec'y and Treasurer. We did all we could, with the aid of the good brethren and sisters, to comfort the needy as they came in with Hand-carts late in the Fall.[29] They got their hands and feet badly frosted. Br. Stephen Nixon and wife nursed and took care of them til they were better. We favoured them br. and Sis. N. by quilting a quilt very nicely for them, as our Society was short of funds then we could not do much, but the four Bishops could hardly carry the bedding and other clothing we got together the first time we met. We did not cease our exersions til all were made comfortable. When the Hand Cart Companies arived, the Desks of the Seminary were loaded with provisions for them.

Just at the session of our Oct. Conference news came where these Hand Cart Co's were. President Young and others were excited and anxious for fear those Co's would be caught in the snow in the mountains. They could not go on with the Conference. The Pres't called for men teams clothing, and provisions, and they were soon on the way to meet the

Companies with Pres't Young himself til he got into the Can[y]on. There he took sick and was oblige to turn back. The sisters stripped off their Peticoats stockings and every thing they could spare, right there in the Tabernacle and piled into the wagons to send to the saints in the mountains. [On the Plains] The Snow was fast falling and the saints were just piling down in a heap with the idea that they must all perish when to their great joy they discovered a light at a distance. Then they took new courge and they had everything for their comfort.

I never took more satisfaction and I might say pleasure in any labour I ever performed in my life, such a unimity [unanimity] of feeling prevailed. I only had to go into a store and make my wants known, if it was cloth it was measured off without charge. My councilors and I wallowed through the snow until our clothes were wet a foot high to get things together give out noticeses &c. We peaced blocks carded bats quilted and got together I think 27 Quilts, besides a great amount of other clothing, in one winter for the needy.

What comes next for willing hands to do? The brethren are called to go into the mountains to stand guard to keep the enemy at bay.[30] They want bedding, socks mittens &c. so we sat up nights and knitted all that was needed til we made out a big load with the Quilts and Blankets which we sent out into the mountains to the brethren.

What next? The Provo Brass Band want a nice Flag. They chose a committee and sent To me desiring me to boss the concern. I said to the sisters less go to the fields, glean Wheat and pick ground Cherries to pay for material and make the Band a Flag. No sooner said than done. We paid br. Henry Maibin part dried Ground-Cherries and banance [balance] in money for the Gilding, part of the silk was donated The rest we paid for in Wheat, which we had gleaned. The middle of the Flag was white Lutestring Silk with an edge of changable Blue and Green let in the shape of saw teeth and a silk fring

269

around the edge of that and sister Eliza Terrill embroidered the corners with a hive and bees, butterflies, roses &c.

The gilding was imitation of two Sacks horns crosed in the middle or centre and gold letters across the top of the Flag (Presented by the Ladies of Provo.)

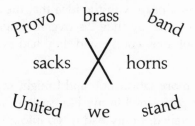

We had a handsome Staff with a beautiful bunch of ribbons on the top and a streamer on the oposite corner. The whole not counting our time or labour cost $76.

I wished to make a speech in behalf of the Ladies of Provo and Present the Flag to the Standard Bearer and have him make a Speech back to me in behalf of the Provo Brass Band, but our President James C. Snow put his foot on it. So we had a Grand Pic Nic Party when I returned from the City with the beautiful Flag. We had a nice supper and finished up with a dance. Our Flag took the prize in the big territorial Fair.

The next thing we must manufacture Carpets for our Provo New Meeting-House. We soon had them made and in position.

I organized and kept up a Sabbath School for many months before the brethern interfered and reorganized although perfect harmony existed among the teachers and children. The children were so strongly attached to me and took such an interest in their singing and other lessons, that I was appointed to take charge of the female portion and a br. to take charge of the males. Our Choirister visited me and wished me to get up some nice pieces and learn the children to sing preparitory

270

for the celebration on the 24th of July. Now here are some of the songs which I composed and I printed off ten coppies with a pen so the little ones could learn them readily, and they made the bowery perfectly ring. They sang with such inspiration that the whole audience were perfectly delighted. Our banners with their appropriate Mottoes were perfectly inspiring. Our children are our glory was one. When our celebration was in marching order we carried a number of blue and white Silk Banners with their appropriate Mottoes, and the boys carried Flags with the stars and stripes.

Br. Samuel S. Jones composed a very nice piece which I took pains to print ten copies with a pen so the small children could learn them preparitory for the celebration, and I felt proud of the little angelic Choir as they sang so sweetly under the bowery on the 24th of July. . . .

Sister Hannah Libbey Smith and I Lucy M Smith did all in our power to provid for the nesitie of our family, as sister Sarah died before John Henry was quite three years old while her husband was away on a mission to help found the County of Iron. As soon as the two boys were old enoug to work they must chop wood tend the stock at the cor[r]al herd cows, spool quill hand ends for me to draw through the harness, and then help wash dishes make pancakes &c.

Charles Warren the Son of Sister Hannah and Apostle George Albert Smith was four months younger than John Henry, and the little fellow would stand out in the snow nearly the whole day and chop wood to get enough to last through the day and have enough to make a fire in the morning. If I would go out to get a little of his wood he would cry poor little fellow. It often makes my heart ache when I think of it, and Jonny tending stock at the coral, nearly freezing, poor boy.

I sat in my loom month after month and wove while Sister Hannah and the boys did the other work, indeed I did all in my power to ease up the burden of my husband as he was President of Utah County for years. . . .

271

Martha Cragun Cox (1852-1932)

"I am proud of the fact that I am one of Utah's early children, having been the first to come to my parents after their arrival in the valley of the Great Salt Lake," began Martha Cragun Cox. At age seventy-seven this veteran schoolteacher and homesteader wrote in longhand an autobiography of nearly three hundred pages. Martha's narrative is really a collection of short personal vignettes, most of them rich in detail and complete with titles.

Martha James Cragun was the seventh child of James and Eleanor Lane Cragun, Indiana farmers who first joined the Latter-day Saints in Nauvoo. Like her parents, Martha lived most of her life on the frontier. Her childhood was spent at Mill Creek, Utah, a small settlement several miles south of Salt Lake City. In 1862 the Craguns were called along with other Mormon families to settle St. George in southern Utah, and Martha stayed in the rugged Virgin River area much of her life.

The vignettes that follow here relate Martha's growing up in St. George in the 1860s and 70s. She did not focus her story on the taming of the desert, though the life of the Saints in Dixie is never far in the background. Her interest lay in conquering personal frontiers, and so she remembered her struggles with the decisions that led her from weaving into teaching and, in 1869, into plural marriage with Isaiah Cox. Writing for a generation of Saints who no longer practiced plural marriage, Martha felt strongly about giving her children and "all who may care to read it" an account of her experience in living "the principle" with "the two best women in the world," her husband's first two wives Henrietta and Lizzie.[31]

The original holograph of the "Biographical Record of Martha Cox" is in the Historical Department of the Church. The manuscript is almost flawless, but where necessary, minimal punctuation has been added for clarification, including the replacement of short dashes with commas and standardization of Martha's rather confusing use of

272

quotation marks. Marginal notes have been included in the text without notation except where they are clearly asides.

Martha Cragun Cox with grandchild. (Portrait Collection. LDS Church Archives.)

I Try School Again in 1868

Bro John McFarlane taught school in our Third Ward. That was a gay season for St George. The influence of School and

273

Study bore light weight against that of Theaters, parties & balls. Whenever it happened that I awoke in time to get off to school in the morning I went. If too much of the morning was spent in restoring the strength lost from the night before, I stayed at home and prepared for the dance on the following night or wove out a few yards of cloth as many people still held to the home weaving. The routine of my life was that of every other girl in school.

The teacher too was interested in Theaters, music, & balls, concerts courts and councils and rarely came into school any earlier than the rest of us. The young lady who assisted the teacher was very frequently absent. As I was about the most steady in attendance among the lady pupils I had the privilege of hearing her classes when she was not there.

During the absence of the teacher at the noon recess we pupils used to dance the waltz in the school room. There were boys and girls a dozen of them just blooming or budding into their teens and I instituted myself their teacher. I was quite proud of this training class when I saw them take their places on the ball room floor always the best waltzers in the room were they. I felt a jealous pang when I saw they did not remember to waltz with their teacher. The theaters and plays in St George were first class. The concerts were also fine. McFarlane was an excellent leader. I had a great love for these things and had I been born with wealth I would have gone to the extreme. I would have travelled much and seen all that my heart desired but my kind heavenly parent placed me where I was out of the way of destruction. I think this school lasted about three months.

I Acquire a Desire to Teach

One day I was taking from the loom a piece of Jeans that I had woven for a pair of pants for Bro Jeffreys, a cultivated English gentleman. It had been made from nappy yarn and I told him did not reflect credit on the weaver. "O well," he said "'twill only be for a little while we'll need it! Twill soon be worn out and then my nappy cloth and the weaver's work will be forgotten. And the weaver too, though she becomes round shouldered over the loom in trying to serve the people with good cloth, will wear out and be forgotten and no one will know that she wove."

The words fell on me solemn like and prophetic, and I pondered on them deeply. "What profit is there finally" I said to myself, "in all this round of never ceasing labor? Weaving cloth to buy dresses to wear out in weaving more cloth to buy more dresses. When my day is past, my warp and woof of life and labors ended and my body has gone to rest in the grave, What is there to mark the ground on which I trod? Nothing," and the thought made me weep. After that I could not throw my schuttle as readily and swiftly as before. If I could only do some undying thing I felt it would move my arm to action. But to write my name on nothing except that that bore the device "Passing Away," was not intended in my creation I was sure of that.

In my dilemma I went to [James] McCarty.[32] I told him what Bro Jeffreys had said to me. "What could I do that my work and myself would not be forgotten?" I asked. He answered: "You might plant." To this I replied, That the day would come when Jos. E. Johnson with all his fine trees, flowers, vegetables etc that he had given St. George would be forgotten by the people & his fine gardens vanished. "Plant in the minds of men and the harvest will be different." He said, "Every wholesome thought you succeed in planting in the mind of a little child even, will grow and bear eternal fruit that will give you such joy that you will not ask to be remembered." His words, though they enlightened brought to me an awful sadness of soul. I was so ignorant. I could realize how dense was my mind. I saw that I had hitherto lacked ambition for I had been content to dance, laugh and sleep my leisure time away, never supposing that I might reach a higher plane than that which enabled me to support and clothe myself.

275

Sympathy for myself led me into a feeling of sympathy for others who were in a like condition of ignorance. And there were many more who were in like condition with myself as far as education was concerned.

I one day passed a group of boys who had stolen out of school to play marbles on the street. The poor old crone who was trying to teach them must have been glad they had played truant for they were of the age and disposition to be most trying in school. And truly, the fact that a great many children were growing up on the streets of St George without schooling or moral training even was truly alarming. I said to the boys mentioned "If I were your teacher I'd be sorry to have you out of school." A big fellow answered. "Oh the old woman's glad we're out." I told the boys I was sorry to see them growing up without education. "If you're sorry for us" they said, "why don't you teach us? We wouldn't stay out of school if you taught us." "I wish I knew enough to teach you," I said "and I'd see whether you would." One bright little fellow spoke up and said "I should think you'd teach us that that you *do* know." Here was a new thought. There were many children who knew less than I. Why not give the little I had, if I could not give much. The bantering words of these rude boys on the street aroused a feeling hard to resist, and I resolved that henceforth as far as it lay in my power to do so I would spread light into darkened chambers. I decided to become a teacher.

But I had much to overcome. I was rough in manner, and though possessed of a good enough heart I was wanting in that pride and dignity so requisite in the make up of a good teacher, which I could never hope to become, but in a quiet way I meant to disseminate knowledge among all those who were poorer than myself in intellectual riches and the thought of doing so gave me happiness.

I had fallen into keeping company with a young man of no very lofty ambition nor striking virtues but had agreeable

276

manners—liked to dance and have a good time, and my family made no objection to our associations. I knew him to be a tippler of wine though I had never known him to get drunk. The fact that he loved wine and that his father was a drunkard did not disturb me much and I gave him reason to expect I would stay by him and marry him, but a conversation I had had once with McCarty on the subject of my marriage would come to me sometimes with such force that it finally took lead in my mind especially when I saw the sparkle in his eyes when he quaffed a glass of wine. McCarty had said to me at the time mentioned that if I married a man who loved whisky as well as my father loved it I could not hope to have a posterity whose natural endowments would be equal to that even of the mediocre among men. I knew enough of the Gospel to realize the responsibility of parenthood and the condemnation I would be under in imposing this curse on my posterity. Again, I had many times said with much earnestness that if a husband ever came home to me drunken and abusive as some men in St. George did to their wives, "I would kill him."[33] And I fully believed that I would do it. Though I knew that no murderer could enter the celestial kingdom.

This gave me much concern and I prayed much to the Lord to teach me what to do, and even that the young man's attentions might be turned away from me. I would have been glad to become distasteful to his sight. But the Lord kept by my side and when the time came I said without a fear "I cannot marry you, I'd lose my salvation if I did." I did not meet this man again face to face till the course of fifty years had run by. His bloated face, and other marks of debauchery during a life of drunkenness in which he lost love of wife & children and loss of all, made me say, "Oh how good is the Lord to me." As I could not summon courage to give an explanation my words created in his soul a sort of contempt for me, or so I thought. But if he wished he might have taken this consolation to himself: I did not quit him for a richer, younger, more popular young man than he for I married one of the poorest men in Washington Co. and one who had already two wives and a family of seven children, and who did not handle as much money in all the years I was his wife as the other handled in six months while a contractor in S.L. City, where he went into all kinds of excesses.

I Decide to Try Plural Marriage

My decision to marry into a plural family tried my family all of them, and in giving them trial I was sorely tried. I had studied out the matter—I knew the principal of plural marriage to be correct—to be the highest, holiest order of marriage. I knew too, that I might fail to live the holy life required and lose the blessings offered. If I had not learned before to go to the Lord with my burden I surely learned to go to him now. Having decided to enter this order it seemed I had passed the Rubicon. I could not go back, though I fain would have done so rather than incur the hatred of my family. If the Lord would have manifested in answer to my sleepless nights of prayer that the principle of plural marriage was wrong and it was not the will of Heaven that I should enter it, I felt I should be happy. But it only made me miserable beyond endurance when I tried to recede from the decision I had made to enter it. My only relief was in prayer, and prayer only strengthened my resolve to leave father, mother and all for—I scarcely knew what. I was sorry sometimes that I had taken up the question at all, but having assumed it I could not recede, and I found relief only in prayer when the Holy Spirit gave me inspiration and made it plain to me that it was the only source thru which I could attain salvation.

When the final decision was made known to my family that I could not recede from my purpose the storm broke upon my head. It was not a marriage of love, they claimed and in saying so they struck me a blow. For I could not say that I had really loved the man as lovers love, though I loved his wives and the spirit of their home. I could not assure my

family that my marriage was gotten up solely on the foundation of love for man. The fact was I had asked the Lord to
lead me in the right way for my best good and the way to fit
me for a place in his kingdom. He had told me how to go and
I must follow in the pathe he dictated and that was all there
was to it.

Meet Wm Smith

Nov 20, 1869. We started for S.L. City to be married. On
Monday Dec 6th we were sealed in the old end[owment]
House. I received my endowments the same day. [*An account of
her trip to the Endowment House, where William Smith was an
officiator, and her work in St. George as a teacher's assistant follows.*]

Tests in Plural Marriage

It had always seemed to me that plural marriage was the leading principle among the L.D.S. and when I came to know how
generally my action in going into it was denounced, especially
the fact I had married into poverty, I was saddened as well as
surprised. When in my mind I took a survey of our little town
I could locate but a very few men, not one in fifty of the
whole city who had entered it at all. One who had been my
admiring friend said: "It is all very well for those girls who
cannot very well get good young men for husbands to take
married men, but *she* (me) had no need to lower herself for
there were young men she could have gotten." And she and
other friends "cold shouldered" me and made uncompli-
mentary remarks. The good kind women whom I had chosen
to share the burdens of life with gave me strength and comfort with their sympathy and love, and I retired within the
home and like the porcupine rolled myself into a ball when
my enemies approached and showed them my quills only. But
when thinking it over soberly I would come to the conclusion
that the public dealt with me as charitably as I could expect it
to do, and I blamed no one not even my own family for their
coolness towards me.

I began to realize my own imperfections now, and I am grateful to my Father that I had wisdom from Him to see [and] know them. Adopting the rules and regulations of my husband's family—an order already established—I had to submit to an almost entire reversal of my nature and habits. The greatest foe I had to meet was the hot Irish temper that had always swayed me when occasion aroused it. Many times the words of McCarty would be brought to my mind. "Remember in your plural home to speak no words when angry." When I disobeyed that injunction it brought me sorrow.

To adopt an early hour for rising and for retiring worked rather a hardship on me. When at the stroke of five in the morning I was obliged to drag my drowsy head from my pillow I would bless my mother for having let me enjoy so many late morning naps when I was at home. And when the clock at nine in the evening sounded the curfew and I had to retire to bed to toss sleeplessly there until near the middle of the night I felt that order and method were hard masters indeed, and I desired to roam once more in the "Happy Valley." Again [came] McCarty's admonition to "conform to all the established rules of the house to which you are going and be careful of how you try to set up your own ideas of government."

To eat a dinner without meat and salt-rising bread without salt in it were two petty trials I had to put under my feet. And I hankered for a sip from my mother's tea-pot. I thank my Father above that He gave me strength to comply with all the rules of our house, the main rule being perfect obedience. The first year of my married life gave me more experience in the duties of life than I had ever learned before.

On 3 Mar. 1870 my 18th birthday Henrietta the Senior wife gave birth to a son. We named him George Washington. A bright lovely child he was and I loved him exceedingly, and his mother was beloved by me. Lizzie's boy Henderson Elias was born 20th of the following April, 1870. Geo. W. d[ied] 5 March 1871.

My First Born

Jan. 11th 1871 I received from Heaven the gift of a daughter, a mite of a creature weighing 7 lbs and 11 oz. As I looked at the waxen figure beside me on the bed I felt I had all I needed in this life to make up my sum of happiness. Two short days she adorned my life. Two short days of unmeasured bliss. But a lingering difficult birth had done its worst for her and on the morning of the 13th the spirit warned me to call the father and family and the elders. They saw no cause for alarm and attributed my uneasiness to the weakened state of my nerves but to humor me they proceeded to bless and name her. Scarcely was this accomplished when the spirit took its flight. This was my first real sorrow and the bitterest disappointment I had ever known. We gave the baby my name and that of my mother: "Martha Eleanor." She died 13th Jan 1871 (b 8:20 PM).

[margin] In this year 1871 B[righam] Y[oung] proposed to build a Temple. Dedication of Temple ground Nov 9th 1871. I attend it. First stone laid 16 Mar 1873. [I attend it.] Temple dedicated Jan 1 [1]877. [I attend it.]

Stricken with Measles

Through the latter part of Jan and thru February Measles prostrated our family one after another only the father of the house escaping. On 5th Mar our little George was taken. This I felt could have been avoided had we understood the disease better, but it was new to us all. The first visitation of it St. George had had.

During April and May I again attended school, to R.S. Horne again. This was at an expense and great sacrafice but I felt that I must get some training as a teacher if I ever succeeded in giving my "street boys" instruction. I had those idle marble players ever on my mind.

281

I ask for a School

In September of this year being reminded again by one of my boys of my promise to teach I applied to the Trustees of school to be permitted to teach in our 3d Ward School house. They would not listen to my proposal. My rude boys would smash the windows, break the benches and in fact make general destruction of the property. Besides they did not think I had the ability to teach.

When I went home Sister Elizabeth Whitmore was there. She who owned the hall wherein McFarlane had kept his school, and where for the past winter the people had danced. She offered to let me have her hall one month free of rent if I wanted it. She felt desirous of seeing me try out my ability as a teacher. I accepted her offer. But the room had no furnishings. Bro Charles A Terry loaned several planks and blocks with which to improvise seats. Sister Whitmore loaned me an old kitchen table of small size for a desk. I mustered up another degree of courage to ask the loan of a black board from the school. Their refusal abashed me so and I felt so belittled for having been turned down the second time. "Auntie" came to my relief. She said "Take the large bread board and paint it, and we'll use the top of the table for kneading dough." This great board four feet by 2½ I carried to Bro Kelsey that very night under cover of darkness and for 50¢ he gave it a good coat of blacking. A piece of white chalk from my husband's tool box and I was equipped. Now for my trial class.

Mrs W. advised me to take the children from the "select" families. She was a Southern woman and felt that "poor white trash" didn't amount to much. I first tried for subscription at the house of a gentleman of culture and education, one of the leaders of the people. His wife informed me that association with the children of the 3d Ward would not be elevating to hers. While Bp. Granger's wife who was present volunteered information and advice: I had married into a poor family—was no better than the other wives—[I should] go home and take hold with them in the work of the family and not be setting myself up for a school teacher. I tried to walk out with the air [of] an independent Republican citizen but I felt "mightily" small. I tried at several of the homes of the well to do and "upper class," but without avail. The last answer I received woke me up. "No, I don't wish to trust my children in a class built up for the teacher's test." I had confessed that I did not know that I could teach. How could I expect the people to support an uncertainty.

When I reached my friend's home and she learned the result of my visit to the "select families" a cloud settled on her face, and she said, "I guess your plan is a failure." I told her: "That is just what Sheriff Hardy says. It will be a failure because I have your house. He will not let his children have the association of yours." Anxious to know the objectionable feature of the association of her boys I had to tell her, "He says your children know nothing except to straddle a horse and swear." (Mrs Whitmore was a "cattle woman," and a very rich one. She owned immense herds of cattle and horses.) This changed her mood somewhat. She said she would not let me have the house if I took Hardy's children in the class.

Just then Mrs Andrus came by. "I hear you are taking up teaching." "Yes" I said, "I'm going to teach." Mrs W. told her she was giving me a chance to try out my ability and see if I could teach. I said with my head held high, "Whatever I do is going to be *teaching,* teaching of as high an order as anyone else's." Mrs Andrus said: "When I heard of your intention I just ran up to see if we can get our children into your class." That settled the matter with Mrs W. The Andrus family was not only one of her best friends but also except herself the richest family in the South. She stood by my school and myself to the end of the month promised. The class filled to overflowing. Some came for the love of learning and others because no fee was attached to the registration. At the end of four weeks I was in a dilemma. So flourishing a school could not be broken up. And I could not raise the subscription price which I meant now to up high enough to cover the expenses of rent: twenty five dollars per month, and seating, and warmth.

Now, the two best women in the world came forward with their helpful advice. During the summer we had built a new room of good size. It was unfurnished, had neither floor or windows yet. They said "Let us put a floor in that room and bring your school home." The father being away from home the task looked impossible. We had the lumber for the floor just from the mills. With the children's help we carried it in and fitted a floor. The uneven edges of the boards made ugly cracks but it was the best we could do. And we were thankful for it. While we were at work a letter came to Lizzie with five dollars enclosed in pay for some obligation. This was from her aunt Annie who came soon after to live with us. With this five dollars we put glass in the windows. With boards and blocks we arranged seats and by the following Monday I was ready for my class. The front yard was given over to the children for a playground.

I received a call one day from the Trustees who told me that my pupils belonged to the Ward School and I should dismiss them and let them go to the Ward. We can see a reason for this claim when we understand that our southern schools were taught on the subscription plan. Hence the more pupils the more money. While I was considering whether I should comply with the request made of me, I received a call from Bro R. Morris head trustee for the 4th Ward schools asking me to come into the 4th Ward School, "and" said he, "We want you to come right down this morning." It was yet early. I sent a runner to tell the trustee who wanted my school to come over at nine o'clock and receive my school. Thus ended that trouble in a very amicable manner. The trustees were pleased. I was pleased to have a ward school to superintend. The women at home were glad to have the children out of the yard and to have the use of the room. The father of the house had come home and was ready to finish the room. So we were pleased all around and had no complaint against anybody.

I Move to the 4th Ward School

1871—Richard Horne was again teaching in St. George. He taught in the 3d Ward School House. The 4th W. school was soon so crowded that an assistant was necessary but teachers were very scarce. There were none to be had. I wonder now how I wallowed through the work of that winter. Bro Horne taught a business course at night school. Rettie [oldest Cox daughter] and I both attended. My school closed in March I think.

29 May 1872 I was again blessed with a little girl. Rettie named her Rosannah. And on the 4th of July following Lizzie's boy Warren came. Just as the cannons were announcing the great Independence Day. "Our twins" we called them. Those were busy days. We had an apple orchard of the very best. Through the fall months we dried and put up much fruit. Peaches were plentiful and we bought and dried many peaches. [margin] Rosannah b. 6:40 Am. Thursday. Weighed 9 pds. 2 oz.

Home Regulations

We had our work so systematized and so well ordered that we could with ease do a great deal. One would for a period superintend the cooking and kitchen work with the help of the girls. Another make beds and sweep, another comb and wash all the children. At 7:30 all would be ready to sit down to breakfast. Lizzie was the dressmaker for the house and she was always ready to go to her work at eight or nine o'clock. She was also the best sales woman of the house. She generally did most of the buying, especially the shoes. She was a good judge of leather. Auntie did darning and repairing. I seldom patched anything. She did it all for me. She never ironed the clothes. I did most of that. When wash day came all hands were employed except the cook. On that day we liked the boiled pudding. Noon saw our family wash on the line.

285

We usually bought cloth by the bolt and whoever needed most was served first. In fact we had in our home an almost perfect United Order. No one can tell the advantages of that system until he has lived it. We enjoyed many privileges that single wifery never knew. We did not often all go out together. One always stayed at home and took care of the children and the house. In that way we generally came home with a correct idea of what was given in the sermon.

Whenever one was indisposed she was not obliged to tie up her head and keep serving about the house but she could go to her room and be down knowing that her children and all her share of the work would be attended to. No one was obliged to bend over the wash tub when she was delicate in health or condition. All stepped into the breach and helped each other.

We acted as nurses for each other during confinement. We were too poor to hire nurses. One suit or outfit for new babies and confined mothers did for us all, and when one piece wore it was supplied by another. For many years we lived thus working together cooking over the same large stove with the same great kettles, eating at the same long table without a word of unpleasantness or a jar in our feelings portrayed. The children we bore while we lived together in that poor home love each other more than those that came to us after the raid on polygamists came on and we were obliged to separate and flee in different directions.

To me it is a joy to know that we laid the foundation of a life to come while we lived in that plural marriage that we three who loved each other more than sisters, children of one mother love, will go hand in hand together down through all eternity. That knowledge is worth more to me than gold and more than compensates for all the sorrow I have ever known.

Chapter Nine

The 1870s:
a Decade of
Collective and
Personal Achievement

"My Sphere of Usefulness
Is Being Enlarged"

It is no coincidence that the three women featured in this chapter
were closely tied to the Relief Society. All three women were writers
who published poems, articles, and books, and all three were suffragists. If the experiences of Emmeline B. Wells, Mary Jane Mount
Tanner, and Susa Young Gates seem to differ somewhat from those of
Latter-day Saint women before them, it is because their lives were
impacted by changes that occurred around the 1870s, one of the most
significant periods in Mormon women's history. The reorganization of
the Relief Society in December 1867 thrust women into expanding
roles of public leadership and increased their opportunities for personal achievement. Brigham Young himself sowed the seeds for this
new era for women, declaring: "We believe that women are useful,

not only to sweep houses, wash dishes, make beds, and raise babies, but that they should stand behind the counter, study law or physic, or become good bookkeepers and be able to do the business in any counting house, and all this to enlarge their sphere of usefulness for the benefit of society at large."[1]

Dormant from 1857 to 1867 because of the general disruption of ward activities caused by the Utah War, the Relief Society became a prominent part of Mormon women's lives in the 1870s. The diaries of Mary Jane Tanner and Emmeline Wells show they both worked with their local societies "looking after some of the poor and the sick." President Young was explicit in directing societies to be organized in wards throughout the territory, not only to carry out such relief, "but for the accomplishment of every good and noble work."[2]

"The subject was home-industries," Emmeline Wells once recorded after "society meeting." With money they had raised from fairs and parties, Relief Society sisters imported knitting machinery, raised silkworms, set up tailoring establishments, bought, stored, and sold grain, made everything from straw hats to shoes, and bought property and built their own cooperatives where they could sell their homemade goods on commission. Home industry was one means by which Brigham Young hoped to preserve the economic entity of the Saints as their geographic isolation faded in the wake of the transcontinental telegraph (1861) and railroad (1869); and it was one means by which women could step forward to build the kingdom "just as much as an Elder who went forth to preach the Gospel."[3]

Having "no house for our meetings," Mary Jane Tanner's Relief Society gathered "at private residences," so she noted in 1874, a time at which many local societies had built halls with their own funds. Women gathered weekly in halls or homes to quilt, sew carpet rags, discuss church history and doctrine, and share testimonies. The impact of the organization spread quickly beyond these meetings, however. "We are going to meet tomorrow evening to choose a president for the Young Ladies Society which will be organized in this ward," recorded Mary Jane. Retrenchment societies, first started by Brigham Young in 1869, were to provide young ladies a way to band together to resist Gentile influences. Later known as Mutual Improvement Associations, these ward organizations were "mothered" by the older

Relief Society women, who helped to staff and direct the young women's meetings. The Relief Society likewise served as a mother organization to the Primary Associations established for children in wards throughout the territory starting in 1878.

"[We are] women of God,—women filling high and responsible positions," declared Eliza R. Snow, "presidentess" or head of these three women's organizations. Encouraging her sisters to take up their new callings in Relief Society, Young Ladies Mutual Improvement Association, and Primary, she also rallied sisters in opposition to local and national antipolygamy campaigns. "Were we the stupid, degraded, heart-broken beings that we have been represented, silence might better become us," she told five thousand women assembled in the Tabernacle in 1870 in the first of many "indignation meetings." Over nearly two decades, through similar mass meetings and petitions and personal visits to Congress, Mormon women made an impressive though ultimately unsuccessful attempt to defend the Latter-day Saint system of plural marriage from legal harassment.[4]

Increased public speaking and public service among Mormon women in the 1870s reflected growing opportunities for American women at large. Latter-day Saints were conscious of the women's rights campaigns being mounted by their contemporaries in the United States, and certainly they were influenced by the widespread concern for expanding woman's sphere. The rigors of frontiering largely behind them, Latter-day Saint women, like their American sisters, turned increasingly to social and cultural pursuits. With the granting of the vote to Utah women in 1870, many of them became involved in politics for the first time. "Political meetings are something new to me," wrote Mary Jane Tanner, noting her attendance with other ladies who said "i [aye] sometimes by way of exercising our rights, and went home feeling the importance of our positions." Their holding of the elective franchise linked Mormon women and the Relief Society with suffragists throughout the country, particularly with the National Woman Suffrage Association. In 1889 Mary Jane Tanner was elected president of the Provo Woman's Suffrage Association. Emmeline B. Wells, who noted in March 1875 "the first time in my life that I ever spoke in public before men," traveled east a few years later to defend the cause of Mormon women before Congress

289

and the U.S. President, organized chapters of the Utah Woman's Suffrage Association in local wards, and attended national suffrage organizations and conventions.

Likewise, Susa Young Gates would eventually serve seven terms as delegate to the National and International Councils of Women (of which the Relief Society and YLMIA were charter members), but in 1879 she was a twenty-three-year-old student at Brigham Young Academy in Provo, and her letters indicate she was "busy with studies and lectures." For several years before the founding of his namesake school in 1875, Susa's father, Brigham Young, had heartily advocated the education of women "without distinction of sex," and his death in 1877 did not stop the movement.[5]

For Susa, academic training was a critical part of fitting oneself "to be a useful member of God's kingdom." Certainly she saw other women about her educating themselves to work in various capacities within the Mormon community: telegraph operators, lawyers, professional teachers. Several Mormon women attended eastern women's medical colleges and returned to Utah as M.D.'s, setting up practices, conducting midwifery and nursing classes, and staffing the Deseret Hospital, established in 1882 by Mormon women's organizations. Such individual achievements brought unprecedented accolades for women from the Mormon community as a whole.

Susa's last letter mentions (with some apology) one of many pieces contributed by her to the *Woman's Exponent*, a semimonthly tabloid owned, edited, and published by Mormon women. Mary Jane Mount Tanner was also a frequent contributor, and Emmeline B. Wells edited the paper for thirty-seven years. From 1872 to 1914 the *Exponent*, as its first editor Louisa Lula Greene Richards indicated, attempted to discuss "every subject interesting and valuable to women." The Relief Society, the Young Ladies MIA, and the Primary Associations were amply featured in its pages, as were reports of suffrage meetings, household hints, notices of current events and special classes, testimonies of the Church and its doctrines, and reams of poetry and personal essays. Early volumes of the *Woman's Exponent* still survive to recount and symbolize the decade when Mormon women began to reach outside their homes to their church and community and even to the nation at large. If they, like Susa, were somewhat self-conscious, they were no longer silent.

Yet, in going public these women did not cease to be private. A brief listing of their external achievements is, as it should be, only background for the drama of their individual lives. In 1874, at age forty-six, Emmeline Wells, an involved mother of five nearly grown daughters, presided over her first meeting and wrote the first of hundreds of *Exponent* editorials. Though two of her girls "were indignant with me for working in the Office, as if I had to earn my living," she was "anxious to acquire a thorough knowledge of an Editor's duties." Prodded by an inner drive, Mary Jane Tanner, wife, mother, and local Relief Society president, continued writing poetry, though it was "tedious work owing to the annoyance of the children," and sought and succeeded at getting it published. Susa Young, leaving behind a marriage that had failed, sensed in 1879 that she had "a destiny in this Church to fulfill." With high sights for herself and her two children, she remained at the Brigham Young Academy in spite of her mother's oft-expressed hope that she would return home to St. George.

In a time of change, these three women found their own personal lives in a state of transition. Emmeline, Mary Jane, and Susa each expressed joy in her new accomplishments, but none sought to substitute her public achievements for her personal family life. Consciously and unconsciously these women battled for balance. Periodic losses of equilibrium were the inevitable growing pains of those who found their "sphere of usefulness . . . being enlarged."

Emmeline B. Wells (1828-1921)

In the rotunda of the Utah State capitol building sits a bust inscribed with the words "A Fine Soul Who Served Us." For nearly half a century Emmeline B. Wells served in civic, political, and religious capacities, proving the truth of a statement printed in an editorial in her own *Woman's Exponent:* "Happy the woman who has the foresight to see that through forty years of experience she has matured the ability to commence a grand, useful second half of her life!" After raising her five daughters, Emmeline deployed her writing interest and talents in the editorship of the *Woman's Exponent* and a lifetime commitment to working in behalf of women.[6]

Born in Petersham, Massachusetts, to David and Deiadama Hare Woodward on February 29, 1828, Emmeline graduated from a "select" girls' school at age fifteen and became a teacher. She had joined the Church the year before, and her mother, fearing that she might be drawn away by her school associates, arranged a marriage for her young daughter with James Harris, son of a local presiding elder. Emmeline traveled with James and his parents to Nauvoo in 1844.

Emmeline's life underwent a dramatic change when she lost her first child, Eugene, soon after birth and was deserted by her husband. She later became a plural wife of Newel K. Whitney and traveled with his family to Utah in 1848. There she gave birth to two daughters before Bishop Whitney's death in 1850. They are Isabel (Belle Sears, in the diary) and Melvina (Millie). Marrying Daniel H. Wells (the Esquire) two years later, she bore three more daughters, two of whom died in young womanhood, and spent the years between 1852 and 1874 closely involved with their growing family. These daughters are Emmeline (Emmie and Em), and Elizabeth Ann (Annie), and Martha Louisa (Lou, Louie). Emmeline's diary abounds with names of both Whitney and Wells family members.[7]

In 1874 and 1875, the period of this diary, Emmeline entered a traumatic period of her life, still heavily involved in family affairs. Because her residence was separate from her husband (Emmeline was the only one of his wives who did not live in the "other house"), she often felt less of his support and association than she desired, which caused her much anguish. Yet she was beginning to find great satisfaction in her service and a challenge in her growing responsibilities in the *Exponent* office. At times her yearning for a strong arm to lean on and a comforting shoulder were replaced by a self-reliance and an independence that made possible her extraordinary achievements.

Emmeline B. Wells, photographed in Washington, D.C., possibly in 1879, during the first of her many trips east to conventions of the National Woman Suffrage Association.   (Portrait Collection. LDS Church Archives.)

As editor of the *Woman's Exponent*, 1877-1914, Emmeline found herself drawn into a public life that would take her back East many times to defend the cause of Mormon women before Congress and the President, and join her voice in the support of better opportunities for women. Active in Relief Society work all of her adult life, she became general president in 1910 and served until three weeks before her death in 1921. She published a book of poetry, *Musings and Memories*, in 1896; it was so popular that another edition was printed in 1905. In 1912 she was honored for her literary efforts by receiving an honorary Doctor of Literature from the Brigham Young University, the first woman to be so honored.

These excerpts are taken from one of the forty-seven volumes of her diary located in the Harold B. Lee Library at Brigham Young University. Minimal punctuation has been added. Some of the abundant semicolons have been replaced with periods, when the thought of a sentence was unrelated to what followed or the sentence ended the daily entry.

> Sat. Aug. 22 [1874]. I went to the fourteenth ward to meeting, had a good meeting. After the close of the meeting Sister E[liza] R. Snow called on me to stay to a meeting of the committee of the Exponent, and they wished me to write an Editorial as Sister [Louisa Lula Greene] Richards was ill in Cache Valley; concluded to send a committee of 2 to call on [James] Dwyer to ask him to take the agency of the Exponent; Sister Woodruff who is going on a visit to her friends in the East, was appointed as a Missionary to preach and teach the Gospel in her travels; she was blessed by the sisters. In the evening Em. went for a ride had a nice time.

> Sun. Aug. 23. Mary Jo's baby died this morn. We are none of us very well today. In the evening Will was here. Mill. went with Lib to the Methodist Church; Mr. Bryant came home with her. Jo Taylor, Rudd, Clawson, Hary Emory, Rulon [Seymour Wells], Heber [Manning Wells] and several others of the young folks were here; enjoyed themselves very much indeed.

Wm. was here drunk both Saturday night and Sunday very much to my annoyance; indeed on Sunday he made me quite sick; when will it all end; I am so worn out with these kind of things.

Mon. Aug. 24. This morning I commenced writing, I seemed concerned about the Editorial for fear I should not please the Committee. For my own part I would not be at all afraid, I love this kind of work. Mr. Wilson came here and spent the evening. Emmie was invited to go riding to Hilt's Farm with Richard Taylor, but the wind was blowing severely and Mr. Wilson being here she could not very well leave him; she missed her music lesson today on account of some difficulty about the key.

Tues. Aug. 25. I am still writing getting on pretty well, been not feeling very well in my mind; and not in health, my head seems confused and I am very nervous indeed; I feel so much care upon me I hardly know how to endure it, but the Lord helps me from day to day.

Wednes. Aug. 26. Today I finished my writing and Annie took it to the Office. I am glad to have it off my mind. In the evening Joshua [Kimball Whitney] came and took tea with us; Mr. Hendrie[8] came after tea, Eliza [Free Wells] came to stay with Annie, he read a little to us; we had a pleasant time; Will[iam] Woods was down stairs with Millie all the evening. I suppose they will soon be married now; Mr. Hendrie did not leave until after twelve.

Thurs. Aug. 27. Little Lou's twelfth birthday. I was taken very sick in the morning continued very bad all day long. I suffered the most agonizing pain got a little easier towards evening. The Lady teachers called Sisters' Reed & Decker. Em. was home all day waiting upon me, and preparing Lou's supper. Annie made a cake, Callie gave her a silver ring Millie a pink neck-ribbon. She was not so happy as she had anticipated on account of my being sick. Mother [Elizabeth Ann Whitney][9] is very sick has had sinking spells they thought she was dying.

Friday Aug. 28. I am a little better to-day. We had a new girl come yesterday Lowena. I hope she will be more help, the last girl run away. I have been reading a little today not able to sit up though; Mother is better too. Will was here in the evening and Rulon Lou, went to a party at Lizzie Young's.

Sat. Aug. 29. This is a very fine day. Annie & Louie have gone to the Springs. I got up about four in the afternoon and went as far as the Globe [Bakery]; took Anie for a walk. Daisie and Louie went down to Mary Jane [Whitney Groo]'s to see Mother. In the evening Miss [Mary] Cook came to see us and staid until half-past ten. Em. Annie went home with her. Lou. went to the Theatre. Chapin was playing with Miss Jean Clara Walters; Will. and Millie Ned, & Lib went to dine at Mr. Robertson's; did not return until about eleven. Very late in the evening a friend of ours called I think he had heard I had been sick; he staid with us very late as little Leslie was very ill.

Sun. Aug. 30. This is another showery day. Em. went to German Meeting—all the others to Sunday school. We had no company except some of the girls from the other house; no one much. Will came in the evening.

Mon. Aug. 31. This is the last day of summer, Miss Cook opened school; Mill. went to Mac.Alister's. I had several calls from lady-friends; in the evening Rulon was here, and Eliza staid all night. Will was here very late indeed. Lou. went to Katie Young's to sleep. Nothing of any importance has transpired with us; the weather is variable. I am troubled considerably about Millie's marriage.

[September 1874]

Tues. Sep. 1. The anniversary of Eugene's birth; he would have been thirty today. It seems almost like a dream when I consider and reflect upon it; if he were living how much happiness he might bring to me; what a rock to lean upon; what a shelter and protection his strong arm might be for his nervous and delicate mother; I feel sure he would have grown up pure and true-hearted, kind and generous. He was beautiful no lily could be fairer than this sweet lad of promise. I can never forget the sensation I felt when I realized I had become a mother; young, childish, inexperienced; always petted and indulged to the very extreme; away from home and friends in a strange city none who had known me hitherto save my husband and he so young, and altogether so unused to the world. We two so unsophisticated alone in a strange place where all were strangers to us, having no idea of the stern realities of life, how hard it was how severely we were put to the test. Our Father in heaven the only one to whom we could go, for comfort, sickness, poverty and all its attendant consequences. When I look back it seems incredible that I should have passed through such hard and thorny places and kept and preserved myself as free from evil and impurity as I have always [been] firm in the belief of the kindness of my Heavenly Father always hopeful believing in the light after darkness; in God's mercy and feeling that somehow it was all for the best. God has been very good to me in many things. He has given me beautiful children, and many kind and true friends, a husband whose interest in the kingdom of God is ever upper most.

Sep. 2. School opened. Em. does not know as yet whether she will teach or not, Miss Cook is undecided, she has fewer scholars. Miss Ida [Cook] was to open school in the 13th Ward Assembly Rooms but it was not ready.[10] It is deferred until Wednesday consequently Miss Cook will not fully organize until that time. The weather is very warm, fruit is ripening and every one is busy with it, I am not well enough to commence as yet.

Tues. Sep 3. No change of any kind. Everything dull in the way of business. I was very sick again similar to the other sickness, indeed I feel as if my health was failing seriously. I suffer with my head all night. I kept the folks up, Em. was very attentive. Millie was not well either suffering all the time with her side.

Sept. Wednes. I was very low-spirited indeed, every time anyone spoke to me I was crying; Annie & Louie commenced to dry a few peaches. I was writing most of the day. Mr. Hendrie called to bring Em. a book, Lile was here and baby, I could not see him. I felt more gloomy than usual. Annie went to ask a friend of mine to call but could not get them, they were engaged. I longed to see my husband who was dead. Why can we not call them to us in our grief and sorrow, why cannot our dead come back to us if only for one sweet hour. In the evening Em. went to the association so did Annie, Millie was at home; Louie slept up with Ruthie Young. Called on several poor people. . . .

Wednes. Sept. 30. One of the very warmest days for this time of the year. I posted a letter today of some importance. O how miserable I am in regard to som of my children, almost heart-broken; every nerve in my whole system is un-strung. All the anguish a mother can feel in seeing her chil-dren do wrong I feel tonight, my heart is bleeding almost. Misery and darkness and I have no one to go to for comfort or shelter no strong arm to lean upon no bosom bared for me, no protection or comfort in my husband. Emmie & the little ones are all tenderness. O what should I do without them. But they are only weak themselves and need to be nourished by me. O if my husband could only love me even a little and not seem so perfectly indifferent to any sensation of that kind. He cannot know the craving of my nature. He is surrounded with love on every side, and I am cast out. O my poor aching heart. Where shall it rest its burden, only on the Lord, only to Him can I look every other avenue seems closed against me. O help me Father in heaven to overcome and resist tempta-tion in every form or shape.

Thurs. Oct. 1 This is the Anniversary of Mill's wedding day seven years ago. How terrible when I look back upon it, and yet we were all satisfied then and thought it a happy marriage.[11] How peculiar were my own circumstances at that time and how changed since then are all things concerning me; how different I have felt since then and how many things have transpired in my life to give me an experience, which is lasting and beneficial. Went to the fast-meeting in the afternoon, or rather the society I should have said. There was some talk about a new-order which some of our sisters who wanted to be very good had been trying to organize but through some misunderstanding it had fallen through.

This morning I went up City Creek to the place of baptism. I enjoyed the walk. My thoughts although solemn were not altogether unpleasant and my heart was fully alive to all the beauties of scenery and the many-hued leaves of autumn always had a charm for me, always reminded me of something pleasant in the past. How wonderfully are our minds impressed by certain objects in Nature.

My heart seemed tuned to harmony with all inanimate things. I did not care to hurry home. I felt I could have wandered among the mountain shrubbery for hours alone, no companion, but my reflections and thoughts. But duty that stern mentor whose calls are paramount recalled me to a sense of the obligations I was under and I turned my footsteps homeward. . . .

[November 1874]

Wednes. Nov. 4. The association met up at Hannah's. Emmie went up to see her father and he came down with her. Will was here; we had a very good time. He was more than usually demonstrative with me, manifesting great love for me and interest in my welfare, said he would get our furniture &c. We shall have to hurry up so little time to make our preparations. It is fully decided that Millie will be married on Saturday evening; Mr. Welch will perform the ceremony at his residence. We shall go up in a carriage with Mill Em. & I.

Ned & Lib in their own buggy, then return immediately and the reception will commence at eight.

Thurs. Nov. 5. Today is sister Ellen's birthday. She is 43. How anxious I feel to hear from her, how neglectful they are about writing to me, so many girls & none of them to pay attention to even a family correspondence. Today we got the cake from the Globe and took it to Brown's.

Friday Nov. 6. We have been expecting all day to get our things. Neve came and measured for our blinds and carpets. It was pouring with rain and has turned to snow, this morning the trees were nearly broken down with the weight of it, they looked enchanting like fairy-work. Weather is cold most unpleasant for a wedding. I have made three jelly cakes and frosted them. Sister Winter & Sarah, Sister Sedon and Clara are all here helping. We had Colt to come and Whitewash all the lower rooms to-day. We got to-day 1 doz. plates 1 doz. cups & saucers ½ doz. tea spoons ½ doz knives & forks 2 gravy boats 1 glass water pitcher 1 coal scuttle 1 tin wash-basin.

Sat. Nov. 7. The morning was fine overhead but the mud was fearful. My sister Mrs. Earl came to help us. Every thing is decided upon, the carpets are come. I am pleased with them also the parlor furniture. I never expected to have been so well off in my life. I am pleased with all, nothing extravagant but all in exact keeping and conformity. At half past seven we were at the residence of Mr. Welch and shortly after they were married, and we returned home, there were no arrivals in our absence. Everything was in complete readiness and we had a moment or two to think before any one came.

The first ones were Aunt Hannah's folks and Dessie; then Martha Lydia Ann Susan Katie & May, Inez and Charlie & Mrs. Tanner; next Joshua and Mary Jane then [unclear] Tibbetts, then about nine we went in to supper. While we were at supper, Ort. Rulie & Heber came then next came my husband. He came and partook of refreshments but took no wine;

after we were through came all the help and last arrival was
Budd. Every one seemed pleased and gratified with the entertainment. Ort played and sang. Lou. sang several of her
pieces; at ten minutes past ten the carriage came to take them
home. They bid us all good evening and left us. Ned & Lib
went with them and so carelessly and indifferently Millie left
her home to which she never expects again to return, as one
of its inmates, to make a new home for herself. May she be
able to make herself a sure place of rest and refuge in her
husband's bosom, and in poverty or sickness always feel
secure in his love and protection.

None but mothers know each other's feelings when we give
up our daughters whom we love and cherish so tenderly to
the mercies of a man, and perhaps even a stranger; Will seems
in every way qualified to make a good husband and to be
ever tender of women but time will tell the story truly.

> O heaven grant it prove a happy union
> Founded on true respect and sympathy.
> May they increase in goodness ever,
> And more abound in unity.
>
> May peace and contentment
> Ever wait upon their happy lot
> And richest blessings which the earth
> Can give, be theirs in wisdom sought.

About twelve the last of the guests left, and we sat alone in
the parlor enjoying the fire and talking over all the events of
this most wonderful day. . . .

[March 1875]

Tues. March 9. Septimus [Sears] is thirty one to-day. Belle
made him a present of Dr. Hollands Poems, and Dot gave him
a pearl handled gold-pen, and Em a paper holder—black
Walnut. Monday was Sep's birthday instead of Tues.

Wednes. March 10. To-day we had our Relief Society party, had a pleasant time. Pres. Young was there. Sat until 10 o'clock, Annie went with me. I danced some the Esq. [Daniel H. Wells] did not dance at all.

Thurs. March 11. Another stormy day. Pres. Young was tried for not paying his fine; and Chief Justice MacKean condemned him to 24 hours imprisonment in the penitentiary and 25 dollars fine. He went accompanied by Mayor [Daniel H.] Wells; and a large company staid his time.

Friday March 12. Will & Mill, Ned. & Lib were here to dinner. The President & party returned about two o'clock. Em. has gone to the Court-House with Rulie. We were alone all the evening.

Sat. March 13. Frankie Wells is 23 today. Swift[?] is getting up a Surprise Party for her; Em. is invited. Mrs. Larsen came here to-day she has left Margaret Young. Br. Joseph Scofield was buried to day his funeral was in the Assembly rooms. Br. George Q. Cannon arrived this evening from Washington; the Esqr. Hanmer & Junius went up as far as Ogden to meet him.[12] Yesterday there was a petition of about nine hundred ladies taken to Gov. [Samuel B.] Axtell to see what he could do towards releasing Prest. Young from his confinement in the penetentiary; the ladies who presented it were Mrs. I.M. Horn, and Mrs. Davis; he received them courteously and promised to aid them to the extent of his ability and the laws and constitution of our country. Tonight the Young Ladies Re-trenchment Society in this ward was organized at the residence of its Prest. Mrs. Elizabeth Thomas; Coun's Mrs. Flora Shipp Miss M. S. MacClean Miss May Wells Miss Ruth Woolley Miss Lucy Stringham Miss Lillie Taylor Miss L. Ashby Sec. Miss Annie Parks Assis; Sec. and organist.

Sun. March 14. A most fearful storm of snow again, wind blowing direct from the North. Millie came up and went up to Lib's; Em. went to Belle's. I staid at home all day but at evening went as far as Horace's [Kimball Whitney]. Found

Helen [Mar Kimball Whitney] alone although the children soon came in; spent the evening pleasantly with her and after Horace came in conversed with him upon portions of his mother's life and so on.

Mon. March 15. The snow is quite deep, and the cold raw wind blows terribly. I went to the Eleventh Ward to a Retrenchment meeting; Sister E.R. Snow and Zina D. Young were there also Bishop McRea and his Counselors'. It was a very good meeting I rose and tried to speak for a few minutes, the first time in my life that I ever spoke in public before men. I called on my sister after meeting. Came home called on Zina, and Elvira; Annie went to the fourteenth ward to the association.

Tues. March 16. Went in the morning to the Exponent Office was there all day correcting and helping the Editor; in the evening was busy writing. A telegram reached us today stating Judge McKean's removal from office, and the appointment of Parker from Missouri.[13]

Wednes. March 17. There is more snow falling at intervals through the day. The Wasatch Club or Literary Association met here this evening.[14] There was an excellent attendance. The weather is moderating.

Thurs. March 18. Went to the Relief Society meeting, the principal subject was the manufacturing and dressing [?] of straw hats, as a branch of self-sustaining home industry. In the evening there was a party for the benefit of the St. George Temple which Louie attended with [Le] Grande Young. I called on Mill.

Friday March 19. Went around to the Exponent Office afterwards to Lib's and took dinner, then up to Mr. Sears in the Eleventh Ward. Called at Olives on my way home, was everywhere welcomed cordially. Lillie walked home with me. Today they put up the ornament on our front porch. In the evening after German Em. went to the Debate and Annie spent the evening with Alice Crismon.

Sat. March 20. Em. went up with Belle this morning in the buggy to spend the day and practice a little on the piano; I went to the meeting in the Fourteenth Ward the subject was home-industries, and the one branch before the meeting and made a speciality was straw hats and bonnets. In the evening Annie & Louie went to the Retrenchment meeting in our own ward. Br. Pond from Cache Valley came and staid all night. We knew each other in the states.

Sun. March 21. Went to meeting with Em. to hear Orson Pratt. He spoke upon the Priesthood. An excellent discourse, and I sorely regretted that there was not a reporter there. In the evening Annie went to meeting, several boys and girls were here.

Mon. A dull drizzly sort of day heavy atmosphere; went to the Exponent Office to work all day copying and correcting reports.

Em. went to the Theatre to see the Lingardes, Annie & Louie to the Fourteenth Ward Association.

Tues. 23. Anna Sears birthday, 7 years old today. Belle came down, and brought both her children intending to stay a day or two. It seems nice to have her home. She is a woman rather superior for her age and the time in which we are living. Sep[timus] came down to see her. Annie went to the Theatre.

Wednes. March 24. Went to the Office again. Belle went down to Mill's and had dinner. I did not return early, called on Sister Eliza and spent the earlier part of the evening, met Miss Cook and Miss Cornelia Cook. Belle and Em. were indignant with me for working in the Office, as if I had to earn my living; it seems out-of-place to them, but I am anxious to acquire a thorough knowledge of an Editor's duties.

Thurs. March 25. Belle went home in the morning. The teachers called and afterwards two of the sisters, and I was very late going to the office. Louie and Mary Larsen went to the Theatre.

Friday March 26. Anie got her face burnt with chocolate, but not bad. Many hindrances. They commenced yesterday to put up the back-porch, are working today. After reading some proof, the first I ever did we called on Aunt Rhoda Richards, and afterwards on Lib. Mell & Bell have both been down to Mary Jane's today. Annie & Louie went to a party in the Court House Annie with Johnnie Spencer Louie with David Hilstead. Em. went to her theatre I was alone all the evening. Went to Elvira's a few minutes; Sister Kimball Adeline were here.

Sat March 27. Was busy all morning went to the Office and read proof about two hours, came home about three. Mrs. Robison and Mrs. Childs, called and staid some time. Harry Emery Jim, Ferguson and Rulie called. Harry staid all the afternoon and evening until after the theatre. Lou. went up to Belle's about noon Annie went to the Retrenchment Meeting. Sister Brooks was here, I went to the Theatre to see Lingard, enjoyed it very much indeed; saw my husband but not to speak to him.

Sun. March 28. Staid at home all day writing and reading. Katie is twenty-two to-day;

Sun. March 28. Katie Wells is twenty-two today. I have been at home all day, looking over old papers etc. and filled with gloomy reflections, looking at dear treasures letters, scraps of poetry, the perfumed essence of the days gone by.

This was Easter Sunday. Mill went with Lib to Church.

Mon. March 29. Stormy and windy, to wet and disagreeable to go out, went to the Post Office. Got my feet wet, felt very sick when I came home.

Tues. March 30. Went up to the other house had lunch in at Lydia Ann's; afterwards came down and was reading all the evening.

Wednes. March 31. A very cold raw air, was writing all the morning. Went out to call, in the afternoon, called on Mrs. Z.

D. Young Mrs. Park Mrs MacLean Mrs. Mussers, Mrs. Barney, Mrs. Herrick.

Engaged a girl from Manti San Pete [County]. Took a lock-box in the Post Office 555. It is said to be the twenty seventh anniversary of Modern Spiritualism today Em. went to the association Annie & Louie to the theatre. Was alone nearly all the evening reading and thinking.

Thurs. Apr. 1. They are trying George Reynolds for poly-gamy here in the district courts, today brought in a verdict of guilty, and found a flaw in the indictment being legally served, consequently it will be necessary to try the case again.[15] Went to the Fast Meeting in the morning had an excellent meeting. Went again in the afternoon to our own meeting over which I preside.

I feel deeply the great responsibility resting upon me in being called to fill this public office; but hope to be guided and sus-tained by the Holy Spirit in this calling and duty that I may keep humble and be qualified to do all things that are required of me and please my husband and gain his good will and favor as also all with whom I am associated.

Mary Jane Mount Tanner (1837-1890)

When Myron Tanner met Mary Jane Mount in Salt Lake City in 1855, he was charmed by the "literary tastes and poetic instincts" of this "refined and intelligent woman." Though he admitted to owning a "rugged, untempered and uncultivated nature" himself, the young Miss Mount found him attractive enough to accept his offer of marriage the following year. The couple decided to move to Payson, Utah, but by 1860 Myron's business ventures had succeeded so well that he bought a mill and two farms in Provo, where the Tanners settled permanently.[16]

Mary Jane's parents joined the Church in Ohio, where she was born February 27, 1837, a daughter of Joseph and Elizabeth Bessac Mount. Her only brother and sister died before the family joined the Saints in Nauvoo. The Mounts were among the first group of Saints to winter in Salt Lake City, having crossed the plains in the fall of 1847.

Of Myron and Mary Jane's first four children, only Joseph Marion, frequently mentioned in the journal, survived childhood. Five years separated him from the other children born to Mary Jane in Provo: Bertrand, Mary Elizabeth (Bessie), Grace Lillian, Lewis, and Arthur. Mary Jane also cared for a niece and nephew, Mary Elizabeth and Joseph Edward (Eddie) Tanner, who were boarding with her while attending school in Provo. A hired girl, first Martha and then Marie, completed the Tanner household. In 1866 Ann Crosby joined the family as Myron's plural wife, for whom he provided a separate home.

While her husband attended to business, civic, and church affairs, Mary Jane divided her time between her growing family and Relief Society responsibilities. Appointed president of her ward Relief Society in 1868, she held the position until her death twenty-two years later. Fond of literature and history, Mary Jane wrote life sketches of the female descendants of the ruling houses of Europe for publication in the *Woman's Exponent.* She also contributed some of her

Officers of the Provo Third Ward Relief Society with Mary Jane Mount Tanner, seated left, as president. Seated center and right, Hanna Clark and Phoebe Pratt. Standing, Sarah Liddiard and Hannah Libby Smith. (LDS Church Archives.)

own poetry, which she compiled into a book, *Fugitive Poems*, in 1880.

Mary Jane's frustration in finding time to write not only poems but in her journal is well chronicled in the following excerpts. Often the demands of husband, family, and church left her little time to compose the poetry and prose that sprung from the depths of her soul.

The following excerpts are taken from a microfilm of Mary Jane's holograph journal. Minimal punctuation has been added. Mary Jane's periods and commas are often indistinguishable and here have been translated as whatever would be appropriate. The original journal and correspondence of Mary Jane Mount Tanner is in the Special Collections of the Marriott Library, University of Utah.[17]

Feb. 11, 1876. My head aches today. I have been busy all the week helping to fit out the missionaries for Arizona.[18] The Relief Society was called on to assist the Bishop and it makes us considerable labor. We did all we could to get Jessie Harding and wife ready, and thought we had the job nicely off our hands, when we were informed that another party wished an outfit. Polly Ann Carter of our Ward is going to be married to William Whipple of the Second Ward, and go to Arizona with him. We got her a few things with means from the treasury, and some donations from the people. I gave something that I thought would be useful, and could, no doubt, collect more if I were able to get around.

May 31, 1876. The weather is raw and chilly, and the wind has blown cold and uncomfortably all day. I have been very busy preparing some of the members of my family to attend the jubilee at American Fork tomorrow. It was nearly night and I had just finished a dress for Mary (my hired girl) when a waggon drove up to the gate and a lady alighted, enveloped in a watterproof and sunbonnet. She was very cold and tired, having rode from Payson. When I had taken her things and made her comfortable she informed me that she had come to teach the District School in our ward, and had been recommended to me to seek board. Her name was Davis, Widow of Dr. Davis of Mona. Her husband had been dead about two years. He left her with very little available means, alone and friendless, in a strange country. She was a lady of intelligence and refinement, but poorly calculated to make her way, or support herself among strangers. I told her I was not prepared to take a boarder, but she should remain with us until she could suit herself better.

June 1st 1876. This is the aniversary of President Brigham Young's birthday. Mary has taken the children and gone on the excursion train to the jubilee at American Fork. We hurried them off this morning. The weather was cloudy and they had just started when it commenced snowing. I fear they will not have a pleasant day. Sister Davis and I are glad to stay quietly at home and rest.

June 2, 1876. The young folks came home last night all right, having enjoyed their trip though the weather was rather disagreeable. The baby grows nicely and we all think him very sweet. My housecleaning is through and we are using the adobie house where Ann used to live for a kitchen, but the weather is so cold that we cannot enjoy the nice clean house very much as we have moved the stove out and cannot have a fire there. Myron is making his home entirely with Ann for a few weeks on account of her health and I feel somewhat lonely but I try not to alow myself to be unreasonable.

June 17. I have coppied my last few entries a little out of place from not being careful in my dates. I find it was in 1875 instead of 1876, that I first made the acquaintance of Sister Davis, and the events just recorded transpired before my mothers death. June 16. 1875 a little boy was born to Ann. She called him William Myron. This is her sixth child, she has burried two. I find no more records until

Dec. 17, 1877. It is Monday, and I arose as usual, assisting with the work and helping wash until three oclock. I sat down to rest and read in Tulledge's new book called "The Women of Mormondom."[19] It carried me back in immagination to the various scenes through which we had passed in colonizing this teritory, and I was led to reflect on the goodness of God to us as a people in bringing us through the trials which had called forth almost superhuman energy and strength of endurance. I know that the colonization of Utah is a marvel to the world, but how much more would they marvel if they knew the various perils we had passed through and the hardships we encountered and which we never could have born but for the hand of an Allwise Providence.

While reading and reflecting on these things I received a call from a gentleman who introduced himself as Mr. Tulledge, the author of the book. He is a small spare man with sharp features and very black eyes. He was canvassing for the book, and we had a long conversation, in which he informed me that he had belonged to the Church for thirty years and had never apostatized as was generally supposed. I showed him my collection of poems and read some, asking his opinion of their merits in regard to publishing as some of my freinds are urging me to do. He said publishing was very expensive business. I would have to bear the expenses and take the risk of pleasing the public. He thought my poems showed considerable merit and had a commercial value. I promised to lend my influence in behalf of his book.

Dec. 18, 1877. I sewed this forenoon and after dinner I went to see some of the sisters about canvasing for his book. Some thought they would like to have it but had not the means at present. No one felt like canvassing for it, but the Teachers promised to mention it when they visited the ward. I called on severel of the neighbors and got home just before dark. Mary and Eddie Tanner, Joseph's children, are boarding with me going to school. They received a letter from home yesterday saying the children were sick. They went home in our buggy and sent it back today with word that their little sister was dead. I feel sorry for them all for I know they will feel the loss deeply. The children are rehearsing for the Christmas exebition, Grace has gone but Bessie is not well and I kept her at home.

Wednesday Dec 19. I sewed on the little girl's' aprons this morning, and in the afternoon I went into my neighbor's where I met a lady of my acquaintance from Salt Lake.

Thursday Dec 19. Today our Relief Society met at the residence of Sister S. A. Davis. We attended to several items of business, and closed early, as we were all busy preparing for Christmass.

Friday Dec. 20. I have been busy all day sewing and preparing for Christmas. Mother Coulson is here visiting and staid all night. I went in the evening and filled a business engagement, then called on Sister Beebe. She wished me to go with her to the School Exebition at the Methodist Meeting House. The performance was very entertaining and I should have enjoyed it if I had not forgotten the brine I was making for the beef. Marion made a fire and put the water over and I had promised to finish it. I got home at ten oclock and found the family in bed. The fire was out and the water nearly cold I knew Myron would be vexed if the brine was not made so I kindled the fire and put in the salt. Marion came in from some of his engagements and finished it. and I went to bed very tired.

Saturday Dec 22. I feel very weary after yesterday's fatigue but I haven been cooking for Christmas.

Monday Dec. 24. I have been very busy all day. I took the buggy about noon and drove around giving a few invitations for dinner tomorrow. I called at the Hall where the Christmas tree was being arranged but as my assistance was not needed Sister Harding and I went to the Second Ward Assembly Rooms to look at their Christmas Tree. It was very prety but not so expensive as ours. I came home and helped to prepare supper as Maria was busy cooking and churning. We all went to the Exebition in the evening. The tree was very nice and proved a success. All the children had nice presents. My little girls had shell boxes. Bertrand had a pocket book and knife, and Lewis a horse on wheels.

Tuesday Dec. 25. Christmas is over at last. The day so eagerly anticipated by the little folks. Owing to the decoration of the tree Santa Claus had but little for their stockings. There were some cakes and apples and little prize boxes, and some trifles that Bessie had made for her brothers and sisters. Bessie had a nice wax doll and Bertrand a pair of skates. I sent the buggy

for Mother Billings and Sisters Tyrel and Merit, some of those
invited to dinner. I did not care to invite those who had
freinds and good cheer at home, but remembered the poor
and the lonely. About ten oclock the band serenaded us. It
commenced snowing about that time and the snow fell all
day. The children were disappointed for they wanted a run,
but they made their playhouse upstairs. We had a nice dinner
and enjoyed ourselves until night when we sent the old
people home with a covered carriage it was snowing so fast. I
went with Myron to a ball at the Acadamy Hall. We enjoyed
the music and dancing until eleven oclock when we came
home thoroughly tired, and glad to close the day and sleep
until the beams of another day should call us to life and
action.

Wednesday Dec. 26, 1877. The snow has fallen quite deep
through the night and is still falling. We slept late this morning resting from yesterday's fatigue. We are reasonably well
and feel comfortable and happy. I received a letter from my
sister Martha, now Mrs. Read, telling us that her husband had
his shop burned down and lost all his stock. It was a saddle
and harness shop and comprised a large stock of goods in that
line, as that was the business he depended on for a living. She
tells me the people are making up a portion of his loss, but
they cannot replace the accumulation of years of industry.

I am trying to write some today but I always find it tedious
work owing to the anoyance of the children. If I sit in the
room with them they play and talk to me, and if I sit in
another room they are continualy coming to the door for
something and keep me answering their questions every few
minutes. It is always so, and for that reason, as well as many
others, I am not able to accomplish much in the literary line. I
work a little and keep my paper in as good shape as possible.
Family cares have taken my attention and long periods have
passed without writing in my journal, and many interresting
incidents are omitted.

Monday Jan. 1st 1878. Another year is ushered in. Another

page has been turned in the history of time, and we begin life as we left in [it] last night when we bade the old year goodbye and closed our eyes to slumber. We awakened, and Lo! another year had commenced. So silent, so stealthy were his steps that no stirring of our pulse told us a change was coming. That a new year was with us, and the old year gone, with all his labors and cares, his sorrows and disappointments. A year ago yesterday Dec. 31. 1876. my father passed away, in the seventy first year of his age. His nephew T. N. Mount of Napa [California] wrote and apprised me of it. His illness was short and he had all necessary care, but it was a great shock to me for I had always hoped to see him again. I tried to get his property for Cornelia and I but we are not likely to succeed. The Lawrences claim it.[20] I have saved the corespondence concerning it but it is too voluminous to copy here.

We have invited company to dine with us today. Myron bought a turkey and wants his freinds to help eat it. I received a letter today with some lines from a paper, speaking disrespectfully of the death of our beloved President Brigham Young.[21] I sat down and wrote some verses that were sudgested to my mind, and they sound very well. We have spent a pleasant day. Sister Newel Sister Bollwinkle and Sister Pratt were here. The children with their company ate their dinner up stairs. We had a pleasant time and felt that our day had been well spent.

Sunday. Jan 13. I have been very busy since New Year's day. I have revised and coppied my poem for press. It is quite a long one, and attracts considerable attention. I receive many compliments about it. Mary and Eddie Tanner have returned from spending holliday at home, and started to school. Bertrand and Bessie have started but Grace has a lame foot and cannot go until it is better. Our ward is preparing for a picnic at the Hall next Saturday. I dread picnics they make so much work. Mrs. Leavitt will help Marie wash tomorrow if her husband is better, he has a very bad finger. I have been coppying some today in my book of poems. I have written one hundred and thirty one pages, and have more to coppy. I wrote a poem today in memory of Sister Whipple which I will present to her husband.

Tuesday Jan 22. Our picnic is over and that seems all that is worth recording. It passed off as such things usualy do, with a great deal of hard work and confusion, but withall quite satis-facterily. The children had a nice time and we did all we could to make them happy as it was especialy for the Sunday Schools. There are 181 children belonging to the Sunday School of our Ward. I have been sick ever since. Mother Tanner is here for a visit. Lewis will be six years old tomor-row. I am invited out to dinner.

Friday Jan 25. Our little Arthur is three years old today. He is the baby and a pet with all the family. We killed two hogs yesterday, and were just starting to try the lard and get the meat taken care of when the door opened, and there stood Aggie Ridges from Salt Lake. I was very much supprised. Dear Aggie: How glad I was to see her. She had just a few hours to stay so I laid aside my work and improved the time by talk-ing. Clara came about noon, and soon after Sister Beebe and Sister Clark came in and we had a good visit and Marie got us a nice dinner. We tried to persuade Aggie to stay and go to the ball this evening, but she could not stay from home so we bade her a reluctant good bye and sent her to the depot. It was certainly a day of supprises, and has passed so pleasantly we can work the better tomorrow.

Monday Jan. 28. I attended a meeting today for electing dele-gates to the County Convention. Political meetings are some-thing new to me. There were severel ladies present, and we said i[aye] sometimes by way of exercising our rights, and went home feeling the importance of our positions. After meeting I called on Frances Clark and took dinner. I came home and helped Marie get supper. Spent the evening knit-ting.

Tuesday Jan 29, 1878. I helped Marie wash Today and am

very tired. Sister Newel came in, and wished me to write to Bro Newel who is on a mission and inform of his release to return home. I have written the letter and read a little. I am so very tired. It is too hard work for me to wash. I called on Sister Holden last Saturday. She was in estacies over my new poem. Said every one was delighted with it.

Friday Feb. 1, 1878. It snowed this morning and I began to think I should have to postpone our proposed visit. We had planned to make Sister Hannah Smith a supprise visit.²² About 8. a m it quit snowing and cleared up so I went in search of some one to harness, as the boys had all gone to school. Mr. Loveless came and harnessed old kate to the buggy, and about ten oclock I started out calling first for Sister [Hannah] Clark had to wait for her to get ready. Then we called for Sister Pratt and then for Sister Beebe, after which we called for Polly Curtes, making five of us for the one horse, but she pulled us bravely through the mud, and with light hearts and merry jests we made our way to sister Smith's, who was as much supprised as we could wish. We sent for Frances Clark, Sister Holden came and we spread the table with the ample good cheer we had brought, and enjoyed our dinner and visit with the best of good feelings. About 4 p.m. Sister Beebe's team came for her, and Sister Carter. I loaded my buggy, going around by Sister Holden's to take her home. I took sister Pratt and Sister Clark home, and we all felt better for our little visit.

I came home and helped prepare supper. I received two letters this evening; one from my cousin in Napa, a very kind pleasant letter. I always like to hear from him although many sad thoughts are stirred, for he lives where my father did and knew something of his life. I did want so much to see my father once more in this life, but it was not to be so. He died suddenly among strangers. I was deeply grieved and many a sad thought was awakened by the circumstances of his death. The other letter was from Bro Whipple acknowledging the receipt of a poem I wrote on the death of his wife. It is very

pleasant to receive such little acknowledgements of kind
feeling.

Sunday Feb. 10, 1878. I am neglectful of my diary, but there
seems so little to write. One day comes and goes, and the
next follows; the same routine of work is gone through, and
the same remains to be done. No change worth mentioning
from one week to another. On saturday I went to the factory
and got part of the flannels they had been colloring for me.
The green was not finished. I called on Sister Holden. Bro.
Holden read me some interresting letters he had received from
the east and the answers he had written. I went to the store
and did a little trading and went to the theater in the evening.
Today has passed as Sunday usualy does. It takes the forenoon
to get the work done, and the children dressed ready for
Sunday School, with an unlimited amount of scolding. At last
dinner is over, the work done and all are gone. I can sit down
quietly to write a few pages, with Arthur climbing on my arm
and pulling my paper. I coppied two pages in my book of
poems, then Myron came and read to me a lecture given by
Moses Thatcher. It is very interresting, but Lewis teases all the
time, and wanders around in search of a pencil. Finaly I get
him one but he soon finds he does not want it, and goes to
the room where the girls are. They raise a fight, and I settle it
by sending them all out of the room. I in the meantime listen-
ing to the lecture but nearly wild and wish there was no
lecture.

Maria gets supper. After supper the usual confusion reigns for
awhile until one after another goes to bed and at eight oclock
Maria is finishing work in the buttry, and I am writing in my
diary. Each Sunday repeats itself with very little variation.
Maria has let the teakettle boil dry and burn and I feel vexed,
but there is not much variety in that. A lady once said to
another, "You do not know anything about trouble for you
keep no hired help." I think sometimes she was right. Marion
preaches at American Fork today. I wish I could hear him. I

think I should be a better woman if I could hear a gospel sermon sometimes. I have a letter commenced, to my cousin which I should like to finish, but I am tired and nervous, so I will drop a line to my sister and go to bed.

Sunday March 10, 1878. I must write a little in my journal tonight. It is hardly worthwhile to write in it daily. Breakfast, dinner, supper, washing ironing and sewing, with now and then an item of gossip and the record is made. Mother Tanner went home Friday the first of March. I was so lonely, it seemed as if some one was dead. John McEwan died the day before and Mrs. Jane Gee died that morning. The next day my head ached, and I felt lonesome. The sun shone pleasantly and I walked out trying to feel better. I called on some of my friends and did not get home until nearly night. Myron invited me to go to the concert. I went although I feared to overtax my strength; but I felt better on Sunday. Monday I had the headache as usual. Mrs. Leavitt helped wash and I got dinner. Severel of us made arrangements to visit Sister Bunnel but it blew up a cold storm and we could not go.

On Tuesday evening the boards of the Relief Societies met at Sister [Margaret] Smoot the Stake [Relief Society] President's to devise ways and means to interrest the ladies in coming to Society meetings. It was resolved that the presidents and counselors were to visit each house in the ward and try to persuade the ladies to attend the Society meetings. I think we hardly realized how heavy the task would be. I am afraid we shall be a long time performing it, for Sister Clark is lame in the feet and I am lame in the head. Sister Pratt is sick a great deal and altogether we are a poor feeble set. I told them our ward was doing well at present and enjoyed a good spirit. I did little sewing and that finished the week.

Today I have headache all day, but that is no variety. I can scarcely tell when I have not had it. I wanted to go to meeting and hear Marion preach, but was not able. The sun shone pleasantly and I walked over to Mother Moss's and sat a little while. I came home to dinner, and while eating, a little girl came in and said Mrs. Hindmersh was sick and wanted to see me. I went to see her and found her up getting dinner. She had been sick in the morning and lain down but did not know that I had been sent for. I stopped a little while at Hannah Clarks and came home feeling so sick that I thought I was hardly fit to visit sick people. My head is so bad I will not write any longer but go to bed.

March 17, 1878. I have been to Springville today. I took Mrs. Leavitt, the Misses Alexander and Bessie. I visited Mrs. Katie Dugal. She is having her new house finished and is nice and comfortable. The weather is lovely and I long to be out fixing up the spring work. Sister made me a visit and we spent a pleasant day. I sewed some and finished the girls dresses. I hope the weather will be pleasant and my health be good so I can do a great deal this week. I have written a long letter to my sister, Martha Read and one to my sister, Cornelia Taylor.

Monday March 18, 1878. Marie washed today and Mrs. Leavitt helped her. I have done some of the house-work and written a little. The weather is damp and cloudy. Mary and Eddie Tanner are boarding with us going to school. They have been home to Payson and came back about noon. Mary said who has been in my room and left the wash bowl dirty. But she did not say who has swept and dusted so nicely and put up clean curtains to make it nice and pleasant. It is human nature. How much quicker we are to find fault and speak of what anoys us than of that which is pleasant and cheerful. How much plainer people's faults show than their virtues. The children have got their suppers and gone to bed and the rain is falling steadily. The clothes willl not be dry to iron tomorrow. I have done no work and if I do as well tomorrow I shall fall short in my calculations for the week. It is after nine oclock and I must retire.

Tuesday March 19, 1878. I laid out some work for today, made a fire in the little stove and commenced a pair of pillow cases. I must do a little writing though and did not sew very fast. Presently Sister Holden came and I laid my work aside.

319

Sister Clark came too and I marked a temple apron and showed her how to work it.[23] Sister Holden felt unwell and laid down. When Eddie came from school he and Bertrand took the horse and scraper and worked awhile at the door yard. Then Eddie took Sister Holden home with the team.

Wednesday March 20, 1878. Myron went to Springville, and I rode down to the store with him and made a few purchases. I called at Halmar Smith's and engaged him to whitewash. Called at Thomas Holdaways and took dinner with them. I made Sister Pratt a short visit. Her and Sister Holden and Sister Clark are going over the river with me to make Sister Bunnel a visit tomorrow. It was half past two when I got home. Maria was ironing. She does up the fine shirts nicely and it is a great care off my mind. I finished my pillow cases tonight. I shall not get much sewing done at this rate. The children have gone to rehearsal. I think exebitions a nuisance they keep them out so late evenings.

Thursday March 21, 1878. Our visit to Sister Bunnel had to be postponed on account of the horse having cast a shoe. The wind was raised this evening so I fear we cannot go tomorrow. I sewed a little and have written some.

Friday March 22, 1878. We had our visit today and enjoyed it very much. I bought some shade trees of Bro. Bunnel. In coming home we forded the river. Bro. Bunnel rode down to the bank and saw us safely across. I took the rest home and called on Sister Smith who is quite sick. When I got home it was nearly dark.

Saturday March 23, 1878. I have been very busy getting the children ready for the exibition. I went to the rehearsal, then to the store and got them some fine shoes. We went to the exibition in the evening. Martha Woodard came and staid all night.

Sunday March 24, 1878. The girls took the buggy for a ride and took Martha to the depot, and the children to Sunday School. I wrote some letters.

Monday March 25, 1878. Jeannett came last night and staid today. She will help me this week to cut carpet rags. Mrs. Leavitt helped Marie wash. It rains hard tonight but the clothes are all in except the flannels.

Tuesday March 26, 1878. Marion is niniteen years old today. We cut carpet rags.

Wednesday March 27, 1878. Washed some quilts and other things this forenoon. I went to Nathan Barrett's to the funeral of their babe. It is the third one they have lost. Jeannett helped Marie with the ironing. I have taken cold and feel unwell.

Thursday March 28, 1878. It has rained all day. We held Society Meeting at Mrs. Bowen's. Rained hard while we were there but slacked in time to come home.

Friday March 29. We are cleaning the chambers. The girls are whitewashing. Mary is not well and did not go to school.

Monday April 1, 1878. I went out today, calling on Sisters Smoot, Smith, Holden and Kimbal. Sister Kimbal entertained me by relating some of her early experience in poligamy. There were many trials in those early days. I stayed until nearly sundown.

Tuesday April 2. 1878. Went to the store with Myron to do some trading. We bought me a new dress, a bolt of bleached muslin, a sack of sugar and severel other things. I was very tired.

Wednesday April 3, 1878. Rested some today and sewed carpet rags.

Thursday April 4, 1878. Took the buggy and [went] to Society Meeting over the river, taking Sisters Clark, Pratt and Garner with me. The bridge is torn up to make a new one and we had to ford the river. Being a little afraid of the water with our light conveyance we women walked over on the timbers of the old bridge and Emery Hill drove the team over for us. We took tea with Sister Bunnel and came back by the lower ford when I drove across myself and got home safely.

Friday April 5, 1878. Sister Clark and a few others came and helped me sew carpet rags. As dinner was about ready Marion came, bringing Bishop Herrington. Myron came in, in a great hurry to start to conference. Mary and Eddy came in a hurry to start home to Payson, and I was so tired and worried that I could hardly get it on the table. Dinner went off all right however and all got away and I sat down with my company and rested awhile. Then my sister Martha Read came with her two children which was a pleasant supprise.

Sunday April 7, 1878. Weather warm and windy. I am tired and stupid. The children have gone to Sunday School and the house is quiet. I should like to lie down and get a nap but I must go to Bro Lydiards and see when he is coming to finish the wash house. I want it cleaned up so I can put the stove out there in the summer. I try to write a little every day but do not progress very fast. I am drafting a narative, or bio-graphical sketch. Have not coppied any for some time. This term of school is out and there will be a weeks vacation. I am glad to have a rest. I want Bertrand to go next term.

Monday April 8, 1878. It was cloudy this morning and rained some, but the clouds cleared and the wind raised, and has blown cold and disagreable all day. I had taken the stove out of the bedroom but was glad to put it in again and make us comfortable while sewing. Martha helped me and we did a nice lot of sewing, made some underclothes for the girls and four pair of pillowcases. The children were very troublesome, having to stay in the house. They played on the organ and made all kinds of noises. William Gill Mills had his store burned last night. It is thought to be the work of an incen-diary as traces were found of the store having been robbed before it caught fire. A warrant was issued to search the city for the goods. Some men came here and I told them they were welcome to search. They looked around a little and went away. It is so cold and windy tonight I shall retire soon.

Saturday April 13, 1878. I went to the weavers with Martha to order a carpet. She went home on the train this afternoon.

Monday April 29, 1878. The time passes so quickly. The weather has been cold and stormy the most of the time since Martha went away. There is still much excitement about the fire. The opinion is gaining that Mills set it himself, for the purpose of attaining the insurance money. A guard is out every night. The citizens taking turns. Marion and his father have both been out. The children have the Whooping Cough, Bertrand, Lewis and Arthur. They cough very hard. William Croff has moved into the Higby House. Mr. Higby has given it to Mrs. Croff who is his daughter. Mrs. Croff called on me today, also Sister Pratt. We are going to meet tomorrow evening to choose a president for the Young Ladies Society which will be organized in this ward on Wednesday evening.

Thursday May 2, 1878. The Young ladies Mutual Improvement Association for this Ward was organized last evening. Mrs. Ella Haws President, Mrs. Pheba Holdaway and Miss Mary Hoover Counselors, Miss Hattie Taylor Treasrer. The secretary is not yet chosen. Br. Lydiard came and fixed the Wash House chimney, it looks better and I hope it will draw better, though he did not turn it upside down as I advised him. I took the horse and buggy yesterday and did severel errands. I drawed Martha's dividend and paid ten dollars on her carpet. It is in the loom and looks very handsome. Called on Sister Smoot inviting her to attend the meeting in the evening. Saw severel with reference to selecting the officers, and went to meeting in the evening.

Sunday May 5, 1878. We got the work done up and I made myself tidy and sat down to rest. Looking out I saw Messre. Tullidge and Crandel, publishers from Salt Lake. They had promised to call and inspect my writings and tell me the cost of publishing a book of poems. I read them my poems with which they were very much pleased, and strongly urged me to publish; selecting such peices as seemed to them suitable. They said I had enough to make a book of a hundred pages that were well worthy of publication. It would cost $350.00 for a thousand coppies. I should like very much to publish, but should be sory to spend so much money and not have the book appreciated. If I could but have a foresight to know how my book would be received I should have more courage to proceed. I read some of my prose writings which also pleased them very much and they encouraged me to proceed with an article I am writing. They staid all night. Myron is in Salt Lake City, but Marion came in and I was proud to introduce him. He conversed with them to good advantage. They talked of science and religion and I was pleased to see him so well informed. I thought he was better than a book and if I did no other work the honor of having such a son is more pride and pleasure than a dozzen books.

Monday May 6, 1878. This morning after breakfast the gentlemen went away. I was glad when they were gone, for trying to acquit myself in a ladylike manner, and cover Marie's awkwardness and the children's rudeness was such a strain on my nerves.

Tuesday May 7, 1878. I went in the washroom today and left Marie to do the work. I always get so tired doing the work on wash-day and I felt so smart & thought I would have a change. It took her until dinner time to do the breakfast work so I let her get the dinner and wash the dishes and then she came to wash. Myron brought the buggy to the door and asked if I wanted a ride. I took Arthur and we called for Sister Moss. We went up the river and over the bench as far as Mr. Carter's. It was a pleasant ride. We could see our farm as we passed. The wheat and lucern looked green and nice. We called on Sister Newel as we came back.

Susa Young Gates (1856-1933)

By the time she was thirteen and a student at the University of Deseret, Susa (or Susannah or Susan), the second of three daughters born to Lucy Bigelow and Brigham Young, had already demonstrated her quick mind, energetic personality, and musical and literary talents.[24] She edited the school's paper, studied telegraphy and stenography, and also took a course in baking. Moving to St. George with her mother and sister in the winter of 1870-71 did not markedly diminish Susa's activities. She taught music lessons, joined the St. George Home Dramatic Group, and organized the Union Club, a social and self-improvement society.

After the dissolution of an unhappy marriage in 1877, Susa worked with her mother in the St. George Temple and then attended the Brigham Young Academy in Provo. Her younger sister Rhoda Mabel joined her a few months later. With Susa also was her young son, Bailey. Her two-year-old daughter Leah had remained in the custody of Susa's former husband, Alma Dunford. Susa attended the academy for only a brief period, but during that time she directed the academy choir, taught piano and voice, and assisted in establishing a department of music. Years later she would also organize a department of domestic science (in which her daughter Leah would teach with her) and serve as a trustee of the academy as well as of the Brigham Young College in Logan.

Her short sojourn as a student at the academy proved to be an uplifting and refreshing experience for Susa. The letters she wrote home from January to June 1879 show a young woman attempting to make a new beginning for herself. Not lengthy, they offer a rare glimpse into the mind and emotions of the person who would become one of the most influential Mormon women. Susa discounted the likelihood of her own remarrying, but she was concerned about the romances of her two sisters, Rhoda Mabel and Eudora (Dora or Dollie). Hoping at this point in her life to be reunited with her daughter Leah and then

325

Susa Young Gates. (Susa Young Gates Collection. Utah State Historical Society.)

devote herself to her children's education, she was determined to rear them "in the fear of God and wrong-doing."

A trip to the Sandwich Islands the next year and her marriage to Jacob Gates in 1880 changed the course she had plotted for herself and her children. Unable to obtain full custody of Bailey and Leah, Susa devoted herself to rearing a new family and entering a life of public and Church service. Eleven children were born to Susa and Jacob, seven of whom died as infants or young children.

Susa founded and edited the *Young Woman's Journal*, a magazine for the YWMIA. Her long enduring interest in temple work led to a genealogical class that she instructed in the Lion House for ten years; and after her appointment to the Relief Society general board in 1911, she helped to incorporate genealogical lessons into the Relief Society curriculum. She also served as first editor of the *Relief Society Magazine* and wrote several novels and numerous poems and stories for local publication. Always an adoring daughter of her beloved father, in 1930 she wrote a biography of Brigham Young.[25]

Tomes of published material distinguish Susa Young Gates as one of the most prolific of Utah's women writers. Many of her personal papers, including holographs of the letters that follow, are in the Utah State Historical Society. Minimal punctuation has been added for clarification.

Provo. Jan 11th '79.

My own Dear Mother and Sister.

You know how I hate letter writing, but am going to write just a word or so to let you know you are always remembered. I must first tell you that Dollie has just gone home. She has been with me a week, and seemed to feel a great deal better. I am in hopes that if John W. [Young] starts soon she will go with him.[26]

The boys are both well.[27] Hope you are well and prospering. I do hope Rhoda will soon resume her studies, for there is no pleasure on earth like that given by a refined and cultivated intellect, lit up by the glorious rays of the spirit of the living

327

God. Dear mother, I am very happy and contented and trying to enjoy all that I can, for who knows when sorrow will come. God give me grace to enjoy the sunshine of life, and to profit by lessons learned in adversity. Shall I have done moralizing? Yes, and come to practical things. Dont fail to send my pillows (you have in your house three of them and the other two are at Dora's) and pillow cases and sheets. Please dont forget this as I may fit up a room and go away from here, to be nearer the Academy. Have started vocal lessons. Kept busy with studies and lectures. Please give my kind love to the Nixons. My regards to all who enquire. Tell Dan, the memory of his true unchanging friendship is about the brightest spot in my rather cool heart. Affection! Thou art dear to me, but Love! Away. Thou art fickle, false! even in my own breast I dare not trust thee. I wish to live for God and His Kingdom. Dear little May [Emma May Bigelow?].[28] Tell her I shall remember her shy farewell kiss. My lips are pressed to others too seldom to not be carefully remembered. God bless and cheer you both. Time will soon be gone then comes the great Eternity. What matters what old Time may bring!

Susa

Provo. March 14th '79.

Dearest Mother.

Your letter came last evening, and I hasten to reply.

First of all, let me set your mind at rest upon one point, Dora will not turn traitor. She started Wednesday afternoon with Aunt Harriet Hanks to California. She did not wish to be here when the trial came on, and would go no where but to Cal. I offered to go along, but she declined. She will be all right I trust, and her abscence from home will serve to open her eyes to the course she has recently taken. So let your mind be at rest. And dear mother, dont be afraid about there being any danger for either you or Bro. [Wilford] Woodruff. Go quietly on with your work in the Temple. That case will pass off with out much more fuss, I think.[29]

Dora will soon be ready to return and I will see her when she does and once more try to persuade her to come down to you. So take all the comfort you can, and be patient. All will come out right. Now dont worry please, but remember God wishes us to devote all our time to the hastening on of His work which is soon to come to an end, and we have no time to spend in mourning over that which we can not help. I have been very much grieved at Dollie's actions, but she assured me she prayed always and wanted to do right, and so I trust to God for the rest. Now Mother, you surely dont wish me to break up all my plans and life, and once more be turned adrift without aim or object. I am contented and busy here. I feel that I am doing some good, and am receiving much instruction. All that we learn in this world counts us so much in the world to come. Dearest Mother, you know my nature well enough to know that without plenty of occupation, my mind would only rust, and I become dissatisfied and reckless.

If there is no absolute need let me remain here and fit myself to be a useful member in God's Kingdom.

Provo. March 21st 79

Dear Mother,

Thought I must write just a few lines.

The little girl down stairs has the diptheria, but we are keeping the children all up-stairs, but her. And giving them constant doses of purifing and opening medicines. We are watching them with great care, and trust in God our Father for the rest. I will telegraph if Baby [Bailey] should come down with it, but am in great hopes that he shall not.

How are you, dear mother? Bless you how often I think of and pray for you. I have tried so hard to do all I could to be a good daughter, but it seems impossible.

Dont sorrow for me. God is with me and I am all right.

How is Rhoda? Why dont she write to us any of us? Is she going to ruin herself, and her whole after life? In all her life she will never find one so noble good and true as Lyman. Tell her I shall endeavor to do all I can to keep him to believe in her truth till it is too late.

Do you know anything about her? Please write to me about her. I am very tired and lonesome, but thankful to God for all. Please write again to me.

Your devoted daughter

Susa

Have heard nothing from Dora

Provo. April 4th '79

My darling Mother.

Rhoda received your letter yesterday. So I thought I would write just to tell you how much we love you, and how often we talk of and pray for our dear mother. Rhoda returned from the City two days before I did, but now we are both here, and commencing school this morning. We are still at Bro. [Benjamin] Cluffs yet, but as they are soon going to the [Hawaiian] Islands we will find another boarding place. I scarcely know what we will do this term, we are not decided. I will let you know as soon as we know ourselves.

Grandma [Mary Gibbs Bigelow] has come down to Conference and is staying here at Provo waiting for Uncle Daniel [Bigelow] to come after her. I got her a few things in the City and sister got her a pair of spectacles.

Dearest Mother Rhoda and I are getting along so well, and we are going to try and be just as good as we know how to be. She is company for me, and we are quite happy. She is going to take music lessons, and I want her to take Vocal Lessons. I hope she will come again next winter as she will make a smart woman with culture. I will let you know if anything goes wrong, believe me.

Now you ask me something about Dan. He was a true kind friend to me in my deepest trial, and my heart will never cease to thank him for it. But mother dear, I do not love any one on earth as well as my precious good Mother, except my little children. I want by next year, (dont mention this to any one) to have my little girl here, and put her into the Kindergarten School, that is to be added to this Academy. Then you know I can devote myself to their education, have them with me, and try to rear them in the fear of God and of wrongdoing. This is my bright dream. This is what I long for in the future. Should I ever marry, my children might not be welltreated. And I must try to do all I can for them. Sometimes they tell me I must be saved by some good man. If that's all, I could be sealed to some one who has proved his integrity and passed away.[30] I am happy, or at least as happy as mortals who have scared hearts and sore memories can ever expect to be. In short I am busy, contented, and useful. I am only twenty-three so there is plenty of time, yes years and years of it for me yet. Let your heart be at rest for me, as long as I am in the Academy I am safe. That is as long as I am a partaker of the spirit that rules in these walls, I am all right.

Now I will not talk of myself any more. Bailey is so fat and seems so happy and well. I have put him in pants. And oh he is so sweet and cunning.

I write simple little letters to my precious "little forsaken," every little while, and thus keep my memory fresh in her mind. I always tell her to pray for the time when she will be with Mama again. She is well.

331

Dora has not written to me at all. Love to my darling Mother

From her   Susa

Bailey sends his love to his dear Grandma. Rhoda will write soon. So will I. Lyman is going home to-day. Love once more

From Susa.

S. L. City April 6th 79

My darling Mother.

Rhoda and I thought we would write. We are staying with Aunt Eliza B[urgess] at conference. My dear mother your letters have reached me and I am sorry to say two received without an answer. I do hope that the heavy clouds of sorrow will be lifted from your mind, and God will graciously give you the light of His Glory. Dearest, do not worry about my dear little sis and I, we are trying to do right, and be quiet and good. Mother, if you really think I can do you any permanent good by coming down, I will willingly do so. But dear, I could not see you now, and the fact of my being there would subject me to a close watch on your account. Let your heart be comforted in knowing that God doeth all things well. Dearest one you will never know how truly I love you, and how much I am willing to do for you, if it is necessary until the Great Hereafter. But I cannot sacrifice all my cheerful labor, happy prospects in my dear Academy, unless I feel I can do you a lasting good. If I can sweeten your bitter cup, if I can soothe your sore heart, and indeed help you with my presence, I am ready to come.

Dearest, how would you like to take nice, comfortable, quiet trip around Soda [Springs] or Bear Lake. Everything being well arranged and everything safe and well. Tell me about this when you write next.

From all accounts I can hear Dora seems to be all right. Dont worry about her. She is the child of God, and He will watch over her. Be comforted my darling Mother and accept the devoted love of your daughter

Susa

Provo April 18 '79

Dearest Mother.

This morning your letter lay on my table, and as I have a few minutes before I will have to go to my students I thought I would *start* at least to answer your letter.

Dear mother I understand fully how you feel about my coming down, and when the time comes that it will be right for me to come, I shall do so.

I decidedly object to my name and Rhoda's being placed alongside of Dora's for being untrue to men. I was *never* under the same circumstances as she. I have not given my heart to any man good or bad, nor am I full of the lust of the world as she is.[31] You do not seem to understand me or my purposes. Is it wrong to want to help build up God's Kingdom? The only desire I know of at present or at any time, is to live so that father will meet and welcome me. Please, my darling mother, do not mention Dan's name to me again, it will be worse than useless. Let us try and think of how much there is to be done in the future, and cease to vainly wish for that which "might have been." Rhoda is very young, and I for one, did not expect such a child to know her own heart. I wish to the goodness she had stayed there and married Dan. For I believe she would have been quite happy with him, and I pay him the compliment of thinking he would be worthy of her. But I see no use in wishing for what cannot be, and so am trying to do what little I can to keep Rhoda straight. She is a dear good sweet girl. . . .

I know nothing about Zina [Young Williams], but as for me I have no desire to be any man's wife.[32] And doubt whether I ever shall. There is very little room in my heart for any one but my darling mother, my precious children, and sisters Zina and May. I care nothing for the fame of the world, but here my few small talents are being daily improved, my sphere of usefulness is being enlarged, and how much happier am I than as though forced to go through a daily routine of work distasteful to me. It is no use talking about recording in the Temple, I could not be contented at that two weeks. If you had not come up here when you did, I should have come any way, and perhaps done much worse than I have done so far.

Yes dearest mother, I am trying to forget all that was, all that might have been, and make myself contented and happy here. I humbly thank God for all his blessings, and want to be worthy of His goodness to me. I enclose three cards. Please give one to Bro. [James G.] Bleak, and one to Bro. [John Daniel Thompson] Mac[Allister].[33]

Your loving Susa

Provo. May 9th 1879

Dearest Mother.

I was so glad to hear from Zina that you are feeling better, and are in better spirits. It will seem so good when everything gets settled down once more, and you can take comfort with your children. I have written to Bro. Taylor about Johnnie and will tell you instantly of the result. I hope the way will open for me to have my children with me this winter, and I do hope Rhoda will come too. Encourage her to come here, for it is the best place on earth for her I feel assured. Is there anything here you want or need, if so let me know.

I neglected to tell you Grandma had been to see us, and I have given her a few things. I was informed that the girl of

Aunt Sariah [Bigelow Cook]'s was desired to be sent to you.[34] Mrs Holliday sent word over for me to tell you that the people who have the child would be glad to let you take her. I give this just as sent, reserving my opinion or comments.

My eyes have been quite bad. Rather dread coming into that hot climate, but guess it will be all right, at least for a week or so. Shall try to come down as soon as I can make the arrangements.

Rhoda sends love and kisses. Hope she'll succeed in Keeping Dan's heart since she wishes to.[35] Thank the Lord, my heart beats only for my children, my mother, and my few friends. It is never disturbed with a throb of love. Guess it never will be. Please darling mother take all the comfort you can, for you will soon meet father.

Your Susa

Provo. June 8th 1879

My darling Mother.

There is a letter down at the schoolhouse now partly written to you. But as I am obliged to do some writing here at home to-night I concluded first to write a few words to her who is more precious to me than fine rubies. And who I love better each day of my happy busy life. I am so vexed with myself for allowing you to go one week without a letter from me. But really mother dear you can scarcely realize the amount of work I have done lately. The Academy Choir (under me of course) learned ten, chorrises, and anthems, in two weeks. I am obliged to sing each part with everyone as I did in the old club. It is indeed *very* wearing on the lungs and nerves. But I love it, and am so glad I can assist the fresh young and often-times sweet singers of Zion to praise God in melody and in song. During the Conference here we sang for the Twelve who were here, and Bros. [John] Taylor, [Daniel H.] Wells, [Brigham] Young [Jr.], and [George F.] Gibbs expressed them-

335

selves highly pleased with our music. Both Bro. Taylor and Sister E[liza] R. Snow expressed the very kindest feelings to me, and seemed to feel a great interest in my course.

God help me to be worthy of the good opinion of all of the true Saints. For verily I want to be as near what father would wish me to be, as it is possible for my weak queer disposition to be. Oh mother, dont you long to see father to[o], clasp his arms around your neck, and hear his blessed voice pronounce those sweet words "Welcome, my beloved, to your home." Oh I know I am young and have a destiny in this Church to fulfill, but how I would love to go to father!

The end of the term comes in two weeks, and we are going to be so very busy. I dread to think of all I must do. I will be somewhat glad if I can have a little rest, but will be ready to work again when school begins again. I hardly know what to do this summer. When I have decided, you shall know of course. There will be only ten weeks and then—school again.

Now mama dont be disappointed, but you know how bad my eyes are down there, and I have had a touch of sore eyes already, and as my business will *oblige* me to come in Aug. or Sept. I think I shall wait till then and come in the grape season. I will, of course, send Rhoda down as soon as school is out. For pity's sake keep her a child as long as you can dont let her "marry in haste and repent at leisure". Set my example before her and let it be a warning. I love the child dearly. She is doing nicely.

Haven't said a word about Br. Mac. Seldom felt so bad as when we heard he was dead. Thank God it was untrue. Give my love to them.

Bailey is well and sends love to his grandma. Had some pictures taken. Will bring some down. I went up to Provo Valley this week after Bailey. Stayed all night with Aunt Lavina [Bigelow Witt]. Zina was with me. Saw Uncle Daniel. All sent love. I urged them to go down there this fall. Please dont worry about Rhoda and I. We are all O.K. so far.

Forgot to tell you that the rhyme piece of "poetry"(?) in the last but one Exponent called the Three "Rain drops" was written by your ambitious but not very wise or talented

Susa

Chapter Ten

Persecution, the Manifesto, and Statehood

Dark Moments—Rejoicing

1896 Opened auspiciously for Utah and its inhabitants. On the 4th [of] January 1896 President Cleaveland issued a Proclaimation admitting Utah into the Sisterhood of States. As soon as the message was recieved 2 oc. PM Guns were fired, Flag hoisted, Bands played, Shouts of joy arose from the heart and lips of all, with ringing of bells and everything which could be used to sound a note of joy was brought into requisition. . . . never had all Utah joined in such hilarious rejoicing.

So wrote Rebecca Elizabeth Howell Mace in Kanab, Utah, personally celebrating the end of nearly half a century of conflict between the Latter-day Saints and the federal government. And well might she rejoice, since the long turbulence and its resolution personally impacted thousands of Latter-day Saints, particularly during the 1880s and '90s. Julina Lambson Smith's mission to Hawaii, Nancy Abigail Clement Williams's settlement in Mexico, Ruth May Fox's effort to bring woman suffrage to Utah, and Rebecca Mace's celebration of Utah's statehood all were tied to Mormon relations with the United States government.

From 1862, when the first federal antipolygamy legislation was passed, efforts to enforce the statute steadily intensified. By 1879 the

U.S. Supreme Court had determined that the statute was not unconstitutional, and finally in 1882 Congress put teeth in the measure with passage of the Edmunds Bill. Aimed largely at the local political power that allowed for "peculiarities of faith" including plural marriage, the law disfranchised polygamists and declared them ineligible for public office and jury service. It also provided for a five-member Utah Commission to administer the territory's elections.

Defining polygamy as a felony punishable with up to five years' imprisonment and/or a $500 fine, the law became the basis for increased legal prosecution, and new appointees to the territory's federal courts began in earnest a judicial crusade against polygamists. Following the lead of Church President John Taylor, many Mormon men and women went underground in an effort to elude federal marshals and nearly certain imprisonment. Sixteen-year-old Nancy Clement Williams entered plural marriage "at a dark hour for the Saints when persecution against that principle raged in its highest." Like others, she traveled to neighboring communities, hid out in friends' homes, and used assumed names. Some Saints left Utah and nearby Idaho, where the "raid" against Mormons also raged. When John Taylor visited Mormon settlements in Arizona, he found similar legal persecution underway and advised Saints there to leave the country. Eventually Nancy and Fredrick Williams were among those who went to Mexico; others fled to Canada.

While President Taylor himself decided to remain in hiding, he suggested that his second counselor, Joseph F. Smith, remove himself to the mission field, and so Julina Lambson Smith accompanied her husband to Hawaii in 1885. "Far off" and in a "strange land, so distant from many of our loved ones," Julina felt keenly that her two-year exile was a result of "infamous persecutions and prosecutions." Like many women who had personally experienced plural marriage, she spoke out in strong opposition to legislation against it. In a letter to the *Woman's Exponent* written from Laie in 1886, she maintained: "I have never felt that I have been guilty of any crime, notwithstanding the action of the courts. . . . It is not a question of any law with us, but a matter of conscience, of religious conviction and of earnest and undying faith in the laws and purposes of God, a matter of happiness or misery, of life or death."[1]

Up against such strong religious conviction and marital loyalty, the federal government exerted greater pressure to force the Saints to abandon plural marriage. The 1887 Edmunds-Tucker law attacked the Church politically and economically. Stringent provisions facilitated polygamy prosecutions, woman suffrage was abolished, and a test oath was instituted for prospective voters, jurors, and office holders. In addition, the Church was dissolved as a legal corporation and its property escheated to the U.S. government.[2]

Upon passage of the law, Joseph F. and Julina Smith returned to Utah. In July 1887, just as the statute was going into effect, John Taylor died and Wilford Woodruff assumed leadership of the Church. After three years of continued turmoil President Woodruff, having prayerfully considered what course the Church should take, declared with solemnity that "by vision and revelation" the Lord had "told me exactly what to do, and what the result would be if we did not do it." Acting upon this prophetic understanding, President Woodruff declared in a Manifesto read to Saints assembled in the Church's October 1890 general conference that his "advice to the Latter-day Saints is to refrain from contracting any marriage forbidden by the law of the land."[3]

It was not without struggle and sorrow that Latter-day Saint men and women let go of plural marriage and of their hopes for a unique political and economic kingdom. Yet, on the eve of the twentieth century they recognized that they stood on the brink of a new era, one of improved relations with the United States and opportunities for unprecedented growth. The Saints began to move into the American mainstream, if not to be totally absorbed, at least to get their feet wet.

The Church-dominated People's Party was abandoned in 1891, and the Saints began to align themselves along national party lines. By 1894, within an increasing array of women's clubs, Mormon women like Ruth May Fox were discussing such national issues as the silver conspiracy. Ruth's prevailing concern, however, was woman suffrage, an issue that dominated her diary and Utah's constitutional convention in 1895. Due to the efforts of Mormon women like Ruth, when Utah entered the Union in 1896, it was the fourth state with suffrage for women.

A year before the century closed, Rebecca Mace closed her diary:

"Farewell 1898 with all your changes and certainly great events have transpired." As the nineteenth century ended, women and men could not help but marvel at the myriad of transitions they had experienced as Mormons. The long-term scuffle over the separation of church and state in Utah ended, and the Saints began to see a manifold increase in its missionary work through the world. The Salt Lake Temple was dedicated in 1893, and the sealing together of family groups and the accompanying genealogical research took on new importance for the Saints.

Within their own households women found continuity. Julina Smith would find cooking to do beyond Hawaii's mission head-quarters. There would continue for Nancy Williams lots of looking after children and grandchildren; Ruth May Fox would be active in organizations for Mormon sisters far into the twentieth century; and Rebecca Mace would "visit the fatherless and widows in their afflic-tion" to the end of her days in Kanab.

Perhaps in praying "God to give us each the spirit and strength, in connection with our companions and fellow-laborers, to do our duty well," Julina Smith sensed the most important continuity: that within individual households of faith, Mormonism's real temporal kingdom existed. There women invested everyday occurrences with dignity and even holiness. The majesty of that investiture endures through this century and continues to be cause for rejoicing.

Julina Lambson Smith (1849-1936)

When Julina Smith left Salt Lake City in 1885 to accompany her husband, Joseph F. Smith, to the Sandwich Islands (Hawaii), she left five children at home, little realizing she would not see them for two full years. Mary (Mamie), Donette (Donnie), Joseph Fielding, David, and George remained with Julina's sister-wives, Sarah and Edna.[4] Year-old Julina Clarissa (Ina) accompanied her mother and father to Laie, Oahu, where the Church had a mission, a six-thousand-acre sugar plantation and about 3500 members.

Joseph F. Smith had served two previous missions to Hawaii, but this mission was not for any designated period, since President John Taylor had called his counselor, President Smith, to remove himself from Salt Lake City in order to avoid enemies who sought to arrest members of the First Presidency for their practice of plural marriage.

Julina, a daughter of Alfred B. and Melissa Jane Bigler Lambson, was born in Salt Lake City, where she spent part of her growing up in the home of her aunt Bathsheba Bigler Smith and uncle George A. Smith. It was in this home, the Historian's Office, that she met Joseph F. Smith, a clerk there. The two were married in 1866 and, over a thirty-year period, had eleven children.[5]

Having graduated from a class in midwifery, Julina was commissioned by the Church to serve as a midwife. She helped deliver the children of her sister wives, and on the mission to Hawaii had more than one occasion to use her obstetrical skill, once when she herself was eight months pregnant! Her son Elias Wesley was born in April 1886, just after the last diary entries quoted here.

This three-month representation of Julina's two-year mission with her husband shows her to be as skilled in the homemaking arts as was her Aunt Bathsheba (see Chapter 5). Julina's constant concern with cleanliness and good meals and her handiness with a needle and thread made her central to the management of the mission's domestic affairs. In addition, she worked hard to learn the native language and served

343

Julina Lambson Smith. (Courtesy Julina and Paul Hokanson, Afton, Wyoming.)

in the mission Relief Society presidency as a counselor.

Five years after her return to Salt Lake City in 1887, Julina was called as a member of the Relief Society general board, where she helped set up the department for temple and burial clothing in 1912.

The excerpts that follow are part of a small collection of Julina's personal records, including three holograph diaries and a reminiscence deposited in the LDS Church Historical Department. Her careful attention to detail makes for an accurate record of a woman's daily activities without precluding a glimpse at her personal thoughts and feelings. Minimal punctuation has been added here for clarification, and where Julina used commas and periods interchangeably, the authors chose whichever mark enhanced the readability of the sentence. Entry dates have been set off with periods.

Laie Friday Jan 1st 1886

Got breakfast for 25. Attended a native feast and meeting in honor of the new year. Jos. F. Smith Geo. Wilcox Jos. S. Hyde and J[acob] F Gates spoke of the foreign brethren, & two of the native brethren. We had a pleasant time. Bro. and Sister [Enoch] Farr[6] & Son, and Bros. [Albert W.] Davis & Wilcox went up in the canyons to look for oranges, but had poor luck. The day has been mild and pleasant. I made May & Rebecca a present each of a silk handkerchief, from home. Gave Geo a knife Hanna a photo of myself and Kalwihaona Napapali and Kaaka a bow made of lace and ribon. I got supper.

Saturday Jan 2nt 1886. Got breakfast then made some mince meat for pies, got Lily Barrell, to chainge work with me. Susie [Young] Gates[7] helping her, and Jos & I went with a company of 56. brethren and Sisters foreign and natives, up to Kaliuwaa. We started about 10. a.m. and got back about 4. p.m. We had a pleasant time and gathered some fearns. I was afraid of the ride on horseback hurting me, so we did not try to keep up with the company but took our time, coming home. I was very tired and lame and expected to go to bed as soon as I reached home, as the folks had promised to get

345

supper, but on my return I found they had made some pies and expected me to get the supper. I did it but realy was not able. The native girles helped me and did the work after. I went to bed but was up & down till midnight, suffering with such pain I was really alarmed, not knowing how it might turn I rested very well the after part of the night.

Sunday Jan 3rd 1886. Fast day. No breakfast to get. Prepaired bread for sacrament. Cooked a good dinner. Did not go to meeting. Can hardly get up and down I am so lame. Jos. brought Kahaana home with him to dinner. I got supper with the help of the girls. Feel some little better this evening.

Mon 4th 1886. We sent out mail to Honolulu by James Kahananni. I wrote to Mamie Donnie Sarah and Edna. I helped get dinner to day to pay Lillie for helping with me work saturday. She is washing to day. I find that I am not the only one that has grunted from their ride. The rest of the women are all complaining. Jos says he never heard me complain so much in his life before.

Tueasday 5th 1886. I did an extra large wash to day. Took a nap after I got through and feel very well. Jos tended Ina and has had a gay time. She had everything she could get in the room to play with.

Wedensday 6th. We spent last evening over to Susie Gates. It was the aniversity of her wedding day six years. We had a very good time playing games &c. Pie and cake was passed around. I did some mending and listened to Jos read the papers this morning. Did my ironing this afternoon. Jos is tired and has gone to bed leaving me up for once since we have been here. I generally go to bed and he writs for some hours after. It will be eleven months on the 10th since we arrived here. Little did I think when I left home that I would have been seperated from my children so long. May we soon meet again in health.

Thursday Jan 7th 1886. I made a pair of pillow cases, and two aprons for my self. A[lbert] W. D[avis] arrived about three Oclock with the mail, and pictures of Mamie Nomie Donnie and Sarah. I cannot tell how it made me feel to see them. The girls have chainged considerably in a year. All are well at home. Albert climed the pali [precipice] last night. It was so dark he had to feel his way.

Friday 8th. Made a pillow and two cases for baby, and started to work a dress for her. I had to draw the patron [pattern] of from a nother. Jos has been writing all day.

Saturday 9th. I have been writing a peice for the Exponent.[8] It has taken me all the time I could get. I feel tired setting so long.

Sunday 10th. Attended meeting this morning. This after noon went with Sisters [Lucy B.] Young [Susa Young] Gates [Marian] Wilcox & bro Gates to see, Carolines baby boy. It was born at three Oclock this morning. She was around as though nothing had happened. Kahaana came home with us from meeting to dinner. Meeting in the evening. They called a vote for the women folks to take turns with the men folks praying and asking the blessing.

Jan Monday 11th 1886. Joseph Albert Enoch and Son bro [Elihu] Barrell and bro [Frederick] and Sister [Ellen (Nellie)] Beesley started to Honolulu this morning. Nellie went to see her husband off. He and bro Barrell are on their way to their field of labor. J and A are agoing to see what can be done about our return tickets. We are also expecting an other mail. I took baby Sister Young accomp[an]ying me and went down to the seashore. Kept her there till twenty minutes past one. She had a good sleep. This afternoon I made a paste board card receiver to hold our photographs.

Tuesday Jan 12th. Did my washing.

Wedensday Jan 13th 1886. After breakfast went back to bed again with a bad headeach. Have not been well all day neither has baby. Robert [B.T. Taylor] came this afternoon with bro

Farr. Jos. and Albert staid. Jos is getting some new gold bows to his specks.

Thursday 14th Jan 1886. Jos. and Albert got here at 12.15 Oclock. We were all in bed. I got up and set them some bread and milk. They had not had any supper. Jos got his specks fixed.

Friday Jan 15. 1886. Did my Ironing. Sent the shirts and my dress to Susan. She brought them back to night. I was not here. Jos baby and I had gone to take a walk on the promentory. I made some zephyr bols for Sister Naau. Meeting tonight. Bros Gates and [George] Cluff were the speakers. Jos spoke a few words after on appostacy. I tried to say the blessing in Native to day noon a[nd] broke down. Sister Wilcox brought some molasses candy over after meeting and we pulled candy. Mabel [Young McAllister] and Cluff got well dobed. Their hair was full and a good portion on their clothes.

Saturday 16 Jan 1886. I paid Sister Farr 1.00 for babies slippers and 50¢ for silk floss, that she got for me while she was in Honolulu. I gave Kaiwi Haone a silk handkerchief. I attended Relief society meeting. Robert was there. He spoke also did Sisters Young, Gates [Elizabeth] Noall and my self.[9] Meeting passed off very well.

Sunday 17. Baby did not rest very well. Papa was up to give her water four times in the night and she dirted her diaper twice. That is something she has never done before since she could talk. I did not go to meeting this morning on her account, but she seems better this morning. Sister Yound [Young] is doing the work in the kitchen this week. She has been trying to churn for four hours, and gave it up. I went and helped her and we soon got a nice lot of butter. We havent had any before for two or three months.

Monday 18th. Baby is not well. I took her down to the sea, worked buttonholes in two pairs of panties then she teased for something to eat. I came back as far as Kekawokas. They were eating dinner. Baby eat with them some pancake and sugar and drank some milk, then I came home and let out the back seam of Roberts breeches.

Tueasday 19th. It was a stormy morning but I started my wash. It soon cleared off. I got my clothes dry. Albert and bro [Isaac] Fox. went for guavas. They got a good suply, but came back as wet as they could be. It rained very hard up in the gulch. I fixed A a bath. Studied my leson for evening.

Jan Wednesday 20th 1886. Baby has felt very bad to day. I tried to sew but she would not let me. Sister Farr went with me. We took her down to Kekawokas she had a nap. We eat breakfast with them about ten Oclock. Baby would not eat. I asked the blessing to day in native. Baby has been very fretful and peavish all day. I made her some sage tea to night. She drank it, but threw it all up. I studied my lesson for school,[10] but it was adjurned on account of the men folks giving bro Miller an alcohol sweat. He has not been well for some days. Nellie's biscuits were taken for *graham,* on account of the *Nuiloa* [great] quantity of soda they had in them.

My Native, Blessing upon Food.

E Ko makou nei makua ma ka lani. Ko nonoi nei makou ia oe, e hoopomaikae mai i keia mau mea ai ia makou pakaki. Oia ka makou e nonoi nei, ma ka inoa o Jesu Kristo—Amene.

Thursday 21st. We took a bugy ride this morning to see if it would help baby. There were four of us Jos. Albert Sister Gates myself and two babies Ina and Carl. We had a good time. The[n] we went by the sea side the waves were very high. It was a grand sight.

Friday 22nt 1886. Jos. took Sister Young Mabel Me and baby for a carriage ride. We went to Punulu. Saw the fragments of a wrecked ship. It was washed to shore by the late high waves. Sister Young got her some specks at a Chinamans store. Baby seems much better. I think taken her out has

helped her. I did my Ironing this after noon. Sent 25¢ worth
to Hanna. Nellie put the boiler of meet on to cook with out
salt and only made enough fire to heat it through. It would
have spoilt if I had not made it boil and salted it. There has
been no interest taken in the work this week. Sisters Nowl
and Beesly were the housekeepers. I take the work in the
morning. Have mixed two batches of bread to night. We Jos
and I Sister Young Mabel and bro Hyde, went down to the
sea for a bath. I swam a little. We are expecting Bro Fox to
night with the mail. I have been to bed and had a nap, no one
could sleep here. There is a terrible noise kept up in the other
room. The folks are anxiously waiting for the mail. Up till
12.30.

Saturday 23rd. Bro Fox did not come. I have done the work
to day and am very tired. Did the scrubbing all my self.
Albert made me a mop stick to do the floors with. The girls
went to meeting both this foornoon and after noon. Their trial
came off this afternoon. They did not proove May to be
guilty but advised Rebecca and Kekawoka to get married.
They have been carrying on very badly.

Jan Sunday 24th 1886. I have done the cooking to day and
attended meeting this after noon. Evening meeting is over and
no Bro Fox yet. The Ship cannot of got in yet. O how we are
longing for good news from home. I have felt very much
worried lately about home.

Monday 25. Jos. and Albert went up Kim's Gulsh this morning and got some *puanas,* and a sack of oranges. I put up pre-
serves this afternoon. Sister Young wants to take the work
half of this week for Susie but I prefur doing it my self for she
would remain here three weeks longer, should her mother
take the work for her. Bro Fox returned this evening with the
mail. Good news from home.

Tueasday Jan 26th. Bro Gates and family moved to themselves
tonight, which will reduce our family by seven souls. It was
like pulling teeth to get them to go. We are now 18 in family.

Wedensday Jan 27th. I had Stued chicken mashed potatoes and *puanas* pies for dinner. I am taken the work alone this week, but will not have to come in again for four w's.

Thursday 28. We had roast beef and custard pies for dinner. I got through with my work in good time. Sister Farr, I and baby went for a ride. I drove. Baby is not feeling well, and I am beginning to feel as though the end of the week was coming, one more day and my time is up. I have to have breakfast ready at six oclock. Albert went to Honolulu this morning in hopes of getting a picture of his family group. It is now 9. Oclock p m. I expect Jos will be writing till late. We have had another class in native to night. I will have to go to bed.

One year this morning since I left my home, and precious children. Little did I think of being away from them so long. Oh how my heart yearns for their presence. When O when can we go home.

Jan Saturday 30. Sister Farr takes the work this morning. I cut Joseph's hair to day, and have tied up some locks to send hom[e] to the folks. He went to meeting. I took baby and went to the sea for a bath. The women folks all went but Sister Farr. I can swim a little. It started to rain before we came out. Papa came with the umberella for baby.

Sunday 31. Went to meeting this morning. Took a nap after dinner and have been copying some of my native lessons since. Have left friday 29th out of my journal. It was my last day in the kitchen. I wrote to Mamie Donnie Sarah & Mother, on that day. Meeting this evening. We read in the book of mormon. Then bro's Noal and Gates spoke. I prayed. Jos. is not feeling well. His stomach is out of order, and head aches. He did not eat any supper. Baby is feeling some better to day.

Feb 1st 1886. Monday. Spent the day coppying my native lessons in a little book. Jos. helped me. I also did some studying.

Tueasday 2nt. Did a two weeks wash, and was two tired to do any thing else after I got through. Did not wash last week on account of being in the kitchen. Could not do both.

Feb 3rd Wedensday. Darned nine pairs of stockings. Took a ride to Haula. It is Election day. It was very quiet. Most of the voting was over when we got there. Sisters Young, Barrell, Bro Fox, and my self and baby went in the carriage, bro Wilcox and wife in the cart, and bro's Taylor and Hyde Sister Beesley and Mabel McAllister went horse back. Jos has been writing to Mother, Sarah and Edna. I wrote the following lines in Sister Lucy B Youngs Album.

Trials are necessary to the perfection of mankind. May your trials be only such as may be necessary to separate the dross of human nature from the pure gold of divine wisdom.

Feb 4th Thursday. Half past ten p m. I did my ironing and mending to day. Have spent a very interesting evening. Jos has been talking of his young days, and of his mother [Mary Fielding Smith] and Father [Hyrum Smith]. Sister Young and Gates were the listeners. They seemed very much interested. Susie is not able to get out much. Expects to go to bed [deliver] in three weeks.

Feb 5 Friday. Jos and Albert went for guaves this morning. Worked hard to get them. Came home soaking wet. Had to chainge all of their clothes, which makes me two extra suits to wash. I made sixteen button holes in sister Wilcoxes dress and sewed the buttons on. We had a good meeting tonight. Bro's Hyde and Taylor were the speakers, after which Jos. made a few remarks to the point. He explained the difference be-tween the gift of the Holy ghost and the Holy ghost.

Feb 6th Saturday. Helped Jos. paste scraps in his scrap book. This foornoon attended relief society meeting and Sister Young, Beesley, Joseph and my self took a bath in the sea. Baby sat and watched us. Seemed to enjoy it as much as the rest of us. I sent one of the babies white dresses to Caroline. She could not have her baby blessed for she had nothing for it to wear. The mail came to night but brought us no letters from home which was a dissapointment to us.

Sunday 7th 1886. I attended meeting this morning. Fast day. Took a nap then wrote to Mother. We had a good meeting in the evening. Jos. and Albert spoke.

Monday 8th 1886. I wrote a few lines to Mamie and Donnie and finished my letter to Mother. Bro Fox started in with the mail this morning. I cut apair of linnen breeches for Jos. and started to make them.

Tueasday Feb 9th 1886. Did my washing. Am not well. Had hard work to get through with it. Went to bed as soon as I had finished, felt much better after a good nap. Fixed the pockets in the breeches and cut a pair for Albert.

Wedensday Feb 10th. Have been sewing most of the day on the breeches. I think I can finish both pair tomorrow if I dont stop to Iron. Jos got me some coal this morning to iron with. He called at Sister Couls, and Vickey let Ina take her dol[l], she has played with it all day. To day is her birthday. She is two years old. It is one year to night since we arrived here at Lanikuli. I am feeling very lonesome and homesick. Oh how I want to see my precious children. We are looking for bro Fox to come with the mail but it is late and I am afraid he will not get here to night. God bless our pets and keep them from all sickness and harm till we can all meet again. I hope we will go home before long.

Feb 11th Thursday. When we got up we found our mail here. Bro Fox got here at two Oclock this morning. Brought some little tin-dishes and a linnen book for baby. I finished both pair of breeches to day for Albert. Wil try to make J a pair this week. Good news from home.

Feb 12th Friday. Did my plain ironing. Susanna did my starched clothes. I paid her 30¢ in Alberts name. I felt very tired and took a nap did not sew much. Lillie overcast the breeches for me.

353

Saturday Feb 13th. Worked steady all day. No time to sleep. Finished Josephs breeches. He was buisy writing home.

Sunday Feb 14. The mail carrier came this morning with the rest of our mail. Some more dishes for Ina a pair of mits for me from Edna a very nice Valentine each (from Edna) for Jos and me, also one from Mamie and another from Donnie. I attended meeting this morning. Staid home to write this after-noon. Tried to write to Edna but did not get my letter fin-ished on account of company. Sister Coles came to be administered to. She has a large lump growing in her *Opu* [stomach or womb]. It pains her consideably. Sister Young anointed the afected part, and Jos. Albert with some of the other Elders administered to her.[11]

Monday Feb 15. Wrote to Melissa J. Davis and Edna. Made a pair of garments for Joseph and cut a bathing suit. Sewed some on it. I cut it to button on the sholder (cross waist) by Enochs say so or at least that is the way he likes them made.

Tueasday Feb 16. 1886. Did my washing, sewed on the bath-ing suit in the afternoon.

Wedensday 17th. Did my Ironing. Mended Roberts and Alberts overalls then I sewed on the suit till after dark. Kekawoka and Rebecca were married to day. Most of the folks went to the wedding supper. I did not go. I was anxious to finish Joseph bath suit.

Thursday 18th. Let Sister Farr have the bathing suit I have made for cloth to make another. She gave me three quarters of a yard extra for my work, the cloth is 50¢ a yard. Joseph thought he would like his to button strait best, and Enoch liked the cross waist best, and it fit very nice. Sister F worked the button holes and sewed the buttons on. I cut and made a suit for Joseph. He likes it very well, I also made a pair of drawers for me. So much towards my suit. Sister Gates sent for me a false alarm.

Friday 19. Finished my suit to day and worked the button holes in Josephs.

Saturday 20th. Albert started to town this morning for the mail. I have been mending and doing od jobs. Attended Reelief Society meeting. We had a good meeting. There were near 40 members present. Sisters Farr Wilcox and I were the only white sisters there. Lilly is quite sick not able to be out coughfs very hard. Sister Young and Mabel went for a horse-back ride. Bros Smith Farr Cluff Noal and Gates, Sisters Smith Farr Noal Wilcox and Beesley went to the sea for a bath. The waves were very high, we crisened our new bathing suits.

Sunday 21st. Attended meeting this morning. Took a nap and wrote to my children in the afternoon. Albert came early in the evening bringing the sad news of little Robert [Smith]s death.[12] Joseph met him at the barn. I stepped out of the door. I could see by their looks that something was [w]rong. They both looked so sad. I asked what is the matter you have brought bad news. Albert answered "Your children are all right. I thought he ment all of Josephs children, so I said is it yours Albert" "no." Is it Mother. "no," it is Robert he is dead. I burst into tears. I felt that it was too hard. Oh, my poor Sister Edna in her touching letter she says, "I am so lonesome no baby to love." Poor girl how my heart aches for her, and poor papa to see his grief seems more than I can bear. O Lord comfort their hearts.

March 7th. Sunday. Joseph Enoch and Robert [Taylor] went yesterday to attend conference. I expect them back to night. Albert started at half past three in for the mail. O how I dread the news he may bring. I fear all is not well. It has been a sad long two weeks since we got our last mail and since I wrote in my journal. Jos has fretted so much and felt so very bad over the loss of his little Robert one of the nicest children we had. At first I thought it was no comfort to him my being here with little Ina, but I can now see that if he had been here alone, it would have been harder. It seems that he can not stand it to be alone.

This last week I have been doing the work in the kitchen. Have been obliged to be out of my room most of the time, and it has made me feel terrible to go in and see his eyes red and swolen with crying, but Ina has been with him much of the time. I took the work saturday, the 27th and worked very hard scrubbing and cleaning all day, for I found every thing was dirty and filthy. A little before twelve oclock in the night bro Gates came for me. Susie was sick. I went over as soon as I could, but was very tired and lame from my hard days work. Her watter had broke but her pains were very light. I staid till half past three then came home and went to bed, got up and went over again at six to see if I could go on with getting breakfast, but found she was getting along nicely and was just going to send for me. I sent word to Sister Farr who got breakfast. Susies ten pound boy was born ten minutes to seven Feb 28th. She had a very easy time. I left both mother and baby comfortable, and got back in time to help wash the breakfast dishes and get dinner. I have had no one but May to help me and have helped wash all the dishes have mixed a big batch of bread every night and done most of the scrub[b]ing. The kitchen dont often look as nice and clean as it does now. This is my second day on another week. It is hard for me but I thought I could do it better now than I could in another four weeks. I will not have to come in again before I am sick [deliver]. The work will not be as hard this week as it was last for every thing is clean an[d] in order. . . .

Monday 15th. Cut three little gowns. I will have the use of the machine, wedensday and thursday. Must get a little ready for fear of needing them before I get the things from home I sent for. I wrote the following lines in Susie Gates album.

Dear Sister Susie In this far off and strange land, so distant from many of our loved ones and the cherished scenes and homes of childhood, with such a wide range for usefulness before us, and so much to be done in the fields of mental and physical labor for the welfare of our race, (and so little power on my part to accomplish my allotted task) I can only sincerely pray God to give us each the spirit and the strength in connection with our companions and fellow laborers to do our duty well.

Hawaiian children with plantation buildings in background. Laie, Hawaii. (Joseph F. Smith family album. LDS Church Archives.)

Nancy Abigail Clement Williams (1872-1954)

Fredrick Granger Williams's proposal of marriage came as such a surprise to Nancy Abigail Clement she "could have fell down." She had worked for Fred and his first wife Amanda for several months, but Nancy "never realized that he ever dreamed of loving me." After personally and prayerfully considering "a question of so great importance," she agreed to enter furtively into plural marriage, a marriage that would be kept absolutely secret for a time, since arrests and prosecution for cohabitation were then at their height.

Nancy Abigail Clement was born May 22, 1872, in New Harmony, Utah, a daughter of Darius Salem Clement and Louisa Kelsey. The Clements moved to Fairview, in central Utah, in 1874, and there Nancy first met Fredrick Granger Williams, farmer, miner, and namesake of an early Church leader.[13] It would seem that most of Nancy's family, including her brothers Easton, Oliver, Jessie, Albert, and Orin, were unaware of her marriage, though her parents and her sister Elizabeth (Lizzie) were in on the secret.

At one point Nancy and Lizzie left Fairview to board a few miles away near the Ephraim Academy, where they had enrolled for classes. After nearly a year of traveling up and down the territory to avoid recognition as Fred's wife, Nancy joined Fred and Amanda and their children in a move to Colonia Dublan, one of the Latter-day Saint colonies in Mexico to which plural families had been moving to escape persecution. Despite her trials and hardships, Nancy remained cheerful and devoted to her husband and the Church.

The excerpt that follows is the first portion of Nancy's reminiscence and journal, written in a notebook along with some of her Ephraim Academy lessons. Nancy kept various notebooks throughout her life, many dealing with family genealogy, others with talks she heard, and some with her poetry and essays. The following selection is taken from the original holograph in the Historical Department of the Church. Minimal punctuation has been added.

Dublan (Mexico) Ward Primary in 1898, with Nancy Clement Williams, standing left of window, as second counselor. Caption written by Nancy reads: "Where I helped to mother all The Primary children In June before Estte was born in July." (LDS Church Archives.)

Jan 3rd [1889]. Eastons boy Sanford aged 3 years old died with croup, & I spent much of my time with them after that. The middle of Jan. I went with him & wife to Manti & tended the baby while they did work in the Temple. We were their a week, and after my return home, father & mother desired that I should board with some one in town & attend school the remainder of the winter. Several women were anxious for me to stay with them. But my parents wished me to go to F. G. Williams. This I feared would not suit their wishes. But father spoke to him & he said they had wished for a long time that I would come but thought it would be imposing on me to ask

359

me to. One Sunday morning I took my clothing & went, prepared for school next morning. My Father gave me good
advice as to what kind of company I kept & not keep late
hours. Said he would not have any occasion to worry while I
was stopping with them as they were very strict in their
releigon. I attended school regular for 2 weeks when Easten
sent for me to help them. Their baby was very sick & I
remained with them a week, when I returned to school.

March 1st. Father decided to go to the temple to do work for
his fathers family, & obtained a reccomend for me & all the
children older. I mentioned it one Sunday morning to Fred
W[illiams] stating that Easton & Oliver were going to be
adopted to Father & Mother.[14] He jockingly ask if he could be
adopted also. I suggested, that they had already more boy's
than girls, & it would be more profitable to adopt girls. "Dont
you understand my meaning, he ask," I told him no. He then
ask me if I would marry him, & share my lot with his. This
was such a surprize to me, I could have fell down. I never
realized that he ever dreamed of loving me. I had found him
to be a true Latter Day Saint, & had great respect for him & if
I ever loved him I never would show it, because I thought he
cared nothing for me. I told him it was a question of so great
importance I could not answer him directly & ask him to give
me untill the following day to answer; this he granted, & I
sought unto the Lord earnestly to know if it was his will.
Having received a testimony that he was the one destined to
be my future husband I gave him the desired promise on the
evening following.

No sooner had I done this than the powers of darkness tried
to thwart my purposes, by discouraging me in every way.
About 2 weeks later I was voted in as ass[t]. sec. in the Relief
Society. I never dreamed of such a thing untill it was done.
Then of course I was powerless to do any thing; but this was
my first and greatest trial. I at first said I would not hold the
position. The idea of a young girl only 16 and unmarried
attending the married sisters meeting.[15] I knew I would be the

laughing stock of all my friends; & it would give more cause for suspiction that I was to be married. However I over came these feelings and attended the meetings & always took minutes, although I felt out of place.

March 25 1889. With my parents, brother Easton & wife & Oliver I went to Manti to do work in the temple. 26 recvd. baptism for my self and several of fathers sisters. 27 had the happy priviledge of receving my washings and anointing and the 2 following days received endowments for the dead.[16] When the elders laid hands upon me for the reception of the Holy Ghost, during my confirmation I was told to keep my promise, and enter the path that had been opened for my footsteps, and keep sacred my covenants and great would be my reward. Said the Lord had heard my prayers, and was pleased with my course. This was a great satisfaction to me, and another strong testimony that I should enter the principle of Celestial Marriage, although it seemed a dark hour for the Saints, when persecution against that principle raged in its highest.

On our return home I made preperations to attend to April Con[ference] in Salt Lake City. My mother, Easton & wife a cousin and several friends were the happy number who started from home very early one morning, arriving S. L. at about 4 P.M. We had bedding & grub and stoped at the tithing house. The same evening I went to a theatre with Bro. Williams. While in the city the time was well spent, attending the various meetings. In the evening of the 8th I was sealed for time and eternity to F. G. Williams, the man of my choice. The same evening we attended a theatre. After it was out we took a short stroll to have a chance to talk, as he was to return home the next morning & I was going to take the train for Ogden. No one of our crowd knew of our marriage, untill the next day I informed my mother, that it had been accomplished, but she ask me no questions.

Next morning we gathered up our things, and went to the D[enver] & R[io] G[rand] R[ailwa]y depot to take the train for the penitentary. We were earlier than needed to be, & my sisterinlaw Malissa [Sanderson Clement] and my self went to Wm. Palmers, (my intended brotherinlaw's) where my mother was, she having staid their over night. At 7-30 we boarded the train and in a short time found our selves at the penitentary guard house, and a fierce wind blowing. At 11 we were escorted into Uncle Sams boarding house; and when the hugh iron doors closed behind us, it made me realize the responsibility I had just taken upon my-self, and a shiver went over me to see so many of our brethern mingling with so many criminals. We were seated in the dinning room, and the men called in that we wished to see. They were Eastons father-in law, H[enry] W[eeks] Sanderson, Bro. Rasmussen, and E. A. Day. We talked across a table with them for half an hour with one of the guards close by to over hear what we said. . . .

[Travels to Ogden; returns to Fairview in April 1889. Engages in domestic service for several families in Fairview. Visits Fred at mining camp.]

Thursday [September ? 1889] Fred went to town, & came back Friday. Said Lizzie was going to Ephriam to school and thought it would be wise for me to go, and escape so much talk. They took me to a shingle mill, and I their got a chance to go on home with a coal team, but strangers to me, arriving home about 4 O clock. I ate some dinner, cleaned my self up and walked to town, got a new dress, underclothing aprons etc. That night and the next day we did up our sewing got all ready for school and the next morning with a crowd of young folks started for Ephriam. We rented a 2 roomed house of Bro. Willardsen; got our things all in, ate supper, then went to the tabernacle and heard a discourse from Wm. Palmer.

Next morning (Sept 9th. 1889) we entered the school house. The first day was spent in arranging classes, and pointing out the duties of students, making them acquainted with the rules of school. We all returned home with the blues, and had them for several days. Every thing looked to be such a task, and the Principal (Alma Greenwood) was such a stern man, with sharp black eyes that would look through a person; their was no

getting around any of the lessons, nor any half way preparation; and we felt our weekness. As time wore on and we got
acquainted with the students and teachers, we grew to love
school. Many a night I have sat and studied until 3 O clock, &
never retiring untill after midnight. Their were 9 of us, from
Fairview, besides a cook. We had our own bedding, grub and
paid the cook for doing all the work. We were allowed to go
home every 2 and 3 weeks.

It was a month after I went before I got to see Fred. He
happened to be in town on my second trip home. One day as
we came out of school I saw his team tied to the wagon
eating hay in the road, but did not see him. I did not say any
thing about it, but one of the girls said she knew it was a
team from home and would like to see the owner. When we
got home I told Lizzie to find something to keep the girls with
her & I would have an excuse to go to the store. I went to the
Post office, then to the store, in hopes of seeing him. He
passed the store while I was there with a load of coal, on his
way to Manti. He nodded, and I returned it. And went home
bluer than I came. Next morning the boys brought me a letter
that had the Manti post mark on; they said they knew it was
a love letter and they was going to read it. I had great difficulty in keeping it from them and had to burn it to do so. He
composed some verses after he had passed me in the store. I
wanted to keep them but could not.

One Thursday evening after school we were all out playing
stink base for exercise. I got to chasing my cousin (Darius San-
ders) & was determined to catch him. I run so hard that I had
to sit down and rest. I turned faint and dizzy and had to go in
and went to bed. I would chill awhile, then nearly burn up
with fever all night. In the morning had a high fever. As soon
as the drug store was opened, my cousin got me salts and
quinnene, which I took, but threw it up as fast as they gave it
to me. Lizzie bathed and soaked my feet, did all she could for
me. She remained from school, also Darius, who went all over
town to hire a buggie to take me home in. They were very

uneasy at the thought of having me so far from home sick. At noon Al Cox came, and him and one of the brethren administered to me, which releived me some. About 4 O clock we started for home in Al's wagon; I had a bed between the seats.

It was just dark when we got into Fairview. The Y.L.M.I.A. were going to give a dance, and as Lizzie was president she remained in town but I went on home. As we were passing Freds shop I noticed a light, and knew he was over. I raised up so he could see me. He did, but did not know wether it was me or Lizzie. So he went to the dance and saw Lizzie, and knew it was me went home. He came their. We were all in bed but he staid untill almost daylight when he had to go. Next night he came again and went on home early next morning. Tuesday he came again and wanted me to go over with him next day. I went and when we were half way up the caynon we met Oliver, but I was under the cover so he did not see me. Next day he fixed up and moved to town. The rest of the week I helped them clean and get moved into the house. Sunday morning Jessie [Clement] took me to Ephriam in a cart. They were all glad to see me back again.

Nov. 15 was the last day of the term of school. I never hated to leave any place so bad in my life as I did their. The ties that endear one to those schools are hard to be broken. Only those who go can realize the trial it is to part from it. It was their I first received and bore testimony to the truth of the gospel. Many tears were shed that day, & I always have joy in thinking of the 9 weeks I spent in the Ephriam Accademy.[17]

Nov. 18 th. Albert [Clement]s, and Mary Ann's first child was born, which they named for Lizzie and I.

Brother Easton was appointed a mission to the Southern States. Was to leave Dec 2nd. The evening of the 29th of Nov. they had his farewell party. In the after-noon I called at all of my brothers to see them the last time for a while. They ask if I was going to the party, I replied that I was. As soon as it was dark I gathered up a bundle of my clothing, Bade father good bye, peeked through the window at my younger brothers and with Lizzie and Mother started to town. As soon as we had got to Freds, he had a team and wagon, ready to take me to Thistle Station. We started about 9 Oclock, arriving their just as day was breaking. To avoid being seen he drove the team about a mile up the track behind the hills. About 9 O clock he went to the ticket office & got my ticket and at 4 O clock drove the wagon as near the station as he could to be safe. As soon as the train came, I went and boarded it, but I had a thick veil over my face, so no one recognized me.

It was 10 O clock when the train reached Ogden. I had been through the city twice before, going and returning from Plain City. The old depot buildings that were their in the spring were removed for large new ones, and instead of the train stopping on the east side as it did before, it stopped on the west. I had been turned around all day, and when I got out of the cars, I was afraid I was lost. Their were no Street cars, or cab's of any kind to take any one up town. I earnestly prayed for the Lord to guide me for I realized He was me only guardian. I started to go east, as I was supposed it was, but found my-self lost among a few scattered houses; and could see tramps bumming around. I entered a house and told the lady I was lost, ask her to show me where the Broom Hotel was. She escorted me around the large buildings where the electric lights made it visible for me to realize where I was. On leaving the train I [had] started west for east, and had it not been for the kind lady I would have wandered around, and probably been insulted by some wretch; as the city was full of rough characters.

As soon as I started up town I realized where I was and went east untill I came to Broom Hotel, then turned north. By this time the lights had gone out. The stores all closed, and only a few police-men and people, whom I suspected had been visiting houses of ill fame were seen on the street. These scanned me as I passed, but I hurried on, and when I came to George A. Lowe's machine shop I knew the next place was my father

in law's [Dr. Ezra Granger Williams]. I knocked and went in.
They were just retiring. I gave them a letter Fred had sent,
and went to bed. As soon as I had got into bed I had to give
vent to my feelings in tears. To think how risky it was for me
to find his place so late at night, all alone; made me feel very
much my dependence on my Heavenly Father. Next morning
the doctor ask me how I got from the depot. When I told him
it almost made him vexed at Fred for not sending him word
so he could have some one meet me. I remained with them
and did their work, never went out in town. Went by the
name of Maggie Granger, and was only known to Ezra [Jr.] and
wife, & the doctor and his wife.

Dec. 11   Fannie Budge (Freds sister) gave birth to a son and
died Jan 1st. The Dr. and wife were with her most of the
time, during her illness, which left me alone with the hired
boy. Several nights I was all alone. The day she was buried I
rode with Hyrum [Williams] in a cutter to Pleasant View
many of the people thought I was his wife. We returned to
Ogden the same day. Two days after her funeral, Fred came.
Had heard nothing of her death untill he got their. My
brother Orien was with them, but he did not knew of my
whereabouts untill he saw me their. The next day they went
on to Pleasant View. The next day Fred came back to Ogden
and the next evening I went with him to Pleasant View to
help clean up. I could not own relationship with Orin, and
said I came from Dixie. The people in Fairview thought I was
in Dixie. I wrote to the girls as though I was at my grand-
mothers. These letters I sent inside a large envelope. He
understood my situation, and would post my letters at his
office, and send them on to Fairview. Of course their would
letters come back to me in his care & he would send them to
me. I wrote to my brothers in the same way but to my
parents, Fred would address the letters to Bro. Peter Sundwall,
and he understood that they were for them, and ma would
have him address all her letters to Fred.

Feb. 21st. Attended the Weber Stake conference. 22nd. Went

to Pleasant View with Sam. Ferrin to keep house for Thomas
Budge. Kept the 3 oldest children; Mandy [Amanda] had the
baby.[18] I could get to see the folks real often here; and often
Fred would come at night when the children were all asleep
and stay until almost morning.

April 5th. I took the children to Freds, and took care of all
the children while him and Amanda went to Salt Lake to
Con[ference]. Next day John Mower from Fairview called to
see Fred. I went in the bed room & had the priviledge of
peeking through the key hole at him. Soon after this I went to
Ogden where I met Lizzie who had been in Salt Lake working
for Edward Anderson, & had moved with them to Ogden
where she still worked. I staid with the Dr. nearly 2 weeks,
helped clean house. One Saturday night Lizzie and I went to
Pleasant View with Fred. She returned early monday morning
but I staid untill Tues morning (May 2nd.) when I went with
Fred before daylight to Ogden. We got in town very early. I
went & saw Lizzie for a few minutes, then back to Ezra's. Ezra
and his father soon came to see me, and Fred took me to
depot in buggie. Here he saw president [Wilford] Woodruff
who told him to go to Mexico as soon as possible. . . . [More
travel to Fairview, Salt Lake City and Pleasant View.]

We remained here untill July 7th. When we removed into
Ogden into a house back of the Dr's. barn. We were very
busy preparing for our journey to Mexico. Lizzie came with
her things from Fairview. I went to Plain City and spent a
week with my folks their. When I returned home Lizzie went
& spent several days. On the morning of the 7th of Aug we
bade the folks good bye & was on our way for Mexico. We
had arranged to leave Ogden at 12. thus arrive in Thistle in
the afternoon. My mother went from Fairview (28 miles to
get to see us once more. But through mistake we had to leave
at 7 in the morning. Thus when she came to Thistle she found
we had gone, which has always been a sore disapointment.
Orien got off here & went home with her. We had a long
tiresome journey. Flora [May Williams] took sick the first day

out and gradually grew worse, untill when we arrived in Deming [New Mexico] on the 10th, She was unable to walk at all. Heber & Joe Farr met us here & took us to where his father [Winslow] had rented rooms. We all piled in a small house (5 small rooms). Their were 31 in all (Bro Farr's 2 famileys) Brigham Binghams 2 families, Bro [William] Staker & wife and our family. We were here for 2 weeks. Flora got very low with spinal disease, her hair all came out and their were large holes in the back of her head.

21st. We left Deming for Diaz,[19] Br Farr leaving his wife Tilda in Deming. The first day out was very pleasant, but the second day was mud to the wagon hubs some times. Those of the women & children who could walked. The drivers pulled off their shoes & socks, rolled up their pants and waded by their teams. The rest of the journey was very pleasant. We traveled with a Bro. David Wilson who was out to Deming from Diaz for provisions. We arrived in Diaz on the 26th. Mud houses & mud fences; the street full of Mosqueat, oh what a home sick crowd. No homes & we could not use our own things untill they were inspected, and there was a large river between us and Assencion the place where the custom house was. We drove our wagons to the very southern skirts of the town to the guard house where a Mexican could watch us. We were then permitted to go with Bro. Wilson to his house where he gave us his large front room. We were here several days when the guard let us have one tent and stove & a few articles. In a few days the river was down enough so the officers could come over and inspected our goods. We then pitched our tents back of Steven Wilson's house. Only 5 tents in all. Ours was 16 by 30 ft. But we found the country two windy & in such a rainy season as it was that year. We found our tent more convenient after it was cut down. For it blew down several times & left us without shelter.

My sister took sick the day we got in Diaz and two days after I came down with Typhoid Maleria. She gradually grew worse until the morning of the 12th of Sept. she passed away.

I was recovering by this time; but this was a terrible blow. Only such a short time since we left our home & parents. In a strange land among strangers. Only 5 teams to the funeral; no friends to mourn with us. No one to speak of her good qualities as they had known her in life. We could only write to them the sad news; which was a very trying ordeal for mother & those at home. Fred went back to Deming for the rest of our furniture & clothes. On his return the men all went up the Casas Grandes river to look for homes.

In Dec. Fred again went to Deming & Josie [Sarah Josephine Williams] & my self went with him to get clothing. Here we met Philip H. Hurst & family on their way to Mexico. On our return we packed up our wagons to remove south. We were loaded in our wagons ready to start in the morning, & during the night several inches of snow had fallen. Our baby took sick who was then about 3 mts old; (Kathena Hazel born Oct 21 1890).[20] Will. Staker had not pulled his tent down & we keep her in by their stove. Flora and Joseph also took sick, & for 2 weeks, we were up night & day, the elders & apostle George Teasdale often comming to administer.[21] Patriarch Benjeman Johnson who had been acquainted with Fred's grandfather F. G. Williams came to see us and gave me the following blessings.... [Nancy was promised children, "the blessings of the earth," opportunities to help the needy, and wisdom.]

Jan 18th 1891. Hazel being much better we started for Dublan arriving their on the 22. The town site had been laid out and we chose a block near the center of town & pitched our tent on the grass which was thick enough to make a nice carpet. At this time our tent was the largest room in town and we very often had pleasant gatherings. On the 29th of March following we had a surprise party for Fred it being his 38th birthday. I put on a play.

April 30th. Fred hoisted our wind mill (The eclipse) which he had bought in Deming.

May 10. I was set apart to act as teacher in the Sunday

School of the Sanfrancisco branch of the Juarez Ward, by
Joseph H. Wright. May 11 we had a surprize party in honor
of Winslow Farr it being his 54th birthday.

May 20 A gentle gale came up and upset our tent as we were
eating dinner, breaking the ridge poll & several others;
riddling it so far as not to be able to live in it any longer. We
borrowed a small tent to put our stove table etc in & moved
our beds and the rest of the things in the shop (blacksmith's).
He had one or two loads of lumber to build with and he
hurried to get the house built and on June 23rd. 1891 it was
for enough completed so that we moved into it, & it seemed
like a palace to us after living in a tent so long. Fred lost one
of his horses while on the mt. for lumber, & he got one of
Edison Porters to put with the other one.

July 19 1891. Apostle George Teasdale met with the Saints
and Set apart Winslow Farr as Bishop in the Dublan ward.
22nd. F. G. Williams, was set apart as 1st. councler & N. H.
Hurst as sec. counclor.

21. Met with the women and organized a Releif Society with
Ida J. Mortensen pres. Lydia K. Young 1st cou & Charlotte
Carroll sec. counclor. Phebe I. Allred. sec. Josepha Wright
ass[t]. sec. Nancy A. Williams treasurer, Kate Porter Chorister.
I was set apart by by George Teasdale. There were 30
members in all. $5.75 were donated that day.

Aug. 5th. The first store (Mr. Halls) was opened in Dublan, in
the new Pratt House.

Aug 11th. Rebecca A. and Ella Hurst went teaching, being the
first to visit as R. S. teachers.

Aug 15 91. The Y.M.Y.L.M.I.A's and the S[unday] S[chool]
were reorganized. I was set apart as sec. counclor to Kate
Porter in the Y L.M.I.A. by George Teasdale. He gave me one
of the best blessings I ever heard, said that my labors among
the young should be one of love, & that I would be a blessing
unto them, in giving unto them words of wisdom and council.

Said my tongue should be loosed, and I should speak as with the voice of an angell. Was set apart the same evening to act as teacher in the S.S.

The same day the first Deacons quorum was organized with Heber E. Farr President, James Hurst first and Albert Mortensen second counclors.

Sept 5th 6 7th. The first conference in the Mexican Mission was held in Juarez. The meeting house at that place was dedicated also.

Sept 23. Peter Mc.Bride & wife Laura came & stayed over night.

" 25. Being Sunday Fred, Amanda myself, Lizzie [Amanda Elizabeth Williams], & Josie all fasted and prayed in my behalf that I might bear children, as I had often felt down-cast that the Lord had not blessed me with children. We did not eat any thing untill at night, when my husband anointed me with oil and blessed me that I might have the desires of my heart, & him also. The Lord heard and answered our prayers, for it was not a week untill I became aware that I was to become a mother. Amanda was just like a mother to me, would not let me make even my own bed, do a lick of washing or ironing or any thing that she thought would injure me. Her own feelings were sacrificed and she only thought of others happiness. About Xmas time Al Cox came from Fairview and brought a lot of fruit my parents had sent. We had a very dry windy winter, no feed on the range and our stock wandered off in search of food, leaving us without milk, & with only a little flour corn meal, beans, & pork.

March 17th. Ezra & Hyrum Williams came with Fred whom had been in Diaz and met them their. They brought a lot of things from ma, which they found in the Deming P. O. We were very glad to see them. But we had about a week of the windiest weather I ever saw. They remained untill the latter part of April when they left & Fred went with them to Sonora

371

where they parted Fred comming home alone, & when in sight of home his other horse died, leaving him without a team.

March 25. Caroline Buchannan gave birth to a pair of twins (a boy & girl, Archie Earl & Carrie Mearl) the first born in Dublan. Fred waited on her this being his first outside his own family.

May 25 1892. In the evening. wensday at 17 minutes to 10 Oclock I gave birth to a little 4# daughter (Premature 1 mt.) She was welcomed by all & when 8 days old her father gave unto her the name of Louie Bell. She was such a poor delicate little thing, only gaining ¼# the first mt. After that I gave her the bottle to nurse and she grew better.

Sept 4 92. Amanda and all the children started for Arizona to visit her mother & folks. Fred worked on the cain mill and got molasses to last us a year. He had raised over 200 bu of wheet that season. Also it was in Sept. that Sis. Thompson & little boy were killed by Indians at Cave Valley.

Dec 4th. 92. My grandmother Abigail Kelsey died at her home in New Harmony, Utah.

In Dec. Fred started for Arizona for the folks, having sold his wind mill for a team to Willard Mortensen. Fred and folks arrived Jan. 8 1893. The Bishop was in Utah and it left the ward affairs all for Fred. He being very desirous to keep the young from falling into errors & from doing wrong constantly earged them to do wright, and some who were inclined to do as they pleased, reguardless of council tried by slander and every way possible to injure his character & that of his family's. But wright is wright; & the Lord assisted us with his holy Spirit to endure through those dark moments; & we had a chance to prove our friends; & those who were on the side of truth and honesty.

Ruth May Fox (1853-1967)

When Ruth May Fox died in Salt Lake City in 1967, she was Utah's oldest living resident, with grandchildren, great-grandchildren, and great-great grandchildren numbering 282. Even a cursory reading of the record she kept as she approached her own "middle age" raises the question of how one who moved so fast could live so long. This particular segment of her diary shows her intense involvement in Utah politics as the territory became a state, a state with constitutionally enfranchised women, much to the delight of ardent suffragist Ruth May Fox. Ever present in this diary segment also is Ruth's activity in the Latter-day Saint organizations for women: the Relief Society, Young Ladies Mutual Improvement Association, and Primary Association. Some thirty-six years later, in 1929, at the age of seventy-five, she was appointed general president of the Young Women's MIA.

Born in Westbury, England, November 16, 1853, Ruth May was a daughter of Mary Ann Harding and James May. After she came to the United States she worked in a Philadelphia factory with her father to earn money for the trip to Zion, and then hiked across the plains beside the wagon she and her father shared with twelve other persons. Her marriage in 1873 to Jesse Williams Fox, Jr., brought twelve children and more prosperous times, though the addition of a second wife in 1888 and the coming of nationwide depression a few years later curtailed some of that prosperity.

A hopeful and energetic writer, Ruth May Fox wrote and published poetry. She was active in the Utah Women's Press Club, founded in 1891 by some of Utah's leading women writers, Emmeline B. Wells, Susa Young Gates, and Louisa Lula Greene Richards. Associating with these accomplished women made her aware of her own educational limitations, so she enrolled in university courses and correspondence classes and studied a great deal on her own. She wrote the texts for several hymns and songs, the best remembered of which is "Carry On," the MIA anthem.

Ruth May Fox at age 33 (1888) with seventh child. From "My Story," by Ruth May Fox, comp. (Leonard Grant Fox, copy of typescript with photos. LDS Church Archives.)

The life of Ruth May Fox is recorded in her own comprehensive autobiography, "My Story." The following selection from her diary covers only a few months in 1894-95, but it well represents the vigor, awareness, and involvement that characterized her long and productive life. The selection has been taken from the original holograph in the Historical Department of the LDS Church, with daily entries set off and minimal punctuation added, including periods after entry dates.[22]

Dec 1894

29. Went to Press Club in the evening. Had a plesant time. Club entertained Phebe Cousins who spoke to us on the sufferage and currency questions.[23]

Sun. 30. Was invited to Dr E[llen] Fergusons where some ladies met to complain of the way they had been treated by the Ter[ritorial] Board of U[tah] W[oman] S[uffrage] A[ssociation]. Questioned the legality of the elections of officers etc. I gained some experience at that time. Made a mistake in signing letter requesting the calling of another convention, although I did it with the best of feelings toward Sister [Emmeline B.] Wells.[24] What [went] to meeting in the evening. Bro Stevenson occupied the entire evening.

31. Miss Cousins was at the Reaper's [Literary Club] to day. Mrs. F[ranklin] S. Richards and I delevered letter to Mrs E B Wells. Was interviewed in the evening by Margeret Caine who thought the letter was wrong.[25] Jet and I sat up with some of the children to see the old year out.

Jan 1 1895. Snowing. Jet and I called on Mrs W. C. Morris, Father, Uncle Gid. Went in cutter. Fine sleighing.

Jan 2. Met E. B. Wells. Had a talk on the sufferage question. Paid my yearly fee.

3d. Very busy making dresses for S. School party. Clara was here and spent the afternoon.

Fri 4th. Got children off to party. Went late to Emily Clawsons to Primary O[fficers] meeting to arrange about Miss

Chapin's [kindergarten] Class which was imediately afterward.[26] I remained and enjoyed it.

Sat 5. In the afternoon went to Mrs. [Phoebe Louisa Young] Beatty's tea she gave to help raise funds to send delegate to Atlanta.

6. Remained at home Jet being poorly.

Mon 7. Went to R[eapers] C[lub] in the afternoon and Y[oung] L[adies] meeting in eve, which met at S. Rockwells. Was asked to write for their paper. Called at Georgie [Fox Young]'s going home to see Lylie about taking part in a Primary entertainment.

Wed. 9. Very busy. Peral. E. left. Daisy and I did work. Attended Ter[ritorial] S[uffrage] executive meeting. I refused to withdraw my name from the letter because the ladies I signed with were not present with the exception of Mrs. F. S. Richards. It was quite late when I returned home being to late for supper.

Thurs. 11 [10]. Frank was sick to day, did not go to Primary. Borrowed $10.00 from Mrs Wimley for Jettie to get his glasses.

Fri. 12 [11]. Worked hard. At 4 o'clock went to Miss Chapins class. Came home in time to get supper. 4 of the children have gone to a party at Mrs. Pollocks.

Sat. 13 [12]. Hurryed all day to get to the club and found it was not to be untill the 15th.

Sunday. Went to hear Miss Phebe Cousin's lecture on the Silver Conspiracy which she did in a very able manner. Jet went also.

Tues. Went to sufferage meeting in the afternoon and P[ress] Club in the evening.

Fri 18 [January]. Miss Chapin class was dismissed as the members were all falling off.

Sat. Worked very hard all day. In the evening finished writing the Ten Virgins.

[February 1895]

Feb 9th. Have been too busy to remember my journal when I might have taken time to write in it. Jan 29 went to Relief Society. Sister E[lmina] S Taylor spoke to us asking our faith and prayers as she was going to Washington to represent the young ladies.[27] Tues Feb 5 Went to S[uffrage] A[ssociation]. Heard Prof Stewart and S. B. Young also a Mr Adams from N[orth] D[akot]a on sufferage. Tried to vote down petition but failed. Feb 8th Went to Sister E Stevenson's birthday party. Had a glorious time. Sister B[athsheba] Smith and Helen [Mar Kimball] Whitney were present. Sister Sarah Phelps spoke in tounges [tongues] with great power insomuch that the floor and the chairs and our limbs trembled. She blessed Sister Whitney who was an invalid for years. Said we should know a year hence whether God spoke or not. The sisters laid hands on Sister W. and prayed for her speedy recovery Sister N[ettie] C Taylor being mouth.

Fri 15. Went to Weiler Horne's funeral. In the evening tended S[alt] L[ake] Co[unty] Sufferage Ass[ociation] entertainment to celebrate Susan B. Anthony's birthday.

Sat eve. Went to P[ress] Club. Sister [Ellis R.] Shipp had gone to Washington. I was chosen to represent the club at the [Utah] Federation [of Women's Clubs].

Sun 17. I have been to evening meeting. Bro Eli Pierce told us that general Carter of Industrial Army fame on the day of his departure made these remark[s]: That slaves were rising up against their masters and would shortly plunge the U. S. in blood. That it was but the sequel to the Civil War. Being a fulfillment of J[oseph] Smith's prophecy (or words to that effect).[28]

Fri. 22. Last Monday at the Reapers Club we voted to send

50 ct apiece as a birthday present to Sister E B Wells who is now in Washington.

Tue. Went to suffrage meeting. We decided to inteview the delegates to the Constitutional convention. Sister Ella Hyde and myself were appointed to see Samuel Hill Richard Lambert and Mr Vanhorne. On thursday attended Primary and changed my name so that it would go on the minutes, from Polly to Ruth M. I thought it would prevent confusion in the future. To-day the children are out of school and I want to do some sewing if I can get time.

24th Sunday. Sick had cramps.

Mon 25. I interviewed delegates. Mr Hill was favorable. Mr Vanhorn did not think the constitution was the place for suf-ferage to come up. Went to see Mrs [Emma J.] McVicker about the federation.[29] I forgot to write that last Friday night Jet told me he was going to the store and he did not come home till next day. I was quite worried was afraid something had happened to him. I don't like to be treated that way.

[March 1895]

I am afraid there are many little incidents my journal will not get. I am so busy I do not get time to attend to it but to day the 6th of March I attended the Federation bussiness meeting. This morning and this afternoon a reception given to the dele-gates, both at the Women's industrial home.[30] Everything went along nicely. I was appointed one of a committee to organize womans clubs throughout the territory, but declined. My home duties are too pressing. Two subjects of the Press Clubs were accepted for discussion at the May meeting in Ogden. Yesterday attended Suff. Meeting.

Mon. Gave my paper [about] Herbert Spencer and Frances Hodgson Burnett at the Reapers.

Sat 2nd. Called at Georgie's. The sewing class met there. Had refreshments then went to Dr. R[omania] Pratt about the Fed-eration.

Fri. Attended Mrs C E Dye's Funeral.

Mar 11. Was called to a meeting on the sufferage question at S[arah] M. Kimballs but could not remain it being to near the dinner hour.

12. Attended Releif Society.

13. Went to W[omen's] Coop[erative] Directors meeting.[31]

14. Saw Dr E R Shipp and decided to pospone Press and Reapers meeting in her and Sister E B Wells honor till Saturday night on account of Bro Hornes party.

Sat 16th. Had a pleasant time at the Club. Mrs E B Wells and Dr. Shipp gave interesting accounts of their visit to the East.[32]

17th. Bro Brigham Young [Jr.] spoke this evening. His theme was to not mix to much with outsiders.

Mon 18th. Met with S. A. in convention at city and county building. Drafted memorial being one of the committee.

18. Presented memorial to [Constitutional Convention] committee on sufferage. Was very courteously treated. We all felt it a great day in the history of Utah. The committee informed us they had passed on W[oman] S[uffrage] being ten to five in favor.[33]

Friday. Am invited to meet the committee in the Probate Court room, when I hope to see inside of State Convention Hall.

Fri 22. Met with committee and decided to ask for a room not now in use for the purpose of holding public meetings for ladies, of course.

Thur 28. A very rainy day but I attended the convention to hear the debate on the sufferage question. Mr. B. H. Roberts was very eloquent but his only argument was that he thought it [woman suffrage] would defer Statehood.

31. It is Grandpa [Jesse William] Fox's birthday. We had all the members of his family to dinner.

April 1st. O dear I have worn myself out to-day. Have been to the convention all day and stood up all the time with the exception of a little while that I sat on the table. Mr Roberts was to give his oration but did not have time so it went over till next day. What a shame he does not use his eloquence in a better cause.

2nd. Attended W. S. meeting. Dr Ferguson thought if we had petitioned it would have been a benefit but we shall see.

Wed 3d. Was called out suddenly to circulate petitions. Met with good success.

Thurs 4. Went with petitions a little while again but did so dislike to visit the business block.

Fri. Press Club met in the evening. Had a pleasant time. Adjourned early to discuss the suffarage question. Everyone present and there were some gentlemen, expressed themselves as being in favor of its being adobted and put in the constitution. The article giving women the Franchise passed in the convention to day 75 to 13 but it is expected to be brought up again so I am afraid the fight is not over.

Sat afternoon. Attended conference. Bro [Lorenzo] Snow and Bro [James E.] Talmage addressed us.

Sun. I went to conference both meetings. The First Presidency occupied the time.

Tue. Went to mutual [Improvement Association].

Wed 9. Have been arround again with petitions to find out who are willing the suffarage clause should remain in the Constitution. Met with very good success.

Apr 14 Sunday. Jette is 21 to-day. Should like to have remembered him but did not feel able.

15th. Clara's birthday. Made her a call after Reapers Club.

Also attended P[ress] C[lub] called for the purpose of considering wether we should entertain officers of Federation.

Tues. Attended S[uffrage] Ass.

Thur. As usual went to Primary.

[May 1895]

May 1st. Have been very busy housecleaning. With that
exception nothing of importance has happened to me personally although the air seems full of misfortune, excepting the
entertaining of the Federation Officers. We had a very pleasant time but was greatly disappointed on account of Sister
E B. Wells being unable to attend also Dr Ellis Shipp, so we
had to do the best we could. I was chosen to preside.

Sun. May 19th. So many things have happened since I wrote
last. In fact I have been too busy to write. There was the
reception given to the delegates to Constitutional Convention,
at the Templeton [Hotel] which I attended and enjoyed very
much. Then the visit of Susan B. Anthony and the Rev. Anna
Shaw whom we met at the depot last Sunday morning on the
12th.[34] We had breakfast at the Templeton, about 40 of us,
and then had a nice ride arround the city using the Utah and
other carriages then it was *meeting meeting* meeting which I
enjoyed very much and now comes the meeting of the Federation of Clubs in Ogden to which I am the delegate from
the Reapers. We go on the 22nd.

May 27. The meeting of the Federation was a success in
every way. The topics were particularly fine. The one by
Anna K. Hardy and Lizzie Wilcox being very creditable to our
clubs. I was made a director of the Federation. Our Press Club
met Fri. 24th. I was chosen on a debate, "Is the double standard of money the one for America?" I am to take the nega-
tive side.

[June 1895]

Sat June 15. The Press Club was entertained by Mrs J Cam-

381

eron Brown. We had a pleasant time. I wrote for the occasion
Two sides of a question which I read and they seemed to
enjoy.

16th. We visited Aunt Prudie her son Gid being very sick.

18. Went to R. Society in the evening. Attended a surprise
party given in honor of Sister Mary Freeze in 14 Wd. It was
unusualy fine but oh! the dressing down Mr B H Roberts got
from Joseph F Smith I realy felt sorry for him.[35]

Sat 22. Went to both meettings of Primary Conference.

Mon June 24. Started to the summer school at the University
[of Utah]. Am taking Grammar and English Literature. Do
hope I shall make a success of it. Shall have to work very hard
to keep up in Grammar.

28. Went to the Temple to do some sealing with Jette.

[July 1895]

July Sun 14. Nothing of importance has happened excepting
that the Republican women are forming leagues.[36] I have been
made Treasurer of the Ter organization. I do hope they will
not engender bad feelings in their division on party lines. For
my part I care nothing for politics. It is mormonism or nothing
for me.

Wed. I am to recite at Saltair[37] for the R. S. I do hope I shall
do it creditably.

July 21. Well I went on the excursion. Gave one of my own
pieces and I guess I did allright as so many people wanted a
copy.

Sat the 20. I was invited with some other ladies to meet with
the gentlemens Co[unty?] Republican Committee. We had a
very nice meeting. In the evening the ladies Republican
League called a meeting which I attended. This afternoon, Sun,
I went to the Tabernacle.

24 July. Pioneer day. Went with Jet to the Lake. Had a bath.

Fri 26th. I was officially notified that I was one of the ladies chosen on the S[alt] L[ake] Co[unty] R[epublican] Committee.

[August 1895]

Aug 23. Since last writing I have been chosen one of the ladies to act on the reception committee [for] Republican Day at Saltair which meets Mon. 26. Yestreday 22, attended Salt Lake Co. Convention. Was there till 3 oclock in the morning. I nominated Mrs. Wells for the [state] House which was carried. Mrs. Lillie Pardee carried for the Senate.[38] Today Emma Empy and myself went to Farmington to a Rep. Convention.

[September 1895]

Sept 1st. I am so busy that I almost forget my journal. Bro Fox and I went to the Lake Republican day. Had a very pleasant time. Tues. 27 of Aug. eve I went to speak in the sixth Ward on registration. Fri. 30th I went to Brigham City with Sister E B Wells to organize a R[epublican] Womens Club. We returned home with Jet who had been to Preston [Idaho] the following day we had a meeting in the Opera House. Staid with Bro. Rich and had a very pleasant time. Today I have been home all day. There was no one to stay with the children so did not go to meeting. I have been invited to speak at the Re[publican?] Ratification to morrow eve. My speeches as yet are very short, not being accustomed to it.

Sept 12. The Y[oung] Ladies M[utual] held their Annl [unclear] this eve. here.

Sept 15. Since I last wrote I have been to Payson Spanish Fork and to American Fork to attend Republican meetings. I also went to speak in the 13 Ward Tues the 10th but did not do very well. I felt very timid. Frank J. Cannon was at this meeting, so I was too frightened to speak.[39] I forgot to state that I was made chairman of the 2nd precinct ladies republican club. I did not want it but because I was a Mormon they wanted me to take it. We were organized Aug 8th 1895.

Sept 17. Gave report of 2nd Precinct in the Grand Opera House where the Republican ladys held a meeting.

Sept 23. Went to South Cottonwood Ward with Mrs E B Wells to talk Republicanism.

24. Was chosen President of the Young Ladies of the 14 Ward.

27. Went to Sugarhouse to the house of Sister Mary Young to speak on politics.

30. Spoke in the 1st precinct to women of the Rep. Club.

[October 1895]

Oct 8. Held a very successful meeting in the 2nd precinct serving refreshments at the close.

Oct 12. Attended Reapers Club. I happened to give in as a current event, [Orlando W.] Powers play against the Priesthood for the democratic party, but withdrew it as our club is divided in politics and some of the ladies thought we should take no note of it on that account.[40] But I think it quite serious.

Sun 20. Mrs Evans has come to pay me a visit. She is 86 yrs old and nearly blind.

21. Went to South Jordan with Mrs Edna Smith to speak at a political meeting. *[in margin]* Pres Smith came to Depot to meet his wife with his whiskers tied back with a [unclear] handkerchief.

25. Went with Young Ladies to take a party to Aggie and Annie Campbell house as a recognition of there efficient labors in the M[utual] I[mprovement] Ass.

Sat 26. Took part in the ladies Republican parade which was a great success. *[in margin]* Mrs Brown rode alone in a chariot in this parade.

Mon 28. Attended Reapers Club. Again a democratic member had a chance to defend Judge Powers.

Oct Tues 29. Discontinued the meetings of the Womens R[epublican] League.

[added later between entries] At this meeting Bro Roberts posed as a blacksmith being [unclear] with a red kerchief round his neck.

Nov Fri 1st. The republican ladies met at my home today to see what we could do about a lunch for the workers on election day and this evening I have been to the theatre to hear B H Roberts speak on democracy. Some of his remarks I enjoyed. Some I could have wept over.

Day before yestreday Bro George Q Cannon was accused of saying a certain thing in Box Elder in a sermon he preached there which he promptly denied and afterward he was told that he did say it by some of the brethren. Though he could not remember it he accepted their statement and made a public acknowledgment and withdrawal.[41] I feel very sorry for him and I felt sorry for Roberts when he said the Church had meddled in politics and he cared not who the meddler was he should be branded as an enemy to the Church and a traitor to the State.

Sat 2. Went to Young ladies in the morning, officers meeting. In the afternoon went to the Walker Pavillion. Settled the affairs of the precinct Rep. Club and found we did not have to serve lunch as the candidates wives were going to attend to it. In the evening went to East Bountiful to speak at a Republican meeting, but did not make myself know[n]. Mrs Clark who should have been there not being forthcomming I staid all night with Elisabeth Fox and visited Jessie Stringham and Eva Grant returning in the afternoon.

Mon eve 4. Went to Rep. Rally in the theatre.

Tues eve. It is election day. Have been to the Y.L.M.I.A. Do not know as yet how it will turn out but do not care much. Beleive we have got Statehood assured so far as the vote is concerned and that means sufferage for women.

Relief Society and Woman's Day at Saltair, ca. 1896. (Charles R. Savage, photographer. LDS Church Archives.)

Rebecca Elizabeth Howell Mace (1833-1917)

"I want you to take my place by the side of my husband, and [be] a mother to my two children." At the request of his dying wife, Rebecca Elizabeth Howell married Wandle Mace in June 1854. Rebecca's decision was made in haste but not without sufficient thought. Throughout the several volumes of her diary written in the 1890s, Rebecca seems well satisfied with the course her life has taken since her marriage as a young woman on the Plains.

Born December 23, 1833, in Norfolk, England, Rebecca was a daughter of John and Sarah Thompson Howell. She was baptized in 1851, and after immigrating to the United States, she found housekeeping work to defray her expenses to Utah. Wandle and Margaret Merkle Mace were among her employers. After Margaret's death and Rebecca's marriage to Wandle, the family—including two of the children, George and Jane—spent some time at Sandusky, Iowa, where they built a mill, then later moved on to Council Bluffs. They came to Utah in 1858.

In 1861 Wandle was called by Brigham Young to take his family and help settle southern Utah. After remaining "twice five years," the family picked up stakes and moved to Kanab, where they raised cattle and maintained the "finest vineyard and orchard" in the town.

Rebecca conscientiously kept both a diary and a journal. She had a mind for accuracy and detail and left blanks for exact names, ages, years, and such when she was unsure of the facts. In addition to her own records, she wrote the "Autobiography of Wandle Mace," a 252-page document "Written as near as possible as told by himself to the writer." Her diary entries often refer to her progress with this work.

After the death of Wandle Mace in 1889, Rebecca remained in Kanab, happily involved with her stepchildren and neighbors and active in the Church. Always interested in learning about the gospel, she recorded her opinions on discourses she heard. Not always agreeing with the brethren, she sometimes sent them her own interpretations of various subjects.

The original holographs of her records and those of her husband are located in the Historical Department of the LDS Church. Minimal punctuation has been added here for clarification.

Rebecca Mace.
(Mace family collection.)

[1895]

March [1895]. It is a long time since I wrote in any journal since the last time on the 28th Dec that I visited the cemetery. Almost three months have fled. Colds and severe cough visited me at the commencement of the New Year and lasted with me so long that I became very weak, I had refrained from my usual beverage 'Tea' for several weeks had quite overcome, but the weakness of my body was so great I took a cup of Tea to stimulate me above the terrible feeling & it had the desired effect and I have continued in its use until now. It has to be done over again. I must again overcome the habit. We are told it is not good then why cling to an evil habit.

I have visited the grave yard again on Sunday, between the afternoon meeting and Sunday School conference, with Sister Jensen a Sister from Orderville who has spent the winter in Kanab and have been at my house quite frequently. She is very deaf and it is very difficult to talk with her. I advised her to use the New Hygeine treatment and she felt much benefitted.

We had a good Conference. The speakers were mostly Young men, three of those young men were especially interesting. They were Elder Meeks and Elders E & A Cutler. I was very much surprised and edified. These young men were raised in the Kanab Stake, I had not thought that we had such talent in our Stake, but I now believe there are many who if oppertunity offered would be bright and valient for the cause of truth.

On the first of March Friday the R[elief] S[ociety] held conference. President [Artemisia] Segmiller Presiding. One of her counsellors E. Pugh was present. The necessity of providing money for the expenses of our representative Sisters in travelling and otherwise to the conventions of the National R.S. was spoken of and also the requirement of 200 dollars per 3 years to be contributed to the national fund.[42] It was necessary for this Stake to contribute by its R.S.s the larger wards one dollar yearly, the smaller Societies 50 cents to have funds to meet all expences of this kind. The members were severally invited to speak upon the subject myself one of the number. I spent much times at Ada [Rhoda Maria Howell Judd]'s.[43] She is quite weak. The General Stake Conference convened on the 2 & 3rd March 1895.

On the 4th & 5 Horse racing took place just out of town about miles. Or as some expressed it the After Conference.

On the 7th the R S meet in a general monthly meeting. There was a good attendance and a good spirit prevailed. Sister Harriet Brown was called upon and she opened upon the evils of Horse racing, and all the sisters sustained her in her

389

position. The Maoris Sisters spoke and Elder B Hamlin interpreted also addressed the meeting. Endorsed the remarks of
the sisters upon horse racing betting & gamblin in general.

10th Sunday attended meeting after which Jane [Mace Ford] &
I went to George [Mace]'s read a letter from John. He is very
pleasant in his correspondence so far. The moon looks very
peculiar, or like blood, it was a total eclipse.

14 With about 22 or 3 other members of R S provided with
Pic nick, surprised Sister Rider and spent the day with her
sewing her carpet rags.

15th Went to Ada's and ironed for her. Her babe was born
on the   th Feb a girl 5½ lb.

17 Sunday We had an excellent discourse from President
Paxman of the Juab Stake. He spoke of duties as stepping
stones and touched upon every duty in a short concise and
spirited manner. Of the work for the dead he said the time
was near when the Temple would be filled night & day with
workers for the dead so anxious were the dead to be released
from prison, that the names of our dead would be revealed to
us that we may go forward and perform this work.

Spoke upon tithing word of wisdom, Politics horse racing card
playing gambling etc. Spoke of the necessity of the reading
those precious books—holding in his hands the Book of
Mormon & Doctrine and Covenants—by the young men and
women telling them of the great work they will have to perform before very long. He said, "There are young women
before me who with others of the Sisters will go forth to
gather in the destitute females who need succor and bring
them in and take care of them." He said a good deal more
than this, and he said it in the name of the Lord.

After meeting by invitation I attend a gathering of the Judd
family at the house of Eli Judd. They met in the order of a
club for mutual improvement. The father of the family
Z[adok] K[napp] Judd presiding, the youngest daughter
Gertrude acting as secretary.

18th Wrote letters to Sisters Swapp & Trump. I spent an hour very pleasantly with L Cutler & Wife.

19 Helped Ada.

20th This morning Bro J Lewis came to invite me to a birthday dinner at his daughters Ida Young it being the 63rd anniversary of the birth of his Wife Emily J Lewis.

Sister Lewis said "I intended to spend the day with Sister Mace, and I want her here with me." I went and visited with them until sundown. . . .

[January 1896]

1896 Opened auspiciously for Utah and its inhabitants. On the 4th January 1896 President Cleaveland issued a Proclaimation admitting Utah into the Sisterhood of States. As soon as the message was recieved 2 oc. PM Guns were fired, Flag hoisted, Bands played, Shouts of joy arose from the heart and lips of all, with ringing of bells and everything which could be used to sound a note of joy was brought into requisition.

Some of our young men formed themselves into a military company calling themselves the Home Guard, and with the Martial Band—George Mace—leader marched and counter marched, serenading prominent men, also Brother Warren Johnson who had been seriously injured a few weeks before from being thrown off a load of hay, breaking his back. He was delighted with the call declaring it done him much good. And thus the day was made one of general rejoicing, from the moment the telegram arrived, never had all Utah joined in such hilarious rejoicing.

On the 6th—Monday, the officers of the new state—who was elected in the previous election held in November 1895—was inaugerated, the day being set apart as a holiday, to be remembered as such forever. It was enjoyed to the utmost.

Guns were fired a daybreak. 10, oc a procession was formed lead by the Band and the Home Guards—followed by citizens, also a juvenile corps, or Bell Brigade. At two oclock the citizens met in the Social Hall and partook of the PicNic Dinner, then followed speach and song closing the day with a grand Inaugural Ball.

The day was all that could be desired. The weather was pleasant and all enjoyed themselves. There was nothing to mar the occasion, and it will be a day long to be remembered by the inhabitants of Kanab both old and young.

I visited Brother Warren Johnson on this particular morning, when Knapp [Judd] came to take me to his home. Ada his wife and children took me home so I could fill an appointment with Jane for the Pic nic dinner. I do not enjoy these public dinners and picnic's but sometimes I feel obliged to attend them. . . .

[May 1896]

18th. Esther Ford came this morning. I potted the plants I received from Burpee.

Tuesday 19th Sister Dr Harris called this afternoon & her two daughters. She went home about 5 oc, and I went to the cemetery and watered my plants. They have not been watered by irrigation since the 11th.

20 A reception was given Elder Asa W Judd. I went to hear the programe an hour. Jane & husband got home about 11-30 PM. Eddie went to meet them and brought his grandmother home in a buggie They reached here about sundown.

21 I went to see them. They were all well. We had the [irrigation] water. George & his son George G & his Brother in Law trimed the Grape vines before taking the water. There is quite a number of Vines dead.

22 Sister Mantripp came to see me this morning. I was surprised to see her so well after her journey. Jane came too. I took home some plants from Burpee's. I went up to Georges this afternoon.

23 This afternoon I went to see Ada and from there I went to the cemetery and watered my plants.

24 Sunday Attended Meeting after taking dinner with Jane. Mrs Mantripp was taken very sick yesterday, but is some better today. Jane has given up her bedroom to her.

26 Visited the 7th & 8th district alone. We are gathering carpet rags to make a carpet for the St George Temple. It will require 100 yds from the Kanab stake as its proportion. Dr Harris bought out the Lot adjoining me. He has been baptized a member of the church. He came to see me on the 27th and I told him I was pleased to heare it, but I told him he would find many stumbling blocks to overcome, but the actions of men does not change the truth of the Gospel.

Conclusion

Orson F. Whitney in his *History of Utah* wrote, "The history of the Mormon community reads like a tragic poem, and the heart and soul of that poem is in the lives, labors and sacrifices of the heroic women of the community."

As we have looked back at these heroic women, the poem that emerges seems more inspiring that tragic, for our perspective gives us a view of the fruition of hopes and dreams that could only be dimly realized by the women who laid the foundation for their completion. It is through illuminating their lives and labors and sacrifices that we have seen a pattern emerge that sets them apart from other women of their time.

First, we see a pattern of complete dedication to the gospel. This commitment enabled women who joined the Church to endure poverty, ridicule, physical and mental hardships, loneliness, and displacement because they were able to see the experiences of this life in the spectrum of eternal life. Separations by death, mission service, and moves to other areas, while painful, could be coped with because testimonies were strong and friends and family were loving and supportive.

Hands that were busy with quilting and washing and writing and building still found time to reach out to sisters in need. Sharing was an important characteristic of these great women—not just sharing yeast and coals and food, but sharing self through being there when necessary, standing up for principles, and giving service in the Church.

A desire for beauty and the ability to recognize it are other common attributes of these great women. As they spent many hours on the prairies and contact with earthly elements, we feel the appreciation that they had for that which feeds the soul. They could love a sunset, a brook, the sounds at night, a rock formation, the smells around them, and display reverence for these gifts from God. This love of beauty could be carried into their homes as they struggled to reinstitute the comforts they had known in far-away homes. Doilies and curtains covered rough unfinished furniture. Flowers appeared around doorsteps. Lacking material, hair was made into pictures, and scraps of cloth became beautiful and serviceable quilts. The special nesting instinct that women possess is very much in evidence in their accounts of setting up new homes.

Familial love was a strong factor in the lives of these women. An almost overwhelming concern for children and husbands runs throughout their writings. In spite of hasty courtships and an environment of reserved personal relationships, there is a special love evident in their lives. This love and concern was honed through the sharing of so many trying and difficult experiences, which not only drove them to their Heavenly Father but to each other as well. And these Mormon women were different than most of their contemporaries in that they believed they were sealed to their husbands and families for all eternity. This conviction gave them a greater courage and resoluteness in the face of tragedy and an even greater calm than others experienced.

Finally, it becomes evident that they lived full, significant lives that deserve to be remembered. Mormon men could not have left homes to serve missions, colonize, and otherwise build the kingdom of God if it hadn't been for the women they left at home to raise the children, grow the crops, care for houses, and educate the offspring. This fact, while frequently overlooked in written histories of this people, is extremely significant. Participation in the community and in the cause of women everywhere proved them able in areas beyond the domain of kitchen and family as well.

The contributions of Mormon women to the Church, to their children, to the community, and to the world, while not as visible as those of men, were in many ways of even greater import partly because of the difficulties they faced.

Louisa Barnes Pratt, a forward-looking pioneer woman, closed her journal with these words: "Ah: but the Lord rules. . . . Let the faithful women trust in Him He will ere long adjust their cause, and help them to fulfill their destiny." Their destiny is ours, too. Commitment, sharing, a love of beauty, familial love, and lives of meaning must be lived anew in each generation. The challenge of their lives is before us.

396

Notes

Chapter 1

[1]Martha James Cragun Cox Reminiscence, holograph, Library-Archives, Historical Department of The Church of Jesus Christ of Latter-day Saints, Salt Lake City, Utah, hereinafter cited Church Archives.

[2]An excellent comprehensive bibliography of historical studies of Mormon women is Carol Cornwall Madsen and David J. Whittaker, "History's Sequel: A Source Essay on Women in Mormon History," *Journal of Mormon History* 6 (1979): 123-45.

[3]In recent years most of these archives have published guides to their women's holdings, including: Christy Best, comp., *Sources for Studies of Mormon Women in the Church Archives of The Church of Jesus Christ of Latter-day Saints* (Salt Lake City: LDS Church Historical Department, 1976); *Women in Utah, Mormon, and Western History* (Salt Lake City: Marriott Library, University of Utah, 1975); and *Women in History: A Guide to Selected Holdings of the Women's History Archives* (Provo, Utah: Lee Library, Brigham Young University, n.d.). Davis Bitton's *Guide to Mormon Diaries and Autobiographies* (Provo, Utah: Brigham Young University Press, 1977) is the most comprehensive and inclusive guide.

[4]A prominent pioneer in woman's history suggests that studies of women's achievements and contributions are initial stages of women's history, followed by a search for the actual experience of a larger number of women. See Gerda Lerner in "Placing Women in History: Definitions and Challenges," *Feminist Studies* 3 (Fall 1975): 5-14.

[5]*History of Sarah Studevant Leavitt, From Her Journal, 1875* (n.p., Juanita L. Pulsipher, 1919), p. 4. A longer excerpt from this journal is contained in chapter 2 of this book. Quotations in the remainder of this introduction are not footnoted if contained within this book.

⁶Eliza R. Snow, "Evening Thoughts of What It Is to Be a Saint," *Poems, Religious, Historical, and Political* 1 (Liverpool: Latter-day Saints' Book Depot, 1856): 4.

⁷The Doctrine and Covenants of The Church of Jesus Christ of Latter-day Saints contains "revelations given to Joseph Smith, the Prophet With some additions by his Successors in the Presidency of the Church," and is hereinafter cited D&C, followed by section and verse numbers. This quotation comes from D&C 29:8.

⁸Angelina Calkins Farley diary, September 22, 1850, microfilm of holograph, Church Archives.

⁹Mary Jane Mount Tanner reminiscence and diary, microfilm of holograph, p. 102, Church Archives. The original holograph of this volume is in Special Collections, Marriott Library, University of Utah, Salt Lake City. An extensive excerpt from the diary is included in chapter 9.

¹⁰Brigham Young sermon, October 9, 1872, *Journal of Discourses*, 26 vols. (Liverpool: F. D. Richards, 1854-86), 15:223, hereinafter cited *JD*, followed by volume and page numbers.

¹¹Eliza R. Snow address, First Ward Relief Society Minutes, June 7, 1877, *Woman's Exponent*, November 15, 1877.

¹²See Leonard J. Arrington, Feramorz Y. Fox, and Dean L. May, *Building the City of God: Community and Cooperation among the Mormons* (Salt Lake City: Deseret Book, 1976).

¹³Cultural developments in Utah are discussed by Bruce E. Campbell and Eugene E. Campbell in "Early Intellectual and Cultural Development," Richard D. Poll et al., eds., *Utah's History* (Provo: Brigham Young University Press, 1978), which includes a good bibliography. See also Ronald W. Walker and D. Michael Quinn, "Virtuous, Lovely, or of Good Report: How the Church Has Fostered the Arts," *Ensign* 7 (July 1977): 81-93, a discussion of cultural achievements among Mormons.

¹⁴Emmeline B. Wells diary, December 10, 1874. An extensive excerpt from this diary is included in chapter 9. The original diary, more than forty volumes, is in Special Collections, Harold B. Lee Library, Brigham Young University, Provo, Utah.

¹⁵The statement is the fifth of the Church's thirteen "Articles of Faith." See B. H. Roberts, ed., *History of the Church of Jesus Christ of Latter-day Saints*, by Joseph Smith, Jr., 7 vols, 2nd ed. rev. (Salt Lake City: Deseret Book, 1974), 4:541.

¹⁶Lerner, "Placing Women in History," p. 13.

¹⁷B[athsheba] W. Smith to George A. Smith, April 13, 1851, George A. Smith Papers, Family Correspondence, Church Archives.

¹⁸Barbara Welter discussed the idealization of domesticity in "The Cult of True Womanhood, 1820-1860," *American Quarterly* 18 (Summer 1966): 151-74. The article was reprinted in Jean E. Friedman and William G. Shade, eds., *Our American Sisters: Women in American Life and Thought* (Boston: Allyn and Bacon, Inc., 1973), pp. 96-123.

¹⁹Martha Spence Heywood to Emmeline Free Young, December 9, [1855], holograph, Church Archives. This letter is published along with the journal in Juanita Brooks, ed., *Not By Bread Alone: The Journal of Martha Spence Heywood, 1850-56* (Salt Lake City: Utah State Historical Society, 1978).

²⁰Marguerite H. Allen, comp., *Henry Hendricks Genealogy* (Salt Lake City: Hendricks Family Organization, 1963), p. 27. An extended excerpt from Drusilla Dorris Hendricks's reminiscence appears in chapter 4.

²¹Eliza R. Snow address, Weber Stake Relief Society Minutes, June 9, 1882, in *Woman's Exponent*, July 1, 1882.

²²Susa Young Gates, "Editor's Department," *Young Woman's Journal* 5 (June 1894): 449.

²³A study of one absentee husband is Randall Leroy Green, "The Joseph F. Smith Family: Life Without Father," MS on file in Church Archives.

²⁴From the original journal of Louisa Barnes Pratt, in possession of S. George and Maria Hunt Ellsworth, Logan, Utah, p. 108, as quoted in Maureen Ursenbach Beecher, "Under the Sunbonnets: Mormon Women with Faces," *BYU Studies* 16 (Summer 1976): 473.

²⁵Mary Haskin Parker Richards diary, April 5, 1847, microfilm of holograph, Church Archives. An extended excerpt from this diary appears in chapter 6.

²⁶Eliza R. Snow, "Sketch of My Life," p. 13, microfilm of holograph, Church Archives. The original is in the Bancroft Library, University of California at Berkeley.

²⁷Polygamy or plural marriage has been discussed at length by many scholars, one of the most important monographs to date still Kimball Young's *Isn't One Wife Enough?* (New York: Henry Holt, 1954). An impressive study incorporating more recent scholarship is *Religion and Sexuality: Three American Communal Experiments of the Nineteenth Century* (New York and Oxford: Oxford

University Press, 1981). Davis Bitton discusses the multitude of works on the subject in "Mormon Polygamy: A Review Article," *Journal of Mormon History* 4 (1977): 101-18.

²⁸Jane Charters Robinson Hindley journal, December 22, 1862, holograph, Church Archives.

²⁹Patty Sessions diary, September 8, 1847, holograph, Church Archives. A more extensive excerpt from this journal appears in chapter 6.

³⁰Emmeline B. Wells, "Woman Against Woman," *Woman's Exponent*, May 1, 1879.

³¹Gail Farr Casterline, "'In the Toils' or 'Onward for Zion': Images of the Mormon Woman, 1852-1890" (Master's thesis, Utah State University, 1974), p. 100.

³²Diary of Rebecca Mace, 9 vols., holograph, Church Archives, April 8, 1897.

³³An excellent introduction to the period is Maureen Ursenbach Beecher, "A Decade of Mormon Women: The 1870s," *New Era* 8 (April 1978): 34-39. Chapter 9 treats the period in greater depth.

³⁴The forming of networks among American women has been insightfully discussed by Carroll Smith-Rosenberg in "The Female World of Love and Ritual: Relations between Women in Nineteenth Century America," *Signs: Journal of Women in Culture and Society* 1 (Autumn 1975): 1-29. Maureen Ursenbach Beecher presents a similar analysis of relations between Mormon women in "Sisters, Sister Wives, Sisters in the Faith: Support Systems among Nineteenth Century Mormon Women," MS in Church Archives.

³⁵Heywood to Young, December 9, [1855].

³⁶*History of the Church* 4:603.

³⁷Claudia L. Bushman discusses the rise and demise of the exercise of spiritual gifts among Mormon women in "Mystics and Healers," in Claudia L. Bushman, ed., *Mormon Sisters: Women in Early Utah* (Cambridge, Mass.: Emmeline Press Limited, 1946), pp. 1-23. Carol Lynn Pearson, *Daughters of Light* (Provo, Utah: Trilogy Arts, 1973) is a collection of Mormon women's spiritual experiences. The most comprehensive study of women and healing is Linda King Newell, "A Gift Given/A Gift Taken: Washing, Anointing, and Blessing the Sick among Mormon Women," *Sunstone* 6 (September-October 1981): 16-25.

³⁸Leonard J. Arrington explains the evolution of Mormon attitudes toward the Word of Wisdom in "Have the Saints always given as much emphasis to the

Word of Wisdom as they do today?" *Ensign* 7 (April 1977): 32. The standard work on Latter-day Saint adherence to the Word of Wisdom is Paul H. Peterson, "An Historical Analysis of the Word of Wisdom" (Master's thesis, Brigham Young University, 1972).

[39]William Mulder, "Mormonism and Literature," as reprinted in *A Believing People: Literature of the Latter-day Saints*, ed. Richard H. Cracroft and Neal E. Lambert (Provo, Utah: Brigham Young University Press, 1974), p. 135. This article originally appeared in *Western Humanities Review* 9 (Winter 1954-55): 85-89.

Chapter 2

Readers desiring additional information regarding the gathering of a covenant people and early Mormon converts are referred to: Gordon Irving, "Numerical Strength and Geographical Distribution of the LDS Missionary Force, 1830-1974," *Task Papers in LDS History*, on file in Church Archives; William Mulder, *Homeward to Zion: The Mormon Migration from Scandinavia* (Minneapolis: University of Minnesota Press, 1957); Wallace Stegner, *The Gathering of Zion: The Story of the Mormon Trail* (New York: McGraw Hill, 1964; and Laurence Milton Yorgason, "Some Demographic Aspects of One Hundred Early Mormon Converts, 1830-1837" (Master's thesis, Brigham Young University, Provo, Utah, 1974).

[1]Gordon Irving, "Numerical Strength and Geographical Distribution of the LDS Missionary Force, 1830-1974," p. 9.

[2]See Galatians 1:8.

[3]Clarissa Leavitt was born in January 1819.

[4]Juanita Brooks's history of Sarah's son Dudley Leavitt explains that the Leavitt family heard about the Mormons from "a man who had attended a Mormon gathering" and "came into town carrying two books, *A Voice of Warning* and The Book of Mormon, which he loaned to the Leavitt family." Juanita Brooks, *On the Ragged Edge: The Life and Times of Dudley Leavitt* (Salt Lake City: Utah State Historical Society, 1973), p. 3. Since Sarah Leavitt was nearly eighty years old when she dictated her autobiography, she may have recalled some events inaccurately. Brooks's history is drawn from several sources and is likely more accurate.

[5]Juanita Brooks says the company left July 20, 1837. She also describes each

wagon in the train of seven. Brooks, *Dudley Leavitt*, pp. 4-5.

[6]Twelve Mile Grove was near the southern point of Lake Michigan. There was free farm land for settlers there. See Brooks, *Dudley Leavitt*, pp. 3-4.

[7]For a discussion of the name of Weston, Idaho, see Lars Fredrickson, *History of Weston, Idaho*, ed. A. J. Simmonds (Logan, Utah: Utah State University Press, 1972), p. 10.

Chapter 3

Additional background and insight into the Kirtland era of the Church's history can be gained by reading the following: Max H. Parkin, "A Study of the Nature and Causes of External and Internal Conflict of the Mormon in Ohio between 1830 and 1838" (M.A. thesis, Brigham Young University, Provo, Utah, 1966); Robert Kent Fielding, "The Growth of the Mormon Church in Kirtland, Ohio," (Ph.D. dissertation, Indiana University, Bloomington, Ind., 1957); Scott H. Partridge, "The Failure of the Kirtland Safety Society," *BYU Studies* 12 (Summer 1972); and Marvin S. Hill, C. Keith Rooker, and Larry T. Wimmer, *The Kirtland Economy Revisited: A Market Critique of Sectarian Economics* (Provo, Utah: Brigham Young University Press, 1977).

[1]See *History of the Church* 2:410-28.

[2]D&C 57:1-3; *History of the Church* 1:196-99.

[3]*History of the Church* 1:261-65.

[4]Rhoda Young Greene was the third child of Abigail Howe and John Young. Brigham Young was the ninth of eleven children in this family.

[5]The brothers of Joseph Smith, Sr., mentioned here are most likely John Smith, later Patriarch to the Church, and Asael (Asahel) Smith, a member of the high council at Kirtland.

[6]Heber C. Kimball, Orson Hyde, Willard Richards, and Joseph Fielding left Kirtland June 13, 1837, en route to Preston, England, to open missionary work there. They arrived in New York June 22, 1837, and set sail for Liverpool on the *Garrick* eight days later. See *History of the Church* 2:492-95.

[7]James Fielding, brother of Joseph, Mary, and Mercy, never accepted the gospel as preached by the Latter-day Saints. Joseph Fielding Diary, 1837-1840, holograph, Church Archives; *History of the Church* 2:499.

[8]See *History of the Church* 2:484-86; *Autobiography of Parley P. Pratt*, ed. Parley P. Pratt, Jr. (Salt Lake City: Deseret Book, 1973), p. 168.

[9]*Messenger and Advocate* 3 (August 1837): 560; *History of the Church* 2:509-10.

[10]Mary Dort was a niece of Lucy Mack Smith. She and her husband joined the Church and moved to Kirtland as a result of Lucy Smith's missionary labors in Michigan. See Lucy Smith, *Biographical Sketches of Joseph Smith the Prophet* (1853; reprint ed. New York: Arno Press & The New York Times, 1969).

[11]Isabella Russell Walton was one of the first converts baptized by Parley P. Pratt in Canada and undoubtedly knew Mary there. The Sister Snider mentioned may be the wife of John Snyder, another Canadian convert. [Samuel Russell], "Laying the Foundation in Canada," *Church News*, July 31, 1937, p. 1.

[12]*History of the Church* 2:508. The quip about not escaping by a basket is a reference to Paul's escape from angry Jews at Damascus. Acts 9:25.

[13]Information on the journey to Kirtland has been taken from Claire Noall, *Intimate Disciple: A Portrait of Willard Richards* (Salt Lake City: University of Utah Press, 1957), pp. 120-26, 161-68.

[14]Joseph Richards–Rhoda Howe family group sheet, Genealogical Library Archives of The Church of Jesus Christ of Latter-day Saints, Salt Lake City, Utah. Helen R. Gardner, comp., *Levi Richards, 1799-1876: Some of His Ancestors and Descendants* (Logan, Utah: Unique Printing, 1973), pp. 88-90.

[15]In May 1837 Grandison Newell accused Joseph Smith of being an accessory in a plot to assassinate him. He denounced Joseph Smith as "the impious fabricator of gold bibles—the blasphemous forger of revelations with which he swindles ignorant people out of their hard-earned money." Joseph Smith was tried and acquitted, and Newell's anti-Mormon bitterness increased. On January 15, 1838, he pressed charges against the First Presidency for indebtedness. See Parkin, "A Study of the Nature of Causes of External and Internal Conflict of the Mormons in Ohio between 1830 and 1838," pp. 269-77, 322.

[16]See *History of the Church* 2:509, 522.

[17]See Jay M. Todd, *The Saga of the Book of Abraham* (Salt Lake City: Deseret Book, 1969), pp. 202-7.

[18]Taken from Joseph Smith, "To the Saints Scattered Abroad," *Elders' Journal* 1 (November 1837): 28.

[19]Two rebellions for independence erupted in Canada during the winter of 1837-38: one in Lower Canada headed by Louis Joseph Papineau, and the other in Upper Canada headed by reformer William Lyon Mackenzie.

Chapter 4

Readers desiring further study into the Missouri period of the Church's history are referred to: Leland Homer Gentry, "A History of the Latter-day Saints in Northern Missouri from 1836-1839" (Ph.D. dissertation, Brigham Young University, Provo, 1965); Alvin R. Dyer, *The Refiner's Fire: The Significance of Events Transpiring in Missouri* (Salt Lake City: Deseret Book, 1972); and T. Edgar Lyon, "Independence, Missouri, and the Mormons, 1827-1833," *BYU Studies* 13 (Autumn 1972): 10-19.

[1]The revelation designating Independence as Zion is D&C 57:1-4. See also *History of the Church* 1:196-99.

[2]Joseph Smith identified Adam-ondi-Ahman as "the place where Adam shall come to visit his people, or the Ancient of Days shall sit, as spoken of by Daniel the prophet." D&C 116.

[3]See Reed C. Durham's "The Election Day Battle at Gallatin," *BYU Studies* 13 (Autumn 1972): 36-61; Gentry, "Latter-day Saints in Northern Missouri," pp. 174-94.

[4]See *History of the Church* 3:171-73, 175-77; Gentry, "Latter-day Saints in Northern Missouri," pp. 273-87.

[5]Though Samuel Avard, leader of the Danites, claimed that he had the support of the top leaders of the Church, evidence indicates that they were not aware of the group's activities. See Leland H. Gentry, "The Danite Band of 1838," *BYU Studies* 14 (Summer 1974): 421-50.

[6]Colonel Pitcher had command of the militia at Independence, which demanded that the Saints surrender their arms and leave the county. See *History of the Church* 1:433-36.

[7]The health Drusilla describes is promised in D&C 89:18-20, where the Word of Wisdom is recorded. Her reference to the strength of Nephite women is from the Book of Mormon, 1 Nephi 17:2.

[8]David Patten was a member of the Council of the Twelve. Another account indicates that his last words were: "Whatever you do else, O! do not deny the faith." *History of the Church* 3:171.

[9]The actual number was seventeen.

[10]Charles C. Rich had anticipated talking to more sympathetic military leaders, Generals Atchison and Doniphan, but was met instead by Bogart. See Leonard J. Arrington, *Charles C. Rich* (Provo, Utah: Brigham Young University Press, 1974), p. 59.

[11]A reference to Psalm 137. Two verses from Parley P. Pratt's "Zion in Captivity—A Lamentation Written in Prison" have been omitted here.

[12]Charles Augustus Nurse was the husband of Harriott Nurse, a sister of Elizabeth Howe Bullard.

[13]See *History of the Church* 4:19, 21, 24-28, 49; also Paul C. Richards, "Missouri Persecutions: Petitions for Redress," *BYU Studies* 13 (Summer 1973): 520-43.

[14]Nancy Haven Rockwood and Mary Haven Palmer were Elizabeth's older sisters. See *Israel Barlow*, p. 173, notes 27-29.

[15]A reference to D&C 1:35.

[16]From the hymn "Hark! Listen to the Trumpeters," *History of the Church* 2:186; *Hymns* (Salt Lake City: The Church of Jesus Christ of Latter-day Saints, 1968), no. 253.

[17]Since Genesis indicates that Eve was fashioned of the rib taken from Adam (Genesis 2:21-23), a wife was sometimes termed a man's rib in the nineteenth century.

[18]Meaning deacon of Holliston's Congregational Church. John Haven had held that position before he was baptized a Latter-day Saint. *Israel Barlow*, p. 172.

[19]See *History of the Church* 3:269-70.

Chapter 5

While there have been over twoscore books relating to the Nauvoo period of the Church's history, those desiring additional background might profitably read the following: David E. Miller and Della S. Miller, *Nauvoo: The City of Joseph* (Santa Barbara and Salt Lake City: Peregrine Smith, Inc, 1974); Robert Bruce Flanders, *Nauvoo: Kingdom on the Mississippi* (Urbana: University of Illinois Press, 1965); and Kenneth W. Godfrey, "Causes of Mormon Non-Mormon Conflict in Hancock County, Illinois, 1839-1846" (Ph.D. dissertation, Brigham Young University, 1967).

[1]David E. Miller and Della S. Miller comment on the renaming of the city in *Nauvoo: The City of Joseph*, p. 35.

[2]A survey of sources of tension in Nauvoo is Godfrey, "Causes of Mormon

Non-Mormon Conflict in Hancock County, Illinois, 1839-1846." Mormon political activities are analyzed by Klaus J. Hansen in *Quest for Empire: The Political Kingdom of God and the Council of Fifty in Mormon History* (Lansing: Michigan State University Press, 1967).

[3]Dallin H. Oaks, "The Suppression of the Nauvoo Expositor," *Utah Law Review* 9 (Winter 1965): 862-903.

[4]George A. Smith was a son of Clarissa Lyman (1790-1854) and John Smith (1781-1854). See Zora Smith Jarvis, comp., *Ancestry, Biography and Family of George A. Smith* (Provo, Utah: Zora Smith Jarvis, 1962).

[5]Melissa Jane Bigler was Bathsheba's younger sister and apparently lived with her during the absence of George A. Smith. Information regarding family relationships has been drawn from family group sheets in the Church Genealogical Archives.

[6]Mary Ann Bogges Bigler, wife of Bathsheba's brother Jacob G. Bigler, died with the ague about three weeks after this letter was written. Jacob G. Bigler autobiography, holograph, Church Archives. Thadeas [Thaddeus] was a son of Nancy Bigler Fleming, Bathsheba's older sister, and Josiah Walcott Fleming.

[7]Caroline Smith (later Callister) was a sister of George A. Smith.

[8]Dr. John M. Bernhisel, educated in medicine at the University of Pennsylvania at Philadelphia, was ordained a Latter-day Saint bishop in New York City while practicing medicine there in 1841. He moved to Nauvoo in the spring of 1843 and figured prominently in church and local government there and in Utah. For a full biographical sketch see Gwynn W. Barrett, "Dr. John M. Bernhisel: Mormon Elder in Congress," *Utah Historical Quarterly* 36 (Spring 1968): 143-67.

[9]This lawsuit perhaps involved Bigler properties in West Virginia. Jacob Bigler recorded, "In March 1843 I returned to *Va* on business." His father, Mark Bigler, had died in September 1839, and settlement of the estate had required some time. Jacob Bigler autobiography.

[10]Amasa Lyman (1813-1877) had accompanied George A. Smith on a mission through Illinois in 1842.

[11]John Lyman Smith was the younger brother of George A. Smith.

[12]Probably Josiah Walcott Fleming, Bathsheba's brother-in-law.

[13]Caleb Washington was the husband of Bathsheba's older sister, Sarah Bigler.

[14]The "Lawites," who broke with the Church in spring 1844, included William and Wilson Law, Austin Cowles, James Blakeslee, Robert D. Foster,

Chauncey Higbee, and Charles Ivins, all of whom had been prominent in church government or business in Nauvoo. Flanders, *Nauvoo: Kingdom on the Mississippi*, p. 308.

[15]Jedediah M. Grant (1816-1856), at this time a member of the First Quorum of the Seventy, was returning to Philadelphia to resume his calling to preside over the Church there. He was, at the same time, to inform the brethren in the East of the martyrdom, though the news traveled so fast he was able to forgo that assignment.

[16]Sarah Bigler Washington was one of Bathsheba's older sisters.

[17]See Flanders, *Nauvoo: Kingdom on the Mississippi*, pp. 144-45.

[18]Charles Thompson, from Elba, New York, a neighboring town to Warsaw, was apparently a Mormon the Randalls had known there. Later in this same letter Sally mentions "them people from Alexander," another town near Warsaw.

[19]Sally's father was George Carlisle, but the George referred to here is likely her brother, since later letters from her son Eli are addressed to "Uncle George."

[20]See D&C 124:29-30; D&C 128; also *History of the Church* 4:446-47.

[21]A revelation to the Latter-day Saints given through Joseph Smith instructed them that "their children shall be baptized for the remission of their sins when eight years old." D&C 68:27.

[22]The "state's arms" referred to here are those of the Nauvoo Legion. Governor Ford demanded their surrender because they had been illegally used in destroying the *Expositor* press and in resisting authorized officers seeking to arrest Joseph Smith. Flanders, *Nauvoo: Kingdom on the Mississippi*, p. 309.

[23]Because the Book of Mormon designated native Americans (there termed Lamanites) as descendants of the House of Israel who would aid in the establishment of Christ's kingdom upon the earth, Latter-day Saints were eager to do missionary work among them, though Sally's reference here to "ten hundred thousand of the Lamanites" is so far an exaggeration as to be fiction. Such statements by zealous Saints prompted non-Mormons in Missouri, Illinois, and Utah to accuse Saints of joining with native Americans in rebellion against the U.S. government.

[24]See Don F. Colvin, "A Historical Study of the Mormon Temple at Nauvoo, Illinois" (Master's thesis, Brigham Young University, Provo, 1962), pp. 115-31.

[25]From fall 1845 through summer 1847, Church agents conferred with lead-

ing Catholic priests regarding the sale of the temple. The sale, due to legal entanglements, failed, and before the end of 1848 the temple interior was destroyed by fire. French Icarians started to rebuild the gutted structure in 1849, but the remains were destroyed by a tornado in 1850. Colvin, "The Mormon Temple at Nauvoo, Illinois," pp. 161-86.

[26]The "false prophet" referred to is James J. Strang, who, following the martyrdom of Joseph Smith, produced a letter purportedly written by the Prophet designating Strang his successor and Voree, Wisconsin, as a new gathering place for the Saints. See Doyle C. Fitzpatrick, *The King Strang Story: A Vindication of James J. Strang, the Beaver Island Mormon King* (Lansing, Mich.: National Heritage, 1970).

Chapter 6

Books providing additional information regarding the history of the Church immediately following the exodus from Nauvoo include: Roberts, ed., *History of the Church*, vol. 7, *Apostolic Interregnum*; James B. Allen and Glen Leonard, *Story of the Latter-day Saints* (Salt Lake City: Deseret Book, 1976), chapters 7 and 8; and Leonard J. Arrington and Davis Bitton, *The Mormon Experience* (New York: Alfred A. Knopf, 1979), chapter 5.

[1]From mid-September 1846 to May 1848 the sexton reported some 359 deaths at Winter Quarters and nearby Cutler's Park. Allen and Leonard, *Story of the Latter-day Saints*, p. 236.

[2]The trail journal of Eliza R. Snow was first published in *Improvement Era* 46 (1943) and 47 (1944). Later *The Pioneer* 5 (1953) and 6 (1954) carried the journal, and *Our Pioneer Heritage* 17 (1974) published excerpts. Nicholas G. Morgan, in compiling *Eliza R. Snow: An Immortal* (Salt Lake City: Nicholas G. Morgan Foundation, 1945), included a large portion of the journal. Maureen Ursenbach Beecher is in the process of editing the journal in its entirety with a biographical introduction and notes.

[3]See Eliza R. Snow, "Sketch of My Life," a holograph autobiography prepared for Hubert Howe Bancroft in the 1880s, now in the Bancroft Library, University of California, Berkeley, California, microfilm of holograph, Church Archives. In the sketch she discusses her marriage to Joseph Smith, pp. 13-14. See also Maureen Ursenbach Beecher, "Leonora, Eliza, and Lorenzo: An Affectionate Portrait of the Snow Family," *Ensign* 10 (June 1980):67.

[4]Sarah Melissa Granger Kimball (1818-1898) and her widowed mother, Lydia Dibble Granger (1790-1857?), were close friends of Eliza Snow in Nauvoo

and in Salt Lake City, where Sarah served as secretary to Eliza in the Relief Society.

[5]Lorenzo Snow (1814-1901) was the first of Eliza's three younger brothers; he and a sister, Leonora, were the only members of the family to accompany Eliza in the Saints' westward trek.

[6]Louisa Beaman and Clarissa (Clara) Decker were wives of Brigham Young. Sarah Lawrence had been a plural wife of Joseph Smith, and after his death, she had married Heber C. Kimball.

[7]This poem has been published. *Millennial Star* 10 (May 15, 1848): 160; also Eliza R. Snow, *Poems, Religious, Historical and Political* (Liverpool: Latter-day Saints' Book Depot, 1856; Salt Lake City: Latter-day Saints' Printing and Publishing Establishment, 1856), 1:161-62.

[8]See Manuscript History of the Church, Brigham Young Period, 1844-1877, March 1, 1846, manuscript, Church Archives. This forty-seven volume work was compiled by clerks and historians under the direction of Brigham Young and others.

[9]Poem published in *Millennial Star* 10 (July 1, 1848): 208; Snow, *Poems* 1:163-64.

[10]Elizabeth Ann Smith Whitney (1800-1882), wife of Presiding Bishop Newel K. Whitney (1795-1850) and Eliza Snow had been well acquainted as "Campbellites" or Disciples of Christ, before joining the Latter-day Saints.

[11]Sarah Ann Whitney Kimball (1825-1873) was a daughter of Newel K. and Elizabeth Ann Smith Whitney.

[12]Amasa Lyman (1813-1877) was a member of the Council of the Twelve from 1842 to 1867 and frequently met with Church leaders and counseled the Saints during the westward trek.

[13]John E. Page and William Smith, the last surviving brother of Joseph Smith, were members of the Council of the Twelve who were dropped from the quorum and excommunicated from the Church for dissenting from the leadership of Brigham Young and the Twelve. James J. Strang, a Church member who claimed to be the appointed successor of Joseph Smith, gathered a number of followers and established a church, and Page and William Smith both followed him for a time. William Smith had earlier made his own claims to church leadership. See Allen and Leonard, *Story of the Latter-day Saints*, pp. 240-41. Orson Hyde, another member of the Council of the Twelve, had remained in Nauvoo to help direct Church affairs there. Luke Johnson, a former apostle who had been excommunicated in 1838, came to Elder Hyde in Nauvoo in February 1846 and requested rebaptism. Manuscript History of the Church, 1844-1977, March 12, 1846.

[14]Poem published in *Millennial Star* 10 (June 1, 1848): 176; Snow, *Poems*, 1:146.

[15]Mary gives a brief sketch of her life in England and her departure for Nauvoo in "The Memorandum of Mary H. Parker," photocopy of holograph, Church Archives.

[16]Henry Phineas Richards was the brother of Mary's husband, Samuel.

[17]The Richards family had formerly resided in Richmond, Massachusetts. Maria Richards Wilcox was the sister of Mary's husband, Samuel, and wife of Walter Eli Wilcox.

[18]Mary met Ellen Wilding in Preston, England, in 1838 or 1839, and apparently the two young English women formed a friendship that endured for several years. Ellen became a plural wife of Edwin D. Woolley in Nauvoo in 1843. See Leonard J. Arrington, *From Quaker to Latter-day Saint: Bishop Edwin D. Woolley* (Salt Lake City: Deseret Book, 1976), pp. 114, 489.

[19]This meeting of the Twelve and the Indians is recorded in the Manuscript History of the Church, 1844-1877, December 12, 1846.

[20]Stephen H. Goddard (1810-1898) was one of three trustees of the concert hall in Nauvoo, where he apparently directed a singing school or choir. He opened a singing school in Salt Lake City in 1848 and directed the choir that sang in the city's Old Tabernacle. Journal History, January 24, 1845; Andrew Jenson, *Latter-day Saint Biographical Encyclopedia: A Compilation of Biographical Sketches of Prominent Men and Women in the Church*, 4 vols. (Salt Lake City: Andrew Jenson History Co., 1901-1936), 4:704-5.

[21]The record of this meeting as contained in the Manuscript History of the Church, 1844-1877, December 20, 1846, corroborates Mary's account, showing her to be a careful listener and reporter.

[22]Henry and Mary Moyer Grow and family lived near the Parkers in Nauvoo. Files of Nauvoo Restoration Incorporated, Salt Lake City, Utah.

[23]In the fall of 1846 Church leaders considered sending three hundred men to the headwaters of the Yellowstone River for the purpose of opening farms there, but plans for settlement still centered on the valley of the Great Salt Lake or the Bear River Valley. See Allen and Leonard, *Story of the Latter-day Saints*, p. 237.

[24]Biographical information pertaining to Patty Sessions and her family is contained in *The Diaries of Perrigrine Sessions*, comp. Earl T. Sessions (Bountiful, Utah: Carr Printing Co., 1967). Claire Noall, *Guardians of the Hearth: Utah's Pioneer Midwives and Women Doctors* (Bountiful, Utah: Horizon Publishers, 1974), pp. 22-51, includes a biographical essay on Patty Sessions. Information

regarding the deaths of her children is from the family group sheet of David and Patty Sessions, Church Genealogical Archives.

[25]See Chapter 1, note 38, for reference on the use of brandy in light of the Saints' commitment to the Word of Wisdom.

[26]The diary of Patty Sessions makes frequent reference to the gathering of women with or without men to exercise spiritual gifts, such as speaking in tongues, healing the sick, or calling down blessings through prayer. This practice among Mormon women is discussed more fully in chapter 1.

[27]Old folks were commonly referred to as Silver Greys, as were older members of the Nauvoo Legion, the Mormon militia that had functioned in Nauvoo.

[28]Poem published in *Woman's Exponent* 14 (June 1, 1885): 2.

[29]An account of the dream is recorded in the Manuscript History of the Church, 1844-1877, February 23, 1847.

[30]Poem published in *Woman's Exponent* 14 (November 1, 1885): 86.

Chapter 7

Studies of the emigration of Mormon converts include P.A.M. Taylor, *Expectations Westward: The Mormons and the Emigration of Their British Converts in the Nineteenth Century* (Edinburgh and London: Oliver & Boyd, 1965), and William Mulder, *Homeward to Zion: The Mormon Migration from Scandinavia* (Minneapolis: University of Minnesota Press, 1957).

[1]See Isaiah 2:2; 11:12; Matthew 28:19.

[2]"Why Do the Saints Gather?," *Millennial Star* 24 (August 9, 1862): 509.

[3]See *Millennial Star* 17 (December 22, 1855): 813, and LeRoy R. Hafen and Ann W. Hafen, *Handcarts to Zion: The Story of a Unique Western Migration, 1856-1860* (Glendale, Calif.: Arthur H. Clark Company, 1960), pp. 29-30.

[4]A sixteen-month-old daughter, Jean Rio, died ten days after her father. This sketchy information was gleaned from the Henry Baker—Jean Rio Griffiths family group sheet, Church Genealogical Archives.

[5]The British Passenger Act of 1849 provided that "the stores, which were to be inspected before the ship sailed, were to include enough water to give each person three quarts a day; and enough bread, flour, oatmeal (or rice or potatoes), molasses, sugar, and tea for ten weeks." Taylor, *Expectations Westward*,

p. 180. An 1855 act varied the ration-scale and described it in detail, including 1½ pounds of oatmeal per passenger per week, with various substitutes permissible. Ibid., p. 182.

⁶Eliza Ann Elliott Baker was the wife of Jean Rio's son Henry Walter. The two had been married on January 5, 1851, just four days before the *George W. Bourne* was cleared to sail. Henry Baker–Jean Rio Griffiths family group sheet.

⁷Though the English generally used the word *chronicles* in reference to histories of their own English kings, here the term probably refers to George Frederick Handel's *Messiah*, an oratorio that chronicles the redemption of the world through Jesus Christ, hailing him as "the mighty God" and "the Lord strong and mighty." See Isaiah 9:6; Psalm 24:8.

⁸Josiah Elliott Baker (1846-1851) was the only passenger to die during the voyage. Elder William Gibson said the boy "was far gone in consumption before we sailed." *Millennial Star* 13 (May 1, 1851): 137. Two of Jean Rio's children and her husband had preceded Josiah in death.

⁹Probably Great or Little Abaco Island in the Bahama Islands.

¹⁰The Belize Jean Rio refers to is probably Balize or Balise, taken from the French word for sea-mark or buoy. Another traveler along the route from Liverpool to the Salt Lake Valley noted: "We entered the [Mississippi] river by the south-west channel, and passed the Balize or Pilot Station on the east, about three miles from the bar." Frederick Piercy, *Route from Liverpool to Great Salt Lake Valley*, ed. James Linforth (Liverpool: Franklin D. Richards, 1855), p. 29.

¹¹By 1854 each Perpetual Emigrating Fund wagon supplied ten people. Taylor, *Expectations Westward*, p. 230. The fact that the Bakers purchased four wagons for eleven people is an indication that they were well off enough to bring substantial personal baggage with them.

¹²In her reminiscence Patience describes her early life in considerable detail. Information was also drawn from the family group sheet of James Loader–Amy Britnell, Church Genealogical Archives.

¹³Patience married John Rozsa in 1858 or 1859. They lived in Utah until John's army obligations took them east during the Civil War. En route back to Utah in 1866, John died, leaving Patience with three sons and a daughter born a few months after John's death. Patience was later married to John Bond Archer.

¹⁴See John Jacques, "Edward Martin's Handcart Company: Some Reminiscences," *Salt Lake Herald*, December 8, 1878.

¹⁵See Hafen and Hafen, *Handcarts to Zion*, pp. 114-15, 134.

[16]George D. Grant was captain of the relief company encamped at Devil's Gate. See *Deseret News*, November 19, 1856, as quoted in Hafen and Hafen, *Handcarts to Zion*, p. 117.

[17]After having borne thirteen children in England, Amy Britnell Loader made the trek across the Plains by handcart. She lived nearly thirty years after her arrival in Utah, dying at age eighty-three. Family group sheet of James Loader—Amy Britnell family group sheet.

[18]Grant's report to President Young indicated that when the rescuers found the Martin Company, they were "in a deplorable condition, they having lost fifty-six of their number since crossing the North Platte, nine days before." As quoted in Hafen and Hafen, *Handcarts to Zion*, p. 114. The loss of life in the Martin Company totaled between 135 and 150. Ibid., p. 140.

[19]Twenty-five-year-old Zilpha Loader Jacques and her husband, John, were also members of the Martin Company. Their two-year-old daughter Flora died November 23, 1856.

[20]John Dalling and Patience's sister, Ann Loader, had been married in Salt Lake City the previous November. Family group sheet of John Dalling–Ann Loader, Church Genealogical Archives.

Chapter 8

Excellent studies of the early years in the Great Basin include: Leonard J. Arrington, *Great Basin Kingdom* (Harvard University Press, 1958); Leonard J. Arrington, Feramorz Y. Fox, and Dean L. May, *Building the City of God: Community and Cooperation among the Mormons* (Salt Lake City: Deseret Book, 1976); and Joel Edward Ricks, *Forms and Methods of Early Mormon Settlement in Utah and the Surrounding Region, 1847-1877* (Logan, Utah: Utah State University Press Monograph Series, vol. 2, 1964).

[1]Using Carroll Smith-Rosenberg's "The Female World of Love and Ritual: Relations between Women in Nineteenth-Century America," *Signs: Journal of Women in Culture and Society* 1 (Autumn 1975): 1-29, as a point of departure, Maureen Ursenbach Beecher has shown that Mormon women, too, formed networks for support, plural marriage being a distinctively Mormon one. "Sisters, Sister Wives and Sisters in the Faith: Support Systems among Nineteenth Century Mormon Women," manuscript, Church Archives.

[2]A family history recounting the life of Amasa Mason Lyman is Albert R. Lyman, *Amasa Mason Lyman: Trailblazer and Pioneer from the Atlantic to the Pacific* (Delta, Utah: Melvin A. Lyman, 1957). In 1851 Elder Lyman took some of his

family with him to San Bernardino, where he and Charles C. Rich, another member of the Twelve, had been called to preside over a settlement of Saints. Eliza stayed in Utah.

[3]Eliza's mother, Lydia Clisbee Partridge Huntington, joined her daughters after the death of her second husband, William Huntington. Lydia's first husband, Edward Partridge, had died in 1840. Two of Eliza's three sisters, Caroline Ely and Lydia, also became plural wives of Amasa Lyman—Caroline in 1844 and Lydia in 1853. Eliza's only brother, Edward, was the youngest of the Partridge children and was fifteen years old at the time of Eliza's writing in 1848. Elder Lyman had other plural families, so he planned to stay with Eliza and Caroline only part of the time. Louisa Marie Tanner Lyman was his first wife, and it was her child who was to stay with Eliza for schooling. Family group sheets of Edward Partridge and Amasa Mason Lyman, Church Genealogical Archives.

[4]The winter of 1848-49 was a severe one. Frequent snows made difficult the care and feeding of cattle as well as the gathering of fuel. Temperatures were unusually cold, and there had been a poor harvest the preceding fall, leaving Saints constantly cold and hungry. See Arrington, *Great Basin Kingdom*, pp. 58-61.

[5]In November 1848 Brigham Young called Amasa Lyman to go to California, hoping eventually to set up a Mormon outpost near Los Angeles to receive and outfit immigrants who would come by ship from Europe to California and then overland to Utah. See Allen and Leonard, *Story of the Latter-day Saints*, p. 266.

[6]Paulina Eliza Phelps Lyman had been a wife of Amasa Lyman since 1846. Apparently she was living in the Old Fort at this time, and so she would have been in close touch with Eliza and her household. Lyman, *Amasa M. Lyman*, p. 302. Louise Maria and her four children were living at Cottonwood, in the southeast area of the Salt Lake Valley.

[7]Eliza had been acquainted with the Hakes family since 1846 when she and Dionitia, a sister-wife, had made the journey from Nauvoo to Winter Quarters in company with Sarah Hakes Clark and her husband, Daniel Porter Clark. Autobiography and journal of Eliza Marie Partridge Lyman, November 9, 1846; Lloyd Clark Ward, "Highlights of the Life of Daniel Porter Clark," typescript, Church Archives.

[8]David Frederick (1809-1886) was one of the members of the Mormon Battalion who returned to the Great Salt Lake Valley after having completed the journey to San Diego, California, in the summer of 1847. See Leonard and Allen, *Story of the Latter-day Saints*, p. 232. Frederick was apparently single at

the time, and it seems that he worked closely with the Lymans while Amasa was away, exchanging labor for board and clothing.

⁹Until 1896 Saints held a special fast day and meeting on the first Thursday of each month. In 1896, as this practice began to interfere with the employment of Saints, the First Presidency instructed members to observe their monthly fast on the first Sunday of each month. Allen and Leonard, *Story of the Latter-day Saints*, p. 425.

¹⁰Cornelia Eliza Leavitt Lyman had been a plural wife of Amasa Lyman since 1846. Family group sheet of Amasa Lyman.

¹¹See note 4 above.

¹²Eliza Partridge Lyman, Emily Dow Partridge Young, Louisa Beaman Young, Sarah Ann Whitney Kimball, and Lucy Walker Kimball all had earlier been sealed to Joseph Smith as plural wives while he was alive. The wives apparently met together frequently, as indicated in Eliza Lyman's diary and the trail journal of Eliza R. Snow, a portion of which is contained in chapter 6.

¹³These two women were sisters-in-law. Helen Mar Clark Callister was a sister of Daniel Porter Clark. The Callisters had joined the Clarks and Eliza and Dionitia Lyman in their journey from Nauvoo to Winter Quarters. Ward, "Daniel Porter Clark."

¹⁴Walker or Walkara, a Ute Indian chief, with twelve of his tribe counseled with Brigham Young and several members of the Council of the Twelve. Chief Walker invited the Mormons to settle in Ute country, and soon over two hundred settlers left for the Sanpete Valley. Manuscript History of the Church, 1844-1877, June 14, 1849; Allen and Leonard, *Story of the Latter-day Saints*, p. 249.

¹⁵The practice of the Word of Wisdom by Latter-day Saints in the nineteenth century is discussed in chapter 1.

¹⁶One of the earliest public works projects was the building of a public bathhouse at the hot springs located in the north part of the Salt Lake Valley, named Warm Springs and later Wasatch Springs. Arrington, *Great Basin Kingdom*, pp. 54, 111.

¹⁷Oscar Lyman was a son of Pauline and Amasa Lyman. Lyman, *Amasa Mason Lyman*, p. 182.

¹⁸A seventh wife, Nancy Clements Smith (1815-1847), died at Winter Quarters. Short biographies of her and the other wives are contained in the family history compiled by Zora Smith Jarvis, *Ancestry, Biography and Family of George A. Smith* (Provo, Utah: Zora Smith Jarvis, 1962).

[19]John Smith (1781-1854) and Clarissa Lyman Smith (1790-1854) were the parents of George A. Smith. John Smith arrived in the valley in 1847 and presided over Saints in the area until October 1848. He was ordained presiding patriarch to the Church in January 1849. Jenson, *Latter-day Saints Biographical Encyclopedia* 1:182-83. Further biographical information on both John and Clarissa is contained in Jarvis, *George A. Smith Family*, pp. 11-32.

[20]Mary Aikens Smith was the wife of Silas Smith, brother of John in note 19 above. She went to Parowan in 1851 and died there in 1877. *Journal of Jesse Nathaniel Smith: The Life Story of a Mormon Pioneer, 1834-1906* (Salt Lake City: Jesse N. Smith Family Association, 1953), p. 1.

[21]Caroline Smith Callister (1820-1895) was a sister of George A. Smith. She married Thomas Callister in 1845. A brief sketch of her life is contained in Jarvis, *George A. Smith Family*, pp. 40-42.

[22]In July 1850 George A. Smith was called to take a company south to Parowan, Utah, to build up a settlement that would serve as a half-way station between the Salt Lake Valley and southern California and also provide agricultural products for the iron mission to be established nearby at Cedar City. The company, consisting of 167 persons, left Salt Lake City for Parowan in December 1850. George A. Smith kept an official journal of the "Iron Mission," running from December 1850 to October 1851, manuscript, Church Archives.

[23]Charles Warren Smith (1849-1903) was a son of Hannah and George A. Smith. John Henry Smith (1848-1911), a son of Sarah and George A., went to live with his mother's sister Hannah after the death of his mother. Family group sheets of George A. Smith, Church Archives.

[24]Lucy is misquoting Shakespeare here. "Ay, there's the rub," is a line from Hamlet's famous "To be or not to be" soliloquy, *Hamlet*, act 3, sc. 1.

[25]The "seminary," a two-story adobe structure to which Lucy refers, was originally built as a residence for George A. Smith and his wives.

[26]A territorial convention convened in Salt Lake City March 17, 1856, for the purpose of preparing a state constitution and memorializing Congress for the admission of Utah into the Union. George A. Smith and John Taylor traveled to Washington, D.C., to present the constitution and the memorial to Congress. Both were ignored. Orson F. Whitney, *History of Utah*, 4 vols. (Salt Lake City: George Q. Cannon & Sons Co., Publishers, 1892-1904), 1:545-46.

[27]John Henry Smith was ordained an apostle October 27, 1880, and was called to preside over the European Mission in 1882. He was sustained as second counselor in the First Presidency in 1910. "Some of the Activities of John Henry Smith," *Improvement Era* 15 (November 1911): 59-60, 77, 83.

[28]The reformation that took place among Saints in 1856-57 was "an effort to persuade the Saints to renew their dedication to righteous living." See Allen and Leonard, *Story of the Latter-day Saints*, p. 279.

[29]The Willie and Martin Handcart Companies were caught in early snows in Wyoming. An account of their difficulties is contained in Patience Loader's reminiscence included in chapter 7, "Some Little Description of My Travels."

[30]As the Utah expedition approached, Mormon militia were sent to Echo Canyon, east of Salt Lake City, to keep the troops from entering the valley. See Allen and Leonard, *Story of the Latter-day Saints*, p. 306.

[31]Henrietta James and Elizabeth Ann Stout were the plural wives with whom Martha spent so much of her time. A fourth wife, Mary Jane Millet, was sealed to Isaiah Cox in 1888. By that time the family had been pretty well scattered by the anti-polygamy "raids."

[32]James Hardwick McCarty was the husband of Martha's sister Lydia. As a young girl Martha spent time with James and Lydia and grew close to them. She refers to James as both brother and uncle, since he was an uncle of her father. Family group sheet of James Cragun, Church Genealogical Archives; Martha Cragun Cox reminiscence.

[33]Dennis Lancaster deals with the drinking of wine in St. George and other settlements in southern Utah in "Dixie Wine," *Sunstone* 1 (Summer 1976): 75-84.

Chapter 9

The last decade has seen a spectacular rise in the number of books and articles regarding Mormon women. Readers who desire further study into this aspect of Mormon history are referred to the following: Jill C. Mulvay (Derr), "Eliza R. Snow and the Woman Question," *BYU Studies* 16 (Winter 1976); Gail Farr Casterline, "The Toils or 'Onward for Zion': Images of the Mormon Woman, 1852-1890" (Masters of Arts thesis, Utah State University, 1974); Maureen Ursenbach Beecher, "A Decade of Mormon Women: The 1870's," *New Era* 8 (April 1978): 34-39; and Sherilyn Cox Bennion, "The Woman's Exponent: Forty-two Years of Speaking for Women," *Utah Historical Quarterly* 44 (Summer 1976): 222-39. For a more complete history, see Madsen and Whittaker, "History's Sequel."

[1]Brigham Young sermon, July 18, 1869, *JD* 13:61.

[2]Eliza R. Snow, "Female Relief Society," *Deseret News*, April 22, 1868.

³Eliza R. Snow address, First Ward Relief Society Minutes, June 7, 1877, *Woman's Exponent*, November 15, 1877.

⁴Eliza R. Snow address, "Great Indignation Meeting," *Deseret News Weekly*, January 19, 1870.

⁵General Epistle, January-February 1868, p. 26, Brigham Young Circular Letters, Church Archives.

⁶A recent biographical treatment is Patricia Rasmussen Eaton-Gadsby and Judith Rasmussen Dushku, "Emmeline B. Wells," in Vicky Burgess-Olson, ed., *Sister Saints* (Provo: Brigham Young University Press, 1978), pp. 457-75.

⁷Bryant S. Hinckley, *Daniel Hanmer Wells and Events of His Time* (Salt Lake City: Deseret News Printing, 1942) contains a chapter by Annie Wells Cannon that provides insight into the "Home and Family Life" of the Wells family, pp. 337-62.

The wives of Daniel Hanmer Wells included Eliza Rebecca Robison, Louisa Free, Martha Givens Harris, Lydia Ann Alley, Susan Hannah Alley, and Hannah Corill Free, and all of them had children.

Newel Kimball Whitney took Emmeline as a second wife, Elizabeth Ann Smith being his first wife. See note 9. A third wife, Anne Houston, was added to the family in 1846.

⁸A handwritten note by one of Emmeline's daughters at the end of this diary reads: "This Mr Hendry so often referred to was very much in love with my sister Emmie. An extremely nice man, educated wealthy good family but not a member of the Church. Mother idolized Emmie and desired her happiness but belief caused difficulties."

⁹Elizabeth Ann Smith Whitney (1800-1882) was the first wife of Newel Kimball Whitney (1795-1850). Emmeline, his second wife, was married to Elder Whitney in 1845. These sister-wives were very close, much like mother and daughter. The relationship is discussed by Eaton-Gadsby and Dushku in "Emmeline B. Wells," Burgess-Olson, ed., *Sister Saints*, pp. 463-64.

¹⁰Mary and Ida Cook were recognized and esteemed teachers, sisters who had graduated from New York State normal schools and arrived together in Utah in 1870. They were baptized members of The Church of Jesus Christ of Latter-day Saints early in 1871, and both the *Deseret News* and the *Woman's Exponent* followed their varied and productive teaching careers with interest. A biographical treatment of the two sisters is Jill Mulvay (Derr), "The Two Miss Cooks: Pioneer Professionals for Utah Schools," *Utah Historical Quarterly* 43 (Fall 1975): 396-409; also reprinted in Burgess-Olson, ed., *Sister Saints*, pp. 242-57. Emmeline seems to have taken a liking to Mary and Ida as well as their sister Cornelia.

¹¹Millie (Melvina) had married William Dunford October 11, 1867, a marriage that apparently ended in divorce.

¹²George Q. Cannon (1827-1901) was Utah's territorial delegate to Congress from 1873 to 1882. He had been ordained an apostle in 1860 and was at this time assistant counselor to Brigham Young in the First Presidency. (Daniel H. Wells was also a member of the First Presidency at this time.)

¹³Five days after Judge McKean sentenced Brigham Young to one day's imprisonment and a fine of $25, a press dispatch from Washington, D.C., announced the removal of the chief justice from office "caused by what the president deems fanatical and extreme conduct." B. H. Roberts, *A Comprehensive History of The Church of Jesus Christ of Latter-day Saints, Century I*, 6 vols. (Salt Lake City: The Church of Jesus Christ of Latter-day Saints, 1930), 5:446-47.

¹⁴Emmeline's daughter Annie Wells Cannon indicated that the Wasatch Literary Association was organized in 1872 in Emmeline's home. See Hinckley, *Daniel Hanmer Wells*, pp. 356-57.

¹⁵Church leaders hoped to use George Reynolds (1842-1909), private secretary to Brigham Young, as a test case in trying the constitutionality of anti-polygamy laws. He was arrested in October 1874, tried, and found guilty, with the conviction overturned for irregularities. When the case came up again a year later, he was found guilty and the conviction was upheld by the territorial supreme court and later, upon appeal, by the U.S. Supreme Court. See James L. Clayton, "The Supreme Court, Polygamy, and the Enforcement of Morals in Nineteenth Century America: An Analysis of Reynolds v. United States," *Dialogue: A Journal of Mormon Thought* 12 (Winter 1979): 46-61.

¹⁶An account of the life of Myron Tanner (1826-1903) as well as some of his and Mary Jane's writings are included in George S. Tanner, *John Tanner and His Family* (Salt Lake City: John Tanner Family Association, 1974), pp. 15-27, 363-65, 401-6.

¹⁷Excerpts from Mary Jane's autobiography, letters, and journal have been published in Margery W. Ward, ed., *A Fragment: The Autobiography of Mary Jane Mount Tanner* (Salt Lake City: Tanner Trust Fund, University of Utah Library, 1980).

¹⁸The history of the Arizona Mormon settlements is set forth in Charles S. Peterson, *Take Up Your Mission: Mormon Colonizing along the Little Colorado River, 1870-1900* (Tucson: University of Arizona Press, 1973).

¹⁹Edward W. Tullidge, *The Women of Mormondom* (New York, 1877; reprint ed. Salt Lake City, 1957).

²⁰Mary Jane observed that her father "was worth considerable property at

the time of his return to Cal. He estimated it at about thirty-five thousand dollars. After his death his property was sold and divided among the Lawrence family according to the will of his second wife, Sarah Lawrence (1826-1875). It was then thirty-five hundred dollars in cash Cornelia and myself received through the kindness of Henry Lawrence, one hundred dollars each." Mary Jane Mount, "A Memorial," Tanner, *John Tanner and His Family*, p. 404.

[21]Brigham Young died August 29, 1877.

[22]Hannah Smith and Hannah Clark were counselors to Mary Jane in the Provo Third Ward Relief Society.

[23]From the time of the Nauvoo Temple, Relief Society members took on the task of sewing temple clothing. A temple and burial clothing department was established by the society's general board in 1912, though even then individual Relief Society women throughout the Church continued sewing the sacred clothing. See *History of Relief Society, 1842-1966* (Salt Lake City: General Board of Relief Society, 1966), pp. 90-91.

[24]Two recent articles on Susa Young Gates provide insight into the complicated life of this complex woman as well as leads to secondary and primary source materials on Susa: Carolyn W. D. Person, "Susa Young Gates," in Bushman, ed., *Mormon Sisters*, pp. 201-23; Rebecca Foster Cornwall, "Susa Y. Gates," Burgess-Olsen, ed., *Sister Saints*, pp. 63-93. R. Paul Cracroft, "Susa Young Gates" (Master's thesis, University of Utah, 1959), is a comprehensive survey and criticism of Susa's literary works.

[25]Susa Young Gates and Leah Dunford Widtsoe, *The Life Story of Brigham Young* (New York: Macmillan, 1930).

[26]This is probably Susa's half-brother John Willard Young (1844-1924), who served for a short time as counselor to Brigham Young in the First Presidency and later as a counselor to the Twelve Apostles.

[27]Like Susa, Dora had two children by her first marriage. Frank Moreland Dunford was born in 1873 and George Albert Dunford in 1875. Either or both of these may have been with Susa at the time, since Dora had recently been there. See note 31.

[28]Emma May Bigelow (1873-1880), a daughter of Lucy's brother Daniel, is one relation who seems to fit this situation, although there is no other indication that this niece was living with her aunt Lucy Bigelow Young at this time.

[29]Susa's references here to "trial" and "case" may well pertain to claims made by seven of Brigham Young's heirs, including Dora, against executors of the Brigham Young estate. The case is discussed by Leonard J. Arrington in "The Settlement of the Brigham Young Estate, 1877-79," *Pacific Historical Review* 21 (February 1952): 1-20.

[30]In Mormon theology, salvation is equally available to men and women, but exaltation is reserved for men and women who marry. Susa's own views on the earthly relationship between men and women varied substantially over the course of her lifetime. See Cornwall, "Susa Y. Gates," Burgess-Olson, ed., *Sister Saints*, pp. 81-85.

[31]Dora's first marriage to Frank Moreland (Morley) Dunford took place against her parents' wishes and in spite of their efforts to thwart it, with an elopement October 3, 1870. Susa says, "Industrious he was, with a sunny disposition . . . but he inherited or developed a deadly weakness of will and lack of self-control. He drank." By 1877, according to Susa, "Dora had left her husband" and returned to St. George. She had two children by the first marriage and six children by a second marriage to Judge Albert Hagen, also a non-Mormon, contracted sometime prior to 1882. See Susa Young Gates, "From Impulsive Girl to Patient Wife: Lucy Bigelow Young," ed. Miriam B. Murphy, *Utah Historical Quarterly* 45 (Summer 1977): 283, 286; also Gates and Sanborn, "Brigham Young Genealogy," *Utah Genealogical and Historical Magazine* 11 (1920): 132-33.

[32]Zina Young Williams (1851-1931) was a daughter of Zina D. H. Young and Brigham Young, a half-sister of Susa. Married in 1868 to Thomas Williams, she had two sons by him. Following the death of Williams in 1874, she moved to Provo so her sons could be educated by Karl G. Maeser. During 1879 she opened the Primary Department at the Brigham Young Academy and served as matron. She married Charles Ora Card in 1884. Jenson, *LDS Biographical Encyclopedia* 3:338-39.

[33]John Daniel Thompson McAllister (1827-1910) was president of the St. George Stake from 1877 to 1888. James G. Bleak (1825-1918) was clerk of the Southern Utah Mission.

[34]Sariah Bigelow Cook, a sister of Susa's mother, died in 1877.

[35]Rhoda Mabel married Daniel Handley McAllister, a son of John D. T. McAllister (see note 33 above), September 7, 1879. She later married a cousin, Daniel Brigham Witt (July 25, 1887), and later a non-Mormon, Joseph Abbot Sanborn (August 2, 1897).

Chapter 10

Some important studies relative to the period of Mormon history covered in this chapter include: Gustive O. Larson, *The Americanization of Utah for Statehood* (San Marino, Calif: The Huntington Library, 1971); B. Carmon Hardy, "The Mormon Colonies of Northern Mexico: A History, 1885-1912" (Ph.D. dissertation, Wayne State University, 1963) and Melvin S. Tagg, *A History of the Mormon Church in Canada* (Lethbridge, Alberta: Lethbridge Herald Co., 1968).

[1]J.L.S. to Editor Exponent, January 9, 1886, *Woman's Exponent* 14 (February 1, 1886): 133-34.

[2]See Arrington, *Great Basin Kingdom*, pp. 353-79, for an analysis of the confiscation of church property and other economic impacts of the raid.

[3]The Manifesto was unanimously accepted by the membership of the Church gathered at the conference and has subsequently been included in the Doctrine and Covenants. Discussions of the declaration include Kenneth W. Godfrey, "The Coming of the Manifesto," *Dialogue: A Journal of Mormon Thought* 5 (Autumn 1970): 11-25; Henry J. Wolfinger, "A Reexamination of the Woodruff Manifesto in the Light of Utah Constitutional History," *Utah Historical Quarterly* 39 (Fall 1971): 328-49; and Gordon C. Thomasson, "The Manifesto Was a Victory," *Dialogue: A Journal of Mormon Thought* 6 (Spring 1971): 37-45.

[4]After his marriage to Julina in 1866, Joseph F. Smith took four plural wives: Sarah Ellen Richards (1850-1915), Julina's sister Edna Lambson (1851-1926), Alice Ann Kimball (1858- ?), and Mary Taylor Schwartz (1865- ?). To these wives and Joseph F. Smith were born forty-three children. The family members are listed in Joseph Fielding Smith, *Life of Joseph F. Smith: Sixth President of The Church of Jesus Christ of Latter-day Saints* (Salt Lake City: Deseret Book, 1969), pp. 487-90. Some insight into the family life is provided in pp. 448-90. For a different view, see Randall Leroy Green, "The Joseph F. Smith Family: Life without Father," MS on file in Church Archives.

[5]The eleven children of Joseph F. and Julina Lambson Smith include Mercy Josephine, Mary Sophronia, Donette, Joseph Fielding, David Asael, George Carlos, Julina Clarisse, Elias Wesley (born in Hawaii, April 21, 1886), Emily, Rachel, and Edith Eleanor. There were also two adopted children: Marjorie Virginia and Edward Arthur.

[6]Enoch Farr (1845-1914) was president of the Sandwich Islands or Hawaiian Mission from 1885 to 1887.

[7]Susa Young Gates and her husband, Jacob Forsberry Gates, arrived in Honolulu in November 1885, and Jacob was appointed secretary of the plantation. He was later president of the Laie Branch. They returned to Utah in April 1889.

[8]J.L.S. to Editor Exponent, January 9, 1886.

[9]Esther Farr, wife of the mission president, was president of the Relief Society and Julina was one of four women who served as counselors. Sand-

wich Islands or Hawaiian Mission, manuscript history, manuscript, Church Archives.

[10]"Through the suggestion of President Joseph F. Smith a theological class was organized in Laie for the purpose of studying the first principles of the gospel." Hawaiian Mission, manuscript history, March 4, 1885.

[11]The participation of women in the administration of healing ordinances is discussed in chapter 1.

[12]Robert (1883-1886), "Robin," was a son of Joseph F. and Edna Lambson Smith. Susa Young Gates wrote a tribute at the boy's death. See Smith, *Life of Joseph F. Smith*, pp. 462-63.

[13]Nancy wrote a history of the elder Williams. See Nancy Clement Williams, *After 100 Years* (Independence Publishing Company, 1951).

[14]Adoption had a peculiar meaning for nineteenth century Latter-day Saints. It was the means by which members were sealed, usually not to their own families but to prominent priesthood leaders. The practice, discontinued in 1894, is discussed by Gordon I. Irving, "The Law of Adoption: One Phase of the Development of the Mormon Concept of Salvation, 1830-1900," *BYU Studies* 14 (Spring 1974): 291-314.

[15]It was common practice at this time for younger women, often even young married women, to attend the Young Ladies' Mutual Improvement Association meetings rather than those of the older women's Relief Society.

[16]Mormon temple ordinances are overviewed by James E. Talmage in *The House of the Lord*, rev. ed. (Salt Lake City: Deseret Book Company, 1971), pp. 79-84.

[17]The academy at Ephraim, Utah, was one of thirty-one high schools started by the Church in Utah, Idaho, Arizona, Canada, and Mexico between 1888 and 1891.

[18]Amanda Burns Williams and her husband, Fredrick Granger Williams, had been married thirteen years and had seven children by the time Nancy Clement entered the family in 1889. Two children had died, one in 1882 and one in 1884. The three oldest were Amanda Elizabeth, Fredrick Ezra, and Sarah Josephine. In 1890, Flora May was three years old and the baby, Joseph Fredrick, eighteen months. Fredrick Granger Williams–Amanda Burns family group sheet, Church Genealogical Archives.

[19]Colonia Diaz, near the Spanish town of La Ascencion, Mexico, was settled by Latter-day Saints early in 1885.

[20]Hazel Kathena (1890-1940) was a daughter of Fredrick Granger Williams and Amanda Burns.

[21]George Teasdale (1831-1907) was a member of the Council of the Twelve who helped direct the settlement of Diaz in 1885 and presided over the Mexican colonies for a period.

[22]The same excerpt of the Fox diary edited by the authors here was edited by Linda Thatcher, "I Care Nothing for Politics: Ruth May Fox, Forgotten Suffragist," *Utah Historical Quarterly* 49 (Summer 1981): 239-53. Further information on Ruth May Fox and her family, her associations with other women, and her personal aspirations can be found in Ruth May Fox, "My Story," comp. Leonard Grant Fox, typescript, Church Archives.

[23]Phoebe Couzins, of St. Louis, was one of two women admitted to the Utah Bar in 1872; she subsequently left Utah for an active legal career in Kansas and Missouri. She was an advocate of suffrage and visited Salt Lake City in January 1895 to lecture. "Phoebe Cousins," *Woman's Exponent* 23 (January 1 and 15, 1895): 228.

[24]Emmeline B. Wells, of whom Ruth May Fox later wrote: "No other woman had so great an influence as she in shaping my life," was at this time president of the Utah Territory Woman Suffrage Association.

[25]Emily S. Tanner Richards (1850-1929) and Margaret A. Mitchell Caine (1859-1929) were both ardent Utah suffragists whose husbands had represented Utah in Washington, D.C., Franklin S. Richards as Church attorney and John T. Caine as territorial delegate.

[26]In 1894, Alice Chapin, a teacher trained in Boston by Elizabeth Peabody, the founder of the first American kindergarten, opened a model kindergarten in Salt Lake City. See Carol Cornwall Madsen and Susan Staker Oman, *Sisters and Little Saints: One Hundred Years of Primary* (Salt Lake City: Deseret Book, 1979), pp. 41-42.

[27]The Second Triennial National Council of Women was held in Washington, D. C., in February 1895. Several Utah women attended, including representatives from the Relief Society and Elmina S. Taylor, president of the Young Ladies' Mutual Improvement Association. Both organizations were charter members of the council. *Woman's Exponent* 23 (January 1 and 15, 1895): 228.

[28]As part of a revelation and prophecy dated December 25, 1832, Joseph Smith declared that "slaves shall rise up against their masters who shall be marshalled and disciplined for war." D&C 87:4.

[29]The Utah Federation of Women's Clubs was organized April 7, 1893. Em-

ma J. McVicker, a prominent non-Mormon appointed to the University of Utah Board of Regents in 1895, was president of the federation.

[30]The Women's Industrial Home, an elaborate structure originally built to house runaway polygamous wives, was at this time the home of various territorial officials and the meeting place of the territorial legislature. See Gustive O. Larson, "An Industrial Home for Polygamous Wives," *Utah Historical Quarterly* 38 (Summer 1970): 263-75.

[31]The Relief Society opened the Woman's Cooperative Mercantile and Manufacturing Institution in 1890 "to promote home industries and help forward the cause of equal rights." *Woman's Exponent* 19 (December 15, 1890): 104. The venture, which lasted until 1912, was the society's second effort to establish a cooperative mercantile. The first was begun in 1876. See also *History of Relief Society, 1842-1966*, pp. 114-15.

[32]Emmeline B. Wells and Ellis Reynolds Shipp had been in the East for six weeks, attending various women's meetings, including the National American Woman Suffrage Association in Atlanta, Georgia, and the National Council of Women in Washington, D.C.

[33]The Committee on Elections and Suffrage began deliberating the subject of equal rights for women March 11, 1895, and presented the majority report eleven days later. See Jean Bickmore White, "Woman's Place Is in the Constitution: The Struggle for Equal Rights in Utah in 1895," *Utah Historical Quarterly* 42 (Fall 1974): 350-53.

[34]"When the convention debate had been at its high point, Emmeline B. Wells had announced the anticipated May 13 arrival in the territory of Susan B. Anthony and Anna Howard Shaw to conduct a woman suffrage conference." The dignitaries arrived after the convention had voted in favor of including woman suffrage, and the Rocky Mountain Suffrage Conference, with representatives from Utah, Wyoming, and Colorado, celebrated the victory. Beverly Beeton, "Woman Suffrage in the American West, 1869-1896" (Ph.D. dissertation, University of Utah, 1976), pp. 143-46, an excellent discussion of Utah's involvement in the suffrage question and very pertinent to this portion of Ruth May Fox's diary.

[35]B.H. Roberts was reprimanded more than once for his political involvement during his tenure as a member of the Church's First Council of Seventy. See D. Craig Mikkelsen, "The Politics of B.H. Roberts," *Dialogue: A Journal of Mormon Thought* 9 (Summer 1974): 25-43.

[36]Even though the proposed constitution granted suffrage to women, it was not clear whether or not women would be able to vote in the November

election. Both the Republicans and the Democrats were interested in the potential participation of women, and several prominent Mormon women had already spoken and campaigned for the Democratic Party. While the Democrats were integrating women into the regular party structure, the Republicans opted to organize women separately, though the organizations petered out when women were not allowed to vote in November 1895. Republican women were assimilated into the party's county and state organizations the following year.

[37]In the wake of the financial panic of 1893, which threw the American economy into a slump, the Church took specific measures to stimulate the regional economy, including establishment of the Saltair bathing resort on the beach of the Great Salt Lake. See Dean L. May, "Towards a Dependent Commonwealth," in Poll, et al., eds., *Utah's History*, p. 238.

[38]The territory's supreme court ruled against women participating in the November 1895 election, and both parties removed women's names from their ballots. Beeton, "Woman Suffrage in the American West," pp. 147-48. Emmeline B. Wells was a Republican candidate for the State Senate in 1896, the first election year for Utah women, but she lost the race, although three other women were winners. See Jean Bickmore White, "Gentle Persuaders: Utah's First Women Legislators," *Utah Historical Quarterly* 38 (Winter 1970): 31-49.

[39]Frank J. Cannon (1859-1933), a son of prominent Church leader George Q. Cannon, left the Church and became one of its most severe journalistic critics. He was a Congressional delegate from Utah in 1894 and was elected on the Republican ticket as a United States Senator in 1896. He later became a Democrat.

[40]Orlando W. Powers (1850-1914) was appointed associate justice of the Utah Territory in 1885, but left the assignment to set up private law practice in Utah. Actively involved in Utah's Liberal Party, he later worked for the Democrats. In 1895, after waging "an energetic campaign," he was unanimously chosen chairman of the Democratic Territorial Central Committee. Whitney, *History of Utah* 4:537-41.

[41]In his discourse to the Box Elder Stake conference at Brigham City, Utah, George Q. Cannon, a member of the First Presidency, cautioned Saints against those who might defame the Church's leadership with lies. Journal History of the Church, October 27, 1895.

[42]On October 10, 1892, the Relief Society was incorporated as the National Women's Relief Society. The organization had become a charter member of the National Council of Women in 1891. See *History of the Relief Society*, p. 36.

[43]Rhoda Maria Howell Judd (1867-1953) was the daughter of Rebecca's brother Robert Thompson Howell.

INDEX

433